Richard's
New Bicycle Book

Richard's
New Bicycle Book

Richard Ballantine

Illustrations by
John Batchelor and Peter Williams

Ballantine Books • New York

**This book is dedicated to
Samuel Joseph Melville,
Hero.**

Library of Congress Catalog Card Number: 86-91563

ISBN 0-345-34182-1

Designed and produced by The Up and Coming Publishing Company, Bearsville, New York.
Technical consultant: Glen Thompson.
Illustration contributors: Heywood Hill, Sherry Rubin, Glen Thompson.

Manufactured in the United States of America

First Edition: October, 1972
Fifth Printing: December, 1973

Revised Edition: First Printing: October, 1974
Second Printing: May, 1976

Second Revised Edition:
First Printing: April, 1978

Third Revised Edition:
First Printing: April, 1982

Fourth Revised Edition:
First Printing: June, 1987

CONTENTS

A daring and foolhardy feat was performed by a bicyclist the other afternoon at Cabin John Bridge. The place is a general pleasure resort about twelve miles from town, over the military road built by Jefferson Davis while Secretary of War. The bridge is said to be the largest single span of masonry in the world. It is 125 feet high, and about 200 feet long, a single magnificent arch spanning a deep and rocky gorge. A good many people go out there to see the bridge, and the man who keeps the little hotel known as Cabin John, just at the end and across the bridge, does a good business, especially on Sunday. Every nice Sunday the sheds about the place are crowded with vehicles of every description, and sporting men, family parties, wheelmen, and gentlemen of leisure, are loafing about the house, getting country dinners or picnicking in the wild gorge below the bridge. As at all such places, there are always a few wheelmen lounging in and out, and a number of machines were stacked in the yard that afternoon, and a lively party within could be heard telling stories and boasting of their personal skill on the road. In the midst of the hilarity one young man suddenly came out alone, and, singling out his machine, mounted, and without a word rode towards the bridge. There is a brownstone coping on the three-foot wall on either side of the road-way. This coping is about a foot broad, and is beveled on the two upper edges for an inch or two. On the inside of these walls is the solid roadway above the duct. On the outside is a perpendicular descent of about 125 feet in the center of the bridge, and of no less than 75 feet at either abutment. The young man stop-ped and dismounted at the end of the bridge and lifted his machine upon the coping. The act was noticed by a couple of gentlemen smoking under the trees, but it was looked upon as a freak, and no particular attention was paid to it. The next moment there was an exclamation of horror, for the young man was seen mounted upon his bicycle deliberately riding along the narrow coping. The sight froze the blood of the ladies and children picnicking in the gorge below, and was enough to appeal to the stoutest heart. The gentlemen in front of the hotel started to their feet and called to the other wheelmen within. It was too late. The young man was already in the centre of the bridge. He never swerved a hair's breadth from his seat. From the end of the bridge he seemed a toy machine run-ning by mechanism, so erect and motionless he sat, and so evenly he rode. "Let him alone," cried one of his companions, "he could ride it if it was a rope." Nevertheless, the fear that interference might hasten the horror that all wished to prevent left the party rooted to the spot. In two places the coping makes a zigzag by the widening of the roadway, and at these places the rider must steer his wheel through a very narrow space at nearly right-angles with his course. The daring fellow had passed the first of these ticklish spots, and, when he carefully wore round the second, not a single one of the horrified spectators could draw a breath for fear. From thence to the end was a short and straight run, and in another moment the young man had completed his dangerous ride, dismounted, and was waving his hand laughingly at the frightened men and women and children who had witnessed it. The young fellow calmly remounted his wheel and rode on towards the city as if he had done a very common thing not worth men-tioning. He was induced to undertake the feat because someone had doubted whether he had the requisite ability and nerve to perform it.

Bicycling News, 10 October 1886

Book
One

Get a Bike!

Zowie! The world is pedaling into the twenty-first century on billions of bicycles. From remote semi-arid plains and mountains to teeming cities the bicycle has emerged as the most efficient, convenient and pleasant form of personal transport. Global production of cycles, now estimated at 100 million units a year, is steadily increasing by about 10 percent annually.

Worldwide, one person in ten owns a bicycle, but the proportion varies considerably in different countries. Bicycles outsell cars in Western Europe, the United States and Japan. In Japan, over 50 million bikes are in use, and congestion is so severe that if one parked bike in a line topples over, the resulting chain reaction of falling bikes can last for several minutes and travel a block. In the Netherlands 80 percent of the population own bicycles. And in China, where one quarter of all the people in the world live and private cars are virtually non-existent, 80 percent of personal travel is by bike. The bicycle, as Stuart S. Wilson of Oxford University says, is the most important modern invention. It was not always thought to be so.

The typical pre-World War II American bike was sturdy but cumbersome. Equipped with massive cowhorn handlebars, a single pedal operated coaster brake and one low, slow gear, these 'balloon tire bombers' hit the scales at 60-75 lbs. Used primarily by youngsters not old enough to drive, they were workhorse machines tough enough to withstand jolting rides over curbs and through fields, frequent nights out in the rain, and a generally high level of abuse. Fond nostalgia permeates memories of these bikes, but for the most part only people who had no other alternative used them. Pre-World War II sales could not have exceeded 500,000 a year.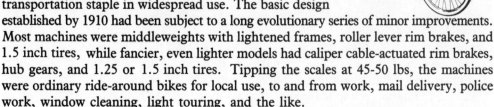

In contrast, in much smaller Great Britain, 1935 saw a record 1.6 million bikes sold. The bicycle was then a transportation staple in widespread use. The basic design established by 1910 had been subject to a long evolutionary series of minor improvements. Most machines were middleweights with lightened frames, roller lever rim brakes, and 1.5 inch tires, while fancier, even lighter models had caliper cable-actuated rim brakes, hub gears, and 1.25 or 1.5 inch tires. Tipping the scales at 45-50 lbs, the machines were ordinary ride-around bikes for local use, to and from work, mail delivery, police work, window cleaning, light touring, and the like.

Everything changed after the end of World War II. Britain went car-crazy and roads, car parks, gas stations, motorways and cars, cars, cars proliferated, transforming towns and villages into mazes of one-way motordromes and elevating Britain to a world leader in numbers of cars per mile of road. The bicycle went the way of the Dodo bird. Sales dropped to less than 500,000 a year.

But the waves of American G.I.s returning home from Europe after the war brought back samples of the new bikes. Called 'English Racers' because of their startlingly better performance over domestic models, they provided the foundation for cycling as an adult activity in the U.S.A. Where the balloon tire bomber needed King Kong on the pedals to get anywhere, the English Racer was a realistic proposition as transportation. In the late '50s and early '60s stores devoted mainly to the sale and rental of bicycles developed steadily. Americans began spending more of their increased free time on afternoon rides in the countryside or parks. Bikes appeared in force on university campuses, and hardier souls began using them as all-around transportation.

In the 1960s came the 10- and 15-speed derailleur gear, drop handlebar racing and touring bikes. Just as there was no comparison in performance between a balloon tire

Like everything else in this war it is Quality that counts. It is because of this that our men in the Army, the Air Force and the Navy to-day ride B.S.A.'s. And when we've won and the fighting is over, B.S.A. will still be the No. I Bicycle all over the world. For B.S.A. Quality is consistent—war or peace.

QUALITY COUNTS   WAR OR PEACE!

B·S·A

stands for QUALITY!

War-time restrictions have affected the civilian supply of ALL Bicycles. But put your B.S.A. on order with your nearest dealer. We will do everything possible to see you get it soon. Write for the "Cycling Annual" to B.S.A. Cycles Ltd., B, Armoury Rd., Birmingham, II

1941 advertisement for an 'English Racer'

roadster and an English Racer, the new lightweight '10-speed' bikes moved far faster and more easily than ordinary bikes. The first models came from Europe, where bike races are more important than baseball is here, and short supply made them very expensive. But adults have the economic clout to buy what they want, and they wanted bikes.

The Great American Bike Boom is a chapter in history now. It was wonderful fun while it lasted. Trading in the bicycle business was like being first in line at the 1849 California gold rush; individual fortunes were made overnight. Annual sales took a decade to double from 4.4 million in 1960 to 8.9 million in 1971, but only 2 years to nearly double again at 15.8 million units in 1973, with a final crest in 1974-5 at nearly 17 million units. The ebb of the boom saw annual sales drop to 8-9 million, and then recover: 10.4 million in 1984, 11.4 million in 1985, and now, in excess of 12 million.

Behind the figures are fundamental changes in the nature of cycling, both as an activity and as an industry. At the height of the Bike Boom people were buying anything that rolled on two wheels, so long as it had drop handlebars, chromed fork blades, quick release hubs, and derailleur gears. Small European and Asian factories produced crude machines for single U.S. retail outlets by the containerload, with no thought of servicing or availability of spare parts.

The times have moved on. Gone are the fly-by-night dealers who did not know a bicycle from a lawnmower, and gone - well, mostly - are the worst of the gilt-covered cheap bikes that were fobbed off on an unsuspecting and unknowledgeable public. Most of the bicycle dealers who have survived have done so by selling good products suitable for the needs of their customers, and by knowing how to service what they sell. Today, you can buy better bikes, for less money, than ever before. And the menu of technical choice is incredibly varied: anything from simple, cheerful single speed cruisers through to bikes - yes, bikes - that can break the national 55 mph speed limit.

The original impetus for the Bike Boom came from European cycle technology and ideas, but American designers, builders and riders are now among the world's best. We win races, break world records, and set technological precedents one after another. The latest and possibly most significant development in cycling is a purely American invention - the mountainbike, a machine that marries the robust construction and go-anywhere nature of the original balloon tire bomber with the light weight and multiple gears of a road racer. It's a bike that can go where there are no roads, clambering up and down mountains, or traversing deserts, that is also perfect for charging through rough, pot-holed urban streets.

When the Bike Boom started gathering force in 1965-66, adult models were but 20 percent of bike sales. Today, the position is reversed: adult models are 80 percent of bike sales. Of these, over half are sporting machines accounting for more than 50 percent of the value turnover. Over 100 million Americans wheel along under their own power. Everybody in America - not just the kids and competition riders - is on two wheels to stay.

There are lots of different reasons for owning a bike, or bikes. Some people cycle when they need to, like opening an umbrella when it rains. They need to go somewhere, they get on a bike. Other people practically live on their machines. They look for places to go. They race, tour, explore or whatever. Each to his or her own. Many are the ways. A bike is a tool that is what you make of it. But as a tool, a bike has some fundamental characteristics well worth thinking about.

Economics

Can you afford not to own a bike? With even moderate use it will pay for itself. Suppose you use a bike instead of public transportation or a car to get to work and back. Say it rains once a week and you live in the Northeast with an 8-month bike season. On public transport that's 128 days x $2.50 = $320, which buys a very nice bike. On a 20-mile round trip @ 45c a mile a car is into it for $9 a day, or $2250 a year (no rain discount). For that kind of money you could ride a different color bicycle each day of the week.

Getting to and from work is just one application. Bikes are just dandy for visiting friends, shopping, nipping down to the movies, and the like. You save money every time and it can add up to an impressive amount - a skiing holiday, say, or some whiz bit of gear. Using a bike marks a lifestyle that makes the most of resources and that does not waste needlessly. And anyway, besides easing your chores and tasks, bikes are worthwhile in and of themselves, so that a bike easily 'pays for itself' in rides taken for fun and pleasure.

Convenience and Reliability

In metropolitan areas for a distance of up to five miles, a bike is faster than a subway, bus or car. In heavy traffic you can expect to average 10 mph, and in lighter traffic 15 mph. In New York City I regularly rode 2½ miles to midtown Manhattan from an apartment on the lower East Side in 15 minutes, usually less. The bus took at least 30 to 40 minutes, the subway about 25 to 35. When I first got into bikes it used to be

my delight to race subway-traveling friends from 120th Street to Greenwich Village - about 6 to 7 miles - and beat them. In London, England, I often do 7 miles between Primrose Hill and London Bridge in 25 minutes, sometimes less if it's a cool, clear night with little traffic, and lots of room for the Speedy (a machine I'll tell you more about later) to stretch out and breathe. The story is the same everywhere. There have been bike versus bus, subway and car contests in many cities, and in each case I know about, the bike has always won.

THE CITY CYCLIST

One reason a bike is so fast is that it can wiggle through the traffic jams that now typify cities and towns. A car or bus may have a higher peak speed, but is often completely immobile. A bike can just keep on moving, posting higher average speeds. Another advantage of traveling by bike is that the journey is door-to-door. Use of public transportation involves walking to the local stop, waiting around for the bus or train, possibly a transfer with another wait, and then a walk from the final stop to your destination. Cars have to be parked. With a bike you simply step out the door and take off. No waiting, no parking problems.

The bike's capabilities make it a real freedom machine. Your lunch hour: tired of the same company cafeteria slop or local hash joint? Getting to a new and interesting restaurant a mile or so away is a matter of minutes. Or how about a picnic in the park? Lots of errands to do? A bike can nip from one place to another much faster than you can hoof it, and has a car beat all hollow in traffic and for parking. What might ordinarily take an hour is only 15 minutes on the bike. And if there is a lot to lug around, it is the bike and not you that does the work. Last minute decision to catch a film? Boom! Ten minutes and you're there before the subway even got going. If, like me, you are at all nocturnal, a bike is a tremendous advantage. Subways and buses tend to become elusive or disappear altogether as the wee hours approach. A bike is always ready to go. There is also a powerful contrast between a journey on a grubby, dirty and noisy subway or bus where you run a definite risk of being mugged or raped, and a graceful, rhythmic ride in which you glide through calm and silent streets or through the stillness of a country night under the moon and stars.

The reliability of a bike does a lot for peace of mind. There is no worrying about: Will the car start? Is there a subway or bus strike today? Do I have enough money for a cab? With a bike you just go. Bikes are little affected by general traffic conditions. The going may be a little slower during the morning and evening rush hours, but only a little experience is necessary to make the timing of most journeys predictable within a minute or two. Best of all, the whole enterprise is under your direct control. If you are late you can pedal faster, and if you have time in hand you can dawdle for a while in an interesting shop or pause for a quick snooze in the park. Freedom.

Health and Fitness

All right, you say. So a bike takes less time than the subway. But I've got to work for a living and the subway (bus/car) is easier, takes less out of me. You expect me to get up in the morning and crack off 5 miles? Finish a day of hard work and do another 5? I'd never make it.

Hm. Most people know that feeling fit is feeling good. But in case you think cycling is like wearing a hairshirt, get this: even a moderate amount of exercise makes life *easier*. It gives your body tone and bounce which makes daily work and chores a breeze. Simply put, this is because exercise increases your range of possible effort, putting daily activities towards the center rather than the peak of your capabilities. So as you go through the day you are just cruising. It's something like the difference between a 25- and 100-horsepower automobile engine. At 60 mph the 25 horse is working hard but the 100 is just loafing. It is important to realise that you can get this increased bounce, verve, and good feeling with relatively little time and effort. Cycling will make your work and day easier, not harder.

Are you familiar with 'cleaning out' a motor vehicle? Cars today often operate in stop-and-go traffic for long periods of time. The engine becomes clogged with carbon and other residue. The car stumbles and staggers, it works harder than it needs to, and gas consumption goes up. The best thing for any such car is to be taken out on the highway and run fast, for at higher speeds the engine cleans itself out. Your body is a machine with similar characteristics, and you will literally become more fagged out and tired just sitting still than if you up and run around the block a few times.

With regular exercise you can expect to:

- live for up to 5 years longer;
- think better (more blood to the brain - if you think this is crazy, go out and run around for a while and then think it through again);
- sleep better, and in general be more relaxed;
- be stronger and more resistant to injury;
- reduce the incidence of degenerative vascular diseases responsible for or associated with heart attacks, strokes and high blood pressure.

As cardiovascular problems account for over 50 percent of all deaths each year this last point is worth some elaboration. The basic deal with the cardiovascular system is movement, the flow of blood through your heart, veins and arteries, and so forth. The heart normally pumps about 5 quarts per minute. If this flow is sluggish and slow, the system clogs up. In arteriosclerosis, for example, the walls of the system become hardened and calcified. This decreases the bore of the arteries and veins, resulting in a diminished capacity to carry blood. The heart must therefore pump harder and high blood pressure results. High blood pressure is a cause of stroke or rupture of brain blood vessels. Arteriosclerosis happens to everybody, but its extent is governed by the rate of flow of the blood. Exercise stimulates the blood flow, and does not permit calcification to occur as rapidly.

Atherosclerosis is a related malady. This is when fatty substances are deposited on the lining of the blood vessels. Clots in the blood may be formed as a result, and these can jam up the system at critical points, such as the brain or heart, causing a stroke or heart attack. Again, exercise by stimulating the blood flow helps prevent fatty deposits.

So, the main benefits of regular exercise are, first, that it will help keep your blood circulation system cleaned out; second, the heart muscle, like any other, responds to exercise by becoming larger and more efficient, so that each heartbeat delivers more oxygen to the body; and third, lung-filling capacity is restored or enlarged. In short, you can do more, and recover more quickly from doing it.

Cycling in particular is a complete exercise. Not only are the legs, the body's largest accessory blood pumping mechanism, used extensively, but also arm, shoulder, back,

abdominal, and diaphragmatic muscles. At the same time there is enough flexibility so that muscle groups can be worked individually, and of course pace can be set to suit the rider.

Being able to go as fast or as slow as you like is mighty handy. If you want to get really fit - biking fit - then you're going to have to hit it hard enough so that it hurts at least a little bit. But we've all got good days and bad days. Sometimes, the buzz is on, and you whirl along out on the edge with all systems go. Other times, stirring yourself up will only make a mess; you're better off taking it easy and enjoying the scenery. On average, you'll still improve. Cycling has natural bite: the more you do it, the better you become, and so the more inclined you are to do it. Naturally.

Cycling is fairly unique in that you can combine exercise and things you have to do anyhow, like commuting to and from work. It's lots of fun to do things like skiing, swimming, tennis, fishing, and a zillion other outdoor activities. But swimming to the bank would be a fair trick. Cycling is something you can mix into regular daily activities. The importance of this feature depends on your circumstances and how you like to live. Some people have heavily physical lifestyles and are already very fit, while others only move fast when racing to the movies. But most of us need more exercise - lots more - and with it, live happier and longer. A word about weight control. Cycling or other exercise will help your body's tone and figure. But a brisk ride does not entitle you to apple pie and ice cream. Cycling burns off anywhere from 300 to 800 calories per hour, depending on the speed and extent of effort. Your body uses up about 150 calories

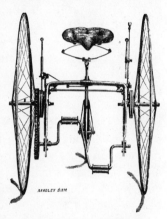

THE "ROYAL METEOR"

per hour just hanging around, which means that in regular cycling the extra burn is only 150 calories per hour. At 3600 calories per pound, it would take 24 hours of riding to lose this amount. There are easier ways.

Of course nutrition and health is much more than just calories. Exercise has a great effect on how the body uses food. You need both to exercise, and to eat foods that burn cleanly and well in your system. If you are overweight because of poor eating habits then cycling may help to change your metabolic balance and restore normal automatic appetite control, so that you eat no more than you actually need.

Ecology

Our country is literally drowning in pollutants and many of them come from transportation machinery. In cities the internal combustion engine is a prime offender that contributes up to 85 percent of all air pollution, and of an especially noxious quality. The effluents from gasoline engines hang in the air and chemically interact with other substances and sunlight to form even deadlier poisons. Living in a major city is the same thing as smoking two packs of cigarettes a day - dangerous to your health.

All city transportation contributes to pollution. Subways run on electricity generated in plants fired by fossil fuels or deadly atomic reactors. But as anyone who has been lucky enough to live through a taxicab strike or vehicle ban knows, cars and buses are the real problem. I shall never forget a long ago winter when a friend and I came driving into New York City late at night after a vacation in Canada. To my amazement, the air was perfectly clear. The lights of the city shone like jewels and each building was clear and distinct. Looking across the Hudson River from the west bank I could for the first (and perhaps only) time in my life see Manhattan and the Bronx in perfect detail from beginning to end, and even beyond to Brooklyn and her bridges. As we crossed the George Washington Bridge the air was clean and fresh, and the city, usually an object of horror and revulsion, was astoundingly beautiful and iridescent. The explanation was simple: enough snow had fallen to effectively eliminate vehicle traffic for a couple of days. No vehicles, no junk in the air. A better world.

Arguments against motorized transport are usually dismissed as idealistic and impractical and on the grounds that the time-saving characteristics of such vehicles are essential. Bilge. Facts are, even pedestrians are easily able to drone past most traffic, and bicycles of course do even better. A saving in physical effort is perhaps realized, but few of us are healthy enough to need this, or to dismiss inhaling the poisons that necessarily accompany the internal combustion engine. Nor do we need to waste time and energy.

Transport uses 25 percent of the energy consumed in America, and 95 percent of this is petroleum derived. We've got three people for each car (as against 22,535 persons per vehicle in China), and 80 percent of all automobile traffic is within 8 miles of home. In other words, most journeys are short and local, use up a lot of gas, take a long time, and smell bad. Walking, roller skating, or cycling is an efficient use of energy and reduces wastage. A cyclist can do 1600 miles on the food energy equivalent of a gallon of gasoline, which will move a car only some 10 to 30 miles.

Facts and figures be as they may, utilizing a 300-horsepower, 5000 lb behemoth to move one single 150 lb person a few miles is like using an atomic bomb to kill a canary. The U.S.A. is unique in its ability to consume and waste. In fact, we utilize something like 60 percent of the world's resources for the benefit of about 7 percent of her population. For example, in South America the forests are being burnt away to make room for beef herds. Do the people down there - who are starving - get to eat the beef? Nope, it's sent up here, to make fast service hamburgers. Anyone who objects gets zapped. And we wonder why South Americans don't like us. Using a bicycle is using less, which is a starting antidote to the horrors of consumerism.

Which brings us to the most positive series of reasons for trying to use bicycles at every opportunity. Basically, this is that it will enhance your life, bringing to it an increase in quality of experience which will find its reflection in everything you do.

Well! you have to expect that I think cycling is a good idea, but how do I get off expressing the notion that it is philosophically and morally sound? Because it is something *you do*, not something that is done to you. Need I chronicle the oft-cited concept of increasing alienation in American life? The mechanization of work and daily activities, the hardships our industrial society places in the way of loving and fulfilling relationships and family life, the tremendous difficulties individuals experience trying to influence political and economic decisions which affect them and others?

What are real values? Sure some people say that they like things the way they are. They find the subway really interesting, or insist on charging around in a chrome bomb. Perhaps they are trying to make the best of matters. But facts are facts. Subways are crowded, noisy, dirty and dangerous, and nearly all cars are ego-structured, worthless junk.

The most important negative effect of mechanical contraptions is that they defeat consciousness. Consciousness, self-awareness, and development are the prerequisites for a life worth living. Now look at what happens to you on a bicycle. It's immediate and direct. *You* pedal. *You* make decisions. *You* experience the tang of the air and the surge of power as you bite into the road. You're vitalized. As you hum along you fully and gloriously experience the day, the sunshine, the clouds, the breezes. You're alive! You are going someplace, and it is *you* who is doing it. Awareness increases, and each day becomes a little more important to you. With increased awareness you see and notice more, and this further reinforces awareness.

Each time you insert *you* into a situation, each time *you* experience, you fight against alienation and impersonality, you build consciousness and identity. You try to understand things in the ways that are important to you. And these qualities carry over into everything you do.

An increased value on one's own life is the first step in social consciousness and politics. Because to you life is dear and important and fun, you are much more easily able to understand why this is also true for others, wherever they live, and whatever their color, language and culture. Believe it. The salvation of the world is the development of personality and identity for everybody in it. Much work, many lifetimes. But a good start for you is to *get a bicycle!*

THE 'ANCHOR,' RIPLEY, SURREY

CHAPTER 2

Bike Genealogy

What kind of bike for you? This chapter overviews the types of cycles and main points in selecting a machine. Read also the chapters on bike anatomy, riding, fitting, touring, mountainbiking, commuting, HPVs, and racing for additional information on the capabilities of various types of cycles and what your particular needs may be before arriving at a final selection.

What's a Bicycle?

Conventional full size bicycles are called 'safety' bicycles, and owe the term to an unendearing characteristic of an earlier design, the Ordinary. In the early 1870s chain technology was too crude for ready use on bicycles.

The Ordinary

Pedals and cranks were attached directly to the front wheel. The only way to make such a machine go faster was to increase the diameter of the front wheel - in extreme cases, up to 60 inches. The rider, perched above the wheel just abaft the center of gravity, was lifted up to between 4½ and 5½ feet off the ground. The view was great and the Ordinary was magnificent, elegant and even rather fast, but any slight impediment to forward progress, such as the then oft-encountered stone, would cause the bike to cartwheel and catapult the rider over the handlebars to 'come a cropper'.

'Coming a cropper'

To move the rider's weight back toward the rear wheel and thereby improve stability, some designers utilized a treadle drive, as in the Singer 'Xtraordinary.

Singer 'Xtraordinary

A different tactic was employed by the famous American Star Machine, which placed the small 'rear' wheel at the front. But the route to go was chain drive and gearing, and the first such machine to gain widespread attention was the Lawson Bicyclette of 1879.

"Here, indeed, is safety guaranteed," wrote the *Cyclist* on 21 April 1880 of the Lawson Bicyclette, "and the cyclist may ride rough-shod over hedges, ditches and similar obstacles without fear of going over the handles. . ." Such machines were advertised as 'safety bicycles', and the conventional high wheeler came to be called an 'Ordinary'. Although the latter had firm adherents, the safety offered incomparably better handling, braking and speed, and the type flourished rapidly; by 1885, with the advent of the

An American Star Machine

second model Rover Safety, the bicycle was recognizably in the form we know today.

Now the applecart is being upset yet again by a new generation of cycles called

The Lawson Bicyclette—also known as 'The Crocodile' because of its shape

recumbents. In these, the rider is positioned as if in a lounge chair, with legs and feet pointing forward and back reclined. Some racing models have the rider fully supine, as when in bed. Lowering the rider reduces the frontal area and hence aerodynamic drag. Maintaining a constant 20 mph on a safety bike takes over one-quarter horsepower, with some 85 percent of this energy needed just to overcome air resistance. A low-slung recumbent has 25 percent less aerodynamic drag than a safety bike, which reduces the energy

requirement for 20 mph to one-fifth horsepower. The really fast machines use streamlined body shells to cut air resistance to the minimum, and are called human powered vehicles, or HPVs for short. They need but one-eighth horsepower for 20 mph, and at full stretch some can break the national speed limit of 55 mph.

The Rover Safety bicycle—1884

Technically, any vehicle with pedals is an HPV. Well, technically an Ordinary is a bicycle. In practice, there is little comparison and it makes sense to differentiate between the broad design categories: upright safeties, recumbents, and streamlined HPVs.

As in the early days of the safety bicycle, the development of recumbent bicycles

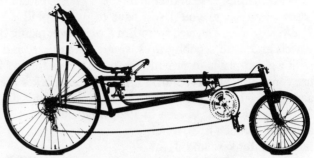

and HPVs is at an embryonic stage and commercial production is limited to individual builders and small firms. There is little doubt that these designs will gain in popularity, and their substantial benefits are discussed in a later chapter. But recumbents and HPVs complement rather than supercede the safety

Avatar 2000 recumbent bicycle

bicycle; each type has advantages and disadvantages. Unlike the Ordinary, the safety bicycle will keep on rolling for millenia to come.

Full Size Safety Bicycles

Bicycles are designed according to the job, or jobs, they are built to do. Some designs are specific, such as track racing bikes without gears or brakes. Others overlap, such

Beach cruiser

as touring and sport touring bikes. In the following quick run-through of categories some of the distinctions and terminology may be confusing. Hang on. Next comes bike anatomy, to explain what makes a bike tick, whatever it is called.

1. Beach cruiser. A modern reincarnation of the classic American 'paperboy' bike, a.k.a. the balloon tire bomber. Built entirely of steel, with a heavy, robust frame, 26 inch wheels with wide 2 inch tires, and a 1- or 2-speed hub

with a pedal operated coaster brake, these are simple, laid-back, comfortable machines for casual fun with little to no mechanical care. Beach cruisers are about style rather than performance. They're usually done up in bright, cheerful colors, and are fine for promenading along a flat broadwalk or boulevard, or

BMX cruiser

splashing through surf. They'll also do as rugged, dependable local transportation, so long as you don't mind taking your time; at a weight of around 50 lbs or more they roll fast downhill, but uphill, you'll have to dismount and push.

Some beach cruiser models are available with alloy wheels, an option that greatly improves riding ease and enjoyment. Others feature 5- or 6-speed derailleur gears, a waste of money as you'll still have to push uphill.

2. BMX cruiser. Derived from BMX dirt track racing bikes, and generally with 24 inch wheels and wide, knobby tires, single speed gear, and BMX-style straight front forks with welded plates to provide mounting holes for the front wheel axle (beach cruisers use conventional curved forks). BMX cruiser bikes are basically BMX for bigger boys and girls. They're OK for fun charging around a dirt track, and not a lot else.

3. Heavy roadster. As seen in 1920. Made entirely of steel, with 26 or 28 inch wheels and wide 1.5 inch tires, roller lever rim brakes, and 1- or 3-speed gears. Weight about 50 lbs. This is the European version of the balloon tire bomber, and is sometimes called an 'Africa' model because of its popularity in developing countries for transporting heavy loads, bouncing across deserts and

Dutch roadster

through jungles and the like. They were used extensively, and very successfully, by the North Vietnamese for transporting supplies during their last war with America. In China, they are the backbone of a national transport system based on pedal power.

In the U.S., models imported from the Netherlands or from China occasionally become available. The bikes are well made and pretty, with a lot of rustic charm, and they ride steadily and gracefully - so long as the terrain is flat. Pedaling them where there are any kinds of hills is hard work.

4. Light roadster. Also called tourist model or English Racer. Lighter weight steel frame and fen ders, 26 inch wheels with 1.375 inch tires, caliper rim brakes, and 1- or 3-speed hub gears. Weight around 35 lbs. Lighter and more sprightly than the heavy roadster and more for per-

Commuter

sonal transportation than carrying things: local errands, shopping, lots of stop-and-go riding, and short trips. Good durability with minimal maintenance.

5. Commuter. A hybrid: flat handlebars and a wide saddle give the familar upright roadster riding position, but the bike itself is a true lightweight with 27 inch wheels and 1.25 inch wide tires, alloy components, and derailleur gears. Weight 25-30 lbs. A nice bike for beginners, with pleasantly brisk performance, that can essay day rides and light touring (25-35 miles) as well as regular commuting.

6. Sports bike. Often called a 10-speed. A general use bike with a lightweight frame,

steel or alloy components depending on model, 27 inch wheels with 1.25 inch wide tires, caliper rim brakes, derailleur gears, narrow saddle and drop handlebars.

Sports bikes vary a lot in quality. At one end of the spectrum, the machine may be an ordinary roadster fitted with derailleur gears and drop handlebars for a peppy appearance. At the other end, the machine may be a genuine lightweight with fairly lively, performance. In general, though, better machines are functionally more specific: fast touring, triathlon, racing and so on. Sports bikes have modest performance and easy, predictable handling, with good directional stability and a comfortable ride over rough surfaces. They're quicker than light roadsters, and good

Sports bike

for general riding, commuting, light touring (35-50 miles) and moderately hilly terrain.

7. Touring. A touring bike will follow the general outlines of the sports bike above, but is particularly designed for a comfortable ride and predictable handling when car-

Touring bike

rying heavy loads. There is provision for fitting fenders and carrier racks for panniers, the gearing is wide-range, with low ratios for easier hill climbing, and the brakes are stout and strong. Machines of this description are of course excellent for general use and commuting, but their proper activity is day after day tour-

ing in the 50-100 mile range. Some models are claimed to weigh as little as 24 lbs, but 27-32 lbs is more likely.

8. Fast touring. Often called sport touring. A touring bike tweaked with narrow 1 inch or 1.125 inch wide tires, and a moderately stiff frame. The result is a machine that is quick, but able to manage light touring loads. This 'best of both worlds' approach is popular with urban riders who want an exciting ride over a regular commuting journey, and a mount that will serve for weekend and holiday touring. Weight from 23-28 lbs.

9. Fast road/training bike. Fast touring bikes can be very quick, but are rooted in touring and carrying things. Fast road or training bikes are essentially derived from racing bikes, and the main emphasis is on performance. There's usually no provision for mounting fenders or carrier racks. The frame is designed for quick handling and rapid translation of pedaling effort into forward motion, and shod with narrow profile 1 inch or 1.125 inch wide tires, has a stiff ride over rough surfaces. Fast road bikes weigh from 21-26 lbs and while intended primarily for sport, are also used by experienced riders for very fast, exciting general transportation.

10. Triathlon. A category created by the great popularity of triathlon (swimming-running-cycling) events. Most of the bikes are simply fast road models fitted with an abundance of water bottles. If the bike is specifically designed for tri events, then the back end will be tight, for quick response to pedal input, but the front will be somewhat relaxed, to help guide tired riders through the bends. Weight 21-26 lbs.

11. Road racing. The business. Strong, tight frame for taut responsiveness and crisp, quick handling. Close-ratio gears, and sew-up tubular tires - narrow, fast and more fragile than the conventional clincher type. Road racing in a pack of riders is often tough and rough, and the bikes are made to be light but strong and reliable. Weight is usually 20-22 lbs, but can go down to 18 lbs. With tubular tires a racing bike is strictly for competition. But it's common practice, and very easy, to substitute wheels with narrow section wire on tires for training and general road riding. A bike set up this way can be motion and bliss incarnate on a smooth, fast road, but painful in a city with jagged, debris-strewn streets. (There are ways and means of coping with this problem, of which more later.)

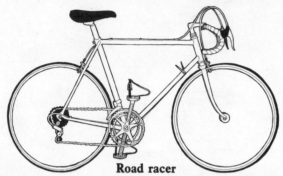

Road racer

12. Track. Made for racing on wooden tracks, these are utterly stark greyhounds with a single fixed gear (the wheels turn when the cranks turn *and* vice versa), no brakes, and a weight of 16-17 lbs. Only the most expert of riders can use these on open roads.

13. Mountainbikes. Also called all terrain bikes, or ATBs. Made for off-road riding and usually fitted with wide, knobby tires, mountainbikes superficially resemble cruiser bikes. This is like comparing a lightning bolt to a candle. Cruisers dress out at 50 lbs weight, mountainbikes are 25-30 lbs, and a really hot-shot competition model can be as scant as 22 lbs.

Mountainbike

Mountainbikes started out in life as the cycling equivalent of Jeeps and 4WD vehicles. In just a few years they have evolved into distinct genres that are very similar to the subdivisions for road bikes. There are mountainbikes for touring, for sport, for competition, and for trials. With modern tires some of these machines are as at home on the street as on the dirt. In fact, for general cycling, mountainbikes are the greatest shot in the arm since the invention of derailleur gears.

The virtues of mountainbikes are worth a book, and there is one down the pipeline. For the moment, we've got to stick with basics: mountainbikes are light, tough, strong and powerful. They've got plenty of gears, and mega-powerful brakes are standard equipment. The wheels are typically 26 inch, with tire widths from 1.375 inch to 2.125 inch. For the most part, they are equipped with wide, flat handlebars for good handling control, and padded anatomic or semi-mattress saddles. Can a mountainbike blow off a road racing bike? Of course not. But in transportation riding (to and from work, the cinema, the hideout) conditions and circumstances are often more important than the distance. A mountainbike is about confidence and the ability to pull through, no matter what. That really counts. The other fantastic thing about a mountainbike is, it doesn't need a road. You can go where you like. It opens up the outdoors, and it also opens up the back alley. A mountainbike is a kind of freedom that is unique.

Summary

Very, very broadly, there are four basic types of safety bikes:

1. Heavy, wide tire cruiser bikes, with coaster (pedal operated) brakes, flat handlebars and wide saddles.

2. Roadster bikes with medium weight tires, hub gears, caliper brakes, flat handlebars and mattress saddles.

3. Lightweight, thin tire road bikes, with derailleur gears, caliper brakes, drop or flat handlebars, and narrow or semi-mattress saddles. These can be general use machines (sports bikes), or more refined racing and touring models.

4. Mountainbikes with medium to wide tires, derailleur gears, strong caliper or hub brakes, flat handlebars and saddles to choice.

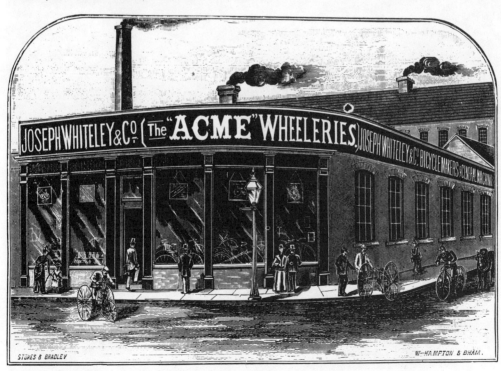

CHAPTER 3

Selection
Part I

Selecting the right bike (or bikes!) for you is a journey through an elaborate spectrum of possibilities. The process may be simple and quick, or complex and long. It depends on what you already know, your nature, and specific needs. This chapter discusses the fundamentals of weight, gearing systems, and road or off-road design. The next chapter, Bike Anatomy, is a whopper that goes into a fair bit of mechanical detail. It's useful stuff to know when messing around with bikes of whatever kind, but if you find your eyes starting to glaze over, then skim on ahead to chapter 5, Selection - Part II, returning back for more information as you need it.

Weight

Bike weight is fundamental. If a machine is heavy, it just cannot be made to go. The limiting factor is the human power plant. Gifted athletes are sometimes able to churn out in excess of 1.5 horsepower, but only for a few seconds. Thereafter, output rarely exceeds one-half horsepower. Ordinary people make do with much less: one-eighth to one-quarter horsepower on a steady basis.

Power to weight ratio is the summary determinant of performance. The effect of bike weight is most evident when accelerating or climbing, and the demarcation line is 30 lbs: bikes at 35 lbs are hard work to move, while bikes at 25 lbs seem to go down the road by themselves. Good quality, general use lightweight bikes are 28-30 lbs and similar grade no-frills sports machines are 24-26 lbs. Really fine racing bikes weigh 21-22 lbs and are joy incarnate.

Bike weight is a function of the materials from which the bike is made. It comes down to money. A heavy material like mild steel is cheap, a light material like alloy steel costs more. Beach cruisers and mountainbikes look much alike,

Rushing a rise

but the former typically weigh around 50 lbs while the latter are usually under 30 lbs.

Some people think that spending money on a bike is frivolous; the whole point is that the thing should be cheap. A bike they can hardly pick up is wonderful because after all, hard work is good for you. This downbeat reasoning misleads them into feeling happier with a rust frozen old hulk than a nice new bike that works. A change of heart is typically very swift: usually, the first time a lightweight sweeps on by going up a hill. Fact is, trudging a heavy bike wears you out while doing little to make you fitter.

The right way

The wrong way

For getting anywhere, and for quality exercise, you need a lightweight machine. Think about it. Would you run better with concrete blocks on your feet? My advice is to save money and get a decent bike in the first place. You get the most fun and turn-on for your money, and you get it right away.

What about durability? Cruiser bikes and heavy roadsters are very sturdy, but for flat-out, bomb-proof toughness it's hard to beat a mountainbike - at half the weight of a heavy roadster. Ultra-lightweight road racing bikes also have extraordinary strength and resilience, but can be damaged by casual abuse or rough off-road riding. And as for light roadsters with hub gears, sad to say, most of these are cheaply constructed and flimsy.

Rider sense and skill also affect durability. Someone who just sits on the saddle like a sack of oats when the bike hits a bump needs a machine that can absorb punishment. A rider who actively moves with the bike, allowing it to pivot underneath him or her over the bumps, can use a lighter and more responsive machine. It's a classic chicken-and-egg proposition that also works the other way. Because heavy bikes are slow to respond, they encourage an inert style of riding. In contrast, the quickness and vitality of lightweight bikes stimulates active riding. It's a partnership: the bike goes, you go; you go, the bike goes.

Bike weight is also a big factor when you are off the bike and have to handle it, for example up and down stairs at home or at work, on and off a car, or aboard a train. Carrying a 35-40 lb heavyweight can be a real chore, but handling a 25 lb lightweight is a breeze. Better yet if the bike is 21-22 lbs. It may be hard to believe that a mere 10-15 lbs makes such a difference, but it does, it does.

Gears

A choice between hub and derailleur gears rests largely with the kind of person you are and how heavily you want to get into cycling. Basically, hub gears are simple, reliable and a bit slow, while in comparison, derailleur gears are more complex, need more frequent servicing, and are extremely efficient - fast.

The crucial difference between hub and derailleur gears is the method of operation: hub gears can be shifted at any time, but derailleur gears must be shifted while the bike is in motion. It's easy once you get the knack, and the efficiency of derailleur gears outweighs the disadvantage of initial unfamiliarity. If you get stopped in a 'wrong' (inefficient) gear, it is easy to shift once you are underway again.

A choice between hub or derailleur gears depends on the kind of person you are and what you want from a bike. Derailleur gears are the route to go if: you're interested in cycling as a sporting, dynamic activity; you need to go places at an appreciable velocity, or for long distances; or any kind of hills are involved. Hub gears are the thing to consider if: you're not terribly interested in cycling and just want something you can stick in the shed or basement to use for local jaunts once or twice a month; you, or the prospective rider, are not at all mechanically inclined and never will be; or if you just want the most worry-free machine possible. There is nothing degenerate about this last state of affairs. A no-think bike is fun: you can leave it wherever, bash it around, loan it to casual friends, and in general never give it a thought.

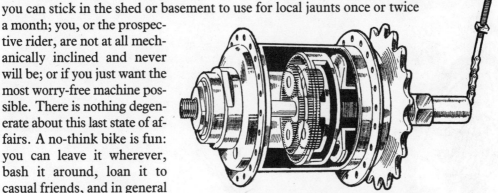

Sturmey-Archer 3-speed hub, 1936

But consider this: Professor David Gordon Wilson of the Massachusetts Institute of Technology has calculated that the energy requirement for maintaining an even 12 mph on a lightweight sports bike is half that for the same speed on a hub gear roadster.

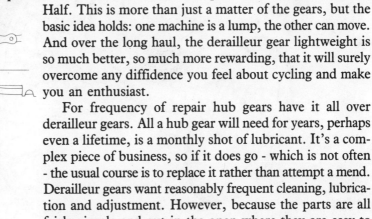

Derailleur gears

Half. This is more than just a matter of the gears, but the basic idea holds: one machine is a lump, the other can move. And over the long haul, the derailleur gear lightweight is so much better, so much more rewarding, that it will surely overcome any diffidence you feel about cycling and make you an enthusiast.

For frequency of repair hub gears have it all over derailleur gears. All a hub gear will need for years, perhaps even a lifetime, is a monthly shot of lubricant. It's a complex piece of business, so if it does go - which is not often - the usual course is to replace it rather than attempt a mend. Derailleur gears want reasonably frequent cleaning, lubrication and adjustment. However, because the parts are all fairly simple and out in the open where they are easy to get at, this is easy to do. In fact, it is part of the fun of riding. You come to enjoy fine-tuning the transmission, and keeping the bike sharp and smooth. What it all comes down to on just about any count other than expense (an item we'll come back to) is a lightweight with derailleur gears.

Road v Off-road

Which leaves road, or off-road. Broadly, road bikes are for going on roads with maximum efficiency, and mountainbikes are for going no matter what. A choice between the two types should not be made at the drop of a hat, however, because many possible permutations and combinations are possible. Road bikes can be set up so that they are very tough, and mountainbikes can be tweaked so that they are very fast. To really understand the options you need to know more about how bikes are designed and built.

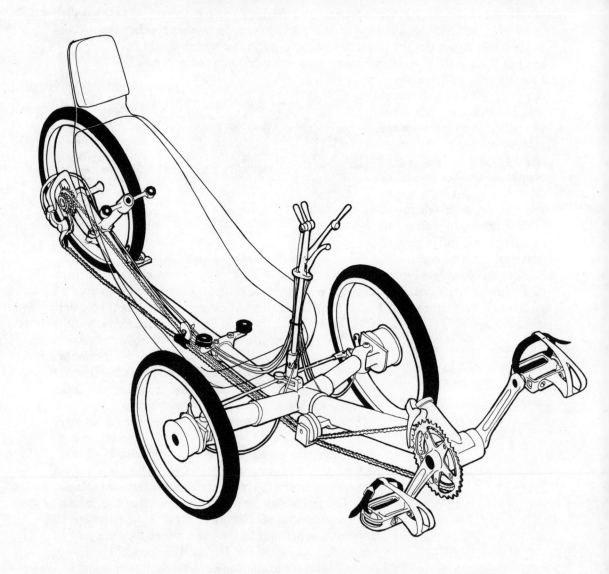

Windcheetah SL.
Fast, exceptionally agile tricycle designed and built by Mike Burrows of Norwich, England. The SL stands for street legal. An optional fiber glass body shell can be fitted, either with a glass hard top, or a fabric convertible top. Popularly known as the Speedy, the machine has been a consistent winner of Practical Vehicle Competitions in America, Canada, and Europe. It is also a wicked contender on tight, twisting racecourses—and in traffic.

CHAPTER 4

Bike Anatomy

In order of importance a bike consists of:
- the frame;
- wheels (hubs, spokes, rims, tires);
- transmission (pedals, chainset, gear changers, chain, freewheel);
- brakes;
- stem, handlebars, and saddle.

The frame carries the maker's brand name - Schwinn, Raleigh, Fuji, Thompson or whatever - and the rest of the components are known as the *specification*. Some manufacturers make their own frames, others buy their frames from outside builders, and many do both. Components are supplied by specialist companies, in various grades of quality. Depending on grade of frame and specification, bikes range in price from under $100 for discount store gaspipe jobs with crude steel parts to well beyond $1500 for fancy superbikes with hand-built frames and finely finished alloy components.

Small bike manufacturers generally concentrate on a few models in one or two categories, while large manufacturers with large distribution networks to satisfy tend to offer models in every category and price range. As a result, comparable models from different brand name 'manufacturers' can and often do have exactly the same specification. If the frames have been bought in as well (a common practice with lower price bikes), it is quite possible for two 'different' bikes to be absolutely identical!

When assessing a frame and/or components the three main factors to consider are design, materials, and quality of building. The interface of these elements determines the usefulness, quality, and value of a product. For example, a racing design frame built from heavy, inert steel is pointless, because the material does not have the performance to fulfill the design. Equally, a grocery delivery bike made from ultralight carbon fiber would be a waste of performance potential - and money. Good bikes are balanced throughout: design and materials for both frame and specification are in harmony with the intended purpose and price range. Quality of construction and assembly is important: a plain bike that works is infinitely superior to a more glamorous model that does not.

The Frame

The frame is the heart and soul of a bicycle. It translates pedal effort into forward motion, guides the wheels in the direction you select, and helps absorb road shock. How well it does these various jobs is determined by the materials from which it is built, the design, or geometry, and the method of construction. There is no way to work around a cheap frame. All of the other components can be modified or changed but the frame endures, and it should be the first focus of your attention when considering a prospective bike.

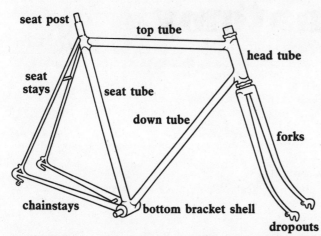

Weight in a bike is pretty well everything, and the most fundamental factor in this department is the frame. Very simply, the better the frame, the lighter the weight for the same or even greater strength. Closely related to weight is a dynamic quality known as resiliency or twang or flex, that gives better bikes springiness and vitality. Frames low in resiliency are wooden and unresponsive - bathtubs. The difference is identical to that between heavy, unyielding cast iron, and light, flexible tempered steel.

Materials

Steel and aluminum are the mainstream materials for bike frames. In years past there were two extremes: low price bikes made in heavy steels by mass production machines, and expensive bikes made in refined alloy steels by individual artisans. The fine metals were strong but required sensitive building techniques beyond the capabilities of machine assembly. Nowadays great advances have been made in the development of alloy steels that are lightweight and resilient, yet compatible with mass production methods, and this has done wonders for the quality and availability of mid-range price bikes. There's been a similar evolution in aluminum metal technologies, and for performance with value for money, aluminum bikes are now in the front rank. Very advanced bikes are made using carbon fiber, Kevlar, and other exotic composites. For a keen enthusiast or professional cyclist the lightness, performance, and comfort qualities of composite frames are often well worth the cost - which is considerable.

There's a good bit to sort out with frame materials, and the starting point is the label on the bike. If the materials are worth mentioning there will be a maker's transfer or sticker, usually on the seat tube just below the saddle. If there is no transfer the chances are that the bike is something very rare, something resprayed, or a bathtub made of low carbon mild steel.

Mild steel is heavy and inert and when arranged in the shape of a bicycle makes a passable small boat anchor. The economic justification for using mild steel to build bikes has been surpassed by modern inexpensive alloy steels, which cost only a tiny bit more. These days, few if any bicycle buying guides even bother to list bikes made with mild steel.

'High-tensile' and 'high-tension' are terms for alloy steels with more carbon and minute quantities of nickel. Frames made from genuine high-tensile steels are lighter and livelier than those made from mild steels. Unfortunately, manufacturers of cheap bikes are particularly prone to describe mild steel frames as high-tensile, slapping on racy stickers such as 'Hi-Ti', 'Hi-Ten', etc., and so unfortunately these terms cannot be taken seriously.

The first grade of quality alloy steels worth spending money on have frame stickers identifying the tubes as Columbus Aelle, Fuji Valite, Ishiwata Mangy-X, Reynolds 453, Tange Mangaloy, or Vitus 181 or 888. The stickers are, or should be, quite specific in the information they provide. Thus, if it says 'Reynolds 453 main tubes' then the seat, down, and top tubes are Reynolds 453, and the forks and stays are probably high-tensile steel. If it says 'Reynolds 453 main tubes, forks and stays' then the frame is uniform in quality throughout.

There are two types of frame tubing: straight- or plain-gauge, and double-butted. Plain-gauge tubing is uniform in wall thickness, or external and internal diameters. Double-butted tubing is uniform in external diameter, but on the inside is thinner in the middle sections and thicker at the ends, for greater strength at joining points. On average, double-butted tubing in place of plain-gauge tubing reduces frame weight by 1 lb. Double-butted tubing is also more resilient.

There are two types of double-butted tubing: seamed, and seamless. Seamed double-butted tubing is made by rolling a flat strip of steel and welding the edges together. In quality it is about one notch below seamless double-butted tubing, but at much less cost. It's often used for mid-price range bikes: Reynolds 501, Ishiwata EXO and EX, Columbus Tenax, and Tange 900, 1000 and Infinity are common brands.

Seamless double-butted tubings in manganese molybdenum (Reynolds 753 and Reynolds 531) and chrome molybdenum (Col-

TUBING

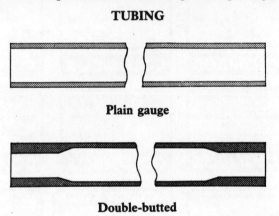

Plain gauge

Double-butted

umbus, Tange Champion, True Temper, and Ishiwata) steels are the top of the range. At this quality level the design and construction of tubing sets is specific to the intended use, as in Reynolds 531 Special Tourist (touring bikes) and Reynolds 531 All Terrain (mountainbikes). Some distinctions are fine but nonetheless real, as in Reynolds 531 Professional (road racing) and Reynolds 531 Competition (fractionally stouter, for road racing, time trials, cyclo cross and track). The categories are not gospel: for example, Reynolds 531 Competition tubing is often used for touring bikes. As ever, much depends on the rider. A lightweight frame that is whippy for a 200 lb rider may be very stiff for a 140 lb rider.

Selection of frame stickers. Each indicates the quality of the tubing used.

Keep a wary eye on plain-gauge chrome molybdenum (chrome-moly, or just cro-mo) tubing, which can vary in quality from equivalent to seamed double-butted tubing down to little better than good high tensile tubing. Like the term high-tensile, cro-mo is an overused bandwagon label that all too many manufacturers use as a matter of course. If the label says 'Cro-mo' and nothing else, be sure to compare the bike (or frameset) with others of known pedigree.

Some bikes use quality tubing for the main frame (top, seat and down) tubes, and more ordinary tubing for stays and forks. It's usually better if the frame is consistent in quality throughout. The forks are particularly important to bike performance. A frame that is Reynolds 501 throughout, or a good cro-mo with Reynolds 531 forks, is likely to be better than a bike with Reynolds 531 main tubes and high-tensile steel forks and stays. The little transfers on the tubes give all the information; be sure to read them carefully. Manufacturers' leaflets with an abundance of technical data are also available in most good bike shops.

Aluminum bikes are rapidly gaining in popularity. Aluminum has advantages in lightness, flex characteristics, and ability to soak up road shock. The technology is very much in development and models from different manufacturers vary a lot in characteristics. American builders generally favor using large diameter tubes that produce frames noticeably stiffer than their alloy steel equivalents. European builders, on the other hand, tend to use aluminum tubes of about the same diameter as conventional steel tubes, so that the frames are very flexible. Likes and dislikes in this area depend a lot on the kind of rider, the conditions of use, and the particular aluminum bike in question.

Big, strong racers frequently dislike aluminum frames with thin tubes, because in sprints the frame 'whips' - flexes back and forth - reducing the rider's control of the bike. (It's often claimed that whip reduces speed by absorbing energy that would otherwise go directly to the rear wheel and immediate forward motion. If this were true, then very stiff frames would consistently win races. They don't.) However, in a long race or when there is a lot of climbing, aluminum's lightness is a considerable advantage. Aluminum frames are also better at absorbing road shock than steel frames, and the reduction of fatigue for the rider often greatly improves performance.

Once the business of snapping away in a sprint as fast as possible is eliminated, aluminum has an awful lot going for it. Lightness and a smooth ride are always welcome assets. People light in body weight obtain the greatest benefit from light aluminum bikes. Most of them do not have enough peak power to start bending things overmuch. Their advantage is in power to weight ratio, and relative to heavier riders, lighter riders gain a greater benefit from reduced bike weight.

The heavy, hairy-chested pedal stomper brigade want to look at aluminum frames with large diameter tubes. Briefly, these do not bend at all. Some makers have even been able to secure patents for the degree of stiffness that can be obtained with aluminum. And yet, the nature of aluminum is such that even these extremely rigid frames excel at soaking up road shock.

On the downbeat side, aluminum is subject to fatigue. It wears out. With large diameter tubing fatigue is not a significant factor. With thinner tubing, one season of hard riding can noticeably diminish the vitality of the frame. But this is for pro grade, working riders spending many hours in the saddle (15-20,000 miles/year) - exactly the people who most value performance and comfort, and least begrudge the cost of proper equipment. In fact, one testimonial for aluminum frames is their popularity with pro riders. Average riders (2-3,000 miles/year) will take a long time to wear out an aluminum frame - and enjoy every moment!

Top of the materials tree and priced accordingly are frames and components made from carbon fiber, which is light but incredibly strong. It is capable of brilliant performance and a level of comfort that ecstatic testers describe as 'too good to be true'. This leading edge of frame technology of course has question mark areas. In common with aluminum, fatigue is a potential problem. Manufacturers claim that in tests carbon fiber frames last as long as steel frames, or well-nigh infinitely. Probably so, but real world confirmation will take time. One unique problem with carbon fiber is delamination of the fibers from the binding resin. The material simply loses cohesion and becomes soft. No one knows just how much of a problem this may, or may not, be.

You only live once. A state-of-the-art carbon fiber bike has got to be one of the most fun things around. If the performance and price tag suit you, then give this kind of bike a try.

Construction

A major element of frame quality is construction, which varies in method for different materials. Mild steel frames are usually just stuck together and welded by machine, leaving a smooth joint. Better quality steels with a high carbon content become brittle and subject to fatigue when heated to high temperatures. Frames of this material are brazed, a joining method that uses lower temperatures than welding. As an aid to accurate assembly, lugs are used to position the tubes. Strictly speaking, lugs do not need to be neat and tidy for a strong joint. However, clean lugwork is a sign of care and thoroughness that bodes well for the rest of the bike. There's a type of lug, by the way, which is internal and therefore invisible.

Tandems, mountainbikes, recumbents, and other machines with odd size tubing or special requirements in frame geometry often cannot use lugs, and have bronze welded (filleted) joints. Many conventional bikes are also made this way. One great advantage of the method is that everything is out in the open, where you can see it.

A decade ago, when frame steels were divided sharply into crude or fine grades, lugs were the indication of a quality bike. The development and widespread use of high grade steels that can safely be machine brazed or welded at higher temperatures has eliminated this easy distinction. By and large, conventional design frames in standard tubings continue to use lugs. To some extent this is a prejudice in favor of tradition,

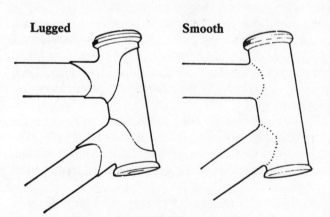

Lugged   **Smooth**

and you'll sometimes hear people decry lugless, TIG (tungsten inert gas) welded frames as crude and somehow less worthy than lugged frames. Phoo. TIG welded joints are strong and the appearance - stippled, like the decorative frosting on a birthday cake - is pleasing. Moreover, you can see for yourself if the frame is properly joined together. I've had more than one disappointment with frames where the lugs concealed inept brazing. A visible check is especially useful in the case of mid-range production bikes, where value for money is a great attraction, but pedigree is usually anonymous.

Example of fine lug and crown work from an early F.W. Evans catalogue

What's the likelihood of problems with steel frames? Very, very slight. Failures do occur - fractures, split tubing, hairline cracks, and other joys. Every bike shop has its tales. But basically, nasty things should not happen, ever, and so there is usually little difficulty in having the manufacturer put matters right. They do not want their pride and joy Wonder Flash out there with a sign: "It broke." As ever, your best protection here is in dealing with reputable people - bike shop, manufacturer, and/or builder - who are serious about their business. But play fair. Just about any bike can be broken if you try hard enough. Bouncing a lightweight racing bike up and down curbs or thrashing it through a rocky streambed is abuse, pure and simple, and if the machine breaks you are not entitled to a refund or free repair.

Aluminum has much less resistance to fatigue than steel. Do's and don'ts of building in aluminum were learned before the computer age, through pragmatic trial and error, and there were some rude, tragic surprises. Around 1981, for example, Lambert bikes with aluminum forks were recalled because the fork blades were snapping apart, with thoroughly nasty consequences for their luckless riders. There were no hidden metallurgical flaws or untoward celestial aspects in the heavens. The designers simply hadn't made the forks strong enough. Lambert are no longer with us, and I think that modern aluminum bikes are no more prone to break than steel bikes - very rarely. The relevant factor here is again not the materials, but the care and skill of manufacture. With reputable companies and respected builders you should be on safe ground.

A more realistic concern with aluminum bikes is involuntary disassembly, or failure of tube joins. Aluminum is not partial to welding. Many aluminum frames are therefore glued rather than welded, and every once in a while a frame does come unstuck. However, there is usually ample warning through the joint loosening rather than parting all at once. It is then very simple to clean the parts up and glue them back together. In any case, bonding processes are improving rapidly, and are frequently stronger than the materials they join.

Welding is an entirely satisfactory method of joining large diameter aluminum tubing, although true skill is essential. It's not a job for the village blacksmith, or even someone who can work well with steels. Mass produced aluminum bikes are a comparatively recent phenomenon, and there may be more information forthcoming on the long-term, in-service durability of welded aluminum joints. My personal preference is for glued joints, as they are simple to work with.

Carbon fiber frames are glued together, usually via lugs made from aluminum. They are light and strong and have performance levels that make questions about wear and tear seem banal. If you want (and can afford) the best, then carbon fiber is an option you must consider.

Design

The design or geometry of a bicycle frame varies according to its intended purpose and the type and weight of rider. The two fundamental types of bikes are road and off-road, or mountainbike, and within each category there is a similar basic choice: going quickly and energetically, or more slowly and comfortably. Sport or utility. Generally, performance bikes have a taut ride and quick handling, while bikes made to carry luggage have an easy ride and slow, predictable handling. Between road and off-road bikes the difference is of degree:

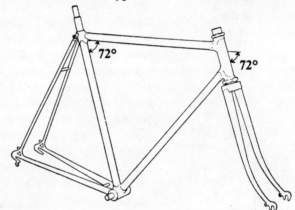

hot, quick off-road bikes are usually relatively tame on pavement, and conversely, docile road bikes used off-road may classify as competition machines.

Dimensions	Racing	Fast Road	Touring	Mountainbike
Angles	73-75°	72-74°	72-73°	68-72°
Wheelbase	38.5-39''	39-41''	40-42''	42-45''
Fork rake	1.4-1.75''	1.75-2.2''	2.2-2.5''	2-2.75''
C'stay length	16-16.5''	16.2-17.5''	16.5-17.7''	17-18.5''
B/B height	10.5-11''	10.5-10.75''	10-10.75'	11.5-13''

The first crude indication of a bike's character is the wheelbase, the distance between the two wheel axles. On road bikes the span ranges from 38.5 inches for racing models to around 42 inches for touring models. On mountainbikes the range is from around 41 inches to 45 inches. Wheelbase is an additive function of the relative angles at which the tubes are joined, and their length. Tightly built, short wheelbase frames with steep angles and short tubes are 'stiff' while long wheelbase frames with more relaxed angles and longer tubes are 'soft'. These terms lend credibility to the simplistic, widespread tenet that stiff frames have a harsh ride, and soft frames a comfortable ride.

More relevant to ride comfort are the wheels and tires used. Variations in frame design are for performance, degree of stability, and room for carrying things. Racing bikes need to be quick and nimble, and there usually isn't enough room to mount fenders, carrier racks and suchlike. Touring bikes want stable, predictable handling - so you don't veer unexpectedly and connect with a tree while enjoying the view - and of course need enough room to carry equipment without entangling the rider. But fast bikes can be comfortable as well as efficient, and one popular model category is the sport, or fast, touring bike, with a wheelbase of 40-41 inches.

Going into all this business a little more deeply, the kick or speed of a bike is largely determined by the tightness of the rear triangle formed by the seat tube, seat stays and chainstays - more simply, the length of the chainstays. On a hot road racing bike this could be as little as 15.75 inches, leaving no room between tire and seat tube for a fender (or on a showroom floor, your finger). On sport touring bikes the interval is 16.25-17 inches, and on machines for fully loaded touring it is 16.5-17.75 inches. Mountain-bikes run hot at around 17.5 inches and more sedately at around 18.5 inches. Simply, short chainstays make for quick acceleration and climbing, and nimble handling; long chainstays reduce snappiness but increase stability and room for carrying things.

The speed with which a bike handles, and its directional stability, is largely determined by the tightness of the front end. This is a function of the head tube angle, and of the fork rake. The tighter the head tube angle, the faster the bike reacts to steering input. Bikes with fork rakes of 2 inches or more tend to be stable, especially at low speeds; fork rakes under 2 inches give nimble handling and better stability at high speeds.

Design elements are often mixed in different ways. The classic road racing bike is tight front and rear, for maximum performance. Many triathlon bikes, however, mix a tight rear with a more relaxed front. This is because in competition, a triathlete is likely to be tired, and welcome a bit of help in staying on course.

Bottom bracket height relates to the center of gravity and stability of a bike, and ease of touching the ground with a foot when seated on the saddle. Touring bikes have low bottom brackets to aid stability when loaded with baggage, and to make frequent stops easier. Racing bikes have higher bottom brackets for pedal clearance when cornering, and mountainbike bottom brackets are the highest of all, for clearance over very rough ground. With a low bottom bracket it is usually possible to start and stop the bike without leaving the saddle. However, the pedals are more prone to ground when cornering - an unpleasant, and possibly very scary experience that can make you nervous about 'laying the bike over'. A high bottom bracket may require that you leave the saddle from time to time when stopping and starting, but adequate pedal clearance when the bike is up and going is a great aid to confident bike handling.

One quick way to annotate bike design and function is via the frame angles formed to the top tube by the seat and head tubes. On a classic touring bike these are likely to be 72° parallel. As the frame tightens and becomes a sport touring bike with more emphasis on performance, the frame angles steepen to say 73° parallel. For road racing they are likely to be 74° parallel. As a progression these figures are broadly accurate, but individual bikes vary a fair bit. Thus, some aluminum racing frames are steeply pitched at 75° seat and 74° head, and yet are comfortable because the material has good shock absorbing qualities. The frame built by Jack Taylor of England for his Superlight Tourist model uses a 73° seat and 71° head. The bike is particularly designed for stability and comfort with heavy touring loads.

The first and most fundamental requirement of a frame is that it fits the rider. If frame angles have to differ from the 'norm', then so be it. For example, women generally have less reach than men, and short women in particular have limited reach. On bikes that are correctly sized for their legs they are stretched out too far for their torsos. It's uncomfortable and can be very painful. The solution is to shorten the top tube, and since you can't just whack a chunk out of it without messing up the rest of the bike, the solution is effected by steepening the seat tube angle to 75° or 76° - a 'stiff', 'harsh riding' racing geometry. Try telling that to those lucky women who have traveled thousands of comfortable miles on properly fitting bikes!

Monocoque frame bike—a new and exciting configuration. Note single fork blade! Designed and built by Mike Burrows.

Frame angles depend on the length of the frame tubes, not the other way round. They do run to pattern, with steeper frame angles for faster, more lively bikes. Most people will find a good fit on standard frames, with the aid of correct saddle positioning and stem length to adjust for minor variations (see Fitting). But go for fit and comfort first, and let the design follow suit.

Diamond pattern frames are with us in no small part because they conform to the narrow definition of a bicycle established by the Union Cyclist Internationale, the governing body of cycle sport. But the death knell is sounding for frames made from sticks. Composites are the new materials, and one enormous asset of these is the ease with which they can be worked and shaped into various forms. Some firms are producing traditional stick design frames in composite materials, but the most exciting configuration is monocoque - single piece, with nary a frame angle in sight. The means to hold the wheels, cranks, forks, saddle, handlebars and everything else are contained in one cohesive unit. Monocoque designs are aerodynamic, light and strong, but the most significant advantage is that strength and flex are almost infinitely variable; in theory at least, it is now possible to build the absolutely perfect bicycle, with every performance characteristic precisely as desired.

At this writing monocoque designs are banned from sanctioned bicycle racing by the UCI, and exist in prototype or custom-built form only. But I've got a funny itch that feels like the first mountainbikes. Monocoque designs are efficient, sleek, and appealing, and I think people will want them, UCI or no. One of the manufacturers of 'outlaw' bikes might well introduce a monocoque model soon, and if so, be sure to look it over. It's the way to go.

Summary

The frame is the most important element in the quality and vitality of a bike. Within reason and the purpose of the bike, you want the best frame you can afford. Alloy steels are the traditional materials for frames, and the parameters for quality, performance, and value are well understood; you'll get what you pay for, from refugee gaspipe through to the finest in ultra-light, ultra-tech tubing. Aluminum frames are a more recent introduction and have advantages in lightness, comfort, and (in large diameter tubing) stiffness. Some models are remarkably economical, and others are quite expensive. Composite frames in carbon fiber, Kevlar, and other exotics are the top of the performance and cost tree, are wildly exciting, and too recent for information on durability.

Wheels

After the frame, the wheels - tires, rims, spokes and hubs - are the most important components of a bike. The frame is the vitality, the wheels the point of translation into motion. Their effect on performance and comfort is enormous. A bike frame is fairly immutable. Once completed and painted, it is very unlikely to go back to the torch for changes and modifications. The range of options offered by wheels, however, are under your direct control. This makes them worth knowing about in some detail.

A bicycle wheel is one of the strongest engineering structures in existence. This is because weight has a greater effect on a wheel than anywhere else on a bike. The best

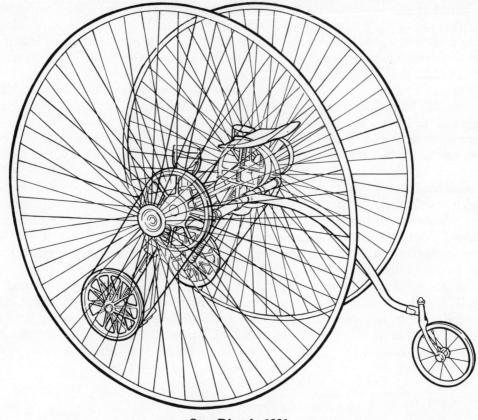

Otto Dicycle 1881

way to appreciate the old saw ''an ounce off the wheels is worth a pound off the frame'' is to hold a wheel by the axle ends and move it around in the air, and then do the same while spinning the wheel. The faster it rotates, the greater the 'weight', or inertia, and the harder it is to move the wheel.

Bicycle wheels are built with spokes and rims to keep weight to the minimum and reduce the effect of gyroscopic force. If weight did not matter they could be a solid one-piece design, like automobile wheels. The other important considerations in wheel design are comfort and durability, and basically it is a straight trade-off: lighter is quicker, stiffer riding, and more fragile; heavier is slower, softer riding, and more durable. The type of bike, rider, and conditions of use determine the balance of priorities. Wheels for racing on smoothly surfaced roads, for example, are lighter and slimmer than wheels for touring with heavy loads on gravel tracks.

A wheel is a package where the components - tire, rim, spokes and hub - tend to follow suit in weight and quality. Stout tires, wide rims, and thick spokes go with touring bikes and mountainbikes. Light tires, narrow rims, and slender spokes go with sport and racing bikes. Generally, heavier wheels are better able to cope with bumps, pot-holes, and rough surfaces, and lighter wheels are faster but harsher riding. Much depends on the rider. 'Comfortable' for a beginner usually means a wheel that does not skitter at the sight of a pebble. The fact that it is heavy and slow is inconsequential. For an advanced rider, however, a slow wheel is usually uncomfortable because it is hard to move. Comfort in such a case is a taut wheel that responds quickly and rolls easily. So far as the drawback of a 'harsh', skittish ride is concerned, he or she would feel lost without it.

Tires

There are two types of tire and rim combinations: clincher or wire-on tires on HP rims, and tubular or sew-up tires on sprint rims. Clincher tires are the familiar type with an open casing, where the two edges of the casing nestle within the lips of a U-shaped rim. The casing edges are reinforced with beads of wire or Kevlar, so that they retain shape and stay inside the rim when the inner tube is inflated. It's a straightforward design that is easy to manage when changing a tire or extracting the inner tube to mend a puncture.

With tubular tires the casing is sewn together, completely encasing the inner tube. A sprint rim has a slightly concave, smooth top with no lips and the tire is held in place with glue or shellac. In the event of a puncture, a complete tubular tire is much quicker to replace than a clincher tire, an advantage when racing. However, mending a puncture in a tubular is a time-consuming, fiddly business.

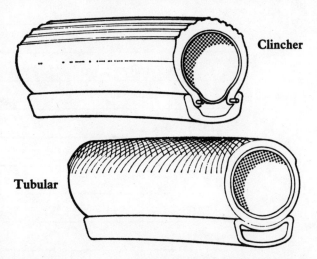

Clincher

Tubular

Where sprints and tubulars - sprints for short - score is in reduced weight. Sprints are inherently lighter than HP's, and the difference this makes in bike performance is very noticeable. The same bike when fitted with sprints handles and responds more quickly than when fitted with clinchers. As a result, sprints - laboriously sewn together casings, sticky glued rims, and all - are the preferred choice for racing.

Sprints are top of the performance tree, but not by much. Clincher tire technology has seen enormous development in recent years. Models range from 26 inch wide, heavy-duty gnarlys for off-road use, down to .875 inch wide, ultra-light treadless road screamers that in terms of rolling resistance (not weight) are just as fast as tubulars. Between the two extremes is a vast spectrum of tires catering to just about every need.

There are two traditional systems for sizing tires and - curses - they are not interchangeable. American and British sizes are in inches: 27 x 1.25 means a tire diameter of 27 inches and a cross section or width of 1.25 inches. Continental (European) sizes are metric: 700 x 28C means a tire diameter of 700 mm and a width of 28 mm. Neither system is accurate: for example, mountainbike 26 inch tires need smaller rims than road 26 inch tires. A more precise metric system of annotating tire sizes is now coming into international use, and consists of a two-figure number, a dash and a three-figure number, as in 32-620. The first figure gives the tire width, the second the diameter of the rim it fits. Both are in millimeters.

Commonly known as	Standard designation
Road	
26 x 1.25	32-597
26 x 1.375 (650 x 35A)	35-590
26 x 1.5 (650 x 35B)	35-584
27 x .875	23-630
27 x 1	25-630
27 x 1.125	28-630
27 x 1.25	32-630
27 x 1.375	35-630
28 x 1.5 (650 x 35B)	35-584
650 x 35A (26 x 1.375)	35-590
650 x 35B (26 x 1.5)	35-584
700 x 19C	19-622
700 x 20C	20-622
700 x 23C	23-622
700 x 25C	25-622
700 x 28C	28-622
700 x 35C	35-622
700 x 35B (28 x 1.5)	35-635
Mountainbike	
26 x 1.5	37-559
26 x 1.75	44-559
26 x 2.125	54-559

The 700C is the same diameter as the sprint rim used for tubular tires, and makes it possible to interchange wheels for clincher or tubular tires on the same bike. This is a handy feature for weekend racers who use their bikes for commuting and training during the week. The 700C is also the common Continental size, a point to note if you plan to tour in Europe.

In America the common size is 27 inches and the usual advice is to use it because replacement tires are easier to find. This idea dates from the days when clincher tires were slow, and little different from each other. The only value was how cheaply a tire could be bought. Modern performance tires are a dynamic component that you select for the balance of speed, grip, comfort, and durability that suits you. Replacement time is a moment of opportunity for contemplating delicious possibilities from the comprehensive ranges stocked in bike shops, not settling for whatever el cheapos are available in the local department store.

An emergency spare is a contingency measure. Basically, if you run good rubber and replace tires before they are completely worn, then you should very rarely suffer worse than a mendable puncture. As for spares when out in the boondocks, you are going to carry one anyhow! It's not much good being out in the Mojave Desert (or anywhere at 5 a.m. Sunday morning) and needing a spare of whatever size. If complete self-sufficiency is important, then carry a spare. Happily, there are lightweight clincher tires that fold to a very compact size, and are easily carried on a bike.

If you are only going to tour in the U.S.A., then 27 inch wheels are fine. If you plan to tour abroad, or run a racing bike, now or perhaps later, then standardize on 700C. Twenty-seven inch and 700C are the sizes for which high performance tires are readily available. Mountainbikes and roadsters generally use 26 or 24 inch wheels, which are stronger because of their smaller diameter and generally more robust construction. But tires in these sizes usually follow suit by favoring strength over speed. Tires for 20 inch wheels are soft and slow, to help cushion the stiffness inherent in small wheels.

In general, wide tires have a more comfortable ride, better traction on loose surfaces such as gravel and in wet conditions, and are the most durable. Narrow tires have a stiffer ride, less traction, and are more vulnerable to punctures and bruising - but go. The mainstream tire width for most 27 inch/700C wheel road bikes is 1.25 inches/32 mm, a category that embraces everything from rugged, heavyweight expedition models through to lightweight, Kevlar-beaded high performance models. Next step up the speed ladder are narrow section, 1.125 and 1 inch/25 and 28 mm wide tires. These are very much for performance, have a stiff ride, and are rather more fragile: one bad hit on a monster pothole can be terminal. But they are great fun, particularly for skilled riders who enjoy zest and sparkle in a bike. Back down the ladder, 1.375 inch/35 mm tires are the job for outback touring with very heavy loads, commuting on really mean streets, slippery conditions, and thick gravel.

The 1.25 inch/32 mm category is very flexible. The tough models are very tough, and the high performance models are very fast, but still practical for durability and traction. For sport riding and race training, narrow section tires give maximum performance - and a few gray hairs if the road is wet and slippery.

Tires for mountainbikes follow similar basic principles except that the width range is from 1.375 to 2.125 inches. The narrow models are usually for pavement or competition, and the wide models for bashing, sand, and mud. There are also dual purpose tires with a pattern or bead for an even thread at the center and speed on the road, and knobs on the sides for traction in dirt.

How a tire is built also affects performance. The tread rubber can be softer, for better grip, or harder, for greater durability. It can be thin, for minimum rolling resistance, or thick, for greater strength. The casing is made of layers of fabric, with the number of threads per square inch (tpi) ranging from around 35 to 106 tpi. A high tpi number indicates a light, supple tire with low rolling resistance and good cornering adhesion, but one that is vulnerable to cuts and bruises. A low tpi number indicates a stout, rigid tire with higher rolling resistance and less adhesion, but better able to resist misfortune.

All these various characteristics can be mixed and matched to meet particular requirements. There are tires made for superior traction in wet conditions, tires with belts of bullet-proof Kevlar in the casings to forestall punctures, and a host of other variations. The point to bear in mind is that tires are a dynamic part of a bike, and greatly increase the range of options under your control.

If the bike you buy is well upmarket and designed for an express purpose such as heavily loaded touring, then it may be fitted with high quality tires. The majority of production bikes, however, must compete vigorously on price, and so in most cases the tires will be merely average - good enough, but easily improved on.

Tire models come and go. Check current periodicals and catalogs for the latest info. Specialized is a leading brand, some would say the best, with a wide range of models to suit every purpose and pocket. Michelin is another top name. IRC and Avocet have good models, and Continental, Clement, Wolber, and Vittoria are all in there pitching hard.

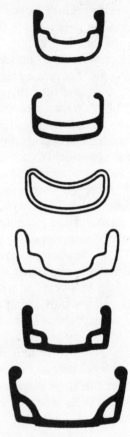

Rim profiles

Rims

Rims are made in steel or alloy. Alloy is what you want. Steel is just too heavy. A bike with steel rims handles like a barrel of nails, takes an age to get into motion, and can take the rest of your life to stop. Most bicycle brakes are the caliper type that work by pressing two blocks against the sides of the rim. In dry conditions this works well with alloy rims, and only just with steel rims. In wet conditions alloy rims have less braking power, but are still functional. In the case of steel rims braking power piffles to almost zero, and it is usually more effective - no joke - to stop by dragging your feet.

In times past steel rims were sometimes recommended for steamroller strength. But like tires, modern alloy rims are available in a range of weights and strengths, and you can pick what you need for the job. Mountainbikes are made to withstand dreadful hammerings - like 30 mph across rocky streambeds - and without exception use alloy rims. For ultimate performance and strength, top line rims are made from specially hardened alloys.

Approximate alloy rim weight	Application
Sprints	
290-325 g	Time trials
325-350 g	Time trials/road racing
350-400 g	Road racing
Clinchers	
380-400 g	Racing/high performance
400-450 g	High performance
450-550 g	Touring

It is important to have a good match between tire and rim widths. For example, most rims made to mount 1.25 inch wide tires will accept a slightly narrower 1.125 inch tire, but not a 1 inch model. Conversely, very narrow rims for .875 and 1 inch tires will sometimes stretch to 1.125 inch tires, but rarely to 1.25 inch. It's more than a simple yes or no fit. A rim and tire work together and have an optimum performance profile. When a tire is too narrow for the rim it tends to take the shape of a wedge, and impact resistance and grip are greatly reduced. The wheel is more easily damaged by bumps, the ride is hard, and handling is skittish and uncertain. There's less of a problem if the tire is too wide for the rim, but sometimes the rim swims about within the tire, so that the bike feels indeterminate and queasy when cornering. When tire and rim are correctly matched the profile is similar to a button mushroom, with the tire (cap) wider than the rim (stem). Ride is firm and handling is certain; the bike is 'willing' to take a corner.

Rim width	Normal tire width range /maximum stretch
Road	
19-20 mm	19-25/28 mm
22 mm	25-28/35 mm
26 mm	28-35 mm
Mountainbike	
22 mm	35-50 mm
28 mm	37-54 mm
32 mm	44-54 mm

Good quality rims are eyeletted: the holes for the spoke nipples are reinforced with metal eyelets, just like shoes. Generally, box or modular section construction gives the most strength for the least weight. Part of the rim is hollow - in cross section, a shallow rectangle or 'box'. Rims that are sturdier all around can use a simpler channel section design shaped like a U.

Top brands with excellent quality in all models are Super Champion, Mavic, and Saturae. Other good names are Ambrosio, Araya, Wolber, and Weinmann. Bike manufacturers understand the performance and durability advantages of good rims, and for the most part, fit models suitable for the type and price range of bike.

Spokes

The most highly stressed parts of a wheel are the spokes. In materials there are three types: galvanized rustless, chrome- or nickel-plated, and stainless steel. Galvanized spokes have a dull finish but are strong. Plated spokes are glittery and pretty but need polishing to prevent rust, and are slightly weaker than galvanized. Stainless steel is generally reck-

oned the best, but is more demanding of wheelbuilding technique. In design, there is plaingauge, the same diameter throughout, and double-butted, with the stressed areas at the ends of the spoke thicker, and the mid-section thinner. Plain gauge spokes are easier to work with, and build a stiff wheel that can carry on for a while even if a spoke breaks. Double-butted spokes are more elastic and supple, and if correctly tensioned will in theory give an even stronger wheel.

Touring bikes and bikes for hard service are usually fitted with plain 14 gauge spokes. Sporting bikes tend towards 14/15/14 double-butted spokes, and light racing wheels often pare down to 15/16/15 double-butted. It's mostly a question of interest. If you want to get around with the minimum of fuss and attention for the bike, then use plain 14 gauge galvanized. If you enjoy bright, clean wheels and don't mind giving them a little care, like a polish job one night while watching TV or chatting with friends, then use double-butted stainless steel. Wheels are lovely things. They deserve to be pretty. It's fun to watch them sparkle in the early morning sunshine, or by the streetlights late at night, and is sort of like having company.

Hubs

There are two types of hubs: steel three-piece, and alloy single piece. Steel hubs malfunction as a matter of course, and should be studiously avoided. You'll only find them on very cheap bikes not worth having.

Alloy hubs are universal on decent lightweight bikes. They attach to the bike with conventional axle nuts, or via quick-release (QR) levers which work instantly. Quick-release hubs are standard for lightweight road bikes, and are a welcome convenience when working on the bike, traveling with it by auto, train or plane, and when locking up on the street (the front wheel is removed and locked together with the frame and back wheel to a rigorously immobile object).

The hub illustrated is a high flange design used for racing and sport riding. The flange is the part with all the holes where the spokes are attached. According to theory, the stiffness of a wheel is proportional to the flange diameter squared. Hence, commuting and touring bikes often use low flange hubs for a softer, less stiff ride. Opinion as to which type is stronger is divided. A high flange reduces the torque load on the spokes, but increases the angle at which the spokes join the rim, trading one problem for another. Tandems require high flange hubs to allow room for additional spokes. For solo bikes, flange size is less important than the overall quality of wheel building.

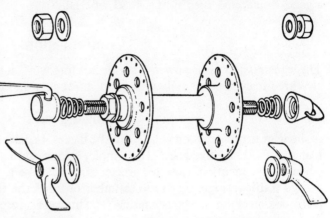

Inexpensive alloy hubs such as Atom, Normandy, and cheap models from the East can deform at the spoke holes, thereby promoting spoke breakage. The top brands are Campagnolo, Shimano, SunTour, Mavic, and Specialized, followed at an interval by Suzue, Zeus, Ofmega, Maillard, and Miche. Most of these manufacturers offer models in several different price ranges.

Many hubs have seals to help protect the bearings from dirt and water. This can be a useful feature, but make sure that the hub is user serviceable. Some hubs can only be serviced at the factory, an unnecessary inconvenience.

Ye Total Wheel

Wheel quality depends partly on the quality of the parts used, and partly on the design, but the thing that makes a good wheel is - a human being. There are all kinds of automatic wheel building machines, and some of them can make a good head start at putting together a wheel, but the final, crucial touch is human. One important function of a bike shop is to check and true the wheels before a new bike is given to a customer. A craft, an art - call it what you will - truing a wheel is something like playing a banjo or guitar. You learn the strings and the notes, you practice, and then your fingers have the music.

A pair of top class, fully handmade wheels can cost as much as a complete basic bike. Yup. But this buys superior performance and strength, and value for money reliability exceeding that of half a dozen sets of cheap wheels. Now very obviously, basic bikes cannot afford handmade wheels with jewel-like parts. In fact, cheap wheels will not stand much more than 6 months of regular urban commuting, and just one long, heavily loaded tour can be finis. One important reason why many people upgrade from cheap bikes after a year or so is, they get fed up with dodgy wheels and broken spokes.

It may be discouraging to hear that wheels can be a source of grief. But the other side of the coin is that wheels can be really good. In fact, wheels can transform a bike - and you are not just limited to one set of wheels. It's increasingly common to run two pairs of wheels, one for heavy going, the other for sport and fun. So, you might buy a very quick road bike with light, fancy wheels, and plan to run heavier, no-nonsense wheels when using the bike for commuting or loaded touring. Or, for economic reasons you might buy a bike with a fairly good frame and so-so wheels, and upgrade the spinners when you can afford to do so.

One basic governing factor for options in wheels is the quality of the frame. Good wheels will not make a dull frame go whiz. This is why first and foremost you go for a good frame, and then next - good wheels!

Transmission

The transmission turns power at the pedals into work at the rear wheel - motion. There are three main types: single gear, hub multi-gear and derailleur multi-gear.

Single gear

A single gear transmission consists of the basics: pedals, cranks and chainwheel, chain, rear sprocket, and freewheel. It's simple, strong and reliable, and fine for flat terrain when you've plenty of time for accelerating the bike to speed. But for hills and stop-and-go traffic a single gear ratio (number of times the rear wheel turns for each complete rotation of the cranks) is limiting. The human powerplant does not churn out slathers of energy. In a low gear ratio (fewer turns of the wheel for each rotation of the cranks) good for climbing hills, you'll run out of breath trying to spin the cranks fast enough for speed on the level. In a high gear ratio (more turns of the wheel for each rotation of the cranks) good for speed on the level, climbing will agonize your muscles and eventually bust your knees. The way to flexibility is a hub or derailleur gear system with multiple gears.

Hub gears

Hub gears are internal; the mechanism nests safely within the hub shell where nothing can get at it. The basic design is nearly 100 years old and is used on utility bikes all over the world. It's as tried and true as they come. Most makes have 3 speeds, with adequate range for ordinary utility use over moderate terrain. Sturmey-Archer also offer a 5-speed model with a slightly greater range.

RIDING FIXED

The most sophisticated and fastest transmission is none at all - riding fixed. There's only one gear, and no freewheel. When the back wheel turns, so do the cranks. The only way to stop pedaling is to stop the bike.

Riding fixed is a traditional European method for winter training. At the end of the road racing season the multi-gear bike is mothballed, and a fixed gear machine commissioned. Sometimes it's a track bike made for the job, but often it is just an old, stripped down road bike that can endure the grunge and grime of winter. The classic gear ratio is 63 inches, which is low and easy to spin.

The bike is used for everything. With only one gear ratio the rider is forced to learn how to spin the cranks at blinding speeds. There's no other way to make the bike move, or to stay with it on the downhills. The rider becomes progressively more supple, fluid - and fast. Come Spring and a return to the multi-gear bike and there's no holding him or her. It is said, with justice, that you do not know how to ride a bike until you have ridden fixed for at least a season.

Hub gears are easy to shift. Three- and 5-speed hub gears are controlled by an external shift lever that can be operated at any time, whether the bike is moving or not. Another type of hub gear is the semi-automatic 2-speed. When pedaling is momentarily paused the unit shifts, up or down as the case may be.

Hub gears are simple and reliable, but have performance drawbacks. One is that the intervals, or jumps, between gears are large, which makes it difficult to maintain a steady, efficient pedaling rate. Another is fundamental: the mechanism itself consumes a lot of the rider's output. The amount of power lost through internal friction is a matter of some debate, but 18 percent is an oft cited figure.

Derailleur gears

Derailleur gears live out in the open air, exposed to wet, dirt, and knocks. They appear crude: to change gear ratio, pieces of metal poke at the chain, knocking it from one set of gear teeth to another. And yet, derailleur gears in good condition can be up to 99 percent efficient in delivering power to the rear wheel. This is why they are the universal choice for performance bikes.

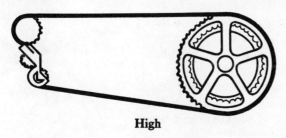

High

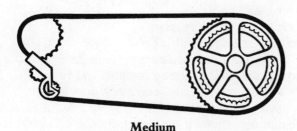

Medium

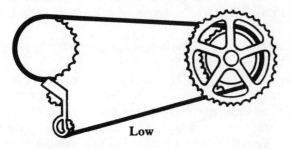

Low

The range of gear ratios in a derailleur system depends on the size of the chainrings on the crankset (the business with the pedals), and the size of the sprockets, or cogs, on the freewheel (the spiky business on the rear wheel). Large on the front to small on the rear makes the wheel go around more times for each rotation of the cranks - speed. Small on the front to large on the rear makes the wheel go around fewer times for each rotation of the cranks - torque. Chainrings and sprockets go up and down in size a tooth at a time, and so derailleur systems are very flexible in size and pattern of gear ratios.

Derailleur systems divide into two general design categories: competition and touring. In racing the need is to keep the human powerplant churning away at peak efficiency. There's one thing to do - go. The gear ratios are tightly clustered in a narrow range: close ratio gears. In touring and general riding the need is to extend the work range as widely as possible. There are many things to do, from lazing along boosted by a tailwind to climbing stiff gradients while laden with baggage. The gear ratios are broadly spaced: wide ratio gears.

Derailleurs

A derailleur (or mech, in bikie parlance) moves the chain from sprocket to sprocket (rear), or chainring to chainring (front). The rear mech also keeps the chain taut by wrapping it through a spring loaded arm. With close ratio gears the sprockets on the

freewheel are near to each other in size, and there is less chain to gather in. A typical competition mech is light-weight and compact, with a short arm, and shifts quickly and precisely. With wide range gears the sprockets are further apart in size and there is more chain to gather in. A touring or mountainbike mech is usually larger and mechanically more elaborate, with a long arm, and shifting is not as whiz as with a com-petition unit.

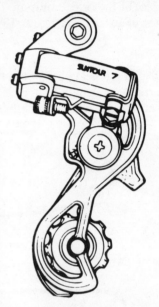

Derailleurs come in good,

Short arm mech   better, and best quality

grades. Just about all of them work. The differences relate to weight, mechanical sophistication, speed of shifting,   **Long arm mech**

strength, finish, and range or capacity. Competition and mountainbike designs are usually strong, touring designs range from simple and strong to complex and vulnerable. For example, the Huret Duopar is a touring mech justly reknowned for smooth shifting over wide range sprockets even when under load, and almost as famous for breaking. The complex mechanical articulation that allows it to zoom from a small sprocket up onto a mega-sprocket is also the means for the unit to destroy itself if something gets out of turn. A mech like the Duopar is fine for a rider who loves precise shifting and knows how to handle the unit. In unskilled hands, however, it can turn cannibal and tear itself to bits.

Such traumas are reasonably rare. Most bike manufacturers prefer to fit reliable equip-ment, and use simple and strong touring mechs. You're only likely to consider a very sophisticated model as a replacement or upgrade. If you enjoy lightness and precision, then by all means try a high tech whizzer. If you want the thing to work even when you make a mistake, then stick with the more robust models made for mountainbikes.

For some years now the cycle components market has been dominated by two major Japanese firms, Shimano and SunTour. They've a running, ding-dong battle for first place, competing vigorously throughout comprehensive ranges from basic budget models through to state of the art models at the forefront of technology. One or the other firm may momentarily forge into the lead, but the other soon catches up. The happy result is that you are on very safe ground with Shimano or SunTour equipment, and likely out ahead of the pack.

The derailleur was invented in 1933 by Tullio Campagnolo, a name that has stood ever since for the pinnacle of elegance and efficiency in cycle components. Many road racing cyclists regard the Campagnolo Record series derailleurs as the best available. Finish and assembly is arguably the finest, and while the design is conservative, it is race-proven for strength and durability. When the chips are down the most important quality is that the equipment works. SunTour and Shimano have the technological edge, Campagnolo the pedigree of victory.

Where the Japanese firms score decisive points is in the important areas of low- and mid-price components - the kind most often seen on production bikes, and that most people use. Savoring top line equipment is fun, but the impressive thing is that you can buy a decent, useable derailleur for the price of a meal - in a fairly cheap restaurant!

Gearing - the size and pattern of gear ratios in a transmission - is a major factor when selecting a derailleur, and this subject is covered under Fitting. Read this chapter before buying a bike.

Shift levers

The shift lever is the means for moving the derailleur from sprocket to sprocket (or chainring to chainring) and then holding it in place. Mechanically, there are two kinds: open and semi-automatic.

An open shift lever depends on simple friction or a ratchet to keep the lever in position. This means that shifting is stopless; aligning the derailleur so that the chain meshes smoothly with the sprocket is done by feel and ear - a knack that comes more easily to some people than others. An semi-automatic shift lever has stops for each correct position; alignment of derailleur and sprocket is completely automatic - a marvellous facility at any level of riding ability.

For semi-automatic shifting both shift lever and derailleur must be designed for semi-automatic operation. Pairing an semi-automatic shift lever with an ordinary derailleur won't work. Another point is that tolerances in an semi-automatic system are stringent.

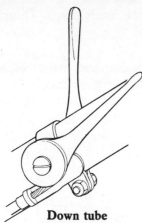

Down tube

All parts must be firmly mounted, the sprockets must be precisely equidistant from each other, and the control cable without slack, or the system will malfunction. Which could be very daunting but for the saving grace: a selector switch for semi-automatic or normal operation. A semi-automatic system can be changed to normal, stopless mode anytime you want. Eat your cake and

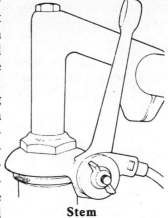

Stem

have it too! This versatility is one reason why semi-automatic shifting systems are gaining so rapidly in popularity.

Generally, shift levers are paired with derailleurs, SunTour for SunTour, Shimano for

Shimano, and so on, and generally, quality is commensurate. A basic mech will have a simple friction lever that moves easily when releasing derailleur spring tension, and that needs more pressure when tightening the spring. A better mech will have a lever with ratchet or clutch mechanism that moves easily in either direction

Shift levers are mounted in various places: on the down tube, on the handlebars, at the handlebar ends, and on the stem. Down tube mount-

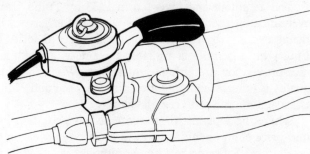

Thumb shifter

ing is the classic method for bikes with drop handlebars. It allows short control cables giving maximum feel and quick response when shifting. One's hand falls naturally to the down tube position, which is on the center line of the bike and thus has the minimum adverse effect on bike stability.

Handlebar end shifters need long cables that give a sloppier response. Mounting on drop handlebars often requires the drilling of holes in the handlebar, and there have been instances where this has led to corrosion and a complete snapping apart of the handlebar while the rider was underway. Handlebar end shifters are a matter of individual preference, as they are fairly rare on production bikes.

Thumb shifters are a blessing from the evolution of mountainbikes. They are designed for flat handlebars and

Bar end

mount just inboard of the brake levers, so that both gears and brakes can be operated without removing hands from the bars. They're lovely.

Stem mounted shifters are a bad idea. They were developed because they look easy to use. But in a crash they can puncture your gut or tear off the family jewels. Thumb shifters are infinitely better, and much friendlier.

Cranksets

Cranks and chainwheels are made of aluminum alloy or steel. Design varies in the method of fastening to the bottom bracket axle. The Ashtabula is a steel one-piece crank, chainwheel, and bottom bracket design, and is most often seen on BMX and cruiser bikes.

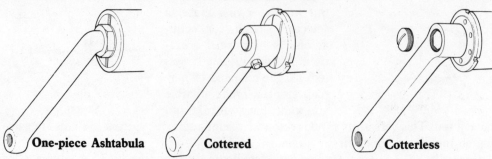

One-piece Ashtabula   **Cottered**   **Cotterless**

Steel cottered cranks are fastened to the bottom bracket axle with a wedge shaped cotter pin, and are usual on cheap roadster bikes. Alloy cotterless cranksets use a recessed bolt to fix the cranks to the bottom bracket axle, and are used for low-price bikes through to superbikes.

Cotterless cranksets vary considerably in type and quality. Bottom line are one-piece cranksets with a fixed chainring. They are used on roadsters, commuting bikes, and cheap sports bikes. When the chainring wears out, the whole unit has to be replaced, at modest cost. Although a fixed chainring limits the possibilities in gear ratios, this is often of little consequence for a utility bike.

Cranksets with detachable chainrings divide into two categories, racing and touring. Racing cranksets are highly stressed, and for maximum strength, long arms are used to mount the chainrings. This limits the minimum size of chainring that can be fitted. Touring bikes need climbing gears, and on touring cranksets the arms are short, so that smaller chainrings giving lower gears can be used.

Competition cranksets are usually doubles, with the chainrings fairly close to each other in size. This gives adequate range for close ratio gears and fast, reliable shifting - the shift lever needs only to banged one way or the other. Doubles can also be used for touring by simply reducing the size of the chainrings so that all the ratios are in a low range.

It's actually best to concentrate gear ratios where you need them most, but a lot of people want it both ways: wide range gearing with low ratios for easy climbing, and big ratios for speed. The range of a double can be extended by using chainrings and/or freewheel sprockets well apart in size, but then there are large jumps between gear ratios and shifting is ragged. A better method for creating wide range gearing is to use triple chainrings. These

CHAINSETS

Competition   Touring

are virtually standard on mountainbikes and very common on touring bikes. Triple chainrings space gear ratios more evenly and make the transmission mechanically more coherent. A triple needs more technique and time for shifting, but is usually smoother and more comfortable than an overextended double. In times past triples were in some disfavor because they were often sensitive and fiddly. The advent of mountainbikes requiring very wide range gearing spurred technological improvements and they now work very well. They are fine for beginners, and for whenever wide range gears are required. See Gearing for more information.

Cranksets with oval shaped chainrings have become quite popular for touring bikes and mountainbikes. These vary the gear ratio during each revolution of the cranks to correspond with the strong and weak parts of the power stroke: lower and easier as the pedals pass through 6 and 12 o'clock, higher and harder as the pedals pass through 3 and 9 o'clock. The net effect is to improve torque but not speed. Put another way, it works, but not for cyclists! Behind that cryptic comment is the quintessential lore of cycling: all through the years aspiring cyclists have diligently applied themselves to

CHANGING THE RINGS

One sin committed by all too many bike manufacturers is the fitting of competition cranksets to less expensive, heavier bikes that will be used primarily for general riding and touring. It is then impossible to fit the lower gear ratios that these bikes so desperately need. Another lingering trap for the unwary are cranksets for which replacement chainrings are unobtainable. Chainring patterns vary from manufacturer to manufacturer and model to model. They divide into a number of compatibility groups of which four or five are mainstream. Parts availability on these is usually very easy. With some of the more obscure models it can be nonexistent. A final point is minimum chainring size. If you're buying a bike for touring and/or off-road riding, then the ability to fit a small 24T inner ring is usually an asset.

mastering the art of spinning, i.e. rotating the cranks at speeds of 100 rpm and more. It's the route to optimum performance. Oval chainrings are not used for racing. Their fast/slow/fast/slow rhythm is not conducive to fast spinning. Optimum efficiency is sometimes a different story. Tourists and mountainbikers have different needs than racers, and the better low speed torque of oval chainrings is often a practical help when climbing, or moving slowly over tricky terrain. Oval chainrings are good for people who pedal slowly.

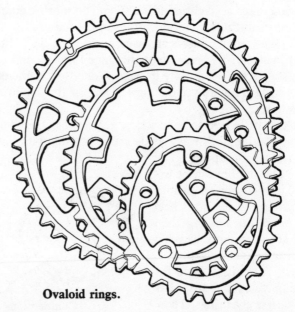

Ovaloid rings.

They do work, some people like them hugely, and it's pretty much a matter of try and see - but not for racing.

Chains

Chains used to be simple, cheap, and black. Nowadays chains come in a variety of colors and designs, and are made with better quality steels using sophisticated hardening and plating processes. They are stronger, lighter and much faster at changing gear. There are two main types: standard width, and narrow width. Narrow chains are

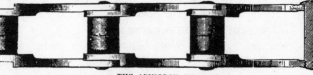

THE ABINGDON CHAIN.

made for use with compact freewheels (see below), and usually also work with standard freewheels. Standard chains are too wide to work smoothly with compact freewheels.

Chains from manufacturers such as SunTour, Shimano, and Regina are designed to be used with their own transmission systems. The area of greatest variety is sideplate shape, which is important to speed and ease of shifting. They all work, but using a chain from one manufacturer on a freewheel from another will sometimes degrade performance, particularly with the new semi-automatic shifting systems. Sedis is a popular independent brand with a comprehensive range of models that seem to always work well.

Freewheels

The freewheel is attached to the rear hub and holds the sprockets, or cogs. These may be five, six, or seven in number. Five sprockets is standard. A 6-speed freewheel may be slightly wider than a 5-speed freewheel, or be a compact design that uses a narrower chain to squeeze six sprockets into the width of a standard 5-speed freewheel. Seven-speed freewheels use a narrow chain and are the same width as a 6-speed freewheel.

In general, 6- and 7-speed freewheels are best suited to fast road and racing bikes. The extra width of the freewheel requires more wheel dish - insetting the hub by using shorter spokes on the freewheel side of the hub - which weakens the wheel.

This is one reason why sturdy touring bikes and mountainbikes favor 5-speed freewheels.

Standard design freewheels thread onto the rear wheel hub. Pedaling winds the freewheel on tight, and it is not always easy to get it back off. A cassette design freewheel slides onto a spline and is much easier to assemble and

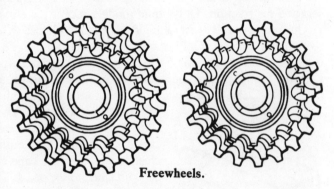

Freewheels.

disassemble. However, a cassette system requires a specially designed hub and freewheel, which precludes using standard freewheels. You're limited to the one system.

HOW MANY SPEEDS?

In Ye Olden days, derailleur gear bikes were called 10-speeds, because the common pattern was a pair of chainrings running to 5 sprockets on the freewheel. These days, you'll find anything from 5 to 21 speeds, with 1 to 3 chainrings running to 5 to 7 sprockets. It sounds good on paper, the availability of 12 or 18 speeds has dazzle appeal, but as a rough rule of thumb more is not always better! You probably already know that a 10-speed only has 8 usable ratios, because it is mechanically harmful to run the chain from the large front to the large rear, or from the small front to small rear. Freewheels with 6 and 7 sprockets magnify this restriction by their greater tendency to produce gear ratios that duplicate each other. Thus, a 2F/7R rig that is supposed to have 14 speeds may still have only 8 different usable ratios! The permutations are myriad but the upshot is: 6- and 7-speed freewheels are best confined to racing bikes with closely spaced gears, and a 6-speed freewheel is the most that should be paired with a triple chainset. For maximum reliability, in wear and in performance, stick with 5-speed freewheels.

Pedals

Pedals are like shoes: intimate, and considerably varied in function, fit and comfort. The pedals on most production bikes are basic and will need replacement within a year. If you have preferences it is probably worth making a substitution at the time of bike purchase. There are three types of pedals: cage, platform, and system (special design).

Parallel cage, or Rat Trap, type pedals have the same shape on each side and can be used either way up. Most models for road bikes can be fitted with toe clips. The pedal is then dual mode: toe clip or open. This arrangement is attractive for people new to toe clips. Parallel cage models for mountainbikes are beefier and the cage side edges are serrated for traction. Only some models accept toe clips.

Quill cage pedals are a racing design made for use with toe clips and cleats. Only one side is right way up. The quill is a small protrusion on the end of the pedal that helps keep the foot in place. The underside of the pedal is rounded, for extra clearance when cornering. Cleats are a device attached to the sole of the shoe. They are about the size

'Bear Trap'

of a matchbook in area, and around a half inch thick. A thin, deep slot across the middle mates with the rear cage side of the pedal. Tightening the toe clip strap snugs the cleat firmly over the cage side and ensures that the shoe stays attached to the pedal. This improves both performance and safety.

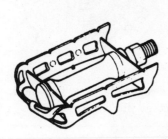

Quill cage

Cage pedals are designed for minimal weight and are intended to be used with cycling shoes that have a stiff sole for supporting the foot. Using them with ordinary shoes may lead to foot cramps on long rides.

Platform pedals have a larger surface area for supporting the foot. Most of the metal and nylon road models are made for use with toe clips and cleats, with a raised ridge to engage the cleat. The off-road models also usually accept toe clips, but not cleats. They often have raised studs on the platform area to help grip the shoe. Rubber platform pedals can be used either way up and do not accept toe clips. They are primarily for simple utility and cruiser bikes.

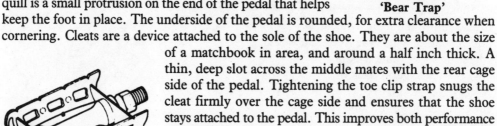

Rubber platform

Metal platform

The toe clip strap and cleat method for attachment to a pedal is classic and works well, but for a secure grip the strap must be tight and this can lead to numbness or discomfort in the foot. Loosening the strap brings relief, but then there is a risk of pulling out of the pedal and possibly losing control of the bike.

The solution to this problem is a system pedal and cleat designed to work as a unit. There's no toe clip or strap. The pedal includes a mechanism that automatically grips the cleat when the rider steps into the pedal. The process is just like a step-in ski binding, and in fact one leading range of models comes from Look, a ski equipment manufacturer. So long as the pedaling forces are vertical, the cleat stays firmly attached to the pedal. The method for disengagement is particular to each make and model, but is usually a simple rolling motion of the foot to the side.

System pedals are lovely. They have a better grip than toe clips and cleats, and yet are usually easier to disengage. There's no toe clip strap cutting painfully into the foot. Weight and bulk are reduced. A really minimalist model like the AeroLite weighs 74 g in steel and but 48 g in titanium, as against a minimum of 200 g for a top quality standard pedal with a toe clip and strap. A system pedal can only be used with a specific design of cleat. This restriction does not matter when the bike is a personal machine used only by you.

Pedals range in cost from a few dollars to over $100. Inexpensive pedals wear out after about 5000 miles. With regular maintenance good quality pedals will turn in 100,000 miles - literally cheaper in the long run. However, if early retirement is forced on a pedal by damage from a fall or grounding on a corner, the economic advantage goes to the cheap pedal.

Names: The SR rubber platform pedal with an alloy body is the best of its type. At peanut prices the parallel cage Lyotard 136 is a favorite standby, and the steel platform Lyotard 23 is known for smooth, reliable performance.

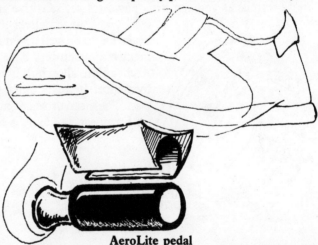

AeroLite pedal

The slightly dearer alloy SR platform pedal is popular for touring bikes. The Campagnolo range of quill pedals is excellent in quality and value throughout. Shimano and Sun-Tour both make fine pedals. I've always had a soft spot for MKS pedals. They work fine and don't cost the earth. In system pedals the AeroLite is miles ahead of anything else.

Selecting an appropriate pedal depends on riding style, the kind of shoes used, and a host of other variables. Many of these are discussed elsewhere in this book. After reading the mountainbike chapter, for example, you should know if you need massive Bear Trap pedals with jagged studs, or slimmer pedals with toe clips. Pedals are personal. Think through your needs, examine and fondle the hardware - and choose whatever you fancy best.

Brakes

Bicycle brake designs differ in balance of braking power, weight, mechanical precision, and expense. They are a dynamic part of bike performance, and it is important to know how different kinds of brakes mix and match with different kinds of bikes. For example, lightweight side pull brakes are fine for road racing bikes, but are a suicide pact when used on mountainbikes. Such machines exist and riding them is terrifying. You can't possibly enjoy yourself on a bike unless you understand and have confidence in the brakes. There are three basic kinds of brakes: hub, disc, and caliper.

Hub brakes

Rear wheel hub coaster brakes are usually pedal operated. They are easy to apply but hard to control and can cause a skid by locking up the wheel. They do not have real stopping power. It's a skid or next to nothing. Skidding to a stop is excessively exciting at high speeds, wears out tires very quickly, and takes too long. Coaster brakes have poor heat dissipating qualities and can burn out on a long downhill descent. In short, they are very Mickey Mouse, and usually found only on beach cruiser bikes and specialized BMX freestyle machines. As a means of stopping they are like dropping down a rock held to the bike with rope - not serious.

Front and rear wheel drum brakes are usually hand operated and, potentially, are as serious as you can get - powerful yet sensitive at all speeds, and effective in all

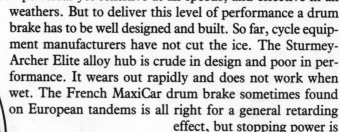

weathers. But to deliver this level of performance a drum brake has to be well designed and built. So far, cycle equipment manufacturers have not cut the ice. The Sturmey-Archer Elite alloy hub is crude in design and poor in performance. It wears out rapidly and does not work when wet. The French MaxiCar drum brake sometimes found on European tandems is all right for a general retarding effect, but stopping power is not electric. The same applies to models from Huret-Sachs.

Good drum brakes are wonderful, and I hope we eventually see viable models from major manufacturers. But at this writing they are obtainable only from custom

Section: Sachs drum brake

engineering builders, at custom prices. The one that I know and can recommend with confidence is a fair distance away: David Wrath-Sharman, High Path Engineering, 54 High Path Road, Merrow, Guilford, Surrey, GU1 2QQ, England.

Disc brakes

Disc brakes are precise and powerful and are used on tandems and tricycles. The commercial models are too heavy for solo bikes. Good lightweight models are custom equipment. Disc brakes work well but tend to be finicky; they need to be kept in precise adjustment, and a few drops of oil or other lubricant on the disc can greatly reduce braking power. For the requisite investment of time, energy, and money, drum brakes give better results.

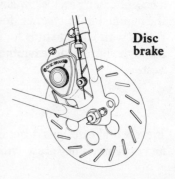

Disc brake

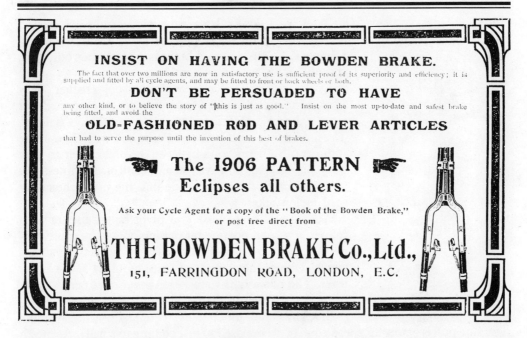

Caliper brakes

Braking for most bikes is through the use of a caliper mechanism to press a pair of blocks (or shoes) against the wheel rim. There are four design types: side pull, center pull, cantilever, and roller cam.

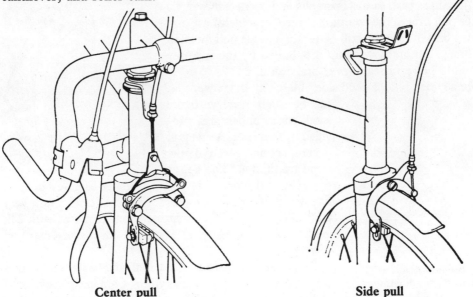

Center pull   Side pull

Side pull brakes pivot two caliper arms on a single bolt and are made in two versions: inexpensive, for cheap bikes, and expensive, for use on quality bikes. Cheap side pull brakes are stamped out of steel and chromed to prevent rust. They are mechanically crude and loose, and have widely set apart, long caliper arms in order to reach around and past fenders and thick tires. The net result is a sloppy mechanism with weak performance. Cheap side pull brakes do work, but only just, and only with constant attention.

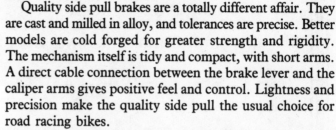

Quality side pull brakes are a totally different affair. They are cast and milled in alloy, and tolerances are precise. Better models are cold forged for greater strength and rigidity. The mechanism itself is tidy and compact, with short arms. A direct cable connection between the brake lever and the caliper arms gives positive feel and control. Lightness and precision make the quality side pull the usual choice for road racing bikes.

Center pull brakes use two pivot bolts, one for each caliper arm, and operate by pulling on a yoke cable connecting the two arms. This gives a mechanical advantage which reduces the amount of force required at the brake lever. The two arms balance each other, and need adjustment less frequently than a side pull design.

Cantilever

Side and center pull brakes stop equally well. The more rigid side pull is better for speed control (as opposed to just coming to a halt). At speed, the slacker center pull brake can be more inclined to snatch and exert more deceleration than necessary or safe. (Mind, this is starting to split hairs. The Tour de France has been won using bikes with center pull brakes. Much depends on quality of manufacture.) In times past, ease of operation and maintenance made center pull brakes the common choice for general use and touring bikes. They are still better than a side pull for such machines, but are now being supplanted by the superior and more powerful cantilever brake design.

For a racing bike, a good side pull has all the power that can be safely used with the small road contact area provided by thin tires. A side pull is compact and aerodynamic - and traditional. The better models stand more as jewel-like works of art than simple mechanical devices. One very upmarket Modolo brake features washers plated with 24k gold. This is actually a legitimate means of retarding corrosion.

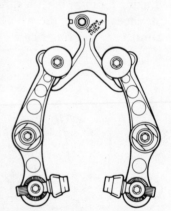

Roller cam design

Shimano 7400 with bearing adjustment

The dominant marque in side pull and center pull brakes is Weinmann. They make everything from inexpensive basic stoppers through to professional grade jewels. Dia Compe also cover the range. For class, Campagnolo, Shimano, SunTour, and Modolo all produce lovely models.

Cantilever brakes pivot on bosses (mounting points) brazed onto the fork blades and seat stays. The two separate caliper arms on either side of the wheel are joined by a yoke cable, which is pulled by the brake lever cable. The design has greater mechanical advantage and better balance than a center pull, and is more rigid and lighter than a side pull. Performance is naturally superior in all respects: sensitivity, ease of application, and sheer raw power. Cantilever brakes are SOP for mountainbikes and heavy duty touring bikes.

Some manufacturers produce 'solo' model cantilever brakes with shorter arms and blocks than the conventional 'tandem' models. These stinge on performance, which is not the idea. If you go for cantilevers, do not settle for less than full-size arms and blocks.

Last but hardly least in caliper brakes is the roller cam design. One of the best known was originated by mountainbike designer and builder Charles Cunningham and is manufactured by SunTour. As with a cantilever, the arms are separate and pivot on bosses alongside the wheels, on the fork blades and chain stays. There is no yoke cable. The ends of the caliper arms nearly touch each other, and in operation are spread apart by a roller cam. The performance is so hot that many bike builders install an roller cam on the back wheel only, and a regular cantilever on the front. Some people have found that a roller cam on the front runs too much risk of locking the wheel and pitching the rider over the handlebars.

Roller cam brakes are fairly well limited to high performance mountainbikes and custom touring bikes. The design is intricate and easily fouled by mud and stones. In fact, it's best to enclose it in a special protective pouch. This kind of fiddling about is all right if you want and can use the performance. If you just want to fit brakes and have them work when required, then the simpler cantilever design is a better bet.

Cantilever and roller cam brakes require brazed mounting bosses, each of a different type, and in slightly different locations. You can't change from one type to the other.

Mathauser hydraulic

A bike without the required mounting bosses can have them added at a later point in time, but this involves stripping down the bike to the bare frame, and then repainting it after the brazing work is done. This is OK for a conversion of an old bike, but not very economic for a new bike.

At this writing the best cantilever brakes are the Shimano models, followed at an interval by Dia Compe. Oddly, the Weinmann cantilever is crude and not very good. For a roller cam brake look to SunTour. A few small builders make their own roller cam or other special design brakes; you have to assess these hands on, and consider availability of parts.

A recent high tech introduction is the W. Mathauser hydraulic brake. This is a caliper design that uses fluid (like car brakes) rather than wire cables. Although the Mathauser hydraulic brake is attached with a single pivot bolt, as with center and side pull designs, it is mounted behind the forks and stays and transfer blocks transmit the very strong braking forces to the frame. Hydraulic systems are the norm for serious power, and down the years many people have chased the goal of a fluid operated cycle brake. Like internal hub gears, it is the use of some quite sophisticated design and engineering to produce a mechanism that, externally, is simple and easy to use. It looks as if Mathauser have turned the trick. Of course this is vanguard technology, and for now at least, very much for people who enjoy high tech and don't mind paying for it.

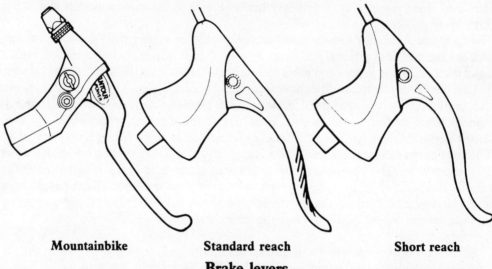

Mountainbike   **Standard reach**   **Short reach**

Brake levers

Brake levers come in two types: flat handlebar and drop handlebar. Simple flat handlebar brake levers as found on roadsters and commuting bikes are basic and simply a means to make the brakes work. Brake levers for mountainbikes are more sophisticated. They are shaped for comfort under steady use, and top models have features like adjustable reach to accommodate different hand sizes.

Brake levers for drop handlebars all have the same general shape, but subtle variations from manufacturer to manufacturer can be important. This is because a lot of riding is done with the hands on the hoods, and the fingers resting on the levers. Make sure that the levers fit your grip, as some makes are only suitable for large hands.

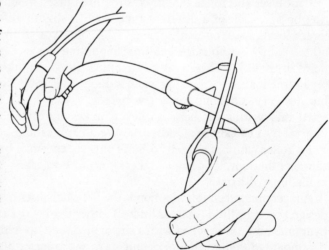

On some bikes the brake levers include a second 'safety' or 'dual' lever underneath the straight section of the handlebars.

These were originally developed for use on touring bikes, to increase the number of positions from which the brakes can be operated and help rider comfort when making long descents. Marketing flacks quickly took to promoting them as 'safety' levers, implying that they could help avoid or mitigate an accident. The truth is precisely the opposite.

Dual levers have to travel a long distance before the brakes engage. If the system is not closely adjusted, it is possible for the 'safety' lever to bang uselessly against the handlebar while you carry on to destruction. Even when adjusted properly, dual levers need 20 to 30 percent more distance for a stop than standard levers. If you're riding top of the bars and an emergency arises, there is no time to change your mind and dive for the standard levers. All you can do is clutch the inferior alternative and hope for the best. What's more, in the top of the bars position, bike control and handling is reduced. This is safety? Finally, hands on the brake hoods is one of the most popular riding positions. The hardware on most dual levers makes impossible the fitting of rubber hoods which are essential for comfort in this position. Bah. You don't find dual levers on good bikes. It's as simple as that.

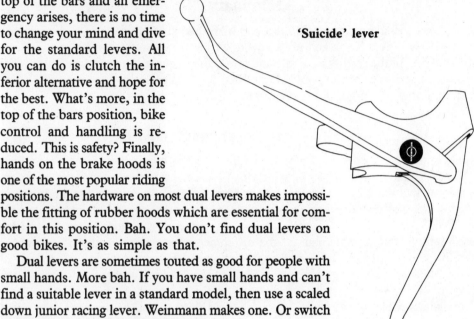

'Suicide' lever

Dual levers are sometimes touted as good for people with small hands. More bah. If you have small hands and can't find a suitable lever in a standard model, then use a scaled down junior racing lever. Weinmann makes one. Or switch to flat bars and mountainbike levers.

Whatever you do, don't settle for second rate brakes. If the bike of your choice has dual levers as standard equipment, insist that they be removed, or that a substitute unit without dual levers be installed. A modest charge for this service is fair, but if the shop becomes tacky, or tries to convince you that dual levers are a good idea, then buy your bike elsewhere.

Brake blocks

With caliper brakes it is essential that the brake block and rim materials are properly matched. Rims are steel or alloy, blocks are rubber, leather or synthetic. Rubber works well on steel or alloy in dry weather, but in wet conditions, poorly on alloy, and sometimes not at all on steel. You haven't lived until you've careened for a few miles down a long hill on a dark, wet night, wondering if each moment will be your last. Rubber blocks are acceptable only for lightweight racing bikes with alloy rims and a minimum of mass to retard. Leather blocks are designed for steel rims only and will chew an alloy rim to bits. They work well in the wet, but badly in the dry, and aren't acceptable for anything. Synthetic blocks outperform all others on alloy or steel rims in the dry, and are in the top performance class in the wet.

The only liability of synthetic blocks is that they can be too effective. A panic-stricken novice rider could clamp down on the front brake too hard and cartwheel the bike. However, synthetic blocks are expensive and the vast majority of new bikes are therefore fitted with rubber blocks. These are more even-tempered in performance and will suffice for a novice rider until he or she becomes adept at braking. But graduation to synthetic blocks, which are stronger in wet conditions, should be an early priority. Aztec, Mathauser, and Kool Stop are good brands.

Summary

When I was a kid most of the neighborhood bikes had sneaker brakes - a foot jammed against the back tire. It worked pretty good. Proper brakes are a lot better, and currently, the best of the readily available and affordable types are the cantilever and roller cam designs. I don't see the point of anything less, except on a road racing bike, or a used bike that is not going to be pressed hard.

Handlebars, Stem, and Saddle

It would make very good sense for bike manufacturers to supply their machines without handlebars, stem, or saddle, leaving selection of these items to the individual bike buyer. It's more than a matter of personal taste or style. These components are the interface between rider and machine and the means for making the bike comfortable and efficient. People are like blades of grass: similar, but never exactly alike. A small variation in stem length, for example, can be the difference between a bike that gives you an aching back after a few miles, or one that you can ride forever. The vital subject of fitting is detailed in a separate chapter. Here, there's just a quick skim through the hardware.

Handlebars come in two basic shapes: flat and downswept, or dropped. The Maes pattern is the most common downswept version and is suitable for racing, touring, and general use. The Randonneur pattern is for touring, with the upswept portions giving the hands firm bracing points when riding in an upright position. The Pista is a pure racing pattern, with little purchase for riding upright.

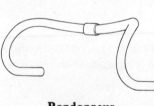

Randonneur

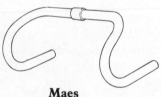

Maes

The fore and aft position of downswept handlebars is determined by the length of the stem (see Fitting). The back end of this item should be rounded, in case you connect with it in a sudden stop. On very cheap bikes the bars and stem are made of steel, but otherwise alloy is the norm.

Flat handlebars come in two general applications: general, and mountainbike. Flat bars for general use as found on roadsters and commuting bikes are sort of like bucket handles: a means to get a grip and steer. They are

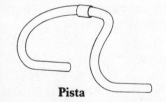

Pista

Bucket

not particularly shaped for comfort, durability, or character. Mountainbike handlebars are a totally different story. They are a dynamic part of bike performance and an essential aspect of comfort. There are two principle types: Bullmoose pattern, with bars and stem as a single unit, and two-piece, with separate bars held in a stem that is either a two-prong Slingshot design, or single-prong four bolt design. Bullmoose pattern bars are extremely strong. They come in various nuances of shape: low, high, short, long, narrow, wide, and the choice has to be right first time out, because it can't be changed. On the other hand, once the shape is right, the pattern is strong and gives a convenient platform for carrying things.

Two-piece bars give greater flexibility in positioning. Different reach stems can be used, and the bars themselves can be rotated for subtle changes in configuration. The whole approach is more minimalist, and currently more favored for competition machines. It flexes more than a Bullmoose pattern, however, and is not as strong.

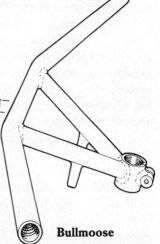

Bullmoose

Mountainbike bars are made in steel or alloy. For once, steel does not indicate cheap. Mountainbikes are made for thrashing and hammering. Steel bars can take repeated abuse more readily than alloy bars, which fatigue much more easily. An alloy bar (of any kind, road or mountainbike) which has had a severe bend should be discarded, because it could fail without warning. Steel can be hammered about with a much greater margin for safety. This said, the weight/performance advantages of alloy bars make them the favored choice.

I'm not big on fancy bars. The best accolade for bars is that they work so comfortably and well that you don't notice them.

There are two basic types of saddles. One is the mattress design, wide and comfy and often fitted with coil springs or other shock absorbing mechanism. It's made to go with flat handlebars and a riding position that puts most of the rider's weight on the saddle. The other type is the racing design, narrow and hard and made for use with drop handlebars. These distribute the rider's weight more evenly and allow a saddle shaped to reduce friction between the legs.

Saddles are about as personal as you can get. Fit and comfort are very individual. What is bliss for one person can be a medieval rack for another. This leaves bike manufacturers in a fix. Even if they supply a good quality saddle, not everyone is going to like it. Partly because of this, and partly because by now the manufacturer has run out of spare change, most production bikes are fitted with indifferent saddles. Some people do not notice; others will be well advised to substitute a better saddle at the time of bike purchase.

There are three essential types of saddles: leather, plastic, and plastic covered with a layer of foam or other shock absorbing material and wrapped in plastic or leather.

Leather saddles are the traditional type and can be very comfortable after 500 miles of riding, treatment with oils,

Racing

incantations, and beatings with a rolling pin. If you get on with a leather saddle you'll never find better, but it takes time and a hard behind. Rain will damage an unprotected leather saddle. If you opt for leather, buy the best - Brooks.

Plastic saddles are cheap, and feel like it. In hot weather they have you swimming about in your own sweat. They have the advantage of lightness, which is good for short distance races where weight is important. They are also impervious to weather, and can be a good choice for utility bikes that will often be left out in the rain.

Mattress

Saddles with a base of plastic, a layer of foam or polymer, and a top cover of leather are the most common type, and with good reason. They need no breaking in and rate very highly for comfort. They are engineered to meet specific requirements: racing models are thin and spartan, touring models are wider and softer. Some have what is known as an anatomic design, with the base shaped to allow extra room and padding where the pelvic bones make contact. These are popular for mountainbikes, as they allow freedom of movement and yet some insulation against shock.

Women have wider pelvic bones than men. This fact has now been recognized by most saddle manufacturers, but many production bikes are fitted with 'male' model saddles. If you are a woman, have it changed to a saddle made for your physique. The difference in pelvic bone width is easily catered for, but I do not know of any saddles that take into account the shallower female pubic arch. One drastic but apparently effective means of dealing with the problem is to simply cut away those portions of the saddle which cause discomfort.

Anatomic

Man or woman, if you buy a bike and the saddle is not to your liking, exchange it immediately for a better one and pay the price difference. You will spend many, many miles and hours on your saddle, and if you pinch pennies on this item you will be so reminded, for truth, by a sore behind and inflamed crotch.

My recommendation for a starter saddle is a fairly soft, foam or polymer filled model. But look out. Only you can say what is a good saddle. Two of my friends set off for India on their bikes, and after two days both were bitterly swearing a blue streak at the discomfort of their saddles - one a leather Brooks Pro, the other a Sella Italia anatomic filled with foam. When raging pain brought them to a halt, they switched saddles as a last resort. Suddenly all was bliss, and the rest of the 6000 mile journey went without a hitch. The only way to know about saddles is to try them for yourself.

General Summary

There are many different brands of bicycles, and each manufacturer usually produces a range of models in different price grades. In the upward progression from basic all steel bikes, you find an increasing use of aluminum alloy for the components, and for the frames, alloy steels, aluminum, and then finally, composites such as carbon fiber and Kevlar. At any point in the progression, a 'good' bicycle is one where design and materials work in harmony to fulfill the intended function of the machine.

Materials can be arbitrarily sorted into four grades:
1. Cheap - Frame of low carbon steel, steel components.

2. Basic - Frame of high carbon steel with small alloy content, alloy components except for steel wheels.

3. Medium - Frame of chrome-moly steel, or seamed double-butted steel, or aluminium, alloy components throughout.

4. High - Frame of seamless double-butted steel, or aluminum, or composite carbon fiber or Kevlar, alloy or carbon fiber components throughout.

This is how it all stacks up:

Design	Materials
1. Beach cruiser - Extra soft frame, 2 inch wide tires, hub brake, 50 lbs.	Cheap to basic.
2. Heavy roadster - Soft frame, 1.5 inch wide tires, hub gears, caliper brakes, 50 lbs.	Cheap but robust.
3. Light roadster (English Racer) - Soft frame, 1.375 inch wide tires, hub gears, caliper brakes, 35 lbs.	Cheap to basic.
4. Commuter (town) - Soft to medium frame, HP wheels with 1.25 inch wide tires, derailleur gears with medium range ratios, caliper brakes, flat bars, 25-30 lbs.	Basic to medium. Anything less is a light roadster, anything more is over the top.
5. Sports (10-speed) - As commuter, but medium to high range ratios, drop bars, 30 lbs. Knock-around general transport.	Cheap to basic. Anything better will be more specific in design and function.
6. Touring - Soft frame, HP wheels with 1.25 inch wide tires, derailleur gears with low to medium high ratios, cantilever brakes, drop bars, carrier racks, 26-30 lbs. Steady, relaxed load carrier.	Basic to high. Quality determines range: basic OK for weekend runs, but not a trip to Alaska.
7. Fast (sport) touring - Medium to stiff frame, HP wheels with 1 or 1.125 inch wide tires, derailleur gears with medium to high ratios, side pull or center pull brakes, drop bars, 24-28 lbs. Lively, performance-minded riding with light loads.	Medium to high. Anything less will shy on performance.
8. Fast road (training) - Stiff frame, HP wheels with 1 or 1.125 inch wide tires or sprint wheels and tubular tires, derailleur gears with closely spaced high ratios, side pull brakes, drop bars, 21-26 lbs. Full on for the fast lane and entry level racing. Baggage: credit card.	Medium to high. Anything less is a joke that manufacturers call a 'look-alike'.
9. Racing - Stiff frame, sprint wheels and tubular tires, derailleur gears with closely spaced high ratios, side pull brakes, drop bars, 18-22 lbs. For joy and racing.	High. Anything less isn't so.
10. Mountainbike (ATB) - Soft to medium frame, 24 or 26 inch wheels with 1.4 to 2.125 inch wide tires, derailleur gears with low to medium high ratios, cantilever or roller cam brakes, flat bars, 24-30 lbs. All terrain - in country or city.	Medium (a taste) to high (real thing).

SOMETHING FOR THE BACK CARRIER —
SUSSEX COAST

CHAPTER 5

Selection Part II

You want a bike suitable for your needs and budget. But in both areas it is usually wise to push a little, so that your bike has some open potential. Suppose, for example, that fitness is a priority, and that you would like to get in some vigorous exercise over a regular 5 mile commute to and from work, and on occasional day rides. A commuting bike would be fine for the commute, but once you were seasoned you would find edge-of-capacity riding out of character for the bike. A good fast tourer would better encourage 'going for it'. On the other hand, suppose the streets and roads for that 5 mile journey are lined with jagged craters, and there are byways - dirt tracks, disused railroads, open fields, who knows what - that look worth exploring. A lively mountainbike is the odds-on choice. You won't go quite as fast on smooth pavement, but you'll have lots of fun and all the room for improving fitness that you can take.

The classic error for novices is to under- or over-buy. They are interested in cycling but shy of 'all the fancy stuff'. They buy an all-steel machine good enough for local use, but that only gives a taste of what is possible when adventuring or going for a turn of speed. A year or so later they are back at the shop laying down the money for a better quality machine.

The opposite extreme is to want the best money can buy. The prospective cyclist buys a lightweight racing bike for commuting and quickly tires of a sore behind, endless punctures, and buckled wheels. The bike spends its life in a shed.

Evaluate and understand your own needs carefully, and then go for a bike that has some fun in reserve. Some bit, some thing, some aspect, that tickles your fancy and scratches a dream. This is the main trick for success with a bike. At root, the reason for cycling is that it is fun. Commuting, racing, touring, hauling the groceries and laundry, off-road bashing - all are experiences. Sure racing is fun. You can also really get off on hauling a heavy load with a nifty trailer. Pick what appeals to you.

One little word of caution. Anti-establishment machines are fun. It's very relaxing to drift down the road on an Old Faithful held together with rust - sort of like joining hands with the stream. The bike is greater than you are. But if you're looking at a bike as a pragmatic tool, then you want a good one that works cleanly and well. That's why I'm big on the No. 1 bike as just that little bit better and more satisfying - a machine that you can move and grow with.

The converse is not to buy more bike than is comfortable. Own the bike and use it, not have it tell you what to do. Hot, fine-tuned machines require a commensurate level of mechanical attention and riding ability. You can't leave them around loose. If your primary requirement is a thrasho utility bike to get you from here to there, and that can stand time spent outside, then buy that sort of machine.

Confounded for choice? You're not limited to just one bike. Start with what you like best. Then later, treat yourself again!

The Exact Machine

The problem with recommending specific bikes is that like people, bicycle manufacturing firms have good times and bad times. A well established company can merge with another, and until the two groups harmonize, product quality may suffer. Or a firm that has been in the doldrums may decide to capture a larger slice of the market, and offer a range of bikes at exceptionally good prices - for a while. Once business picks up, so do the prices.

Select a bike by first working out a solid idea of the design, quality level, and features you want. Then look around and see what's going. Without being tiresome, seek as many opinions as possible. Your most likely sources of advice and counsel are bike shops. These people want you as a customer. Of course they have particular lines of bikes to sell. But this cuts both ways. There are many reasons why a shop will have certain bikes and not others. If the shop looks halfway decent then the fact that they stock a machine can be a recommendation in itself. If you can't find that Wheelie Wonder that is supposed to beat any rival by at least $200, it may because the thing is a mangled pile of garbage that no dealer in town wants to touch with a barge pole. Listen to what the shops say. Yes, they will try to sell you what they have. But like food in a restaurant, what's on for the day may be the best thing.

The design, quality level, and features you want may cost more than you can afford. This is where matters can get really sticky. Be realistic. It is not a good idea to buy on price. In the end you pay, one way or the other. Better a good basic than a poor medium. If your budget is limited, then look to a used machine (see Buying a Bike).

Don't let price chasing lead you into a department or discount store. These places do not sell worthwhile bikes. In Buying a Bike I explain some of the vital role of a bike shop in making a bike work. This applies double to cheap bikes. Even if all you want is a basic, all steel runabout, buy it from a bike shop! The one you get from a discount store is likely to break, and when it does and you take it along to the bike shop for fixing, odds are they will say no. The reason is that the bike is wrong from the ground up and not worth trying to fix. It's a waste of your money. If you cannot afford a bike from a bike shop, buy used.

Women

Unless you have a very particular need for an open frame without a top tube, go for a diamond frame. An open or 'woman's' pattern frame is structurally weaker and less responsive than a diamond pattern frame. There are fewer models and sizes, and all too often the 'woman's' version of a production bike has an inferior specification in comparison with the 'man's' version. Worse, while the lack of a top tube may help preserve your genitals, it does not change the length of the bike for a better fit. All the way around it is not much of a deal, and my advice is to go for the better value and performance of a diamond frame.

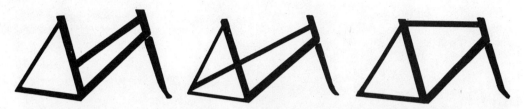

Conventional woman's frame   **Mixte frame**   **Triangulated frame**

If you are on the short side you may have a problem finding a diamond frame production bike in your size. They are made; finding one is a matter of persistence.

One builder specializing in bikes for women is Georgena Terry (140 Despatch Drive, East Rochester, NY 14445, for leaflets and list of dealers). She has several models and a neat solution for the smallest sizes: a 24 inch front wheel. This allows the bike to be proportioned correctly for length without fouling up the handling qualities, and to have a head tube of reasonable size. I've not personally examined her bikes, but the cycle press reviews are full of praise, and her literature and ideas are really together. If you are among the some 75 percent of women who are 5'7" or less, then Terry Bikes or similar machines are really worth investigating.

Custom bikes

One grand bit of fun is to build up your own bike, starting either with a frame off the shelf, or a frame custom built to order. Strictly speaking, off the shelf frames will serve the needs of most people, but the satisfaction of having a unique made to measure frame, finished and decorated exactly as you wish, can be tremendous.

The old-time master frame builders are a dying breed and their work is in great demand, but there are also many young, new frame builders who turn out excellent products at very competitive

The Terry bicycle

rates. Many of them are to be found in smaller communities and rural areas where overheads are low, and many are into participation and dialogue. They'll talk with you, analyze your needs, and let you see the frame actually being built. It's wonderful fun all around, but bear in mind that time is money and be prepared to pay a fair price for custom service. A cardinal rule is, never ask a frame builder to do something he or she does not want to do. The responsibility for ultimate success rests with the builder, and it is not fair to press for a scheme that could turn out wrong.

A custom bike is one of life's great pleasures. But in view of the cost you may want to leave this one until you have run a bike or two and have a sound idea of what you want.

CHAPTER 6

Special Bicycles and Tricycles

Small Wheel Bicycles

Mini-bikes with open, step through frames and 16 or 20 inch wheels are heavy and slow, unstable, and have lousy brakes. On paper, a mini-bike looks appealing: a one size fits all machine that can haul groceries or serve as a general runabout. Many models are shopper versions with baskets front and rear that come off quickly so that they can be carried around in the store. Neat. But because small wheels are stiff, mini-bikes use wide, soft tires to give an acceptable ride. This makes them slow. A weight of around 40 to 50 lbs adds to the drag. But the real wash-out is the first time the brakes are applied in wet weather. Nada. Zilch. The ride is perhaps forever. Small steel rims and crude caliper brakes are marginal in performance when dry, and utterly worthless when wet.

Small wheel shopper

If you need a general runabout suitable for all the family, look for a small frame beach cruiser or mountain-bike with alloy wheels. If some people in the family are small, models with 24 inch wheels are available. Fit a long seat post with a quick release clamp for instant size adjustment. For hauling things, equip the bike with big mesh carriers, such as the Eclipse Commuter Baskets.

Folding Bikes

A folding bike can be a viable means of dealing with specific situations and conditions. In fact, it can be a real treat. But it is not a means to eat your cake and have it too.

The key to success with a folding bike is that the ability to reduce in size serves a useful purpose. If not, you are better off with a regular bike.

One oft seen 'folder' is a standard mini-bike, hinged at the middle of the frame. It's one of the great tortures. The thing is a disaster as a bike, and folded, it is an awkward,

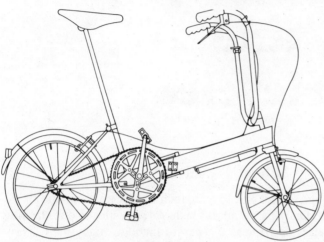

The Bickerton

unmanageable mangle of sharp protrusions and filthy greasy bits. There's no good way to get ahold of the thing, and when you finally do, it's too heavy to move more than a few feet at time.

If you want a bike that folds compactly so that you can store it easily, or put it in a car trunk, consider the Hon. It reduces to 8 x 18 x 28 inches, or about the size of a small suitcase. When folded, a third castor wheel comes into service, and this allows the whole package to be trundled along the ground. Good, because the Hon is too heavy to carry for any distance. It's a useful machine where the problem is storage: in your home, at work, or in a car,

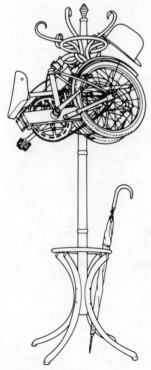

boat or airplane. In comparison with other folding bikes the performance and ride of the Hon is very good. One weak point is the rear brake, which is not fierce.

If portability is the prime requirement, one very good bike to consider is the Bickerton, an aluminum folder with 3- or 5-speed hub gears that weighs in at around 23 lbs, lbs, and reduces to a compact 9 x 20 x 30 inches. A stout fabric bag on the front handlebars will hold up to 40 lbs of groceries or whatever, and doubles as a carrier for the bike when it is folded.

At 23 lbs the Bickerton is easy to manage. It's no trouble at all to take along in a taxi, train, bus, or airplane. It can be checked into cloakrooms and other places that would never touch a regular bike. Storage in a home with limited space is a snap.

As a bike, the Bickerton is good, but unusual. It has the fundamental asset of light weight, which gives responsiveness and good hill climbing. Design and materials give the frame surprising flexibility, so that despite the use of small wheels, the ride is very comfortable. You can go all day on it. One 55-year-old grandmother rode her Bickerton across the entire United States.

The chief disadvantage of a Bickerton is that when underway it feels loopy, like it was made out of rubber bands. If you pour power into the pedals and heave mightily on the bars, the bike indeed does go twang, sometimes in several directions at once. You can't have everything. The Bickerton is a great folder and all right as a bike so long as you work with it, slipping in the power steadily and smoothly. On descents it is best to keep the speed down; the small wheels make for fast, tender handling. But they are alloy, and the braking is adequate if not fantastic.

If full-size bike performance is paramount, the one to consider is the Montague (Montague Folding Bicycle Company, 3042 Newark St. NW, Washington, D.C. 20008). This is a lightweight 26 lbs 27 inch wheel bike with a diamond frame, that reduces to 12 x 28 x 32 inches - a neat trick accomplished by using two seat tubes, one inside the other. Folding is literally three snaps: the quick release levers for two seat clamp bolts and the front wheel. I've never had a ride on one, but reviews in the cycle press are good.

Another option to consider if you like a full size bike is - a full size bike! I travel a fair bit, and rarely without a bike. The usual first choice machine is a lightweight mountainbike that I can strip down very quickly with just two Allen key wrenches. The lot pops into a bike bag padded with a sheet of air-bubble plastic and some extra clothes, zip zip, and I'm gone. If they nick me at the airport the excess charge is for an item of sporting equipment, and costs only a few dollars - a bargain. The bike has no racks or fenders and so the package, while substantial, is manageable on a train or bus, and will easily slip into a car trunk. At

Montague folding bike

journey's end the dividend is a versatile, full-on bike that can go wherever, on or off-road.

Folding bikes raise all kinds of possibilities. Londoner Paul Fagin did a 20-city tour of China by airplane - with a Bickerton. What a combination! He covered a lot of ground and a wide range of cultures and environments, was able to explore each area in close-up detail, and was fully mobile, with the ability to use any type of transport.

There are many reasons for using a folding bike: ease of storage, mobility when traveling, commuting mixed mode together with a car, plane or train, ease of storage, etc. Priorities are up to you. But if you go for a folding bike, make sure that it will do what you want.

If you've a deep pocket, another possibility for a portable bike is the Moulton AM, discussed below.

The Moulton AM

The Moulton AM is a unique design justly described as an engineered bike. The most obvious innovative feature is full independent suspension for both front and rear wheels. Unlike other small wheel bikes which use squishy tires for a comfortable ride, the Moulton design small diameter wheels are narrow, hard, and very fast. Moultons are both extremely comfortable and efficient.

Many advantages accrue from the suspension and small wheel combination. There is room for wide, platform carrier racks that can manage bulky, heavy loads. Perhaps most exciting of all, there is room for a generously sized Zzipper fairing. This means greatly improved aerodynamics and a new dimension in speed. The Moulton AM-14/S has a gear range of 30 to 117 inches, and can use it. Other things being equal, catching one needs another AM-14/S, or a full bore HPV. A standard racing bike hasn't a hope. The fairing is also excellent protection from rain and dirt.

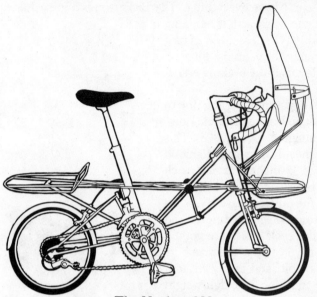

The Moulton AM

A disadvantage of the suspension is that the bike bobbles like a trampoline if you hammer it hard. The suspension is adjustable, and can be tuned to suit a strong rider, but the AM is still a bike that wants a smooth riding technique. Over a distance, the reduction in fatigue awarded by the suspension is worth a lot more to performance than the ability to snap off in a sprint.

The Moulton AM does not fold, but only a single Allen key is needed to disassemble the bike into two halves. There's an optional bag to carry it, and while the package cannot be classified as slim and neat, it is manageable enough for traveling.

There are three models. The AM-2 has a 2-speed, pedal operated hub gear. It is a simple town bike, and very disarming; you'd have to be wealthy indeed to buy an AM just as a light runabout. Most people want something more flash: either the AM-7 with 7-speed derailleur gears, or the full house AM-14/S with 14-speed derailleur gears. I agree. At this level, you should go all the way.

The Moulton AM is a class machine. It's beautifully made and handsomely finished and is an assured classic. And it costs a bomb. No more than any other really top-flight superbike perhaps, but a hefty sum.

The real issue is not so much the cost, which in raw mechanical terms is fair enough, but what you want. For many people, owning an AM is a passionate affair filled with satisfaction, delight, and adventure. Other people agree that the bike is very gee whiz, fun, and useful, but have other things they'd rather spend their money on. It is a question of temperament and interest, not right and wrong. If you enjoy innovative engineering and superb building, and can write four digit checks without flinching, then look over a Moulton.

Tandems

Tandems offer a number of advantages and disadvantages over solo machines. Two strong riders can move a tandem along very briskly, as overall weight is less and wind resistance is cut in half. A tandem will outrun a solo on a downhill run. Uphill, a tandem is slow. But over gently undulating terrain the greater mass of the tandem increases momentum and helps to iron out small hills. A long wheelbase gives excellent stability, and a smooth ride.

FIG. 60. — INVINCIBLE' TANDEM.

Two riders of unequal strength can have rest periods for the weaker rider on the easy parts of a ride, and put in the muscle together when climbing hills. Togetherness is a definite plus feature of tandem cycling; it is easy to talk, and there is something very pleasant about the shared physical effort. There's a whole new collection of skills to learn before the pilot (front) and stoker (rear) work together smoothly. It's a process that is the making of some people, and the undoing of others.

Tandem disadvantages stem chiefly from sheer size. A tandem handles awkwardly in traffic, needs a roof rack for transport by automobile, and takes up a lot of storage space.

Only a lightweight (35 to 45 lbs) derailleur gear tandem is worth owning. The heavyweight (90 lbs) models are just too much work to pedal. With the weight of two riders a tandem has to have first class brakes. At the minimum, cantilevers with over-size blocks. This would be for a lightweight racing tandem for use by experienced riders. Touring tandems should have cantilevers, and a drum or disc brake. The latter is primarily for speed control on long descents, so that the caliper brakes do not overheat the rims and cause a tire to burst.

Wheel quality is critical. The hubs should be made for tandem use, with 11 or 15 mm axles; standard 9.5 mm axles are not strong enough. There should be at least 40 spokes, better yet 48, in 13 or 14 gauge. The rims should be renowned for strength, for example the Super Champion Module 58.

It's well worth figuring out just what you'd like to do with a tandem. For sport and speed you've got to go a quality and fineness route similar to that for a solo racing bike. It's not a machine for lumping around. For casual fun and games a more robust model with 26 inch or 650B tires is a better bet; the ride is more comfortable, and handling is good enough even for unpaved roads. In fact, there are even tandem mountainbikes!

Look carefully into the whole business before you buy. A good tandem is expensive

TANDEM FRAMES

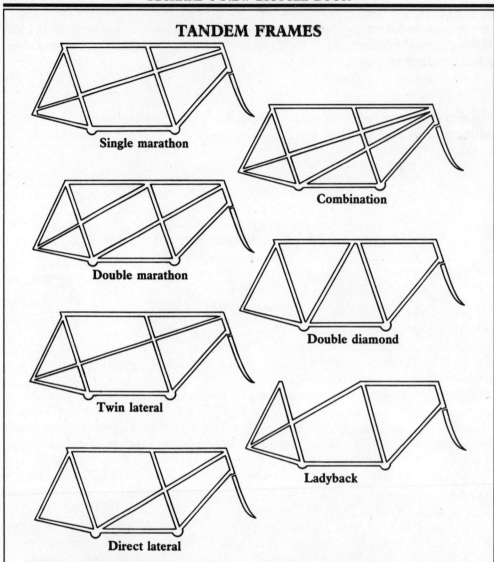

Single marathon

Combination

Double marathon

Double diamond

Twin lateral

Ladyback

Direct lateral

Tandem frames are designed to reduce side-to-side flex while still retaining a reasonably comfortable ride. Two popular compromises are the marathon and twin lateral designs. Both use long diagonal tubes running from the head tube all the way back to the rear drop-outs. These provide lateral bracing against the flex caused by powerful pedaling and sharp changes of course. With the marathon, a single tube splits at the seat tube to run on either side of the rear wheel; with the twin lateral, two thin tubes are used for the entire length.

The double marathon has two diagonal bracing tubes for a very stiff and strong geometry. The direct lateral, which is popular with US builders, uses a single diagonal tube from the head tube to the rear bottom bracket, and beefy chain stays. The stiffest and heaviest is the combination, which uses both marathon and direct lateral tubes. Double-diamond frames are common, because they are easy to build, but tend to flex at the front bottom bracket. Ladyback tandems look all right on a TV show, but are much too flexible for serious riding.

and any compromise on quality will cost dearly. A tandem must be soundly engineered and constructed in order to stand the stress of two riders. Historically, large manufacturers have not done well with tandems; the good ones come from smaller, specialized firms and builders. It's best if the people who make and sell the equipment use it as well. Then you get straight information. See if there is a bike shop within reachable distance that specializes in

Santana tandem

tandems, and check adverts in cycling magazines. The Tandem Club of America, c/o Peter Hutchison, Route 1, Box 276, Esperance, NY 12066, may be able to help. One well known firm run by enthusiasts is Santana, Box 1205, Claremont, CA 91711, Tel: (714) 621 6943. Ask for a catalog and dealer list.

If you are venturing to Britain, try:

Jack Taylor Cycles, Church Road, Stockton-on-Tees, Teeside TS18 2LY, England.
Bob Jackson, 148 Harehills Lane, Leeds, West Yorkshire LS8 5BD, England.
Mercian Cycles, 28 Stenson Road, Cavendish, Derby DE3 7JB, England.
Tony Oliver, Maes Meredydd Uchaf, Rhosybool, Amlwch, Anglesey, Gwynedd, Wales.
George Longstaff, Albert Street, Chesterton, Newcastle-under-Lyme, Staffs ST5 7JF, England.
Ken Rogers, 37 Berkeley Avenue, Cranford, Hounslow, Middlesex, England.
Swallow Frames and Cycles, 2 Stannetts, Laindon North Trade Centre, Essex SS15 6DJ, England.

Side-by-side

A tandem in a class of its own is the companion, or sociable, bicycle, with the saddles set side-by-side rather than in-line as with an ordinary tandem. It looks weird but works a treat and is easy to ride. Anyone who can ride an ordinary bike can just get aboard and go.

A large frontal area gives poor aerodynamics and precludes using a side-by-side for long or quick journeys. However, at speeds up to 15 mph on local excursions and on tours where speed and distance are not the object, it is a complete stone gas. You can talk, hold hands, and even kiss.

Some very lovely side-by-side bikes were made by Barrett Cycles, Angola, NY 14006. They might still be going. A recent introduction comes from Buddy Bike, 77 Mowat Avenue, Toronto, Ontario, Canada M6K 3E3 1T4. The models I've seen are a touch basic, but seem to work perfectly well.

Tricycles

There are trikes and there are trikes! The type popular in retirement areas usually has 20 inch wheels to keep the weight down low and are quite stable as long as they are not pushed hard A large rear basket handy for carrying groceries, gold bricks, golf clubs, or whatever is a popular accessory. People with poor balance or coordination, brittle bones, or other problems, should seriously consider a tricycle. Bear in mind, though, that many old folks do just fine with conventional two wheelers, and there are a number of bicycle clubs whose members are all over seventy.

One type of tricycle has a fixed gear, so that the pedals and wheels always move together. People with limited motion in their legs have sometimes found that the exercise provided by this arrangement improves leg mobility.

People with a taste for the unusual might want to consider a lightweight racing or touring tricycle with 26 or 27

Low rider tricycle

inch wheels. In no way is this an old age toy. Many an experienced bicyclist has come a cropper first time out on a trike. It must be steered around a corner, a sensation completely at odds with the handling of a bicycle, and rider weight must be counterbalanced to the inside on even a moderate bend. It is quite easy to lift a wheel, and downhill bends must be approached with caution. Changes in the camber of the road also easily upset balance.

Part of the appeal of trikes is that they are challenging to ride. Many adherents are crack bicyclists out for still more thrills. But trikes also

Higgins tricycle ca.1950

have practical advantages: they're good for carrying things, can stop and park without difficulty, and stay upright under slippery conditions. We've had the good luck to run a big tandem trike as the 'family' cycle for some years, and the different combinations of adults, kids, and babies that can be hung on the thing is quite dazzling. At the moment, the machine is back with the man who made it. He is well into his 70s and still likes a nice 35 mile spin two or three times a week. His wife has arthritis, and can't ride on her own, so now they go on the tandem trike. It really is a very useful machine.

Kits for converting solo and tandem bicycles into trikes are available from Rogers, Swallow, and Longstaff (see below). These work, but you need to be mechanically proficient, or have the services of an able shop. The process involves fiddly details that are essential, such as new arrangements for braking.

In Britain, a trike is called a 'barrow', and dedicated adherents have banded together

as: The Tricycle Association, 37 York Close, Market Bosworth, Nuneaton, Warwickshire.
Builders include:
Jack Taylor Cycles, Church Road, Stockton-on-Tees, Teeside TS18 2LY, England.
Bob Jackson, 148 Harehills Lane, Leeds, West Yorkshire LS8 5BD, England.
George Longstaff, Albert Street, Chesterton, Newcastle-under-Lyme, Staffs ST5 7JF, England.
Ken Rogers, 37 Berkeley Avenue, Cranford, Hounslow, Middlesex, England.
Swallow Frames and Cycles, 2 Stannetts, Laindon North Trade Centre, Essex SS15 6DJ, England.

At the opposite end of the scale from the racing and touring trikes are the utility machines. These are workhorses that often weigh 100 lbs unladen, but that can manage loads of up to 500 lbs. One increasingly favored application is as a mobile stand for hot dogs, ice cream, vegetables, or whatever is going. Many are lovingly decorated and maintained by their owners and are really pretty. I'm prejudiced of course, but feel that pedal power and street trading are a balanced combination that hang together well. The people who go in for motorized premises always seem pressed, and a bit wan. Pedal power has low overheads.

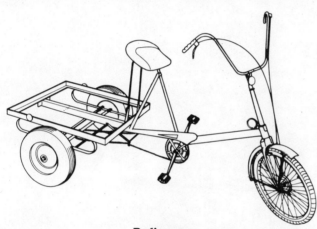

Pedi-porter

Load-carrying trikes have a great variety of industrial and commercial uses. A few examples would be: moving gardening equipment and lawnmowers around estates and parks; moving anything that a human being can pick up around a warehouse or shipping depot; and collecting rubbish from small bins. There are a zillion other applications - just look at countries like the Netherlands and China. The great point in favor of utility trikes are that they are highly economical, and use only the amount of power needed for the job at hand. They are also noise and pollution free. If you can think of and suggest an application for a utility

A COUNTRY POSTMAN.

trike where you live or work, you will be doing yourself and everybody else a big favor. One utility trike is called the Pedi-Porter, and is made by Alco Cycle Products, 451 3rd Street S.E., Largo, FL 33540.

Sailing Tricycle

The Rans Company, 408 Milner, Hays, Kansas 67601, manufactures sailing tricycles. These have a sail (about 30 square feet) just like on a boat, and will see 50 mph - be sure you have enough room!

Reproduction Antiques

From time to time small firms or builders take up producing reproduction antique cycles. If you are interested in something really different, this may be for you.

Rideable Bicycles Replicas, 2447 Telegraph Avenue, Oakland, CA, have been making various models for a number of years. In 1981, one of their machines completed a 1000 mile tour down the length of England without a hitch.

If you opt for a machine like an Ordinary, or Star, get ahold of a book like *Collecting and Restoring Antique Bicycles* by G. Donald Adams (Tab Books Inc., Blue Ridge Summit, PA 17214), with directions for riding. It is just as easy to 'come a cropper' with a modern Ordinary as an old one.

If you like the flash and thunder of mock gas tanks and coil spring shock absorbers, cast an eye on Columbia's re-issue of their 1952 Five Star model: two-tone green and cream paint, long streamlined chrome bullet headlight, white wall tires - ooh!

Children's Bicycles

Children need and deserve good bikes. For children, bikes are motion and growth incarnate. Freedom, and a means to learn all kinds of new skills and accomplishments. Bikes are incredibly important tools for children.

Unfortunately, it is common to treat children's bikes as cheap toys. The market is littered with worthless junk. Tin can assemblies with sleeves of plastic for bearings. Even King Kong would have trouble making one of these things go. Try turning the cranks of one with your hand and see. Your little nipper with tiny legs no longer than your forearm hasn't got a chance. Of course he or she will leave the stupid thing to rot. It isn't even worth giving away. Cheap kid's bikes are a complete waste of money.

A better bike costs a reasonable piece of change, because it costs just as much to make as a full size bike. But it works! The return value in terms of play and work is incredible. I've watched many young children (under age 4) play with bikes for oh, one or two hours at a stretch, every day, for months on end. They just keep on whizzing and whizzing. If you're looking for something to get the kids out of your hair, a bike is one of the best things going.

VIGOR'S
"Our Little Ones."

A good bike gives genuine play value, and it lasts. You can pass it down in the family, or sell it for a recovery of a lot of the purchase price. If you are on a tight budget or have a swarm of offspring to mount, then buy used. Basic quality is more important than new paint and anyhow, joint participation in sprucing up a bike is far more interesting for most children than spending money at the store. Local classified adverts, 3 x 5 WANTED cards at laundromats, PTA meetings, etc., will do the trick.

A child can enjoy a bike at age 2 or even sooner, but not necessarily as a means of transport. The initial use may be as a house or study in mechanical engineering. Let the child move at his or her own pace and they will eventually figure out what the thing can do. Keep a careful eye on matters. A toddler can easily catch a finger in moving bits. A proper tricycle is far more stable and safe than a bicycle with training wheels, which upsets easily.

A child is ready for a bicycle at about age 4 or 5, depending on individual development, coordination, and interest. Don't use training wheels. They are dangerous, and retard learning. The best way to teach anybody, young or old, to ride a bike is to let them do it themselves. Remove the pedals, and lower the saddle so that he or she can reach the ground with their feet when mounted. Show them how the bike steers. Let them push with their feet, as with a scooter. After a little progress, put them on a bit of ground with a gentle downslope. The individual scoots will each become longer and longer. When they can go for a good stretch without touching the ground, replace the pedals and watch them go. Keep them on level ground until they also learn how the brakes work.

The ideal first bike for a youngster should have:

● Pneumatic tires for a comfortable ride, easier pedaling, and effective braking. Solid rubber tires are three times harder to pedal, provide a harsh, jolting ride, and give bad braking.

● Ball bearings for the headset, bottom bracket, and wheels. Plastic sleeve bearings give bad handling and steering, poor efficiency, and wear out quickly.

● A large seat range adjustment so the bike can grow with the child.

● Brakes that work. It's surprising how many do not. The type is a matter of the individual child. I prefer caliper rim brakes, because they are easy to tune and service, but many young children do not have hands large and strong enough to work the levers. If this is the case, go for a pedal operated coaster brake.

Once a child is about age 7, a whole new world opens up - BMX. This started as small fry, dirt track racing. It's now blossomed into incredible developments like freestyle, with levels of bike handling that have to be seen to be believed. It's sort of like fish underwater, spinning and darting, diving and swooping - except these people are doing it on terra firma and in the air!

The whole thing about BMX is that it is real time. A lot of the development and spread of adult mountainbikes is due directly to BMX technology. Mechanically, most BMX bikes are far superior to most adult bikes. They have to be. In the broadest sense, BMX is like truth. You can't fake a bunny hop or placing in a heat. And junk iron doesn't cut the ice.

All you have to do is pick up a good BMX bike to appreciate why any kid would

want it. It's light. It'll go. And it's unbelievably tough. It is made to leap into the air, zoom off things, crash - and come back for more. Does your little nipper have a chance of being hurt doing this kind of thing? You bet. But not mortally. In fact, not even seriously, if he or she uses the right equipment. BMX is a microcosm of the big world. You can only show off if you've got the stuff - and that takes dedication and work. In BMX, jerks are not well regarded, because they are not working with the reality.

BMX is wired up short, just like kids are. It's on a scale that they can manage, and safely. All they need is a bit of ground someplace and they're off, messing around and learning new tricks. I've never really believed in the business of aping adult activities by putting a kid on a junior road bike, and dragging them on a 50 mile tour. Yes kids like riding, sometimes for long distances, but I don't think roads are the place for it until they are age 13. Until then, they simply haven't got the attention span to cope with the many dangers. Too many get wiped out; per mile cycled, the highest accident rate by far is for under-16s.

One reason I'm an off-road fan is that the whole family can do it, dogs and all. Whether it's the park next door, the seacoast, or a run in the mountains, we can all be together, and yet each of us can ride as hard or as softly as we want. But I'm getting ahead of myself.

The main point is that children deserve good bikes. Adults have cars, they have money in their pockets for public transportation - kids generally just have a bike. It should be a good one. There are lots of options. BMX of course. There are also junior mountainbikes with 20 inch wheels that are really a treat. Tough, lots of gears, mega-brakes, and easy to handle. My eldest daughter has one, and loves it dearly.

How do you pick out a good kid's bike? The same way you pick out a good adult bike. You're looking for quality tubings, alloy components, and good building. And it can cost. Junior mountainbikes and road bikes aren't so bad. Some of the BMX machines can break your back. If little junior starts getting into serious competition you may be in for some real life and death dramas about iron. I think that here, you start to get into what family is all about. Working out what the resources really are, and how they can be distributed, is part of learning how things happen. How much or how little money is less important than how you both handle it.

FIG. 6.—THE RUDGE TRIPLET TANDEM QUADRICYCLE DIRECT STEERING ROADSTER.

TESTIMONIAL.

To Messrs. HILLMAN, HERBERT & COOPER, LTD.

Ghostland, December, 1889.

Dear Sirs,—I left the old world through an accident, the result of a fall from a so-called safety bicycle by one of the too numerous jerry makers, who, being without the means to build cycles with limbs of steel, resort to the fatal practice of casting in large pieces.

My present object in writing to you is to express my unbounded gratitude for the "Premier" cycle you made for me. It carries my weight well, and although the roads are full of clinkers and other rough products of combustion, the grade of steel of which it is composed is so fine, and its temper so excellent, that the 5,000,000 miles I have traversed upon it have not impaired it to any appreciable extent.

In contrast to this I have seen machines brought here by ill-advised Ghosts, which I will simply describe as not "Premiers," made of such common soft material that they have melted like butter in the sun.

You will be somewhat astonished at the number of miles I have ridden in this land, but the fact is that one has to take a deal of exercise to keep one's form as a Ghost, and I prefer to take all mine on a "Premier." Besides, a Ghost has to be in many places at one time, and that means fast travelling.

I congratulate you on that wonderful ride on a "Catford Premier" safety by Holbein!!! **324 miles at one go!!!** If ever that man comes to these parts, where the physical conditions are so different to those you are familiar with, and gets down to the weight of a healthy Ghost, he will do about 1,000 miles a day.

I have learnt with great satisfaction that you have made more cycles than any other maker during the past season: that your factories are the largest, and your machinery the finest in the world. I should wonder how your rivals find purchasers were it not for the fact that I know all cyclists are not able to get your wonderful machines, the supply, great as it is, being limited.

I enclose my photo, taken by an old gentleman in these parts who has only just commenced the photographic art. The likeness is not a very good one: you may therefore not recognise the features of,

Yours very truly,

JOHN NOTELEKS.

FOR LISTS APPLY TO

Hillman, Herbert & Cooper, Ltd.

PREMIER WORKS, COVENTRY.

London Office & Depot: 14, Holborn Viaduct, and 5, Lisle St., Leicester Square.

CHAPTER 7

Buying (and Keeping) a Bike

The best place to buy a new bicycle is a bike store. You can sometimes save money at a department or discount store, but you are virtually guaranteed disproportionate headaches and problems. In the first place, the quality of merchandise is almost always inferior. Secondly, manufacturers assemble bikes only up to a point; final assembly, adjustment and tuning is left to the person who sets the bike up for use. Department and discount stores do not employ trained bicycle mechanics, and so the bikes they sell are often unassembled, or have been put together by some cretin who has literally done more harm than good. And even the finest machines can have a defect or other problem requiring expert attention. It takes a good bicycle mechanic to assemble a new bike without damaging anything, check all the parts, and iron out the inevitable defects. Even then, problems are not likely to be over. If a department or discount store gives a guarantee - few do - they have no mechanics to take care of in-service problems. And if there is some totally basic defect in a machine you buy, it takes weeks for a refund or replacement.

A bike store will assemble the machine. Although you must check their work, chances are they'll do the job right. If some problem comes up later they are available right away to fix it, and so are replacement parts. You get a guarantee on parts and labor good for a year and more. Three-year guarantees are not uncommon.

The more local a shop you can deal with, the better. Any bike store must meet certain basic requirements in quality of bikes and in service, but convenience means a lot. A guarantee on a store 50 miles away is useless for anything except a major disaster. If there is a local shop and they don't have what you want, talk it over with them. Perhaps they can order a bike for you. If their brand of bike is not the one you had in mind take a good look at what they offer. All other things being equal, as they may well be since many manufacturers use the same components, the convenience of a local shop is an excellent reason to switch brands. Just make sure you get a fair value. Ask about servicing and parts. If their guarantee isn't good enough, explain the problem. Don't expect, however, that they will be able to offer as good a deal as a high-volume super-powered bike store. What you pay a little extra for is the fact that they are around the corner. Also, perhaps the general feeling and vibes are better.

At any rate, stay away from discount and department stores. I have not regaled you with horror stories about machines purchased from such stores, but they are legion, and cover everything from kids' tricycles to ultra-fancy racers. The tiny bit extra you spend in a bike shop buys an awful lot.

Check the Yellow Pages, ads in cycling magazines, and any local oracles for the locations of bike shops near your home. Visit them. Bike shops can vary a good bit in character. Some are dedicated strictly to racing, others to plain utility machines. The important thing is that you are made to feel welcome, and are offered service. These are the things you want to know:

- Does the shop have the sort of bikes you are interested in? Ask for leaflets that you can take home and study.
- Will you be able to take a test ride? (Nice days only, so bike does not get wet and dirty - mountainbikes excepted!)
- What sort of servicing does the shop offer? What are the guarantee terms? Do they include a free post sale service?

The Buy

Once you've boiled your options down to two or three bikes and one or two shops, you're ready for the main event: the buy. To ensure the best attention of the shop, avoid doing this on Saturday, Friday evening, or Monday morning, when they are likely to be busy. Wear suitable clothes and shoes and have a bit of tissue or rag handy in your back pocket.

Before whizzing off on a test ride (or on any strange bike, for that matter) check that the handlebars and saddle are tight, the brakes firm, the gears operational, and the wheels free running and true. Simple stuff, yes, but many an experienced rider has had an unhappy surprise from a loose or poorly adjusted component.

Vary the pace of your test ride: try out low speed handling, a turn of speed, ride over a rough surface, cornering, and braking, but don't press the bike too hard, or expect too much. Any new bike feels strange for a while. If you are actually uncomfortable, and the feeling persists, ask the advice of the shop. Sometimes an adjustment of saddle height or stem length will cure the difficulty. If not, try another bike. When you've found the bike you like the most, buy it.

If you are interested in substitutions, this is the time to specify what you want. You might need a shorter stem, drop instead of flat bars, or a better saddle, to name a few common swaps. Although you are trading one item for another, the shop is entitled to charge for labor, and any difference in value. Then there are accessories such as racks and lights. Sort it all out and get the money down to the bottom line. The shop may ask you to return for the bike, later that day if there is time, the next day if not, and are entitled to a deposit. Ensure that the sales receipt has the frame number of the bike, and your name and address.

Taking Delivery

Anticipate that any new bike will have something wrong with it. Dealing with a good bike store minimizes this possibility but by no means eliminates it. When I picked up a new dream machine from one of NYC's finest stores I was too bedazzled to give it

THE NEW MOUNT.

anything but the most cursory inspection. As I accelerated away from the store the rear hub and freewheel exploded in a blizzard of metal flakes and chips. Most problems you are likely to encounter are not apt to be so spectacular, but the point cannot be emphasized too strongly that a thorough inspection of any new bike is necessary.

Collect the bike at least two hours before store closing time, so you have plenty of time to sort out fine points and adjustments if necessary. Look the bike over carefully, checking that all the bits are tight and tidy, and of course that the brakes and gears work. Take it out for a good spin, and check the following:

● Frame for straightness. Stand behind or in front of the bicycle and see that the wheels are in line. Next, hold the bicycle by the saddle only and wheel it around. If the frame or forks are bent, it will tend to veer to one side. Finally, at some point when you are clear of traffic hold the handlebars as lightly as possible, even riding hands off if you have this skill. The bicycle should go straight, in control, without pulling to one side. Reject any bicycle which fails these tests. A bicycle which will not track accurately is tiring and unsafe to ride.

91

- Wheels should spin easily. When held off ground weight of valve stem should pull wheel around so valve is in 6 o'clock position. Wheel should be centered in fork arms or chain stays. If wheel can be moved from side to side and there is a clicking sound, hub cones are out of adjustment. Check that rim is true by holding a pencil next to it and spinning the wheel. Brace the pencil on a fork arm of chain stay to keep it steady. Side-to-side movement of wheel rim should not exceed ⅛".
- Pluck spokes. All should be evenly tight and give the same 'twang'.
- Brake blocks should hit rims squarely and not drag when released.
- Gears should work smoothly and with no slippage. Test first with wheels off ground and then on a ride.
- Pedals and chainwheel should spin easily but without side-to-side play.

You may think that all this is a lot of trouble to go through. I have bought a fair number of new bikes for myself, family, or friends. There was something wrong with every one of them, and a few I rejected outright. You will save yourself a lot of grief if you invest some time at the outset on careful inspection.

A bike inspection is something that a good bike shop will regard with tolerant amusement. A bad shop will register irritation and this is immediate grounds for concern. Your interest and participation should be welcomed, not fobbed off. But be fair. You can't expect some basic machine to sing with quality, or for the shop to spend all day fiddling with it. What you do have the right to expect of any bike, whatever the amount of money, is that it is roadworthy.

After you purchase a bike, check that all nuts, bolts, and screws are secure. Every last one. After riding 50 miles or so, repeat this operation. New bicycles 'bed in', and it is very common, for example, for the brake bolts to work loose. Cranks, particularly the cotterless type, are bound to need tightening. See the appropriate section under Maintenance for details.

Used Bikes

Used bikes are a good way to save money. Expect to pay about 75 percent of list price for a machine in excellent as-new condition, and about 50 percent of list for one in average conditi Sources of used bikes depend on where you live and your own initiative. A lot of the bikes sold during the Bicycle Boom now moulder away in garages, attics, and sheds. They often have some minor fault like a broken brake or gear shift cable, and are no problem to make roadworthy. If you just start asking around in your neighborhood, put up WANTED notices in laundromats and on bulletin boards, you may well turn up a prize bike for a song.

Some bike shops sell used machines. Most cities and counties have local classified publications listing all kinds of stuff - including bikes - for sale. Check also the classified ads in the regular papers. Often a sale of household effects includes a bicycle. Auctions are sometimes good. A good bet in the spring are local bulletin boards at universities and colleges. Put up some cards yourself or take an ad in the student newspaper. Naturally, the more prosaic a bike you seek, the faster you will be likely to find it. But if you just put the word out wherever you go something will eventually turn up.

Understand exactly what sort of bike you are looking for. Converting a racing bike to a touring bike can be expensive - new freewheel, chain, chainwheel sprockets, and possibly new derailleurs and new wheels. Be particularly careful of winding up with a lemon. Try to find out the history of the machine. It's best if you can talk to the owner. Was he or she interested in the bike and in taking care of it? Or did they just leave it out in the rain? Where did they ride? I would rather pay a little extra for a well-loved bike than save a few dollars on a machine with a dubious or unknown past.

In inspecting the bike, cover all the points listed for a new bike. Pay particular attention to the frame. Wrinkled paint on the forks or where the top and down tubes meet the head tube can indicate that the bike was crashed. So can a coat of nice new paint. I know of instances where badly repaired crash damaged bikes have fallen apart, killing their unfortunate new owners. What you want to see are a certain number of inevitable nicks and scrapes, but no major dents, rust spots, or welds.

Count into the cost of a used bike a complete overhaul and lubrication, including possible replacement of cables, chain, and sprockets. Read the sections on Maintenance and Repair in this book to learn how to assess components for wear and useful life.

A final word about used bikes related to the next problem, keeping your bike. There are plenty of stolen bicycles for sale. Newspapers publish articles about marketplaces for stolen machines, and in some areas you can even order the type of bike you want. Price is usually about 25 percent of the list, often less. With such a flourishing industry it hardly seems a crime to get a bike that way. It is. Legally and morally. Simply put, you are helping to steal. Additionally, it is not some giant dollar-hungry corporation's candy bar or rip-off piece of junk which you are stealing, but a possession somebody quite probably loves and cherishes.

Keeping Your Bike

The figures on stolen bikes are impressive. As near as I can figure out, about 20 percent of the bikes in use at any given moment will be ripped off within a year. Conditions are barbaric. One day I came out of school to find a gang of urchins swarming over my bike. They had a long steel bar filched from a construction project with which they were busily trying to break the chain. I noticed with some amusement that not only were passers-by oblivious to the drama, but so were two cops in a patrol car directly across the street. In fact, should your bicycle be stolen and recovered by the police, there is still a good chance that you will not get it back. Many police forces have not got the time or inclination to check serial numbers against lists of stolen bikes.

The point is, you can expect little help. You have to rely almost entirely on out-thinking the opposition, and on the strength of your locking system. There's only one answer here: a Citadel, Kryptonite, or similar lock with a performance warranty that pays you back if your bike is stolen as a result of the failure of the lock to prevent the theft. Ordinary cable and chain locks are no good, because they can be cut in seconds with ordinary tools.

I once arranged a bike theft for a magazine article. We locked a bike to a fence railing on a busy street, positioned a photographer on the first floor of a building directly opposite the bike, and sent in our very own professional 'thief'. The dirty deed was accomplished within seconds. A voluminous raincoat concealed the actual snipping of a cable lock, which the thief tidily tucked away in a pocket before absconding with the bike. People only yards away did not notice a thing. We could hardly believe how easy it was. We repeated the experiment six times, progressively making the theft more and more obvious. On the final go, the thief marched directly up to the bike, hauled out the snippers and cut the cable lock in full open view of nearby pedestrians, and still got away with the bike. One person took notice of what was happening, but did nothing about it.

A good lock is your baseline for security, but is only a start. When locking up on the street you should:

- Lock your bike to seriously immovable objects like lamp-posts, parking signs, heavy fences, etc.
- Lock the frame, and both front and back wheels.
- Be very selective about where and when you lock the bike. Slum neighborhoods are a bad bet at any time. Even if the bike itself is not ripped off, kids will often strip away the seat, handlebars, brakes, and other components. Business and industrial districts are OK during the day. Always try to pick a busy spot with plenty of people around. NEVER leave your bike locked on the street overnight.
- Try to enlist help. The cashier for a movie theater will usually keep an eye on your bike. Newsdealers and other merchants will often help, and particularly if you do business with them. The local greasy spoon may give you indigestion, but if the cook waves a cleaver at anybody who bothers your bike the place is worth cultivating.

Successfully locking your bike is only one part of the problem. Depending on your age, sex, and the value of your bike, you are also subject to direct assault while riding. Usually this crime occurs in parks and other semi-isolated places, and to a lesser extent on slum streets. In form it can vary from seemingly friendly and casual interest on the part of strangers who would like to 'try your bike out', to people leaping out of the bushes, knocking you flat with a club, and riding away on your bike. This once happened to an entire pack of racers in New York's Central Park. The attacking gang got away with 10 bikes.

Once assaulted, there is little you can - or should - do unless you are an action freak or have experience in physical combat. No bike is worth a cracked skull or a knife in the gut. You would not have been jumped in the first place if your opponents did not have an advantage.

On the other hand, it is sickening and degrading to be ripped off. If you're up against three guys armed with knives and clubs, then quit. If you are simply up against an aggressor who is forcing you into the role of victim, then fight. On principle. It's OK to lose a bike, the crown jewels, or a million bucks. You are worth more. What's not OK is to lose your own self-respect. There are lots of circumstances where you can and should fight, win or lose. Where you draw the line is up to you. Fighting takes experience. Foolish bravery can get you killed. In any case, do not let a violent encounter take you by surprise. Think about and prepare for it now.

For example, one kind of attack consists of a group of people fanning out across a street with the obvious intention of stopping you. What do you do? Stop and negotiate? You might as well just hand your bike over. Is that what you want to do? There may be room enough for a quick U-turn and fast sprint away. Suppose there isn't? William 'Sundown Slim' Sanders (a fun bike journalist) has a succinct answer: CHARGE! Pour on the power, yell like a maniac, and head directly for one of the people blocking you. Don't aim at a gap between people, aim at somebody and genuinely try to hit them. In the end, most anybody will make a scrambling effort to get out of the way. This is the kind of thing you can do only if you are prepared. Otherwise you will just roll to a dumb stop, wondering what if anything you can do, and one of the crowd will 'try your bike out'.

Of course if you can avoid confrontations in the first place, so much the better. Stay out of isolated areas in parks at any time, and stay out of parks altogether at night. If you travel through slum areas move along at a smart pace, and try to stick to well-lit streets. Stay out of lonely business and shipping districts at night. Above all else, be alert. Look for likely ambushes and for people who seem unduly interested in you. Keep moving in areas you think are dangerous. You can do 30 mph and easily outrace people on foot.

In weighing the pros and cons of owning a bike you have to make a realistic evaluation of your own situation. If you work in a crummy neighborhood and your employer won't let you bring

... gone!

your bike inside, you're screwed (and should get another job). If you are a woman in a major metropolitan area you are a more likely victim of direct assault. I think that the advantages of owning a bike outweigh the disadvantages. But it would be unfair not to tell you about the problems you may encounter.

If you do get a bike you must accept the possibility that it will be stolen. I succeeded in keeping one bike for years and years. It went when my apartment was ripped off. It can hurt a lot when a cherished and loved bike that you have shared all kinds of experiences with suddenly vanishes to feed some junkie's habit. Try not to forget that it can happen to you, accept it, and the elaborate security precautions you must take will have a slightly less paranoid tone.

A final word about attitude: I used to forgive thieves on the grounds that they were poor. Now that I have seen plenty of places where poor people do not steal this idea is invalid. Still, if you catch somebody trying to steal a bike I think the best thing to do is just tell them to split. Punitive measures, if you are capable of them, will accomplish little, as will moralizing or sermonizing. Calling the police or authorities will only result in teaching the thief how better to steal. Do what you have to do, but the drift of what I am saying is not to blow your cool. You'll only become frustrated. The old slogan was: LOVE AMERICA OR LEAVE IT. The other possibility is to change it.

CHAPTER 8

Fitting and Gearing

Getting the most out of a bike requires a good fit; the right frame size, with correct placement of the handlebars, seat, and controls. The various formulas and methods listed here have historic precedent. At first, a riding position that is 'according to the book' may feel odd. Give yourself at least 50 miles to get used to the new arrangement before making alterations. You may find the 'odd' position considerably more efficient and less fatiguing than a supposedly comfortable position. On the other side, everyone is a little different, and some variation from the norm may be in order. Just give the orthodox position a fair trial, and make changes gradually.

For how to make the alterations in the position of seat, handlebars, stem, and brake levers, look up Adjustment under the relevant heading in the Maintenance and repair sections.

Fitting

Frame

Frame size is measured from the seat lug to the center of the bottom bracket axle. There is no single infallible method for calculating correct individual frame size. For example, three popular rules of thumb are:

1. Inside length of leg from crotch bone to floor, measured in stocking feet, less 9 inches for heights to 5'10'', 10 inches for heights 5'10'' to 6'1'' and 11 inches for heights over 6'1''.
2. Height divided by 3.
3. Two-thirds inside length of leg.

Thus, a person 68 inches tall with a 32 inch inseam would have a frame size of (1) 23 inches, (2) 22.6 inches, and (3) 21.3 inches! In fact, correct frame size is a matter of trial and error, and experience in what is right. The start has to be with a live human being. A man and a woman of the same height, for example, have different leg lengths (hers are longer). A man and a woman with the same leg lengths have different arm lengths (hers are shorter). Each one of these people has different needs.

Some bike shops have fitting machines - static gadgets that you climb aboard, and that are then adjusted until fit is ideal. You know the correct frame size, saddle height, stem length, handlebar rake, and so on. Great stuff, but I'd like to walk you through how it is done by eyeball.

Firstly, a diamond frame size is selected that you can comfortably straddle with your feet flat on the ground. If the top tube digs into your crotch, you can be sure sooner or later of a nasty slam where it hurts the most. There should be an inch to spare, more if you are 5'10'' or taller.

Next, the saddle height is set so that when you sit on the bike with your heel on the pedal, your leg is almost straight. Between 2 and 4 inches of seat post should be exposed; if less, try a smaller frame, if more, a larger frame. In general, women will be happier favoring a smaller frame and longer seat post, because their (comparatively) shorter torsos and arms will be more comfortable on a smaller bike.

Novices are prone to select a frame which is too large. An oversize frame, particularly when touring, feels a bit more secure and steady. It may also have a slightly easier ride, as small frames tend to be stiffer than large frames. A novice may have had only a few rides, and 'feel right' on a frame that in fact is a little too big. Only with time and miles does the rider come to appreciate the deftness and responsiveness of a correctly sized frame.

It pays to carry out the sizing exercise first thing, before looking at bikes or frames. You might be one of those lucky people who fits a common size without a hitch. Or you might be someone who really needs a frame at say, 19.5 inches maximum. This requirement eliminates a lot of bikes that would be a waste of time for you to consider.

There is little harm and possibly even merit in undersizing slightly. A longer seat post and stem will put matters right. But do not oversize by more than one-half inch. An excess of 1 inch or more will adversely affect handling, speed, and most importantly comfort.

A mountainbike is harder to size than a road bike, because the bottom bracket height tends to vary more. The rough rule is 3-4 inches smaller than a road frame. A lot depends on what you are going to do with the bike. For town and road riding a larger frame is fine. For serious off-road work a smaller frame is essential. There should be at least 4 inches of daylight between your crotch and the top tube. This may dictate a sloping top tube. Again, the usual tendency is to go for too big.

Saddle

The position of the saddle determines the fitting of the rest of the bike. For most riders the correct fore-to-aft position is with the nose of the saddle 1.75 to 2.5 inches behind a vertical line through the crank hanger.

When comfortably seated on the saddle with feet on the pedals and with cranks parallel to the ground (3 o'clock/9 o'clock), a plumb line (weight and string) from the center of the forward knee should pass right through the pedal spindle.

The taller the person, the further back the saddle. However, there are many variations. Touring riders often use a slightly rearward saddle position together with handlebars set on the high side. They are interested in comfort and steady power over long distances. Sprint riders and traffic jammers who use brief bursts of sharp energy use a more forward saddle position. This is one reason why sprint frames come with a steeper seat tube angle. For around-town use, if you are a vigorous rider, you may like a more forward saddle position. For extended going and best overall efficiency, however, stick to the normal postion.

The horizontal tilt of the saddle, i.e. height of the front relative to the rear, is crucial. There is, in your crotch, a nerve. Pinching it even just slightly over a long ride can disable you with numb crotch for weeks. Start with the saddle dead level, and if you

experience any discomfort, immediately lower the nose a degree or two. It can make all the difference. This is where a good quality seat with micro-adjusting bolts is important.

You may find yourself trying out different kinds of saddles. Each type may need a slightly different horizontal tilt. For example, padded anatomic saddles have a tendency to bounce the rider forward, and the usual recourse is to tilt the nose up a degree or two. This position could be very uncomfortable with a harder saddle. Don't be afraid to make changes and experiment. With time you will know by feel what is right for you.

Most saddles are set too low. A rough rule of thumb is that while sitting on the bike with your heel on the pedal at its lowest point, your leg should be almost straight. This means that when riding with the ball of your foot on the pedal, your leg is almost but not quite fully extended at the bottom of the stroke.

A precise formula for the best saddle height has been worked out in a series of tests. Measure inside leg length from crotch bone to floor without shoes. Multiply this length (in inches) by 1.09. Example: 32 inches × 1.09 equals 34.88, or 34⅞ inches. Set saddle so that distance A from top of saddle to center of pedal spindle in down position with crank parallel to seat tube is 34⅞ inches.

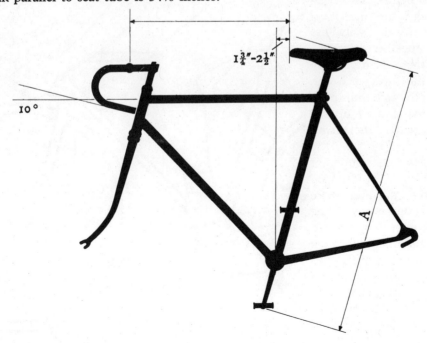

The 1.09 formula was put together by experts. They found that an alteration in saddle height of 4 percent of inside leg measurement from the 1.09 setting affected power output by approximately 5 percent. Once you've set the saddle height by this formula, leave it alone for a while before making changes.

Handlebars

By and large, dropped bars are more efficient and comfortable than flat bars.

1. A much greater variety of positions is possible. Not only can you select the best position for conditions, such as low down when headed into the wind, but being able to shift about and bring different muscle groups into play greatly increases comfort, to say nothing of power.

2. Because weight is supported by both the hands and posterior, road shocks and bumps rock the body rather than jar it. With conventional flat bars the whole weight of the body rests on the saddle. With dropped bars, not only is a portion of the weight supported by the arms, but because the saddle is forward, it tends to pivot at the hips going over bumps. As it happens this is desirable from an anatomical point of view: leaning forward stretches the spine, allowing the absorption of shocks. Flat bars force the rider into a stiff-spined position where the individual vertebrae of the spine are pinched together. Further, because there is no pivoting give at the hips, each and every jolt and bump is transmitted directly up the spine, greatly increasing fatigue.

3. The better distribution of weight allowed by dropped bars makes the bike more stable, and improves handling and steering.

One important exception to these remarks are mountainbike handlebars. Some competition riders use dropped bars on mountainbikes, but flat bars are customary.

Unlike the flat bars on a 'sit up and beg' roadster, flat bars on a mountainbike support part of the rider's weight and are very much an active feature of the bike. They are usually wider than dropped bars, for greater leverage, and the single riding position keeps the brake and gear levers literally at the rider's fingertips. The configuration is expressly designed for maximum bike handling and control, and is excellent for use in traffic provided the bars are not too wide. In the big open spaces wide bars are great; in traffic they tend to snag car rear view mirrors, trucks, pedestrians, and what-else. Bars that are too wide are usually easily trimmed with a hacksaw.

Drop bars range from 38 to 42 mm in width, with 44 mm sometimes available. If you have wide shoulders, bars with a narrow span will compress the chest and impair breathing. If you have narrow shoulders, wide bars won't do any harm.

Handlebar height is very important. For conventional use handlebars should be set so that the uppermost section is just level with the saddle. Sprint bikes have the bars a whole lot lower, and if you do a lot of traffic riding you may want to set yours down a bit. Be careful of an overly 'fierce' position, however; the gain for short-term speed will be at some cost to overall efficiency.

The stem should position the bars so that the distance between the nose of the saddle and the rear edge of the center of the handlebars equals the distance from your elbow to your outstretched fingertips. Take the trouble to get this one right, particularly if you are female. There are two ways to check:
1. Sit on the bike in your normal riding position while a friend holds the bike steady. Without changing position, remove one hand from the handlebars and let the arm dangle fully relaxed. Then rotate your arm in a large arc without stretching. If, as your hand comes back to the bar, it is ahead of or behind the other hand, the bars need to be moved.
2. When comfortably seated on the saddle with both feet on the pedals and with cranks parallel to the ground (3 o'clock/9 o'clock), and hands on the hooks of drop bars, a plumb line (weight and string) from the nose should pass through the headset.

Brakes

Brake levers on flat bars should be set between 30° and 45° below horizontal to prevent damaged fingers in the event of a fall.

On dropped bars set up for racing the hands are often primarily on the hooks, inside 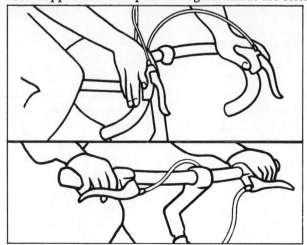 the curved section of the bars, and the brake levers are usually set at approximately 3 o'clock within ready reach of the fingers. Tourists and urban riders, however, tend to use a more upright position and place their hands on the tops of the bars, or in traffic, on the brake lever hoods.

For comfort, and a secure grip when braking hard, the levers should be set at around the 2 o'clock mark. With this

101

arrangement I like to have the ends of the bars raked 10° from the horizontal. This allows the 3 o'clock racing position to be created by simply rotating the bars until the ends are horizontal.

Toe clips

Use them! Toe clips are what cycling is all about. They are essential for full pedaling and riding skills. You might be worried about being trapped to the pedal. This is extremely rare. In fact, for safety reasons it is far, far more important to have your feet firmly attached to the pedals. Toe clips may look awkward, but with a little practice you'll soon slip in and out of them without a thought (see Riding). Be sure to have them correspond to your shoe size: small for small, medium to size 8-9, and large for size 9-10 and up. Go for larger if you tend to wear bulky shoes. To avoid scratching up fancy shoes, either fit toe clip pads or tape the clips with cloth tape.

Cleats

Cleats are metal or plastic strips fastened to the soles of cycling shoes. Used together with toe clips they hold your foot to the pedal with a vengeance, and are unsafe for traffic riding unless you use very loosely set straps. But they are essential for racing and great for touring. To fit cleats, first ride your bike for a few miles so that the soles of your shoes take an impression from the pedals. Then simply position the cleats so cleat gap is aligned with the pedal mark. Many cycling shoes have adjustable cleats that allow you to experiment with different positions.

Be careful not to force your feet out of natural alignment. If you twist them a little one way or the other, you can really wreck your knees. If you experience discomfort while using cleats, I strongly recommend seeking professional advice from a qualified bike shop or sports coach. Don't use cleats if they hurt.

Crank length

The cranks on Ashtabula and cottered cranksets are usually 165 mm long. Cranks for cotterless cranksets range in length from 160 mm to 180 mm. The usual size on road bikes is 170 mm. Some bike manufacturers supply 165 mm cranks on small frames, and 175 mm cranks on large frames. Many mountainbikes are fitted with 175 mm cranks for extra torque.

Correct crank length is a function of rider size, riding style, and skill. A person 6'4'' tall is not going to be too happy twiddling short 160 mm cranks, and a person 5' tall is going to have a long stretch to spin 175 mm cranks. Broadly, long cranks are for slow pedaling and delivery of torque through leverage and short cranks are for fast pedaling and delivery of torque through momentum. Another element is clearance when cornering or going over rough ground. It's surprising how much difference a few millimeters can make. Long cranks on a touring bike with a low bottom bracket, for example, give a machine that is tender in corners. If you are an old codger with no intention of hurrying anything, then longer cranks will provide a bit of welcome advantage. If you like to whiz and dive, stay off long cranks unless the bike is a criterium racer or mountainbike, with a high bottom bracket.

Unequal legs

A number of people have legs that are different in length. The result can be inexplicable back, hip and leg pains. If a qualified orthopedist or sports physician confirms that this is the problem, the method for compensation is to use pedals of different heights. TA has an Piste Orthopedic pedal with interchangeable cage plates of different heights. Your bike shop might be able to get them. Alternatively, any good engineering workshop should be able to modify pedals with removable cage plates.

Gearing

Fitting also includes the selection of gearing. Understanding this subject requires some knowledge of basic riding technique. Some of the information I am going to give you now is rather technical. Just use it as you need it.

When I bought my first derailleur gear bike I was surprised to find that the gear ratios, instead of each having a separate range like on a car, overlapped considerably. One gear wasn't much different from the other. The reason for this is that there is a rate of cadence - the speed with which the cranks are spun around - which is the most efficient. For most people this rate is from 65 to 85 strokes per minute. Racers run 120-130 and up. The idea behind a multitude of gears is to allow the rider to maintain the same cadence regardless of terrain.

In consequence, a racing bike will have close-ratio gears, each one much the same as the next, while a touring bike will have wide-ratio gears, with much greater differences between each gear. The reason for this is that touring bikes frequently pack heavy loads up steep grades. They are also more likely to be used by novice riders. Only expert riders in good condition can comfortably use close-ratio gears.

What determines ratio? The number of teeth on the front chainring divided by the number of teeth on the back sprocket (or cog). Thus 60 front to 15 rear is a 4 to 1 ratio. For competition a typical set-up might be a rear cluster of 23, 21, 19, 17, 15, matched to front chainrings of 49 and 52. For touring it might be 28, 24, 20, 17, 14 rear and 40 to 50 front.

To make everything a little simpler, gear ratios are expressed as a single number. The formula is:

$$\frac{\text{Number of teeth on front sprocket}}{\text{Number of teeth on back sprocket}} \times \text{wheel diameter} = \text{gear ratio}$$

In general, 100 is the top range and is hard to push, 90 is more common, and 80 the usual speed gear. 60 and 70 are the most often used, 40 and 50 are for hills. Below 40 is for extremely steep terrain and heavy loads. Most people gear too high and pedal too slowly. This increases fatigue. It is much better to pedal briskly against relatively little resistance.

There are other factors besides range to consider in setting up gears. Ease of transition from one gear to another is important. If you have to shift both front and back sprockets every time, it is laborious. For example:

Rear		14	17	21	26	31
Front	52	100.2	82.3	66.9	54	45
Front	47	90.4	74.5	60.2	48.6	40.8

means that to run up through the gears consecutively requires continuous double shifts. On the other hand, a set up like:

Rear		14	15	17	19	21
Front	54	104	97.2	85.6	76.7	69.4
Front	38	73.2	68	60	54	49

means that you can run up through the gears using only one shift of the front derailleur. (Never use the small front to small rear or big front to big rear. I will explain why later.)

If you use wide gaps front and rear there is almost bound to be some duplication of gears:

Rear		14	17	21	26	31
Front	52	100.2	82.3	66.9	54	45
Front	42	81	66.7	54	43.5	36.4

and yet curiously enough, many good bikes are set up this way. It really depends on what you want the bike for, because in balancing the various factors of range, ease of shifting, and number of different gears, you are just going to have to make compromises.

Stock gearing on many production bikes is definitely a compromise:

Rear		14	17	20	24	28
Front	52	100	83	70	58.5	50
Front	42	81	67	57	47	40.5

This selection of ratios is adequate for town riding, but the bottom 40.5 inch gear is not low enough for touring in hilly terrain or carrying heavy loads.

Tourists want lower gears spaced closely together, and the classic method for doing this is to use smaller front chainrings and a modest spread of cogs:

Rear		15	17	19	21	23
Front	46	83	73	65	59	54
Front	28	50	44	40	36	33

By dropping the sprockets a little more and widening the range of cogs, we come to a little whizzer known as the Montague:

Rear		14	16	18	20	22	28/30
Front	42	81	71	63	57	51.5	
Front	26		44	39	35	32	25/23

These patterns have a lot going for them: four close ratios at the low end of the range for climbing hills, a simple shifting sequence, and four good ratios for level ground. The drawbacks are a big jump between the small and large chainrings, and a limit on top speed.

One way of obtaining low ratios while still keeping speed gears is to use a big 34T rear cog:

Rear		14	18	23	30	34
Front	52	100	78	61	47	41
Front	42	81	63	49	38	33

This gives a wide range, but the large jumps between ratios make it difficult to maintain an even pedaling cadence, and many of the ratios are duplicates. Another method is to reduce the size of the small chainring as:

Rear		14	17	20	24	28
Front	52	100	83	70	58.5	50
Front	36	69	57	48.5	40.5	34.7

The advent of 6-speed blocks and narrow chains makes it possible to have both fairly close spaced gears, and a 'stump-puller' for hills:

Rear		13	15	18	21	26	32
Front	52	108	93.6	78	67	54	44
Front	42	87	75.6	63	54	43	35

This arrangement gives a reasonable hill-climbing gear, a good spread of middle and high gears, and an 'overdrive' for zooming down hills.

Racing and fast road bikes want narrow jumps between gears, as in this 14-speed arrangement.

Rear		12	13	14	15	17	19	21
Front	52	117	108	100	93	82	73	66
Front	42	94	87	81	75	66	59	54

The main points to bear in mind when working out a selection of gear ratios are:
1. Emphasis - for touring and mountainbiking, a good range of low gears; for competition, a good range of high gears; and for town riding, a good range of middle gears.
2. Bottom low - for touring in hilly terrain this should be around the 20 inch mark. A gear this low is thought by some to be for weaklings and called a 'granny' gear. With it, however, you will be able to pedal when others have to walk. Some of the strongest riders I know use a bottom gear of 19 inches for touring. Town bikes want a bottom gear in the low 30s, and competition bikes can start with a 45 or 50 inch gear.
3. Top high - there are many world champion riders who like to use big gears. In general, however, most racers gain speed by pedaling faster, not harder. The great Eddy Merckx, for example, used a 77 inch gear when he broke the 1 hour time trial record. For practical purposes anything over 100 inches is an overdrive giving more speed on downhills. Fine if you like excitement or are racing, but otherwise, consider the hard work - and

VISCOUNT BURY, K.C.M.G.

From a Photograph by the Hon. A. Keppel

main need for gears - is going UP the hill. Let gravity do the work down the other side, while you relax and enjoy the view.

Consider also the long term. In Europe, juvenile (under 16) racers are limited to a maximum gear of about 76 inches. This is to prevent injury to their legs and force the development of correct riding techniques. I wish this had happened to me. I would have stronger knees, and be a much better bike rider.

4. Shift sequence - make it as simple as possible. You want it all to happen easily. Double (front and rear together) shifts are fun when you want to be artistic, but not when you are panting for breath and fighting for a tight edge of momentum.

5. Derailleur capacity - this is a function of the difference in size between the large and small sprockets, and large and small chainrings. (A 14-28T block has a 14T difference, and 52/42 chainrings have a 10T difference, for a total of 24T. The arm of a rear derailleur

The Osgear (Constrictor Tyre Co.)

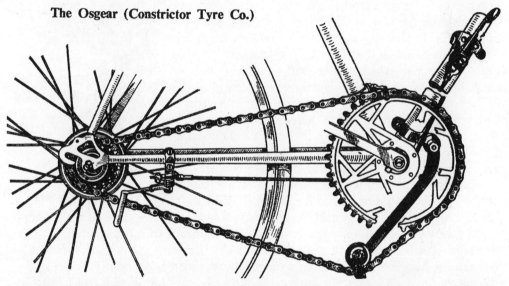

for use with this system must able to wrap 24T worth of chain.) Competition derailleurs with short arms usually range from 22T to 28T capacity. Touring derailleurs run up to 32T or 34T, and the big 'uns hit 38T.

Another aspect of rear derailleur capacity is maximum front chainring difference. This can be from around 12T to 18T and is generally linked to overall chain length capacity; a derailleur that wraps a lot of chain will usually also cope with large differences in chainring sizes.

Front derailleur capacity is a straightforward function of the difference in chainring sizes. Competition units are as low as 14T, and hefty units for use with wide range triple chainrings are 26T or more. Note that some of the mega-capacity front changers do not work properly unless there is a minimum difference of 6T.

American product liability laws require that derailleur gears on production bikes must be idiot-proofed by being capable of shifting to any possible combination of front chainring and sprocket. This means that many gear systems are needlessly bulky and awkward in terms of chain length, and size of derailleur needed to manage it. In real life it is silly (and harmful, see below) to pair the big chainring with the largest rear sprocket, or the small chainring with the smallest rear sprocket. If you eliminate these combinations which you should never use, the system can be set up with less chain, and a lighter, more responsive derailleur.

6. Derailleur sprocket size - the largest size rear sprocket that a derailleur can handle. If a derailleur is marked for a 30T sprocket, it is usually unable to mount a larger sprocket such as 34T. This is a function of the mechanical range of the derailleur itself, and not the amount of chain to wrap. Broadly, competition derailleurs work best on close-ratio freewheels kept well within capacity. Touring derailleurs work well on wide-ratio freewheels and indifferently on close-ratio freewheels.

7. Number of gear ratios - 6- and 7-speed freewheels (which give 12 and 14 speeds with double chainrings, 18 and 21 speeds with triple rings) are not uncommon on production bikes. Set up with close-ratio cogs they are great for competition, but are more trouble than gain when set up with a wide range of cogs for a town or touring bike. For one thing, gear ratios have a greater tendency to duplicate, negating the point of the exercise. For another, a narrow chain is required, which makes shifting more fiddly. To make room for the 7-speed model freewheel, and certain of the 6-speed model freewheels, the wheel must have more dish (off-set of the hub) and is therefore weaker - not the thing for bumpy urban streets or heavyweight touring. Finally, a 7-speed block matched to double chainrings in actual practice gives 10 speeds at most and not 14.

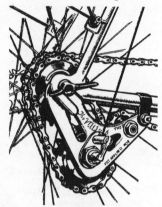

Villiers 2-speed gear

Why? Because even with a 5-speed block and double chainrings you should never run the big front chainring to big rear cog, or small front chainring to small rear cog. It causes the chain to cut across at too severe an angle, creating excessive wear, a tendency to rub the derailleur cages, and reduced efficiency. With a 7-speed block the problems are even worse. At most you can use only 5 of the 7 rear cogs on each front chainring, and it is better to limit the number to 4 - a rather anemic total of 8 speeds out of a possible 14. Throw in a couple of duplicated gears and you are down to 6 usable ratios - the minimum that even a poorly designed 5-speed block/double chainring combination will produce!

Triple chainrings

For really effective wide range gearing, the route to take is triple front chainrings. You will not gain all that many more ratios, but they will be exactly where required and certain types of difficult gear shifts will be easier. With a triple the inner chainring should be the smallest available, say 28T, 26T, or even 24T. This allows the use of a moderately sized largest rear cog, saving weight and improving shifting. It is always much easier to drop the chain from a large to small front chainring than to lift the chain up on to a large rear cog. With a triple, shifting into low range is a simple matter of banging home the shift lever for the front derailleur.

The next advantage of a triple is that the middle chainring can be ideally sized for level cruising, and be used on all five (or six) rear cogs without chain deflection problems. Most of the time you just run on the middle ring, and have only one shift lever to worry about.

When there is a tail wind or downgrade it's up onto the big chainring and go. Since the middle range is nicely taken care of by the center chainring, you can afford to have a selection of final drive ratios plus an overdrive ratio off the big chainring.

A triple is a bit tricky when shifting to the middle chainring. At first, you will have to look at and center the derailleur with each shift. But with practice you'll be able to do it by feel. Another factor is that a long chain, and long arm derailleur to keep it under control, makes for slower shifting. It takes a while for all that hardware to settle into place.

If you want a triple chainset, sort matters out at the time of bike purchase. Triple rings require a longer bottom bracket axle to adjust the chainline and keep the inner chainring clear of the bike frame. Some double chainsets can be converted to triples, but getting everything to work properly can take a lot of fiddling about. Better if the bike is set up as a triple in the first place.

Summary

A bike is an extension of your body. It is all right for cycling to hurt because you are riding vigorously, or hardening yourself and extending your range. But the bike itself should be comfortable. If there are aches and pains that do not go away with a bit of riding and conditioning, then carefully review the fit of the bike.

PATENT INTERCHANGEABLE GEAR

For all our Safeties, enabling the rider, by keeping an extra gear wheel (cost 7s. 6d. only), to change in a few minutes from a road to a racing gear or *vice versa*, the choice extending from 45in. to 66in. This gear is also fitted to tricycles at a cost of 10s. each, and is a boon to those who cycle for health as it enables them to change the gear from time to time, as they may regain strength or the condition or nature of the roads may render advisable.

GEAR RATIO CHART FOR 27 INCH WHEELS

Number of teeth on sprocket

Number of teeth on chainring

Sprocket \ Chainring	24	25	26	27	28	29	30	31	32	33	34	35	36	37	38	39	40	41	42	43	44	45	46	47	48	49	50	51	52	53	54	55	56	57	58
12	54.0	56.3	58.5	60.8	63.0	65.3	67.5	69.8	72.0	74.3	76.5	78.8	81.0	83.3	85.5	87.8	90.0	92.3	94.5	96.8	99.0	101.3	103.5	105.8	108.0	110.3	112.5	114.8	117.0	119.3	121.5	123.8	126.0	128.3	130.5
13	49.8	51.9	54.0	56.1	58.2	60.2	62.3	64.4	66.5	68.5	70.6	72.7	74.8	76.8	78.9	81.0	83.1	85.2	87.2	89.3	91.4	93.5	95.5	97.6	99.7	101.8	103.8	105.9	108.0	110.1	112.2	114.2	116.3	118.4	120.5
14	46.3	48.2	50.1	52.1	54.0	55.9	57.9	59.8	61.7	63.6	65.6	67.5	69.4	71.4	73.3	75.2	77.1	79.1	81.0	82.9	84.9	86.8	88.7	90.6	92.6	94.5	96.4	98.4	100.3	102.2	104.1	106.1	108.0	109.9	111.9
15	43.2	45.0	46.8	48.6	50.4	52.2	54.0	55.8	57.6	59.4	61.2	63.0	64.8	66.6	68.4	70.2	72.0	73.8	75.6	77.4	79.2	81.0	82.8	84.6	86.4	88.2	90.0	91.8	93.6	95.4	97.2	99.0	100.8	102.6	104.4
16	40.5	42.2	43.9	45.6	47.3	48.9	50.6	52.3	54.0	55.7	57.4	59.1	60.8	62.4	64.1	65.8	67.5	69.2	70.9	72.6	74.3	75.9	77.6	79.3	81.0	82.7	84.4	86.1	87.8	89.4	91.1	92.8	94.5	96.2	97.9
17	38.1	39.7	41.3	42.9	44.5	46.1	47.6	49.2	50.8	52.4	54.0	55.6	57.2	58.8	60.4	61.9	63.5	65.1	66.7	68.3	69.9	71.5	73.1	74.6	76.2	77.8	79.4	81.0	82.6	84.2	85.8	87.4	88.9	90.5	92.1
18	36.0	37.5	39.0	40.5	42.0	43.5	45.0	46.5	48.0	49.5	51.0	52.5	54.0	55.5	57.0	58.5	60.0	61.5	63.0	64.5	66.0	67.5	69.0	70.5	72.0	73.5	75.0	76.5	78.0	79.5	81.0	82.5	84.0	85.5	87.0
19	34.1	35.5	36.9	38.4	39.8	41.2	42.6	44.1	45.5	46.9	48.3	49.7	51.2	52.6	54.0	55.4	56.8	58.3	59.7	61.1	62.5	63.9	65.4	66.8	68.2	69.6	71.1	72.5	73.9	75.3	76.7	78.2	79.6	81.0	82.4
20	32.4	33.8	35.1	36.5	37.8	39.2	40.5	41.9	43.2	44.6	45.9	47.3	48.6	50.0	51.3	52.7	54.0	55.4	56.7	58.1	59.4	60.8	62.1	63.5	64.8	66.2	67.5	68.9	70.2	71.6	72.9	74.3	75.6	77.0	78.3
21	30.9	32.1	33.4	34.7	36.0	37.3	38.6	39.9	41.1	42.4	43.7	45.0	46.3	47.6	48.9	50.1	51.4	52.7	54.0	55.3	56.6	57.9	59.1	60.4	61.7	63.0	64.3	65.6	66.9	68.1	69.4	70.7	72.0	73.3	74.6
22	29.5	30.7	31.9	33.1	34.4	35.6	36.8	38.0	39.3	40.5	41.7	43.0	44.2	45.4	46.6	47.9	49.1	50.3	51.5	52.8	54.0	55.2	56.5	57.7	58.9	60.1	61.4	62.6	63.8	65.0	66.3	67.5	68.7	70.0	71.2
23	28.2	29.3	30.5	31.7	32.9	34.0	35.2	36.4	37.6	38.7	39.9	41.1	42.3	43.4	44.6	45.8	47.0	48.1	49.3	50.5	51.7	52.8	54.0	55.2	56.3	57.5	58.7	59.9	61.0	62.2	63.4	64.6	65.7	66.9	68.1
24	27.0	28.1	29.3	30.4	31.5	32.6	33.8	34.9	36.0	37.1	38.3	39.4	40.5	41.6	42.8	43.9	45.0	46.1	47.3	48.4	49.5	50.6	51.8	52.9	54.0	55.1	56.3	57.4	58.5	59.6	60.8	61.9	63.0	64.1	65.3
25	25.9	27.0	28.1	29.2	30.2	31.3	32.4	33.5	34.6	35.6	36.7	37.8	38.9	40.0	41.0	42.1	43.2	44.3	45.4	46.4	47.5	48.6	49.7	50.8	51.8	52.9	54.0	55.1	56.2	57.2	58.3	59.4	60.5	61.6	62.6
26	24.9	26.0	27.0	28.0	29.0	30.1	31.2	32.2	33.2	34.3	35.3	36.3	37.4	38.4	39.5	40.5	41.5	42.6	43.6	44.7	45.7	46.7	47.8	48.8	49.8	50.9	51.9	53.0	54.0	55.0	56.1	57.1	58.2	59.2	60.2
27	24.0	25.0	26.0	27.0	28.0	29.0	30.0	31.0	32.0	33.0	34.0	35.0	36.0	37.0	38.0	39.0	40.0	41.0	42.0	43.0	44.0	45.0	46.0	47.0	48.0	49.0	50.0	51.0	52.0	53.0	54.0	55.0	56.0	57.0	58.0
28	23.1	24.1	25.1	26.0	27.0	28.0	28.9	29.9	30.9	31.8	32.8	33.8	34.7	35.7	36.6	37.6	38.6	39.5	40.5	41.5	42.4	43.4	44.4	45.3	46.3	47.3	48.2	49.2	50.1	51.1	52.1	53.0	54.0	55.0	55.9
29	22.3	23.3	24.2	25.1	26.1	27.0	27.9	28.9	29.8	30.7	31.7	32.6	33.5	34.5	35.4	36.3	37.2	38.2	39.1	40.0	41.0	41.9	42.8	43.8	44.7	45.6	46.6	47.5	48.4	49.3	50.3	51.2	52.1	53.1	54.0
30	21.6	22.5	23.4	24.3	25.2	26.1	27.0	27.9	28.8	29.7	30.6	31.5	32.4	33.3	34.2	35.1	36.0	36.9	37.8	38.7	39.6	40.5	41.4	42.3	43.2	44.1	45.0	45.9	46.8	47.7	48.6	49.5	50.4	51.3	52.2
31	20.9	21.8	22.6	23.5	24.4	25.3	26.1	27.0	27.9	28.7	29.6	30.5	31.4	32.2	33.1	34.0	34.8	35.7	36.6	37.5	38.3	39.2	40.1	40.9	41.8	42.7	43.5	44.4	45.3	46.2	47.0	47.9	48.8	49.6	50.5
32	20.3	21.1	21.9	22.8	23.6	24.5	25.3	26.2	27.0	27.8	28.7	29.5	30.4	31.2	32.1	32.9	33.8	34.6	35.4	36.3	37.1	38.0	38.8	39.7	40.5	41.3	42.2	43.0	43.9	44.7	45.6	46.4	47.3	48.1	48.9
33	19.6	20.5	21.3	22.1	22.9	23.7	24.5	25.4	26.2	27.0	27.8	28.6	29.5	30.3	31.1	31.9	32.7	33.5	34.4	35.2	36.0	36.8	37.6	38.5	39.3	40.1	40.9	41.7	42.5	43.4	44.2	45.0	45.8	46.6	47.5
34	19.1	19.9	20.6	21.4	22.2	23.0	23.8	24.6	25.4	26.2	27.0	27.8	28.6	29.4	30.2	31.0	31.8	32.6	33.4	34.1	34.9	35.7	36.5	37.3	38.1	38.9	39.7	40.5	41.3	42.1	42.9	43.7	44.5	45.3	46.1
35	18.5	19.3	20.1	20.8	21.6	22.4	23.1	23.9	24.7	25.5	26.2	27.0	27.8	28.5	29.3	30.1	30.9	31.6	32.4	33.2	33.9	34.7	35.5	36.3	37.0	37.8	38.6	39.3	40.1	40.9	41.7	42.4	43.2	44.0	44.7
36	18.0	18.8	19.5	20.3	21.0	21.8	22.5	23.3	24.0	24.8	25.5	26.3	27.0	27.8	28.5	29.3	30.0	30.8	31.5	32.3	33.0	33.8	34.5	35.3	36.0	36.8	37.5	38.3	39.0	39.8	40.5	41.3	42.0	42.8	43.5
37	17.5	18.2	19.0	19.7	20.4	21.2	21.9	22.6	23.4	24.1	24.8	25.5	26.3	27.0	27.7	28.5	29.2	29.9	30.6	31.4	32.1	32.8	33.6	34.3	35.0	35.8	36.5	37.2	37.9	38.7	39.4	40.1	40.9	41.6	42.3
38	17.1	17.8	18.5	19.2	19.9	20.6	21.3	22.0	22.7	23.4	24.2	24.9	25.6	26.3	27.0	27.7	28.4	29.1	29.8	30.6	31.3	32.0	32.7	33.4	34.1	34.8	35.5	36.2	36.9	37.7	38.4	39.1	39.8	40.5	41.2

Number of teeth on chainring

Number of teeth on sprocket

GEAR RATIO CHART FOR 26 INCH WHEELS

Number of teeth on sprocket (rows) × **Number of teeth on chainring** (columns)

Sprocket \ Chainring	24	25	26	27	28	29	30	31	32	33	34	35	36	37	38	39	40	41	42	43	44	45	46	47	48	49	50	51	52	53	54	55	56	57	58
12	52.0	54.2	56.3	58.5	60.7	62.8	65.0	67.2	69.3	71.5	73.7	75.8	78.0	80.2	82.3	84.5	86.7	88.8	91.0	93.2	95.3	97.5	99.7	101.8	104.0	106.2	108.3	110.5	112.7	114.8	117.0	119.2	121.3	123.5	125.7
13	48.0	50.0	52.0	54.0	56.0	58.0	60.0	62.0	64.0	66.0	68.0	70.0	72.0	74.0	76.0	78.0	80.0	82.0	84.0	86.0	88.0	90.0	92.0	94.0	96.0	98.0	100.0	102.0	104.0	106.0	108.0	110.0	112.0	114.0	116.0
14	44.6	46.4	48.3	50.1	52.0	53.9	55.7	57.6	59.4	61.3	63.1	65.0	66.9	68.7	70.6	72.4	74.3	76.1	78.0	79.9	81.7	83.6	85.4	87.3	89.1	91.0	92.9	94.7	96.6	98.4	100.3	102.1	104.0	105.9	107.7
15	41.6	43.3	45.1	46.8	48.5	50.3	52.0	53.7	55.5	57.2	58.9	60.7	62.4	64.1	65.9	67.6	69.3	71.1	72.8	74.6	76.3	78.0	79.7	81.5	83.2	84.9	86.7	88.4	90.1	91.9	93.6	95.3	97.1	98.8	100.5
16	39.0	40.6	42.3	43.9	45.5	47.1	48.8	50.4	52.0	53.6	55.2	56.9	58.5	60.1	61.8	63.4	65.0	66.6	68.3	69.9	71.5	73.1	74.8	76.4	78.0	79.6	81.3	82.9	84.5	86.1	87.8	89.4	91.0	92.6	94.3
17	36.7	38.2	39.8	41.3	42.8	44.4	45.9	47.4	48.9	50.5	52.0	53.5	55.1	56.6	58.1	59.6	61.2	62.7	64.2	65.8	67.3	68.8	70.4	71.9	73.4	74.9	76.5	78.0	79.5	81.1	82.6	84.1	85.6	87.2	88.7
18	34.7	36.1	37.6	39.0	40.4	41.9	43.3	44.8	46.2	47.7	49.1	50.6	52.0	53.4	54.9	56.3	57.8	59.2	60.7	62.1	63.6	65.0	66.4	67.9	69.3	70.8	72.2	73.7	75.1	76.6	78.0	79.4	80.9	82.3	83.8
19	32.8	34.2	35.6	36.9	38.3	39.7	41.1	42.4	43.8	45.2	46.5	47.9	49.3	50.6	52.0	53.4	54.7	56.1	57.5	58.8	60.2	61.6	62.9	64.3	65.7	67.1	68.4	69.8	71.2	72.5	73.9	75.3	76.6	78.0	79.4
20	31.2	32.5	33.8	35.1	36.4	37.7	39.0	40.3	41.6	42.9	44.2	45.5	46.8	48.1	49.4	50.7	52.0	53.3	54.6	55.9	57.2	58.5	59.8	61.1	62.4	63.7	65.0	66.3	67.6	68.9	70.2	71.5	72.8	74.1	75.4
21	29.7	31.0	32.2	33.4	34.7	35.9	37.1	38.4	39.6	40.9	42.1	43.3	44.6	45.8	47.0	48.3	49.5	50.8	52.0	53.2	54.5	55.7	57.0	58.2	59.4	60.7	61.9	63.1	64.4	65.6	66.9	68.1	69.3	70.6	71.8
22	28.4	29.5	30.7	31.9	33.1	34.3	35.5	36.6	37.8	39.0	40.2	41.4	42.5	43.7	44.9	46.1	47.3	48.5	49.6	50.8	52.0	53.2	54.4	55.5	56.7	57.9	59.1	60.3	61.5	62.6	63.8	65.0	66.2	67.4	68.5
23	27.1	28.3	29.4	30.5	31.7	32.8	33.9	35.0	36.2	37.3	38.4	39.6	40.7	41.8	43.0	44.1	45.2	46.3	47.5	48.6	49.7	50.9	52.0	53.1	54.3	55.4	56.5	57.7	58.8	59.9	61.0	62.2	63.3	64.4	65.6
24	26.0	27.1	28.2	29.3	30.3	31.4	32.5	33.6	34.7	35.8	36.8	37.9	39.0	40.1	41.2	42.3	43.3	44.4	45.5	46.6	47.7	48.8	49.8	50.9	52.0	53.1	54.2	55.3	56.3	57.4	58.5	59.6	60.7	61.8	62.8
25	25.0	26.0	27.0	28.1	29.1	30.2	31.2	32.2	33.3	34.3	35.4	36.4	37.4	38.5	39.5	40.6	41.6	42.6	43.7	44.7	45.8	46.8	47.8	48.9	49.9	51.0	52.0	53.0	54.1	55.1	56.2	57.2	58.2	59.3	60.3
26	24.0	25.0	26.0	27.0	28.0	29.0	30.0	31.0	32.0	33.0	34.0	35.0	36.0	37.0	38.0	39.0	40.0	41.0	42.0	43.0	44.0	45.0	46.0	47.0	48.0	49.0	50.0	51.0	52.0	53.0	54.0	55.0	56.0	57.0	58.0
27	23.1	24.1	25.0	26.0	27.0	27.9	28.9	29.9	30.8	31.8	32.7	33.7	34.7	35.6	36.6	37.6	38.5	39.5	40.4	41.4	42.4	43.3	44.3	45.3	46.2	47.2	48.1	49.1	50.1	51.0	52.0	53.0	53.9	54.9	55.9
28	22.3	23.2	24.1	25.1	26.0	26.9	27.9	28.8	29.7	30.6	31.6	32.5	33.4	34.4	35.3	36.2	37.1	38.1	39.0	39.9	40.9	41.8	42.7	43.6	44.6	45.5	46.4	47.4	48.3	49.2	50.1	51.1	52.0	52.9	53.9
29	21.5	22.4	23.3	24.2	25.1	26.0	26.9	27.8	28.7	29.6	30.5	31.4	32.3	33.2	34.1	35.0	35.9	36.8	37.7	38.6	39.4	40.3	41.2	42.1	43.0	43.9	44.8	45.7	46.6	47.5	48.4	49.3	50.2	51.1	52.0
30	20.8	21.7	22.5	23.4	24.3	25.1	26.0	26.9	27.7	28.6	29.5	30.3	31.2	32.1	32.9	33.8	34.7	35.5	36.4	37.3	38.1	39.0	39.9	40.7	41.6	42.5	43.3	44.2	45.1	45.9	46.8	47.7	48.5	49.4	50.3
31	20.1	21.0	21.8	22.6	23.5	24.3	25.2	26.0	26.8	27.7	28.5	29.4	30.2	31.0	31.9	32.7	33.5	34.4	35.2	36.1	36.9	37.7	38.6	39.4	40.3	41.1	41.9	42.8	43.6	44.5	45.3	46.1	47.0	47.8	48.6
32	19.5	20.3	21.1	21.9	22.8	23.6	24.4	25.2	26.0	26.8	27.6	28.4	29.3	30.1	30.9	31.7	32.5	33.3	34.1	34.9	35.8	36.6	37.4	38.2	39.0	39.8	40.6	41.4	42.3	43.1	43.9	44.7	45.5	46.3	47.1
33	18.9	19.7	20.5	21.3	22.1	22.8	23.6	24.4	25.2	26.0	26.8	27.6	28.4	29.2	29.9	30.7	31.5	32.3	33.1	33.9	34.7	35.5	36.2	37.0	37.8	38.6	39.4	40.2	41.0	41.8	42.5	43.3	44.1	44.9	45.7
34	18.4	19.1	19.9	20.6	21.4	22.2	22.9	23.7	24.5	25.2	26.0	26.8	27.5	28.3	29.1	29.8	30.6	31.4	32.1	32.9	33.6	34.4	35.2	35.9	36.7	37.5	38.2	39.0	39.8	40.5	41.3	42.1	42.8	43.6	44.4
35	17.8	18.6	19.3	20.1	20.8	21.5	22.3	23.0	23.8	24.5	25.3	26.0	26.7	27.5	28.2	29.0	29.7	30.5	31.2	31.9	32.7	33.4	34.2	34.9	35.7	36.4	37.1	37.9	38.6	39.4	40.1	40.9	41.6	42.3	43.1
36	17.3	18.1	18.8	19.5	20.2	20.9	21.7	22.4	23.1	23.8	24.6	25.3	26.0	26.7	27.4	28.2	28.9	29.6	30.3	31.1	31.8	32.5	33.2	33.9	34.7	35.4	36.1	36.8	37.6	38.3	39.0	39.7	40.4	41.2	41.9
37	16.9	17.6	18.3	19.0	19.7	20.4	21.1	21.8	22.5	23.2	23.9	24.6	25.3	26.0	26.7	27.4	28.1	28.8	29.5	30.2	30.9	31.6	32.3	33.0	33.7	34.4	35.1	35.8	36.5	37.2	37.9	38.6	39.4	40.1	40.8
38	16.4	17.1	17.8	18.5	19.2	19.8	20.5	21.2	21.9	22.6	23.3	23.9	24.6	25.3	26.0	26.7	27.4	28.1	28.7	29.4	30.1	30.8	31.5	32.2	32.8	33.5	34.2	34.9	35.6	36.3	36.9	37.6	38.3	39.0	39.7

Number of teeth on chainring

Number of teeth on sprocket

111

CHAPTER 9

Riding

Anybody can ride a bicycle. You just get aboard and pedal. Heh! Try following an experienced tourist on an 100 mile run or a competition rider around the track. Physical condition of course plays a part, but here technique counts more than anything else. Fifty-year-old grandmothers can and do run rings around fit young adults. Attention to the basics of technique will make riding easier and more enjoyable, and help you realize your capacities and abilities. Riding well is part of the fun - and there is always room for improvement!

This chapter concentrates on basic mechanical techniques for bike operation and control. Of course even basic technique varies somewhat with conditions, and there is a lot more to riding than mere technique. The following chapters on traffic jamming, commuting, touring, and mountainbiking amplify considerably on the information you need in order to cycle safely and comfortably.

Shifting

Broadly, shifting is a matter of synchronizing pedal pressure and crank rotation with movement of the shift lever. There are pre-select systems which allow you to move the shift lever before pedaling, but they operate slowly, and are mechanically more trouble than they are worth. It's better to use a conventional system and let your skill develop gradually. Back off if you start to get damaging 'clunk' sounding shifts. These are caused by incorrectly timed pedal pressure. The way to do things fast is to do them right. Once you get the knack, smooth, split-second gear changes will be second nature.

Hub gears

To shift up to a higher gear, ease pressure on pedals while continuing to rotate cranks, move selector to next gear, and resume pedal pressure. Extra fast shifts may be made by maintaining pedal pressure, moving the selector, and then pausing pedaling momentarily when the shift is desired. If done too hard, this may damage gears. Going down to 1st from 2nd or 3rd and coming to a stop, back pedal slightly. If not stopping use same procedure as for upshifts.

Derailleur gears

Shift derailleur gears only while pedaling. To see why, hang your bike up so that the rear wheel is off the ground, rotate the cranks, and manipulate the gear shift levers so you can see how they work. Shifting a derailleur without pedaling may result in a bent or broken chain or gear teeth. If you park your bike in the street, always give the gears a visual check to make sure passers-by have not fiddled with them. It happens often.

113

Ease pedal pressure when shifting. The exact amount depends on the kind of shift and equipment involved. For example, in a front changer downshift the chain is knocked off a larger chainring down onto a smaller chainring. This is mechanically easy and is usually quick. In an upshift from a smaller to a larger chainring, however, the chain must climb up while overcoming the spring tension provided by the rear derailleur. If the difference in chainring sizes is large, upshifts will take a bit of time.

There are three types of shift lever mechanisms: simple friction, friction with a clutch or ratchet device, and semi-automatic. Semi-automatic levers automatically stop in the right place for each gear. Friction shift levers do not have stops for the different gears, and you have to learn where they are by feel and ear. Do not let the front derailleur cage rub the chain. Sometimes a front changer will shift only if it is overset; once the shift is completed the lever must be reversed slightly to reposition the changer and prevent the chain from rubbing the cage. It's easy to do, because you can look right down and see what is happening.

Aligning a rear changer so that the chain meshes smoothly with the cog is not as easy. It's a matter of ear and feel; no untoward grinding or chattering noises, and a smooth sensation at the pedals. Some old fashioned rear derailleurs need back and forth shift lever movement; a generous motion to initiate the shift, and then a slight reverse direction adjustment to bring everything into alignment. Many modern designs, on the other hand, are very responsive and shift with just a touch of the lever. Experiment with your own system to see what works best.

Do not run the big front chainring to the big rear sprocket, or the small front to the small rear. It causes the chain to cut across at too severe an angle, greatly increasing wear and reducing efficiency. Proper shifting should also take into account the demands of cadence (see below).

Pedaling

Ride with the ball of your foot on the pedal, not the heel or arch. The fundamental technique for easy cycling is called ankling. This is where the foot pivots at the ankle with each revolution of the crank. Start at the top of the stroke (12 o'clock) with the heel slightly lower than the toes. Push with the ball of the foot and simultaneously pivot at the ankle on the downstroke so that the foot levels out between 2 and 3 o'clock, and continue this motion so that at the bottom of the stroke the toes are lower than the heel:

The main thing to strive for is smoothness and steady, even pressure. Practice this slowly, in a high gear, and away from traffic so you can concentrate on watching your feet.

Toe clips are a great boon. They allow you to have a feather-light touch on the pedals with no fear of losing grip. In fact, you cannot spin properly without them. They are completely safe. Smooth-

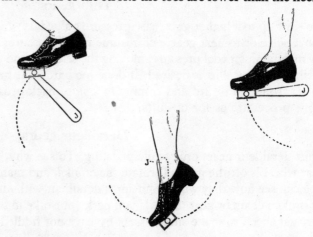

soled conventional shoes can always be slipped out of the pedal even if the straps are tight. If using cycling shoes with cleats or ridges, keep the straps loose in traffic.

The technique for getting underway is simple: start with loose straps. Straddle the bike, slip a foot into a pedal at the 1 o'clock position, and tighten the strap. Push off, using the downstroke of this crank to get you underway, and simultaneously reach down with the free foot, give the pedal a light tap to spin the toe clip around to the proper position, slip in foot, and tighten strap. It sounds more complicated than it is. The key is the deft, light tap to the pedal to bring the toe clip around so you can slip your foot in. Practice will soon make it second nature. When coming to a stop, reach down and loosen one strap so you can get your foot back in easily when underway again. Do not worry about being trapped by toe clips. I have made zillions of emergency stops and have always been able to get my feet free. On the other hand, do not tempt fate by riding in heavy traffic with ultra-tight straps. And if you use sneakers or other soft-soled shoes (bad - not enough support), or cleated bicycling shoes, keep the straps loose when conditions warrant.

Cadence

This subject was mentioned in connection with gearing. Briefly, human beings pedal most efficiently at a certain number of strokes per minute. The optimum cadence varies with the physical condition and technique of the individual rider. Generally, novices run from 60 to 85 strokes per minute, experienced tourists approach 100, and racers run 120-130 and up.

Most people gear too high and pedal too slowly. They don't think they are going anywhere or getting any exercise unless they are pushing against resistance. It is precisely this pushing which creates fatigue. It is much better to pedal rapidly against relatively little resistance. Especially when first starting with a bike, always try to pedal as rapidly as you can without going into orbit. As a rough rule of thumb, if your legs are on fire, you are pushing too hard; if you are gasping for breath, you are spinning too fast. Maintaining a comfortable balance is one of the primary reasons for having lots of gears; always shift up or down as necessary to maintain an even cadence. Learn to shift just before you need the new gear. Do not let a hill slow down your cadence, for example, but shift just before you hit it, and as needed going up. The way you will be able churn along will be absolutely amazing.

Bumps

When you come to bumps, pot-holes, cables, etc., put most of your weight on the pedals and handlebars. This allows the bike to pivot underneath you, reducing shock for both you and the bike. You know how motorcycle scramble riders stand up on the pegs? Like that.

Braking

Try to use your brakes as little as possible. This will help you to 'look ahead' and anticipate traffic conditions in advance. Be careful of braking too hard and skidding, or pitching yourself over the handlebars. It is the front brake which does most of the work, and the more rapidly you decelerate, the more work it can do. This is because weight is transferred forward, increasing the coefficient of friction between the front tire and the road surface. Simultaneously, weight on the back tire is lessened slightly, decreasing the coefficient of friction and making it more liable to skid. The technique for a rapid or panic stop is thus one of moving body weight rearward while progressively increasing pressure on the front brake and simultaneously holding pressure on the back brake just below the point where the wheel will lock and skid. It is a coordinated sequence of events that can only be learned by practice. Start with quick stops from low speeds and gradually increase velocity. Really throw your butt back as you hit the brakes, transferring most of your weight onto the pedals. This helps lower the center of gravity. Get to the point where you are stopping the bike just as fast as you can. Then have a friend give you stop signals at unexpected moments.

Once you master hard braking, keep your technique fresh and sharp with regular practice. Knowing is not enough. The reflexes have to be actively kept in shape so that in a real emergency, you make the right moves as quickly as possible. Some people feel foolish doing this sort of thing - cowboy. Foo. Better to burn some rubber and have an idea of what you can do with your bike.

In slippery conditions or when banked hard over in a turn favor the rear brake. The rear wheel does have a greater tendency to skid, but if it goes you may still be able to keep yourself upright, and at worst will land on your hip. If the front wheel washes away you've a good chance of landing on your face.

In wet conditions frequently apply the brakes lightly to wipe water off the rims. Don't get caught napping, otherwise you may need four or five times the distance for stopping with dry brakes.

Going down long hills avoid overheating the wheel rims by pumping (on-off-on-off-on etc.) the brakes. Always be able to stop. If you find yourself wondering if the brakes will work - say on a very steep pitch - find out at once. Ride within your experience. If the descent is longer or steeper than you've made before, periodically stop and check the rims for overheating.

On the other side of the coin, if you've got a clear road don't be afraid to let the bike move out and breathe. Past 20 mph you've got a free speed control - air resistance. For speed, a racer will tuck into a full crouch, tighten in the elbows, and hold the pedals at 3 and 9 o'clock. If you sit bolt upright with arms and legs splayed apart, you'll find that air drag is often all you need to keep speed at a comfortable level. An important advantage in using this technique is that the mechanical brakes are kept fresh and ready.

Turning

If you ride a bicycle then by definition you can turn it. But there are different methods and styles of turning.

Underway, a bicycle is in a constant state of imbalance. A tendency to lean one way will be corrected by the rider, the bike will move through center of balance to a lean the opposite way, and the rider will correct again. Most turning consists simply of taking advantage of a lean in the desired direction. Instead of correcting, the rider allows the lean to continue and thus effects a turn. The feeling is that the rider has changed balance and the bike has followed suit, and in that bicycle geometry is designed for a certain amount of self-steering, the feeling is accurate enough. The rider does in fact change balance. This type of turn has two faults: it is slow, and it puts rider and bicycle weight in one single line down to the point of tire contact with the road.

In racing, and in traffic riding, it is often necessary to turn - FAST! This can be done by hauling back on the handlebar end opposite to the direction in which you wish to go. The bike will move out from under you, you will start to fall, and then you will TURN. Can you see it? In the 'normal' turn you topple to one side gradually; in the 'haul handlebar' turn you snatch the bike out from underneath you, and immediately fall into a turn. It is very handy for avoiding unexpected obstacles such as broken glass. In effect, you go one way, the bike goes the other, and afterwards you catch up with each other. Like panic braking, this type of turn must be learned slowly, and with lots of room for maneuvering.

Another type of turn consists of laying down the bike, while you remain relatively upright, i.e. the bike 'leans' more than you do. This is useful when the road surface is rough, because then a percentage of the rider weight pivots as the bike moves up and down, lessening the load on the wheels. Better for the bike, better for you. It is also a quick turn, although not as fast as hauling handlebar.

Another type of turn consists of leaning the body more than the bike. This is a very standard technique for fast riding on shale and gravel, and is thought to lessen the chances of skidding. When I unexpectedly encounter a wet manhole cover or oil slick while turning I throw the bike up while keeping my own weight down. This, and the lay down turn, can be done by moving the whole bike underneath you while you pivot sideways at the hips, and can be accelerated by hauling on the handlebars as well.

Haul, lay down, and set up turns are esoteric in description but relatively simple in practice. You can learn them in a backyard or empty parking lot. For your own safety you should be able to execute a haul turn instantly, whenever circumstances require.

Climbing

Climbing technique depends on the length and pitch of climb, the kind of bike, and the condition and nature of the rider. A racer is more likely to 'honk' - stand up out of the saddle and use body weight to help drive the cranks around. A heavily laden tourist is more likely to drop into bottom gear and twiddle up - stay in the saddle while spinning the cranks lightly and rapidly. Unless you know that you can attack a hill and win, it is generally better to start calmly and moderately and keep some strength in reserve. On very long climbs do not look at the top; concentrate on the immediate moment and surroundings, and on maintaining a steady rhythm. If there is a long downgrade after the crest, keep pedaling as you coast down, to prevent stiffening up.

CHAPTER 10

Fast is Safe

Every rider must know how to ride on streets and highways shared with motor vehicles, the same way if you walk you have to know how to cross the street. Beyond this, for many people 99 percent of their riding is in traffic, and they might as well make it as safe and as enjoyable as possible. There is no way, however, that I can tell you riding in traffic is safe. In plain fact it is dangerous. The people frightened away from cycling by fear of an accident with a car have ample justification for their fears.

Nervousness when first venturing into traffic indicates a sound mind. With time and experience you can learn to ride with a level of knowledge and skill that greatly reduces the risk of accident. The outcome of riding in traffic depends less on the situation than on what you do. But the element of risk is constant. Something can happen out of the blue, through no fault of your own, that wipes you off the face of the earth in a twinkling.

Taking a bath is also a risky affair. And people die unexpectedly in bed. The amount of traffic riding that suits you is entirely your decision. Although the basic principles are the same, there is a considerable difference between mixing it up with heavy weekday commuter traffic and cycling a few blocks to the park on Sunday. I'll help you best as I know how. But the go/no go decision is yours.

The most important thing to understand is that efficient, safe riding in traffic requires attentiveness. You must be alert at all times and know everything that is going on, from the size of the pebbles on the road to the debris which might fall on you from a construction project to the number and type of vehicles before and behind you - absolutely everything. Traffic riding requires total concentration. There is no place for woolgathering or idyllic pastoral pleasures.

Some people are just born inattentive. If you are one of these and a survivor, you've probably learned to steer clear of risky places and situations. You prefer walking perhaps, to cycling or driving a car, because it does not need a lot of attention and leaves your mind free to wander. Great, but if you ride a bike then it should be off-road, or on cyclepaths. Because if you do not pay constant attention when cycling in traffic, you may only survive as a statistic.

It's not all downhill. Attentiveness has benefits. Total engagement is refreshing. For example, I like physical challenges but spend a lot of time pushing a keyboard. For me the change of pace jamming through traffic is often exhilarating. As they say, it takes your mind off your troubles. More to the point, once you gain experience you are still alert, but relaxed. Moving easy. Is crossing the street a C. B. DeMille production for you? In a more relaxed state attentiveness is fun; you see more, notice more, feel more. Every once in a while I give a ride a miss, because I'm feeling bad. I might be unhappy, and not paying enough attention. Or angry, and likely to be too aggressive.

But if I'm feeling good it is hard to keep me off a bike. And if I'm marginal, I know from experience that a bike ride will probably set me up.

There are at least two drawbacks to riding in traffic that have no redeeming features: air pollution, and harassment.

Air Pollution

The inhalation of exhaust fumes and other pollutants is a serious health hazard for cyclists. Motor vehicles contribute up to 85 percent of all air pollution in urban areas. In traffic you are at nose level with the source, and it cannot possibly be good for you. As a cyclist you have the advantage of physical activity, which increases the effectiveness of the body's own natural defense mechanisms against airborne pollutants; in comparison with motorists in the same traffic, cyclists have lower blood levels of lead and carbon monoxide.

What are you in for? It's difficult to say exactly. One statistic that has been around for years is that the average urbanite inhales the equivalent in particles and poisons of two packs of cigarettes a day. I've got a much more personal index. I used to do training rides in the local park early in the morning, before it opened at 7 a.m. and cars entered the road. On each outing I went for a few seconds off my best time for lapping the park. It was edge of performance riding, and if I was late and the park opened and just one lousy car got on the road, I felt the difference. Even if the car went completely out of sight, the fumes hanging in the air made me dizzy, cut down on the amount of oxygen I was getting, and slowed my time.

Motor vehicles are pretty well the beginning and the end of the air pollution problem. They emit lead, unburnt gas, nitrogen oxides, sulfur oxides, carbon monoxide, and grit. Worst for the cyclist are lead and carbon monoxide. In a negative sense, Americans are lucky. The 1970 Clean Air Act established requirements for vehicle emissions and introduced unleaded gasoline. In Europe they have not been so quick off the mark, and it is now estimated that at least one in every three children is suffering damage from lead pollution.

How dangerous is lead? Very. The list of possible damages is amazing, and ranges from headache through a string of severe disabilities including arthritis, gout, and heart disease, through to simply shortening your lifespan. But perhaps the worst is that lead makes you stupid. Researchers the world over have shown that children exposed to high lead levels are associated with low intelligence, low verbal skill, bad hearing, and slow reaction times.

In terms of immediate risk, carbon monoxide is the greatest hazard for the cyclist. It is a classic poison which interferes with the oxygen-carrying capacity of the blood. Long before it kills, this action results in decreased alertness, headaches, vague dizziness, and nausea. Just the thing for riding in traffic. For bonuses, heart problems, memory loss, emphysema, and cancer.

One note of cheer is that your chances are a lot better if you take in an adequate amount of vitamin C. It reduces the toxicity of all sorts of things, including lead, carbon monoxide, and nitrogen dioxide. Some people feel that the alleged benefits of vitamin C are a lot of hogwash. Others - some of them pretty smart - think the stuff is useful. A well balanced diet with as much real, fresh food as possible, will help in equipping you to deal with pollutants. One nice thing about cycling is that your fuel is important, and this helps to create a predisposition towards foods that are actually nutritious. So to some extent, matters take care of themselves.

But your advantage as a cyclist in comparison with motorists in the same situation does not mean that air pollution is good for you. Try to avoid congested routes by traveling back streets and through parks, and if you can, avoid the peak traffic rush hours. Worst of all are steep hills, where cars really pour out the junk.

Harassment

Motorists routinely harass cyclists. Sometimes it is unintentional, and sometimes it is deliberate.

Traffic involves many points of conflict where resolution is up to the road users themselves. Driving a car in traffic requires controlled aggression; an indication to other road users of what is to happen next, followed by action. In light traffic this give and usually goes smoothly enough, but in heavy traffic it can easily get out of hand. Just as when the mouse population in a cage is intensified and the mice become progressively more and more frenetic, motorists in heavy traffic tend to be more aggressive. The more retarded the journey, the angrier they become.

Matters are made worse by the fact that only a few people treat motor vehicles strictly as a means of transport. Ego, status, and territory are all closely intertwined with motor vehicles. It is these psychological factors, rather than mechanical aspects such as braking capacity, which are the main cause of 'accidents'. Driving a car is a sexually based expression of power and potency. That this leads to risk-taking is clearly reflected in insurance premium rates: higher if you are young, male and/or operate a powerful car, lower if you are experienced, female and/or operate a vehicle of modest power. The common denominator is greater or lesser aggressiveness.

Traffic is an environment of regularized confrontation involving fundamental instincts and emotions - a sanctioned madhouse. It doesn't have to be that way, but it often is. In such circumstances the physical vulnerability of a cyclist is a serious disadvantage. Motorists have strong metal

FEMALES - WARNING

Female cyclists are subject to harassment from motorists and passers-by. In form, this ranges from insulting lewd comments to outright assault, where a motorist will reach out and knock a moving female cyclist to the pavement. I do not have statistics on this sort of thing, but it most definitely happens and any female cyclist must take warning.

In a fantasy world, an endangered cyclist would be a reincarnated Bruce Lee, and beat the attacker senseless. In real life it is hard to get up after being knocked off your bike because someone goosed you, or clouted you with a baseball bat or length of 2 x 4 timber. This kind of thing happens, to both men and women.

Please be scared now, it might help you to be careful.

cocoons; cyclists have nothing. In any direct confrontation, they lose. And as the insurance premiums show, some motorists are much more aggressive than others. Many will not hesitate to cut up a cyclist.

For beginning cyclists the confrontative and competitive aspects of riding in traffic appear stupid and daunting. What's the sense of stacking up a bike against a car? A common reaction is to ride very timidly, making matters even worse by failing to take right of way when open.

Intermediate cyclists know enough moves to feel victimized when a motorist is too aggressive. At this stage, frustration with the unfairness of it all can be acute, and the reaction to abuse from a motorist one of extreme and unsettling anger. If the first instinctive reaction to danger is to cower, the second is to strike back. Often this is a great idea. For many motorists who endanger cyclists, the fact that they can be yanked out of their protective shells and hurt is a shocking revelation. But this method of operating has serious drawbacks.

Methods of dismounting from a Bicycle.

In most bike-car confrontations the cyclist is helpless to do anything but preserve life and limb while the motorist escapes. When the cyclist finally does catch a motorist, the accumulated frustration can erupt in violent anger that is out of all proportion to the circumstances. Sometimes it is rough justice, and sometimes it is wrong. Either way, in the long run it is debilitating and at odds with having a good time. And while venting your spleen may make you feel better, it is likely to make the motorist more wrong in an effort to be right.

Part of becoming a skilled cyclist is learning to stay out of trouble in the first place. You'll ride careful but comfortable. Most of the potential bad incidents can be spotted in advance and avoided, including the unconscious or deliberate evils of motorists. Your own skill is what determines if your journeys are smooth and easy, or jerky and hard.

But there is one category of motorist for which there is no good answer: killers who deliberately mow down cyclists. It happens more often than most people imagine.

Homicidal intent with a car is difficult to establish. Typically, when a cyclist dies at the hands of a motorist, the worst charge is negligence, and the penalty a fine and perhaps a period of time for which the motorist's license is suspended. Often there is no penalty at all. Killers know that if they off someone with a gun, they are in trouble. If the instrument is a car, it is called an accident.

It is one thing to dice with a motorist for space and territory, and quite another to find that someone in a car is trying to kill you. I have given this problem a lot of thought and do not have any good answers. In practical terms counterattacking is usually impossible; you are too busy trying to stay alive. If matters do get to the state where you fight back on a physical level, you may well wind up facing criminal charges. If a motorist attacks and fails, there is no proof of malicious intent, even if you are injured. But if you pull a motorist out of a car and beat him or her senseless, and/or use weapons, then an attack is clearly evident, and you may be the one who goes to jail. Do not confuse life and justice. There are times when you should retaliate, and later on I explain some of the methods for doing so. But in general, responding to the threat of danger with anger is non-productive, serving only to destroy your peace of mind and, possibly, get you into trouble.

Why am I telling you all these wonderful cheerful things? How would you like it if I said to go swimming in a stretch of ocean, and neglected to mention that the waters were infested with sharks? The analogy is interesting, because the patterns are very similar. Cars and sharks alike have their ways of moving and doing things. Sharks are feared out of proportion to the actual danger they present. People with the right temperament who know what is going on can handle sharks comfortably. There are right moves and wrong moves - but sometimes sharks just up and bite. Cars are the same. There are right moves and wrong moves for riding in traffic, but sometimes cars just bite. If you ride in traffic there is always a chance that you won't come back. Thousands of cyclists are killed every year. No matter how good you are, you might be one of them. If you cannot accept and deal with that possibility, then do not ride in traffic.

Riding

There are innumerable physical hazards to look out for when riding in traffic, but motor vehicles are your main concern. Theory says that bikes have the same rights and privileges as other types of vehicles. The facts are otherwise.

A motor vehicle is an inherently rapid piece of equipment. For motorists, anything which obstructs forward progress - such as a slow moving bicycle - should not be there. They may be wrong, but it is essential to understand how they think. As a cyclist you are a relative nonentity. As often as not, motorists will cut you off, make turns right in front of you, or sit on your tail when there is no room to pass. It never occurs to them to put on the brakes and give you room to maneuver, as they would for another car or truck.

Many motorists are incompetent, under the influence of alcohol or drugs, or all of these things. Any cross-section of drivers will find elderly, obese, and otherwise infirm people with the motion capacity of a frozen sloth. They may think they are all right when in charge of a motor vehicle, or even hot stuff (drunks especially), but the truth is that their control of a vehicle is marginal. If something untoward happens they are unlikely to react in time, or correctly. Such people are also unlikely to be cyclists themselves, and are therefore unfamiliar with how cyclists behave.

Come on, there's no one about!

oh Law!

Please Sir, the road was so muddy.

Riding successfully in traffic requires a blend of determination and knowing when to give in. For example, try never to block overtaking cars. But if it is unsafe for you to let them pass, then do not hesitate to take full possession of your lane so that they *can't* pass. Both you and the other person have exactly the same right to use the street or highway. Possession of a motor vehicle confers no additional rights or privileges. It is very important that you understand and believe this. You have nothing to apologize for. You are not blocking or in the way. If anything, you are owed a vote of thanks for using a minimum amount of energy, not polluting the environment, and not endangering lives. At the same time you have to be practical. A lot of motorists are outright maniacs. No matter how right you are, any confrontation with a motor vehicle will see you the loser.

What about the rules of the road? It depends on where you are. In England, for example, the vast majority of cyclists obey all the traffic regulations. Even if there is no one else in sight, they stop for red lights, signal turns, and so on. The reason is that the rules cut both ways. It is very rare, for example, for motorists to run a red light. The British have their nutcases too, and problems particular to the country, but the general standard of driving is good enough to make rules useful.

Now look at a town like New York City. Anarchy. You couldn't possibly count all the people who charge red lights as a matter of course. You are not long for this world if you count on a red light for protection. If there is a way for someone to get you, you have to assume that they will. The only rule is to survive.

Rules are relative. I've cycled in a lot of different places, and most are pretty good. In general, if you can abide by the rules, do so. We'll all be better off. But if it is safer to break the rules, then do so. For example, it is often better to jump a light so that you have time to get out of the way of faster vehicles. In countries like Holland, early start green lights for cyclists are the norm. Do note, however, that you can get a summons for traffic violations on a bicycle, and if you supply a motoring license as identification (which you are not required to do), any convictions become part of your driving record. Many people cheerfully lie in their teeth about who and what they are.

If you have never cycled or driven a car in traffic, riding with a friend who can show you the ropes can be very helpful. It's also possible to take professional instruction. The very useful book *Effective Cycling* by John Forester (MIT Press, Boston) is the foundation for a teaching program of the same name. A certified Effective Cycling instructor can give you riding lessons, much as a ski instructor gives skiing lessons. It may sound a bit daft, but the idea that anyone automatically knows how to ride a bike just isn't so. The Effective Cycling people are sometimes pedantic, but they know their stuff. For information, contact Bicycle USA, Suite 209, 6707 Whitestone Rd., Baltimore, MD 21207.

Rolling

- Hands near or on brake levers at all times. With modern synthetic brake blocks you should be able to exert the maximum braking force the tires will stand. If you are on a bike with poor brakes and must stop or die, try twisting the front wheel as you apply the brakes. So long as you're not going too fast, the bike will melt into the ground in a controlled crash as the wheel and forks buckle.
- Keep your eyes constantly moving both fore and aft. When looking behind do not twist your head; duck it down. Easier to do, quicker, and smoother. Do this constantly. At any moment you might have to swerve to avoid an obstacle, and must know if you have the room to do so. Any bike used regularly in traffic should have a rear view mirror. The contribution this makes to safety, comfort, and speed is immense.
- Be definite. Save meandering for country lanes where you can see for a long way in both directions. Ride in a straight line. Signal all turns clearly. Make right turns from the right lane and left turns from the left lane, if on a wide street. If you are going to do something, do it. Being definite takes the form of a certain amount of aggressiveness. Don't get bulldozed into immobility - nobody is going to give you a break. Make and take your own breaks. As far as most motorists are concerned, you either don't exist or are some alien foreign object which they want behind them. Draw attention to yourself and be super-clear about your intentions. Colorful clothing is a good idea.
- Always assume the worst. You can't see around the stopped bus? *Assume* a pregnant woman who is the sole support of 21 children is going to come prancing out. There is a car waiting to cross your lane? *Assume* it will, because *it will.* In 4 out of 5 accidents involving bicycles and motor vehicles, the motor vehicle committed a traffic violation. Always ride within a margin of control which allows you to stop or escape should absolutely everything go wrong.

- Look for openings in traffic, driveways, streets, garages, etc., that you can duck into should the need arise. Try to plan where you would go should you and the bike part company. The natural tendency in a collision situation is to try desperately to stop. Many times your interest will be better served by launching yourself over an obstacle. Far better to hit the road at an angle than a car head-on.

- While not exceeding a speed which gives you control, try to keep moving. Within reason, avoid using brakes. This will have the effect of making you figure out well in advance what traffic situations are going to occur. There is a car double-parked in the next block. Are you going to be able to swing out? Also, a lot of the danger from other vehicles in traffic comes from differences in velocity. If you are going slow, cars bunch up behind, crowd, become impatient, etc. A racing bike can easily keep up with and pass a lot of traffic. You may find it a bit unnerving to run neck and neck with cabs and lorries at first, but it is safer than offering a stationary target. Try to integrate yourself with the traffic.

- To this end, always be in a gear low enough to give you power and acceleration. In heavy traffic an even cadence is difficult to maintain, but try to keep your feet churning away and avoid getting stuck in a 'dead' high gear. As a cyclist, you have only a fraction of the power available to the motorist. To stay integrated with traffic requires that you be prepared to accelerate hard and quickly.

- On the other hand, do not tailgate. Car brakes are better than bike brakes. Most bike accidents consist of the bicycle running into something. Leave plenty of room up front. This is where motorists accustomed to running bumper-to-bumper will try to pressure you from behind, even though you are moving at the same speed as the car you are following. Maintain position and if they give you the horn, give them the finger.

- Be extra-cautious at intersections where you already have right of way. Cars coming from the opposite direction and turning left will frequently cut straight across your path. Even if the vehicle is seemingly waiting for you to pass, don't trust it, for at the last moment it will leap forward. Letting a motor vehicle precede you to clear the way is often a good tactic.

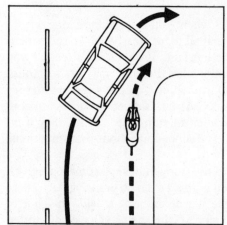 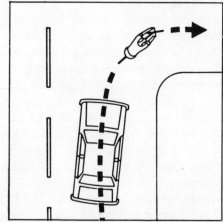

LOW SIDE. Selfish and dastardly, the car grinds the cyclist into the curb.   **HIGH SIDE. The cyclist forces the car to follow behind.**

Another danger at intersections is cars coming up alongside from behind and then making a sudden right turn. One way to stop it is for you to be in the center of the lane. However, if the intersection you are entering has a light which is going to change soon, then traffic from behind may be storming up at breakneck pace. You'd better be out of the way.

● In any city anywhere in the world, taxi drivers are a hazard. All things are relative and in London, for example, most cabbies are decent. In America cabbies have the highest ulcer rate of any occupational group, a necessary concomitant of their working conditions and driving skills. Abilities vary, but most are just no good. New York City cabbies are the bottom of the barrel.

The cab driver is your enemy. He is *accustomed* to bulldozing and bluffing his way around by main force. It is second nature, and does not even require hostile intent on his part. It is just something he does. Every day. You, on a 30 lb bicycle, just haven't got a chance against his 5000 lb cab. And many cabbies do take do take a perverse pleasure out of screwing you up. Perhaps they are resentful of anyone having fun on a bike. Who knows. At any rate, if there is anybody who is going to cut in front of you, brake suddenly, etc., it is the cabbie. Cabs are the enemy.

● Very often you will be riding next to parked cars. Be especially careful of motorists opening doors in your path. Exhaust smoke and faces in rearview mirrors are tips. Even if a motorist looks right at you and is seemingly waiting for you to pass,

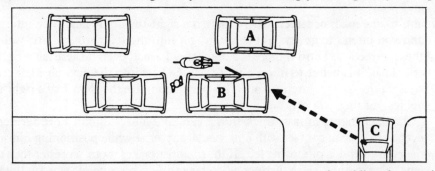

LOW SIDE. Hemmed in by car A, the cyclist has no way of avoiding the opening door of car B. He is invisible to the driver of car C waiting at the junction.

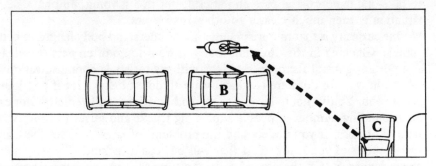

HIGH SIDE. Cyclist is well clear of opening car door, and visible to driver of car C.

give her/him a wide berth. Believe it or not, you may not register on her/his consciousness, and she/he may open the door in your face.

● The law requires you to ride to the right of the right lane as far as is consistent with
safety. This is a very elastic and sometimes abused definition. Cyclists have been
ticketed for causing an obstruction by riding too far to the left, and there have
also been instances of opening car door/cyclist accidents where the cyclist was held
to be at fault. Always allow enough maneuvering room to avoid road litter and
pot-holes. Pass parked cars with room to spare should a door open. If somebody
objects to your 'obstructing', ignore them. You are not obliged to risk your life
for their convenience.

If the road or street is too narrow for overtaking vehicles to pass you with enough
room, then ride bang out in the center of the lane. Do not let them pass, or if
it is a two-way road or street, make them pass in the opposite lane. You want room.
Vehicle drivers may hoot and fume, but this is far safer for you than letting them
pass with only inches to spare. You are equally entitled to road space and safe
passage.

A common problem is a double parked car or other obstacle that narrows the
road space, bunching traffic into a single line. If you are to one side with the vehicles
passing by in a steady stream, joining the line takes good timing. Blocking a motorist
is all right if you obviously have no alternative, but not for long. The trick is to
pick a gap that gives you reasonable clearance for the obstacle, signal your move,
and go.

● On multi-lane roads or streets where there is a right-turn-only lane at an intersection,
and you intend to go straight through, get into the left through-lane well before
the intersection. Ditto if there is a bike lane. In fact, even if there is no right-turn-
only lane, it is better to move out of the bike lane into the next lane left for going
straight through an intersection. This helps minimize the chance of a right-turning
vehicle cutting you off.

Lane changing in fast, thick traffic can take muscle. John Forester does it by
eyeball to eyeball contact with a particular motorist while positioning himself with
the clear intention of moving left. If the motorist makes room, Forester then changes
lane. The method has a distinct advantage in that both hands stay on the brakes,
where they belong in heavy traffic. However, if you have enough room in front
to take one hand off the bars and stick it out in a jabbing, emphatic signal, the
situation is then much clearer to other road users.

One curiosity is that motorists sometimes understand body language better than
signals. Glancing in the direction that you want to go often gets the idea across.

● The important general factor in relations with motorists is communication: here is
what you want to do, here is what I want to do. It helps a lot if you know what
is going on. You've got to be able to read other drivers and vehicles. For example,
an astounding number of people expect big trucks and buses to contravene basic
laws of physics. If you understand the problems of large vehicles there are many
little courtesies you can extend that will be repaid in kind. Professional drivers
appreciate craft. On the other hand, don't expect someone grinding along with
a load of screaming kids in a wreck that can barely stand up to have much of a
grip on what is happening. It's not that they mean harm, the problem is that they

are not there in the moment. Keep track of neighbors. A young kid in an old heap with go faster stripes who keeps flooring the gas and brakes is someone to stay away from. If something goes wrong he or she is likely to foul up. The big moving van of a nationwide company may be awesome in size, but is better close company because the driver is more likely to have his or her mind on the job.

● Keep an eye on the road surface. Watch out for broken glass, stones, pot-holes, etc. Plenty of bumps and pot-holes are big enough to destroy a bike - and you. Going over bumps, cables, etc., get off the saddle and keep your weight on the pedals and handlebars. This is when toe clips and straps are reassuring.

● Quite a few things can dump a bike:

Oil slicks in the center of traffic lanes at busy intersections and on sharp curves. When cars stop or turn hard, a little oil drops off. The resulting slick can send you off the road or sliding out into the middle of a busy intersection.

Newly wet streets. There is a light film of oil which until it is washed away mixes with the water to make a very slippery surface.

Wet manhole covers and steel plates can dump you in a hurry. So can wet cobblestones, wet autumn leaves, gravel, and sand. Many storm sewers are just the right size to swallow up a bicycle wheel.

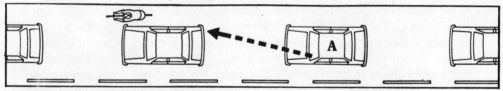

LOW SIDE. With no room to spare, the cyclist cannot avoid broken pavement or road litter, and is invisible to the driver of car A. If car A is moving faster than the bike, and the driver happens to glance at the instruments or at a passenger, the cyclist may be hit.

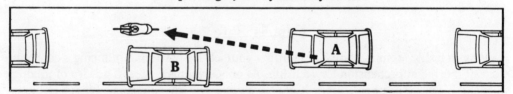

HIGH SIDE. The cyclist has enough room to move around holes and litter, and is visible to car A in time enough for the driver to make a little extra room. The fact that car B has moved out slightly also helps tell the driver of car A that the cyclist is there.

● Ride with the traffic. Sometimes when there is no traffic coming the other way, it is better to ride in the opposite lane.

● The velocity of traffic on freeway style streets which have no parking is usually too high to permit safe cycling. If you run in the center of the lane, you block traffic. If you go to the side, cars whizz by you at high speeds with only inches to spare. Stick to streets with parked cars and look out for opening doors.

● Cars and trucks have a habit of pulling out unexpectedly and without signaling. Look out for driveways, building entrances, construction projects, cab ranks, and any other possible source of a vehicle. Remember, you don't exist for many drivers.

They look right at you, the image is flashed on their brain, but they don't comprehend. They don't *see* you.

And perhaps some do. One time in New York City I had the lights in my favor at an intersection with a police car waiting on the cross street. The eyes of the driver fixed steadily on me and he waited until I was just going through the intersection before pulling through a red light and right in front of me. Expect the unexpected.

- Pedestrians are awful. They don't think 200 lbs of bike and rider coming towards them at 30 mph means anything, and will frequently jaywalk right in your path. The other side of this coin are cyclists who run red lights, hurling themselves past pedestrians with inches to spare. They don't always make it. Any collision between a cyclist and a pedestrian is going to be a painful affair for everyone. Respect the right of way of pedestrians. When you have the right of way, use a whistle or yell - and give way if you have to.
- Kids. As much of a hazard to the cyclist as to the motorist. Any child has the potential to race out suddenly into the street.
- Other cyclists. The fact that someone is riding a bike does not mean that they are on your side. Like other road users, many cyclists do stupid things. Stay clear of other riders unless you know them, or they obviously know what they are doing.
- Lights. Although lights at night are a legal requirement, the vast majority of American cyclists do not use them. I've seen plenty of riders wearing helmets, but with no lights. This is insane. Lights help make you visible to motorists. Rear reflectors and pedal reflectors are useful. Wheel reflectors and front reflectors are useless and can be heaved into the garbage. Lights are what might help you to be seen. The various kinds are discussed in Accessories. CAUTION: using lights does not mean you are safe. Some motorists will take no notice even if you are lit up like a starship. I know a lot of people who had to be convinced of this the hard way.

Fast is Safe

Cycling in traffic seemingly involves girding yourself for battle and inducing a constant state of morbid apprehension for your life. At one level this is true. The idea of mixing cars and bicycles together is crazy. Cars are an atavistic idiocy responsible for millions of deaths and injuries. It is entirely logical to want nothing whatsoever to do with them.

However, once you have a working appreciation of the hazards to be encountered in traffic, you will find that the situation can be made to work to your advantage. Riding fast promotes your own safety. This is because moving quickly demands that you anticipate and avoid the troublesome situations that would otherwise retard your journey. The best way to do this is to ride what I call the high side.

So long as you shift along quickly enough to keep pace with the other road users, riding in the mainstream of traffic is safer than trying to stay out of the way by keeping to the low side. Riding the high side largely eliminates hazards such as road litter, opening car doors, cars overtaking and turning right across your path and stray pedestrians stepping off the sidewalk. All of these are a greater danger than the risk of being struck from behind by a motorist. Furthermore, on the high side you are more visible to motorists than when on the low side.

Emotionally, riding the high side is more satisfactory than hiding in the gutter and waiting to be hit. Clear assertiveness diminishes rather than increases tension for the cyclist. The aim is to pass along smoothly, neither accelerating nor decelerating excessively. The mark of a good traffic rider is that she or he is in the right place at the right time. This skill is a function of awareness and a positive orientation, whereas tension is the negative outcome of worrying about finding yourself in the wrong place at the wrong time. Just reducing the need to slow down or stop will itself make for a more relaxed journey.

This is not an endorsement of a wholesale speed trial or kamikaze style of riding. Initially, the approach to learning about cycling hazards must be defensive. First save your neck. Once you have learned the ropes, however, riding the high side in urban traffic will provide a creative and therefore enjoyable method for maximizing average speed and ease of passage.

CHAPTER 11

Bang!

An accident is a surprise. It is not the same thing as losing control of a bike because you pressed a corner too hard. An accident is something you didn't consciously anticipate. You need to know what to do if an accident starts to happen. The problem is not so much knowing what to do, as being able to do it.

Most people react to an imminent crash with panic. They may freeze into immobility and do nothing, or blindly clamp down on the brakes and lose directional stability. This can make a bad situation fatal. For example, if a car is about to hit you from the side and you death grip the brakes, the rear wheel is likely to lock up and send you down in a slide, to be rolled up underneath the car. But if at the moment of impact you try to get clear of the bike and make a dive for the hood of the car, you may slide along to the windscreen and perhaps even over the roof. Not fun, but the survival chances are much better than if you are underneath the car.

Panic-induced muscular tension increases physical damage in a crash. The person who falls or is thrown and is able to stay loose and relaxed will suffer less injury than a person who tenses and tries to save him or herself.

The ability to exercise the best of a series of bad options, and stay physically relaxed in a situation offering damage, can only be learned through experience and practice. I have been an avid skier since I was 4, a high diver since I was 7, and when I suddenly find myself flying through the air upside down I am automatically loose, looking to tuck and roll when I hit.

If you do not know how to fall, try to have someone with training - fighting experts, skydivers, skiers - give you some pointers. I find that fast woods riding with an old trasho bike is useful. A few spills are inevitable, and as long as they are in loose dirt, usually little damage results. This kind of play is even better on winter snow and ice.

Practice the braking and turning techniques discussed in the Riding chapter. Think of how to use them in various circumstances. If a car pulls up alongside you and then unexpectedly turns right, cutting you off, sudden application of the brakes will simply pile you into the car. A rapid haul turn, however, just might avoid an accident, and if you do hit, you will both be going more or less in the same direction. Suppose a car pulls out in front of you from a side road or driveway. There may be enough room for a haul turn so that you hit the car a glancing blow. If there is not enough room to turn, then brake as hard as possible without skidding, and just before hitting the car launch yourself clear of the bike. You may be able to sail right over the car. Stay loose and roll when you hit the pavement.

If you are hit from behind. DO NOT BRAKE. Try to get away by steering to the side.

Having It Back

When a motorist does you dirt, one acceptable response is an explosive yell. It's the cycling equivalent of blowing a horn to signify potential or immediate danger.

A good yell can help you to release some of the adrenalin energy that danger generates. It can make a motorist just a touch uncomfortable, and is more effective if there are passengers in the vehicle. A lot of ruckus and commotion means that the motorist is doing something wrong, and the more passengers as audience, the greater the awareness of discord.

One of the most frequent sins of the motorist is to overtake a cyclist and then suddenly brake and turn right. The motorist knowingly creates trouble for the cyclist, and hopes to get away with it through sheer greater size. This is a moment of opportunity. The cyclist is usually in the blind rear quarter of the vehicle and invisible to the motorist,

"AN AGÈD WOMAN ON HER BACK,
TWO BABES IN GUTTER PRONE."

who will be under some tension about the outcome of his or her misdeed. In such circumstances, a well timed yell can startle a motorist a clear 6 inches off the seat up into the air, and cause a momentary loss of vehicle control. If there is a nearby obstruction, the motorist may hit it.

Another unsettling tactic in a situation where a motor vehicle is actively risking an accident is to hit it hard with the flat of your hand. This makes a tremendous bang especially if done on the roof. The best time for a direct attack is when a vehicle entering the roadway from the right and turning left cuts across your path. By swerving behind the vehicle, you create the welcome safety of diverging trajectories and with good timing you can give it a good noisy bash. Do not use this ploy without a clear escape route. If you bang on the roof of a vehicle which is running alongside and crowding, you are just asking for the motorist to panic and do something wrong, or for a hot-head to give that little twitch of the wheel that will smear you forever.

One defense is attack. At close quarters you have the advantage of knowing where you are to the inch. Few motorists are that good. If someone starts to crowd you, one tactic is to call their hand by moving in close, paintflake to paintflake. You can run very tight if need be. Most motorists can't handle it and will give way. In heavy traffic this technique can also be used to brush motorists into giving you enough room. Another effective trick is a deliberate wobble that suggests you might do anything next. The motorists' instinct is to shy away.

I have friends who regularly go out and deliberately pick fights with motorists. Sooner or later they get more than they bargained for. David and Goliath routines are fun as games, or if you are angry and don't want to back down, but if you get hurt doing this kind of thing, don't complain.

It is sometimes tempting to deliberately have an accident. The most appealing moment is when a motorist noses out in front of you from a side road, forcing you to slam on the brakes to avoid a collison. Sooner or later it will cross your mind to deliberately slack the brakes just a little and hit the side of the vehicle, rolling on your shoulder and back over the hood to a safe landing, but thereafter continuously complaining of an unspecified pain in your back. You must never do such a terrible thing.

CHAPTER 12

Urban Commuting

Road racing, cyclo-cross and track bicycles each have distinctive characteristics appropriate to their intended use. So does the urban commuting bicycle. Many city streets are obstacle courses filled with bumps, pot-holes, uneven surfaces, 'temporary' steel plates which are slippery when wet, broken glass, bits of sharp metal, and other rubbish. In heavy traffic there is often not enough room for a cyclist to avoid an obstacle. A machine for these conditions must be tough. Theft is a constant problem in cities. An obviously expensive bicycle is more likely to be stolen, or stripped for parts. Finally, most regular commuters prefer a bike that requires a minimum of maintenance.

Several different types of bicycle are best capable of coping with urban conditions. Each has advantages and disadvantages according to your particular situation and needs.

The classic chunker offers a soft frame design which helps to iron out the worst of the bumps, robust tires which have a fighting chance of surviving glass and other road litter, and an upright riding position which allows a good view of traffic conditions. However, at 50 lbs weight, chunkers are hard work to pedal, and are not suitable for long journeys or steep terrain.

The 3-speed hub gear roadster is lighter in weight and uses narrower, faster tires, but is still not much of a speed machine or hill-climber. One performance improvement is to fit alloy rims and high pressure tires. An inexpensive way of improving hill-climbing ability is to fit a larger rear sprocket of 22 or 24 teeth. This limits top speed to around 20 mph, but this is adequate for most traffic conditions. The bike is then more suitable for off-road riding. Roadsters are not the most valuable of bicycles, but are easy to re-sell. Security is a problem.

Derailleur gear road bikes are one obvious choice for long journeys and/or steep terrain. Models made expressly for commuting usually have alloy components, flat bars, fenders, and a comfy saddle. Another good choice is a touring bike. A generous wheelbase and fork rake, strong rims with thick spokes, and stout tires, will maximize comfort and stability over rough surfaces. Sealed bearings for the bottom bracket, headset, hubs, and pedals will help minimize maintenance.

Security is a problem. The best answer is someplace inside at work. If not there, see if you can promote something in another building. For locking up on the street, the only answer is a lock such as the Citadel or Kryptonite (see Chapter 7 for details). Some people keep a collection of locks at their work parking place, and carry a small lock in case of need. Many people disguise high quality frames with a coat of dull looking, sloppy paint, and substitute low grade components (saddle, derailleurs, chainset). The resulting bike looks like an old banger but still goes fairly well. Some people booby-trap their bikes by slacking off the brakes or wheels, or removing the saddle. These are last ditch measures.

The ultimate machine for urban cycling is the mountainbike. On an ordinary lightweight road bike, the sight of a jagged, yawning pot-hole will set your senses screaming with alarm. On a mountainbike you can laugh and attack the thing. Wide tires and handlebars give a sure grip and utterly superior low speed handling. The only thing that will stop quicker than a mountainbike is a long wheelbase recumbent, and I wouldn't

A PRACTICAL DEMONSTRATION—I.
County Councillor (to distinguished foreign guest): ''You will get an admirable idea of how we sand the roads on an extensive scale. With this huge van we can cover the ground in one-third the time, and distribute ten times the quantity of ——

A PRACTICAL DEMONSTRATION—II.
Councillor: ''Great Sahara!!! —— !!!''
Visitor: ''Ah! Malheur!! —— a mort!!! —— sacre-e-e-e-e-e-e-e!!!!''

want to live on the difference. When it comes time to snap away from a traffic light, a good surge through the extra long cranks will leave even a pure road racing bike in the dust. You can go where you like - blazing down the fast lane, up and down curbs, along canal towpaths, straight through parks - the mountainbike will do it all and more.

Many mountainbike tires run well enough on pavement. If you want to be more precise, run two sets of wheels, one with road tires, the other with big gnarly knobblies for off-road bashing. For minimum fuss when making a switch, use the same size rims and freewheel type. I prefer 22 mm rims, as they are very good with the 1.4 inch wide Specialized Nimbus tire, and will also mount 2 inch wide knobblies. The more usual 28 mm rims do not match happily with tires less than 1.75 inches wide. The Nimbus is a wet weather tire that grips the road like a leech. It's pretty good off-road too.

One way to bypass the security problem is to use a lightweight folding bike. These machines go where you go and can be tidily tucked away under a desk or in a restaurant cloakroom. If it suddenly starts to pour cats and dogs and you do not feel like getting wet, a folding bike is little trouble to take on a bus, train, or taxi. This makes such a machine the favored contender for mixed mode transport.

In performance, lightweight folding bikes need make little apology. They will go. But there is no way that small wheels will give the stability of large wheels over bumps and through pot-holes, and braking capacity is not of the first water. If you can, ride large wheels.

Routing

Bikes move in different ways than other vehicles. They can cut down alleyways, zip through parking lots, and what have you. Even if you know the territory over which you plan to commute, it is worth obtaining a map and giving it a good study. Very often, things are not what you thought they were. Working out good commuting routes is a matter of trial and error. What you are looking for are streets and roads that allow you to keep moving, but that do not embroil you in the worst of the traffic. Start by drawing a straight line on the map between home and work. Pick out a trial route, bearing in mind whatever you know about the area. A direct route, for example, might crest three hills that you could avoid entirely with a slightly longer route. Or, perhaps there is a way to have one short, sharp climb, and then gentle downgrades the rest of the journey.

Hard and fast rules are difficult to suggest, because it all depends on where you are. Vancouver, B.C. is not at all similar to Woodstock, NY, and neither is anything remotely like New York City. I think the best method is trial and error. Work out an approximate route, and explore it. For the first few journeys allow at least twice the time you think you need. This gives a comfortable margin for problems, rest stops, sorting out parking, and so on. Relate what you discover to the map. You'll usually find that there are one or two obvious options to check out. After a week or two you'll probably have the optimum route down pat, but keep on exploring. You never know what you might find and anyway, it is fun to have different routes to run.

In many areas you are required to use bikeways if they are available. This can be a real problem, because the majority of bikeways are badly designed and very dangerous. They are littered with broken glass, cross-traffic, pedestrians, parked cars, and who knows what else. They were built to get bikes out of the way of cars, not for bikes to run on. On the other hand, you might be lucky and be able to route on a bikeway built by people who knew what they were doing. Lots of them are really lovely, and in some places you can cover a lot of ground without ever seeing a car. There's no way I can predict the exact conditions in your area. But if the bikeways run parallel to the roads, with a lot of cross-traffic for driveways, shopping centers, and such-like, you will go much more quickly and safely on the roads.

CHAPTER 13

Touring

Touring is the real joy in biking. The only better way to see the country is to walk or rollerskate. A bike has advantages in mobility and luggage carrying, however, and the aesthetic sacrifice is not too great. Touring can be done in a tremendous variety of ways. You can go for an afternoon's jaunt or spend a summer or more traveling thousands of miles. You can go as a self-contained unit with your own camping gear, or ultra-light and stay in inns and motels. You can count the miles traveled, or concentrate on the scenery (yeah!). Your journey can include transit by auto, bus, train, boat, and plane, so that you can hop from one interesting place to another. You can have a plan, or absolutely none at all. Touring is a call to adventure, beauty, new sights and experiences.

There's a lot to touring, and plenty for you to think about. At the same time it can be kept simple. Any bike headed for the boondocks should have a tool kit, unless you don't mind pushing your bike a few miles to a garage and/or the possibility of an overnight stay until it opens. Equipment makes a difference, but the main thing is to get out there. My greatest, happiest tour was on a battered 1935 BSA whose vital parts shed like water.

Part of the fun of touring is figuring it out and planning or not planning for yourself. Some people insist that the only way to tour is with a meticulous and detailed plan;

' A merry heart goes all the way,
Your sad tires in a mile, a.'—*Shakespeare.*

others heave map and compass into the bushes and go wherever fancy takes them. For some the fun and relaxation comes as a result of planned and concentrated effort; for others it is through not thinking about anything. There is no 'right' way to tour. Each to his or her own. Accordingly, this chapter tries to simply give basic information about touring. It is not a step-by-step guide. It's up to you to decide where and when you want to go, and what sort of equipment you expect to need.

One source of detailed information is books. One of the best is *Bike Touring* by Raymond Bridge (Sierra Club Books). Good reading is *Bike Tripping* by Tom Cuthbertson

(Ten Speed Press). A tome full of basic information is *The Bicycle Touring Book* by Tim and Glenda Wilhelm (Rodale Press). The Bicycle USA *Almanac* is a 'where to go' with state-by-state info on climate, terrain, maps, contacts, etc. There are lots of other books and booklets, many are regional publications with exact particulars on local

resources and conditions. Magazines come and go, but a pretty one with the emphasis on touring is *Bicycle Rider*, P.O. Box 52377, Boulder, CO 80321-2377.

A good way to get into heavy touring is to join a society or organization. You get a planned tour, the benefit of a group leader who will set a pace within your capacity, and lots of free friendly help and advice. Tours can vary a good bit in character. Some are spartan and fast, others are gently paced and followed by a sag wagon to carry baggage and spare parts for the bikes.

●American Youth Hostels, 1332 I Street N.W., Suite 800, Washington, D.C. 20005
A somewhat straitlaced but nevertheless very good outfit with over 4000 hostels in 47 countries, about 100 in the US. Good equipment and books. Hostels are sometimes spartan but always serviceable. Tours in the US and abroad. Inexpensive.

●International Bicycle Touring Society, 2115 Pasco Dorado, La Jolla, CA 92037
An easy going outfit for adults only. Tours are followed by a sag wagon, overnight stays in motels and inns at moderate rates.

●Touring Cyclists' Hospitality Directory, 13623 Sylvan, Van Nuys, CA 91401

A mutual cooperation scheme where you agree to provide cyclists with sleeping or camping space, and thereby obtain a list of people willing to do the same for you.

●Bikecentennial, PO Box 8308, Missoula, MT 59807

Born with the Bicentennial in 1976, this organization has gone from strength to strength in helping and serving cyclists of all types. They are particularly big on touring, and have publications, organized tours, route services, and who knows what else. Well worth contacting.

●Bicycle USA, Suite 209, 6707 Whitestone Road, Baltimore, MD 21207

Run by the League of American Wheelmen, a touring and general cycling activity organization that is over 100 years old. They've got publications, all manner of tours and events, cycling instruction, and most everything else. Well worth contacting.

There are many other touring organizations, both private and public. The Bicentennial *Yellow Pages* and Bicycle USA *Almanac* both list local touring clubs.

Holiday Tours

A number of holiday resorts offer bike tours either based from the resort itself, or stopping over at selected inns and hotels. Tours are graded for different levels of rider ability and strength, and rental machines and equipment are often available.

As with any other type of package holiday, there are good outfits and bad, and a colorful brochure does not necessarily indicate that you will have a good time. A simple test for any prospective resort is to ask for the names of two or three people in your area who have been there. A quick telephone call or visit will then produce all the information you need. Here are some established firms:

●Country Cycling Tours, 380 Lexington Avenue, New York, NY 10168, Tel: (212) 687 6565

●Country Roads, P.O. Box 10279, State College, PA 16805

●Sierra Club, 530 Bush Street, San Francisco, CA 94108, Tel: (415) 981 8634

●Vermont Bicycle Touring, Box 711, Bristol, VT 05443, Tel: (802) 453 4811

There are many, many others. Check adverts in the cycling press, particularly in the spring.

Where

Where you go depends on your own temperament, interests, physical conditions, and available equipment. I would suggest that you make your initial rides about 20 miles or so, and work up to longer hours and overnight stays as you get used to it. If you favor back roads off the beaten track and camping, you are going to have to deal with equipment for both you and the bike; touring on better roads and sleeping in inns means less and lighter equipment.

Riding

I recommend taking the smallest, least traveled roads practicably possible. Not only are they almost always more interesting, but the fewer cars the more comfortable you will be. Safe country riding is largely a matter of common sense. Most of the rules for traffic riding apply here also.

● Always carry identification and your health insurance card if you have one. Leave a motor vehicle operator's license at home, as it can be endorsed with traffic offenses committed on a bicycle.

● The cardinal rule is 'what if?' Look and think ahead. Don't, for example, time your riding so that you and an overtaking car reach a curve at the same time. If a car - or worse yet a truck - comes the other way there just isn't going to be enough room.

● Bear in mind the tremendous relative velocity of cars. In traffic you can pretty much keep up, but in the country cars will have up to 70 mph over your 5 to 15. If you crest a hill and there is no oncoming traffic, move over into the opposite lane for a while. This avoids the hazard of overtaking cars who cannot see you over the crest.

● Try to have a hole to duck into should everything go wrong. Where will you go if that tractor pulls out? If a car comes around the corner on your side of the road are you going to try for the ditch or a tree? You may wreck a bike going off into a field, but this is a lot better than colliding with a car. Think about this as much as you can and try to make it an automatic process. This way when an emergency arises, instead of freezing in panic you may be able to save your life.

● Be particularly wary, when you have speed up, of people doing odd things. Cannonballing down a hill you may be doing 40 mph, a fact that many motorists and pedestrians do not comprehend. They see a bicycle, and automatically class it as slow and unimportant, dismissing it from mind (as you can be sure they would not do for a large truck), and step or drive out onto the road, or pass, or whatever. This capacity for visual recognition with no subsequent cognitive comprehension may seem bizarre, but I assure you it is so. Never trust other road users.

● After running through puddles or wet grass, dry your brakes off by applying them slightly as you ride. Running down steep hills do not hold the brakes steadily,

which can cause overheating, but pump on and off. This tells you if you have stopping power in reserve - which you always should.

● Run to the right, but leave room to maneuver in case you encounter road litter, potholes, or whatever.

● On two-lane roads watch out for overtaking motorists coming towards you. They often do not see or just plain ignore a bicycle coming towards them. If you move out to the center of your lane most motorists will return to their lane. Some will not

and you must be prepared to stop on the shoulder of the road. You might care
to have a few rotten tomatoes handy for such moments.
- Beware the Hun in the Sun. At sunrise and sunset motorists with the sun in their
eyes may not see you.
- Rural farm traffic is a law unto itself. Many farmers operate machinery on local public
roads as if they were in the middle of a field.

- Watch for loose gravel, dirt, or sand, and especially at driveway and side road entrances.
- Bridge gratings, cattle guards, railroad tracks, etc., can all swallow up a bicycle wheel
and send you flying.

Dogs

Dogs and other creatures of the field and air are a menace to the cyclist. I was once
attacked by a determined and large goose. Dogs are the main problem, though, and
you need to keep a constant lookout for old Towser.

There are many theories about why dogs attack two-wheeled vehicles. I think that
the spokes make a noise which drives them nuts. There are also a number of dog owners
who take a not-so-secret pleasure in having vicious attack-prone animals, and others
who should not even try to take responsibility for a cockroach. One couple expressed
puzzlement to me after their dog bit my riding companion. Every time the dog was
disobedient they beat it until their arms hurt: why wouldn't it obey? With treatment
like that, any dog will become vicious and irrational.

Understanding that old Poochie may not be directly at fault does not make being
bitten more fun. Dogs are livestock, fully the responsibility of the owner, and excep-
ting dogs crazed by disease, can be trained to leave cyclists alone. I like dogs very much
and accept that some adjustment to their particular natures and quirks is necessary if
they are to be around. I do not accept being knocked off my bike by some giant hound.
If the owner will not control the dog, I will, and with force if necessary.

Most dogs attack according to a pattern. They circle to the rear of the cyclist and
come up from behind. So sometimes you can outrun a dog. Often this is not possible,
but 99 times out of a 100 there is still no serious problem. Many cyclists become hysterical
on the subject of dog defense, and recommend whips, car aerials, clubs, and other weapons
that will really hurt a dog. This is not necessary. It really isn't the dog's fault. Nine
times out of ten he is normally friendly. All you have to do is stop, dismount, and face

145

him directly. That's all. Simply stop. Often he will come up wagging his tail. When you leave, walk away like all 'normal' (to the dog) people do, and the matter will be forgotten.

It is important to get the reflex of stopping if you are not going to outrun or spray the dog. People do get bitten, but the majority of injuries happen because the cyclist panics, loses control of the bike, and crashes.

The tenth time, when a dog still threatens attack: the main thing when dealing with a vicious dog is to have *confidence*. As a human being you are one of the largest mammals on earth and a formidable contender in a fight. Suppress your fears and radiate the notion that any dog that messes with you will regret it for the rest of his days, if he lives that long. It is only the rarest of dogs that will attack a human obviously prepared for self-defense. Speak to the dog in firm tones, keep your bike between you, and slowly walk away.

Flying Yankee Velocipede

If the dog attacks: one defense is aerosol pepper sprays made for exactly this purpose. They have a range of about 10 feet and are light enough to clip to the handlebars or your belt. The drawback is that they don't always work. You have to be accurate and get the stuff in to the dog's eyes, not always an easy trick when there is a lot of excitement and action. Even when the spray is accurately directed, there have been plenty of instances where dogs (and people too) have come back for more.

There isn't a dog alive that will come back for another faceful of water mixed with chili sauce or powder. The solution can be sprayed from a water bottle or ex-container for detergent, shampoo, etc., all of which are easily carried on a bike. An advantage of this method is that you can practice spraying until you are proficient. Also, although a pepper solution will make a lasting impression on a dog, it won't do any permanent damage.

If you have no weapon and can't or won't climb a tree, get a stick or large rock. No? The bicycle pump. In any event, don't cower or cover up, because the dog will only chew you to ribbons. *Attack*. Any small dog can simply be hoisted up by the legs and his brains dashed out. With a big dog you are fighting for your life. If you are weaponless try to tangle him up in your bike and then strangle him. Kicks to the balls and which break ribs are effective. If you have got a pump or stick hold it at both ends and offer it up to the dog horizontally. Often the dog will bite the stick/pump and hang on. Immediately lift the dog up and deliver a very solid kick to the genitals. Follow up with breaking the dog's ribs or crushing its head with a rock. If worst comes to worst, ram your entire arm down his throat. He will choke and die. Better your arm than your throat.

If you are bitten and the dog gets away, make every effort to find the dog and its owner. If the dog cannot be quarantined you will have to get a long series of painful rabies shots. Ask around the area, check with local gas stations, stores, etc. In any event, get immediate medical treatment, even for a light bite. Then notify the dog warden or police of the incident. If the dog owner is uncooperative about paying for the doctor and any other related expenses, just get a lawyer. The law is completely and absolutely on your side.

If you successfully fend off an attack, notify the dog owner and dog warden or police. This is a very real responsibility because the next person might not be as well prepared as you. A little girl, for example, like the one down the road from my parents' place who was pulled down and killed by three dogs.

Technique

Cadence plays an extremely significant part in the technique of long-distance touring. In short sprints you can drain your body's resources and strength, but on a long tour output must not exceed ability to continuously replenish fuel and oxygen. Which makes it sound simple: just take it easy and have something in reserve. Not quite.

If you are interested in covering a lot of ground (not everybody is) and in feeling comfortable, then you must strive for an exact balance between energy output and the body's ability to synthesize and store energy. There is a *pace* which works best. Go too fast and the result will be fatigue and possibly strained muscles that will dog you

147

throughout the tour. But go too slow, and you will become sluggish and lethargic, and mistake this for genuine tiredness.

A rough indicator of pace is respiration and heartbeat. You simply cannot sustain for long periods effort which noticeably increases either. Thus, the exact pace you can maintain depends on your physical condition, not on your strength.

I particularly recommend that you take it easy at first, sticking to the lower gears and not pushing hard against the pedals. This will help you to find your own cadence

and pace, and perhaps avoid excessive initial effort. Most people tend to lean into it hard the first day. The result is strained and sore muscles, and the next day they can hardly move. You'll go farther and faster if you take it easy at the start.

Riding position can make a tremendous difference. Going into the wind try to get low down. With a strong tail wind straighten up and get a free push. In Europe many riders use home made 'sails' resembling kites strapped to their backs. These are effective even with a quartering wind. Position determines the muscle groups in use: hands high on the bars eases the back, stomach, arms, and hands; down positions do exactly the opposite and are the best for hill-climbing.

Equipment

Choice of bike depends on the kind of touring you do. A hub gear roadster is durable, but heavy weight and inefficient gear train make it a poor choice for distance work. For all round use, a derailleur gear road bike is best by far. It can be set up to favor durability and carrying heavy loads, or performance and speed. Proper touring bikes have wide range gears and are usually equipped with cantilever brakes. Many general use sports bikes can be modified for touring, and the discussions of luggage, lights, etc., below will suggest what bits and pieces are necessary for your needs. The most important thing is for your bike to be geared correctly for the terrain you will encounter (See Fitting and Gears).

Personally, I love touring with a lightweight mountainbike. Tires can be mounted that are reasonably swift and fleet on pavement, but that can cope with dirt tracks and country bashing. I don't mind trading a bit of speed for the ability to go where I please. Tourists who mix transportation modes frequently, going by bus, train, plane, or auto from one place to the next, may find a portable folding bike the most convenient.

Tires

The development of narrow profile high pressure clincher tires precludes the use of tubulars by all but a handful of affluent fanatics. For poor roads and/or very heavy loads use a 1¼ inch heavyweight tire, or at the ultimate, a 650-B 1¾ inch tire. For more performance, use a lighter 1¼ inch high pressure gumwall, and if you really want to blast along, then use a 1⅛ inch high pressure (90 psi) tire. Remember: the narrower and harder, the faster, and the more punctures.

Tool kit

What you need depends on how far you go and how you maintain your bike. I keep a basic tool kit and expand it with extra tools and parts when necessary. At the minimum, have:

    Tire repair kit including levers and spare valve
    4 inch adjustable wrench
    Screwdriver
    Chain tool and spare links
    Brake and gear cables, long
    Any special Allen keys required for your bike.
    A few assorted nuts and bolts, and a bit of tape
For longer journeys add:
    Spoke key
    Freewheel remover
    Cotterless crank extractor
    Lubricants, including grease
    Any special gizmo you might need.
Sounds like a lot, but it can all be packed into a compact bundle. On group rides cut down on the number of spare parts per rider, and share one set of tools. Your lighting system as a matter of course should carry spare bulbs. Include a bit of wire and tape for longer runs.

For mending yourself, a basic first-aid kit. I generally also carry: a multi-purpose pocketknife, compass, waterproofed matches, button thread for clothing repairs, game snares, or fishing line, and, when appropriate, a snake-bite kit. If you are fond of following sudden fanciful notions and exploring odd by-ways when riding a bike, then a lightweight reflectorized survival blanket is worthwhile insurance.

Lights

A requirement at night. Many tourists like generator lights as they are consistently bright and less expensive than battery lights. However, some people do not care to pedal against the resistance of a wheel or hub generator, and wiring tends to snag and break at inconvenient moments. Unless fitted with a storage battery adding 14-16 oz weight, generator lights go out when the bike stops.

Battery lights are simple, can be used off the bike for map reading or roadside repairs, and left off the bike altogether on a fast daytime run. They are best for off-road riding, as they do not dim if you go slowly, and there are no wires to snag.

Generator lights are brighter than ordinary battery lights. Specialized rechargeable battery systems, however, are bright and can also be generator powered if necessary. They are the route to go if you want to be definitive. See the lights entry in Accessories for details.

I strongly suggest using a warning flasher unit such as the Belt Beacon (see Accessories). A useful item is the Matex flashlight, which straps on the arm or leg and shows a white light to the front, red light to the rear. It will also do as a camp light or for roadside repairs.

Fenders

A great pleasure in wet going and on rough back roads. Plastic models are light and easily removed when not needed, but eventually warp. Alloy and stainless steel models are sturdier, and offer mounting points for lights and other knick-knacks. They tend to transmit sound, but this can be cured with a coat of undercovering paint from an auto shop.

Bicycle shoes and cleats

There are two basic choices: shoes made to be used without cleats and suitable for walking when off the bike, and shoes made for use with cleats and suitable only for cycling. In theory, if you are really rolling on the miles and want the strongest possible shoe, then cleats give the maximum get up and go. In fact, there are many ultra-long distance tourists who are perfectly happy with dual purpose cycling/walking shoes, and they have the advantage of not having to carry an additional pair of shoes for use when off the bike.

Start off with a pair of dual purpose shoes. They'll be useful anyhow for general riding. If you find them suitable for touring, fine. If not, buy a pair of proper cycling shoes with cleats. In my experience nothing beats these for comfort and efficiency.

Baggage

Loading a touring bike is an art. There are two cardinal principles: load low and load evenly. Piling gear up in a high stack or all in one place creates tremendous instability for the bike. Bicycle carriers are designed to distribute loads properly. There are three basic kinds: handlebar bags, saddlebags, and panniers. People traveling light can get by with a saddlebag. These fasten to the seat and seat post and are available in various sizes, from little larger than a wallet to bags that can hold a lot of gear.

An alternative is the handlebar bag. These give ready access for maps, food, cameras and other things you need often. On drop handlebars the weight has an adverse effect on steering, but I've not had this problem with flat handlebar mountainbikes.

A revolution in cycle baggage occurred with the introduction of the Jim Blackburn Low Rider front pannier rack. Instead of holding the panniers up high, these center the panniers on the front hub. The improvement to bike handling over standard front pannier racks has to be experienced to be believed. Front panniers will carry more than a handlebar bag and are not that difficult for access. Maps can be held to the handlebars with a spring clip. The only

need for a handlebar bag that comes to mind is when carrying sophisticated cameras. In such a case the handlebar bag should be of a type which is held by a wire frame slung from the handlebars, and secured by elastic tension cords to the front forks. This will help minimize the tiny sharp vibrations which are particularly harmful to cameras.

Campers will want rear panniers, and for the best load distribution, front panniers as well. Panniers come in one of two basic designs: single bag, which allows maximum cramming in of gear, and multi-compartment bag, which separates gear for easy access. Most panniers made today are quick on or off the bike, and some can be converted into backpacks.

Good brand names are Karrimore, Kirtland, Bellwether, Eclipse, Cannondale, Recreation Equipment, Gerry, Kangaroo, and Touring Cyclist Shop. I have used Karrimore and Eclipse with good results, but different models suit different uses. You really need to go to a bike shop and inspect the merchandise personally.

Panniers want the support of a stout rack. Those supplied on production bikes are often flimsy. There are two types: aluminum alloy and steel. Aluminum alloy racks are light and strong, and while breaks are very rare, they have been known to happen. In such an instance special equipment is needed for a repair. The original Blackburn racks have many copies, and with these you get what you pay for. So far as I am concerned, there is no substitute for the real McCoy.

Steel racks are less expensive and of course heavier than aluminum alloy but have the advantage of being easy to repair with ordinary welding equipment. The Karrimor rack has been around for many years and is a proven performer.

When you load your bike, put heavy gear at the bottom of the bags, light bulky stuff like sleeping bags at the top. Give yourself a few shakedown trial runs. The extra weight takes getting used to, and nothing is quite so irritating as rebuilding a luggage rack in the middle of a tour. After the rack bolts and screws have bedded in, use a locking material such as Loctite to hold them firmly in place.

Maps

A compass is not only useful in conjunction with a map, but can itself guide you in the general direction you want to go without strict routing. Sometimes it is fun to dispose of maps altogether. Just go where fancy takes you, and ask directions along the way. You get to meet people, and often they can suggest really interesting routes, scenic attractions, swimming holes, and the like. But have a map in reserve.

As well as keeping you on a desired route, maps have the vital function of keeping you off main traveled roads and out of industrial areas. Gas station maps are not detailed enough. The best source is the US Geological Service, who publish contour maps for each state. If you know the exact area you'll be in, they also have local maps down to 1:24,000, a scale which shows walls, footpaths, tiny streams, etc. These are too detailed for any but the most local use, but are extremely interesting. Many map stores carry the USGS maps, or you can order them direct (for local maps ask first for free state index map):

East of the Mississippi, US Geologic Survey, Washington District Section, 1200 South Eads Street, Arlington, Virginia 22202

West of the Mississippi, US Geological Survey, District Section, Federal Center, Denver, Colorado 80225.

Clothing

This is rather obviously a function of climate. There is a quite real danger of hypothermia if you are ill-clad while topping a high alpine pass in conditions of freezing rain; and equally, you can be fried cherry red if you ride unprotected under a blazing sun. The best guide for this sort of thing is simple experience gained on short excursions.

Wash and wear synthetic garments provide a high convenience factor. However, they are often uncomfortable to wear during sustained physical activity, and my own preference is for clothing made of cotton, wool, or silk. For raingear, see the discussion in Accessories.

Camping gear

Personal experience and preference are the main basis for scope and choice of camping equipment. Some people need a prepared campsite with johns, showers, and even a

TV set. Others get by with a bivvy sack and a candle. If you are unfamiliar with living outdoors, do some research before investing heavily in a lot of paraphernalia. One excellent and definitive tome is *Backcountry Bikepacking*, by W. Sanders. There are

camping equipment stores in most cities and towns, but be selective. A lot of the gear is designed to be carted around in an automobile; cyclists require light weight and quintessential function.

1. Sleeping bag. Tents and stoves etc. can always be improvised with fair success, but only the most skilled can keep warm in a bad bag. A poor

bag weighs more, and if you freeze and can't sleep, this will give you ample time to brood on the economic and practical merits of having gotten something that would do the job in the first place. Get the best bag you can afford. Also, although your bike has carrying capacity and most of your touring is apt to be in warm weather, I suggest you keep other possibilities such as backpacking or tours in the autumn (fantastic!) in mind.

The best bags, pound-for-pound, are of down. Down has the greatest range (temperatures at which the bag will work), resiliency (bag packs small), recovery (gets

loft back when unpacked), wicking properties (carries moisture away from body), and moral character. The less expensive, lighter (filled with 1½-2½ lbs of down) models are OK for warm weather. I suggest a multi-layered and/or openable bag that will also take a flannel insert. This gives optimum range and comfort.

The least expensive bags contain synthetic fillers such as 'Dacron 88' and 'Astrofill'. These weigh about 6 lbs, and are somewhat bulky, but are OK for warm weather and low altitudes.

2. A ground sheet such as a triple-purpose (rain cape, tent) poncho.

The remaining equipment listed here can always be improvised. The trouble with this is that garnering boughs for a bed or building fires is rather wasteful and ecologically unsound. There are enough campers now so that the total destruction can be devastating. In many areas you are not allowed to do these things. So, drag that it may be, it is both practical and considerate to be as self-sufficient as possible.

3. Sleeping mattress or pad. Air mattresses (avoid plastic ones) are comfortable but bulky. Pads such as ensolite are fine.

4. Tents come in all shapes, sizes and grades. Conditions and personal preference dictate choice. Tents are good for protection against bugs, rain, and to ensure privacy. Bivvy bags are minimalist and give a good view of the stars. Polythene sheets can be rigged into a decent shelter with only a little effort and are extremely cheap and light. A poncho is just as good.

5. Cooking stove and utensils. The days of scrounging up bits of wood for a cheery campfire are fairly well gone. Open fires are not allowed in many areas because of the risk of a general fire. Also, if enough campers pick over an area there can be ecological damage.

To be sure of a means for cooking, you'll need a stove. Cheapest are the solid fuel jobs such as the Esbit, which will fold and actually fit into a pocket. The flame on these cannot be controlled, which means no cooking inside a tent, and in windy conditions matters can get impossibly out of hand.

More tractable are gas stoves with throw-away cartridges. These burn clean and pack tidily, but the cartridges have an annoying habit of running out when least expected; for regular use you will need to carry a spare refill.

Liquid fuel stoves variously use kerosene, meths, white gas, diesel, or gasoline. Some will run on only one type of fuel, others will digest the lot.

Operating a kero stove is something of an art. First the burner must be pre-heated with meths. Then you prick the jet with a wire to clear any possible obstruction, open a tap and, if all is well, the emerging kero vaporizes and ignites. If something is amiss, then the stove goes out and you are enshrouded in a cloud of oily black smoke. Kero stoves are one of the few mechanical devices known to possess intelligence. They always wait for the key moment when your back is turned before malfunctioning and erupting in a ball of flame (although there is no particular danger, so long as you are within quick striking distance of the controls).

Meths stoves are simple and reliable. An excellent make is the Swedish Trangia, which comes complete with its own frying pan, two saucepans, handle, and kettle. The Trangia is clean and will cope with high winds. The snag is the cost and availability of meths. In fact, with kerosene, white gas, and meths you will have to always plan ahead, and ensure that you have an adequate supply. This can make your life miserable with, for example, a compulsory Saturday morning ride in a torrential downpour to make town before the shops close.

Gasoline is more easily available and is relatively cheap, but can blow you to kingdom come. So long as you are careful there should not be a problem, and many experienced tourists swear by the excellent performance and economy of stoves such as the Optimus 99. I think a gasoline stove is fine if you are using it all the time and well in the habit of following the necessary precautions. For sometime use, white gas, meths, or kerosene stoves are better, as their quirks are merely inconvenient and amusing rather than fatal. As for gas stoves, I abhor a world filled with empty gas cylinders.

The stoves put out by MSR, Box 3978 Terminal Station, Seattle, WA 98124, are luscious. Their X-GK is an expedition grade corker that will burn anything, anytime. The WhisperLite model runs on white gas and is popular because it is inexpensive (but not cheap), lightweight, and compact.

For utensils I prefer a steel pot, a steel fry pan that will serve as a lid for the pot (and simultaneously keep its own contents warm) and a steel cup that can also go on the fire. Avoid aluminum utensils, they are toxic. Skewers can be used on their own, or to form a grill, and are very compact.

6. Food. Dried lightweight foods are extremely convenient and quite palatable. I suggest carrying enough for emergencies only, however, and trying for fresh food along the route. Stock up on supper and breakfast at about 4 o'clock. Mixtures of dried fruit, grains, dried milk, protein powders, yeast, etc., are nourishing, tasty, and easy to carry. Many health food shops have a dried fruit and nut mixture called trail food. Always have something more advanced than a candy bar in reserve, just in case you get stuck.

Most any city has a camping equipment store. Mail order outfits I have done business with to complete satisfaction are:

LL Bean, Freeport, ME 04032

Not deadly cheap, but always quality equipment which *works*.

Herter's, Route 1, Waseca, MN 56093

My favorite. Chest-thumpers, but sound equipment at very low cost.

Recreational Co-op, 1525 11th Ave., Seattle, WA 98122

Excellent equipment at good prices. Nice knapsacks.

Gerry, 5450 North Valley Highway, Denver, CO 80306

Expensive, but first-rate equipment which works really well.

Please

If you camp or otherwise hang out in the countryside, please be tidy. Litter is not only aesthetically vastly unpleasing to other people, but is also very dangerous for animals. Livestock and wild creatures can cut themselves on tin cans and glass, and choke to death on plastic bags. Take away all your rubbish and if you find extra, do yourself a favor and take away as much as you can of that as well. In a very real sense the countryside belongs to everybody. But the people who live and work there are getting increasingly fed up with the sloppy ways of tourists and 'outsiders'. In popular holidays areas there are farmers and other locals who really hate tourists, and with good cause. As a result, more and more real estate is being closed off. Do your bit to reverse this trend.

Getting There

Other forms of locomotion complement bicycles very well.

Cars: A bike with wheels off will fit in the trunk of many economy cars and certainly on the back seat. For carrying several bikes you can buy or make a car carrier. There are two types, rear end and top. The rear end version holds 2 bikes and is easy to load. It is hard to get at the trunk, however, and the bikes get a lot of road grit and scratch each other.

Top mounted carriers hold 4 to 5 bikes, and require that each bike be strapped down. But machines are kept clean, separate, and out of harm's way. Available from any good bike shop.

Most any auto store has luggage racks which can easily be adapted for bikes. Or you can make your own, and have something exactly suited for the job.

When loading, alternate direction for 3 or more bikes. Seat on one cross-bar, handlebars on the other. Careful of brake and shift cables. Lash down with toe straps or elastic luggage straps at contact points, and especially the handlebars, since these hold the bike upright. Guying, running straps from the side of the car to high points on the bike (like with a sailboat mast), is a *good idea*.

Mixing up a tour with public transportation, or even just complementing a trip with a bicycle, is a great way to travel. You get the same benefits of mobility and covering a lot of ground, but at the same time a bike lets you examine interesting areas in detail. Preparation of your bike for travel depends on the kind of carrier you will use.

Airlines: These handle bikes routinely and some provide special bike boxes. Remove the rear derailleur if you have one, and loosen stem and twist handlebars parallel with front wheel. They may ask you to remove or reverse the pedals. Protect the frame and chainwheel with a broken-up cardboard box. Deflate tires to ½ pressure. Airlines sometimes let bikes on free, and sometimes charge.

Buses: Here your bike lies flat on its side in a luggage compartment with a lot of other junk that can bang into it. I strongly recommend picking up a box from a local bike dealer and stuffing yours inside. If you are leap-frogging, send the box on ahead.

Railroads: In Europe you can load a bike into the baggage compartment yourself. In the US the make-work contingent has rigged it so a baggage handler must do the job - badly. Stories of bikes mangled into oblivion by baggage handlers are legion. Insist on personally supervising loading or don't go. Hang the bike from the ceiling or side of the baggage car if possible, and in any case see that it is lashed down securely and that no heavy stuff can fall on it.

Boats: Same story. One boat-loading crew broke an internal gear on a motorcycle of mine, I never did figure out how.

If you regularly travel mixed mode, invest in a bike bag. These are available in light, soft versions, and heavier, fiberglass models.

Touring Abroad

'Going foreign' with a bike is a particularly satisfying way of traveling, as it allows you to explore and savor a country to a degree not otherwise possible. In most places people admire and respect cyclists, and are exceptionally helpful and friendly. For uninteresting or arduous sections of the journey you simply use public transport.

Great Britain

The CTC Route Guide to Cycling in Britain and Ireland by N. Crane and C. Gausden (Penguin Books) will spell out most of what you need to know for a good tour.

General information is available from:

- British Tourist Authority, 64 St. James Street, London SW1 1NF, England
- Scottish Tourist Board, 23 Ravelston Terrace, Edinburgh EH4 3EU, Scotland

First and foremost of the touring organizations is the Cyclists Touring Club, Cotterell House, 69 Meadrow, Godalming, Surrey GU7 3HS, England. Membership (write for cost) includes the *Cycle Touring Club Handbook*, a thick list of 3,000 recommended accommodation addresses, places to eat, cycle repairers, and CTC local information officers for Great Britain; a list of overseas touring correspondents; information about touring areas, equipment and travel by air, rail, and sea, including ferries, tunnels, and bridges; a catalog of the books and maps for Great Britain, the Continent, and Morocco available through the bookstore; and a complete exposition of club services. For the tourist, the most important of these is the touring department, which has available a large library of comprehensive, personally researched tours complete with maps. The touring department will also plan and suggest tours for routes and areas you request, and will advise on cycle and personal equipment, gears, maps, and travel books. Other CTC services are too numerous to mention. Get in touch with them if you plan to tour abroad.

A WELL-KNOWN SPOT ON THE GODSTONE ROAD.

The ROSE & CROWN Riddlesdown

- The Youth Hostel Association, Trevelyan House, 8 St Stephen's Hill, St Albans, Herts AL1 2DY, England

Hostels are sometimes spartan, but always serviceable. You provide your own sleeping bag, and help a bit with the chores. Inexpensive, and you can cook your own food. The association stores sell camping and touring equipment, have a tourist service, and run guided tours. An essential organization for the economy minded.

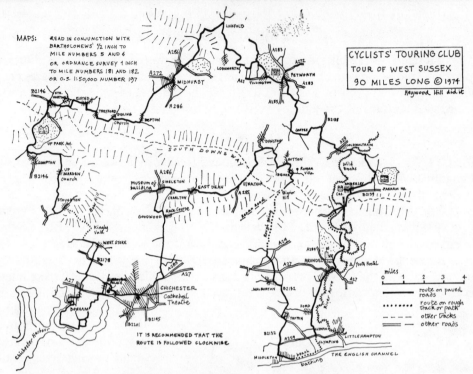

MAPS: READ IN CONJUNCTION WITH BARTHOLOMEWS' ½ INCH TO MILE NUMBERS 5 AND 6 OR ORDNANCE SURVEY 1 INCH TO MILE NUMBERS 181 AND 182 OR O.S. 1:50,000 NUMBER 197

CYCLISTS' TOURING CLUB TOUR OF WEST SUSSEX 90 MILES LONG © 1974 Heywood Hill did it

● Bike Events, P.O. Box 75, Bath, Avon BA1 1BX, England
Guided tours in G.B. and on the Continent. A fun outfit.

Riding

The word on British roads is to take the smallest you can find. These reduce automobile speeds down to a level where a cyclist can co-exist with cars in relative comfort. On the main through routes (called 'A' class roads), vehicle speeds are high, and there is often no room for a cyclist to maneuver. There will be no shoulder, for example, only a solid earthen embankment. Anyway, the smaller roads ('B' class and under) are far more scenic and interesting. The British are a nation of social drinkers, and on Friday and Saturday nights after 9 o'clock the roads are full of tipsy drivers going home from pubs. Don't be out on a bike at that time.

In Britain you are required by law to obey the rules of the road and all traffic regulations. You must have lights front and rear at night, and a reflector. These rules are enforced with fines. Pick up a copy of the *Highway Code* at any (British) newsagent or bookshop to familiarize yourself with the regulations. The British drive on the left side of the road. This can be a terrifying prospect for some people, but in actuality it is quite easy.

Equipment

Fenders are pretty much a requirement for British and Continental touring. The weather tends not to steady downpours that last all day (in which case fenders make no difference since you are soaked anyhow), but to a bit of wet here or there.

Although not alpine, many hills in Britain are steeply pitched. Gear low. For a 5-speed, the Cyclists' Touring Club recommends a 13-15-18-23-31 to 40 front, and for a 10-speed,

15-17-19-21-23 to 28 x 46 front (read up on gearing in Chapter 8 if you do not understand what these numbers mean). These combinations concentrate the gears in a low range, without large gaps.

Technically, it is more practical to sort out your bike before traveling. But many people use a trip abroad as an opportunity to buy a bike. Economically and aesthetically, this route is worthwhile only if you go first class and buy a quality machine from a small shop or builder. Here are a few:

Condor Cycles, 144 Gray's Inn Road, London WC1

FW Evans, 77 The Cut, London SE1

Bob Jackson, 148 Harehills Lane, Leeds LS8 5BD

Harry Hall Cycles, 32 Cathedral Close, Manchester M4

Mercian Cycles, 28 Stenson Road, Cavendish, Derby DE3 7JB

Jack Taylor Cycles, Church Road, Stockton, Teeside TS18 2LY

There are many, many others; check in the local cycling press, with friends, etc.

Maps

Ordnance Survey maps are best. A catalog is available from the Director General, Ordnance Survey, Romsey Road, Maybush, Southampton SO9 4DH. The 1:25,000 scale maps are extremely detailed, showing individual buildings, walls, tiny streams, and the like, and give an endless amount of information about the area covered. They are wonderful for detailed exploring; but for overall route planning, ½ inch or 1 inch scale maps are better. These still show virtually all roads, footpaths, villages, rivers, and other stuff, like youth hostels, inns, National Trust properties, windmills, public rights

A COUNTRY CLUB RUN

of way, and more. There are also a number of tourist maps made up especially for popular and scenic areas, and archeological and historical maps.

The privately published Bartholomews's ½ inch series, the most useful size, is obtainable in bookstores or from John Bartholomew, 12 Duncan Street, Edinburgh, EH9 1TA, Scotland.

Both Ordnance and Bartholomew's maps are available from the Cyclists' Touring Club at a reduced price for members.

Camping

The Camping Club of Great Britain and Ireland, Ltd., 11 Lower Grosvenor Place, London SW1W 0EY, England. Membership includes an International Camping Carnet, insurance services, a handbook on camping, and a guide to 1,500 sites in Great Britain and Ireland. Site lists are also available from the British Tourist Authority, Thames Tower, Black's Road, Hammersmith, London W6 9EL, England.

Railroads

The British rail system is extremely comprehensive, and great for skipping around the country. On most local trains the bike goes for free. On fast long distance trains there is a charge and space must be reserved in advance. Load and unload the bike from the luggage car yourself, using elastic straps to keep it upright. Never ship a bike alone via British Rail unless it is heavily insured against any possible contingency.

The Continent

The book to have is *Cycling in Europe* by Nicholas Crane (Pan Books, Cavaye Place, London SW10). It's full of all the info you need, and a fun read as well. There are

plenty of others: *Adventure Cycling in Europe* by J. Rakowski tells everything you need to know for 27 countries. *Cycle Touring in Britain and the Rest of Europe* by P. Knottley is another useful book with many practical tips from a veteran.

The best single source of current information is the Cyclists' Touring Club. They have information sheets, pre-planned tours, maps, and insurance and travel services which make them unbeatable value for the tourist. They also conduct tours. So do the Youth Hostel Association, and membership includes a number of useful guides and handbooks.

And then there are always the traditional aids to travel - the Michelin Guides and various sight-seeing tomes. One of the nicest things about cycle touring is that you are not obliged to make a plan and stick to a schedule. Even in crowded holiday areas you should not have much difficulty in finding accommodation if you just veer off the beaten track.

AWHEEL IN FRANCE.

USEFUL ADDRESSES

You can write to various national tourist offices and cycling organizations for information:

Albania - Federata Sportive Shgiptare-Bruga, Abdi Toptani 3, Tirana.

Austria - Osterreichischer Radsport-Verband, Prinz Eugenstrasse 12, 1040 Vienna.

Belgium - Ligue Velocipedique Belge, 49 avenue du Globe, 1190 Brussels.

Bulgaria - Federation Bulgare de Cyclisme, Boulevard Tolboukhine 18, Sofia.

Czechoslovakia - Ceskoslovenska Sekce Cyklistiky, Na Porici 12, 115 30 Prague 1, CSSR.

Denmark - Dansk Cyklist Forbund, Kjield Langes Gade 14, DK-1367 Copenhagen.

Eire - Irish Cycling Federation, 5 St Christopher's Road, Montemotte, Cork.

France - FUBICY, 7 avenue de la foret noire, 67000 Strasbourg; Federation Francaise de Cyclotourisme, 8 rue Jean-Marie Jego, 75013 Paris.

Holland - ANWB, Wassenaarseweg 220, 2596 EC Den Haag; Netherlands Cycletouring Union, PO Box 240, 2700AE, Zoetermeer.

Hungary - Hungarian Cyclists' Federation, Budapest 1146.

Northern Ireland - Northern Ireland Cycling Federation, 9a Great Northern Street, Belfast.

Norway - Norges Cykleforbund, Hauger Skolevei 1, 1351-Rud, Oslo; Syklistenes Landsforening, Majorstuveien 20, Oslo 3.

Poland - Polska Zwiazek Kolarska, 1 Plac Xelaznej, 00136 Warsaw.

Portugal - Federacao Portuguesa de Ciclismo, Rua Barros Queiroz 39-10, Lisbon.

Spain - Federacion Espianola de Ciclismo, Calle Ferraz 16-50, Madrid 8.

Sweden - Cykelframjandet, PO Box 2085, 103 12 Stockholm; Svenska Cykelsallskapet, PO Box 6006, 163-03 Spanga.

Switzerland - Comite National du Cyclisme, PO Box 930, 1211 Geneva 3.

W. Germany - ADFC, Postfach 101123, D-2800 Bremen.

USSR - USSR Cycling Federation, Lougenetskay Naberognay 8, Sportcomite, 119270 Moscow.

Africa

Bicycles are a common form of transport for Africans, but their machines are of course extremely stout and sturdy, as often there is simply no road at all. In Morocco, for example, south of the Atlas Mountains and into the Sahara Desert, the roads are dirt tracks resembling streambeds. Most of the locals simply cycle over the desert itself. However, in Northern Morocco the roads are quite negotiable, and there are not many cars. I should imagine that similar varied conditions prevail throughout Africa.

Unless you run a local bike, parts are a problem, and in many areas so is thievery. Cyclists in Africa have been trapped in disease quarantine areas. There is always an ongoing selection of wars, revolutions, famines, and other excitements to interest the tourist. In many places life is less than cheap. Still, I would say the prospects for cycle touring are good. Beyond odd articles in the cycle press there is not a lot of annotated information, but I know a fair number of people who have toured in Africa. They all seem to share the characteristics of being self-reliant, energetic, and able to get on well with people.

Asia and the Pacific

China - Cycling Association of People's Republic of China, 9 Tiyuguan Road, Beijing, Tel: 75 1313.

Much the same story as for Africa. Many people have cycled out that way, and most of them have a hair-raising story or two to tell. There are organized tours for India, Mongolia, China, etc., on a fairly frequent basis. Try China Passage, 168 State Street, Teaneck, NJ 07666, Tel: (201) 837-1400. You can also just decide on an area, grab a mountainbike, and catch the next plane out.

The Americas

Canada - Canadian Cycling Association, 333 River Road, Vanier, Ottawa KIL 8B9, Ontario.

Mexico - Todo en Bicicleta, c/o Morales, Pirineos 239, Col Porteles, Mexico 13 DF.

A DANGER BOARD

CHAPTER 14

Mountainbike!

The mountainbike is an invention which is changing the world. It's the cycling equivalent of a Jeep, with thick, stout tires, a profusion of gears with up to 18 speeds, and mega-powerful brakes. There have always been bikes for hard work and rough roads. Bikes were important in the development of remote, wild areas such as the Australian Outback and Alaska, and most of the Third World relies heavily on bikes for transport. But the bikes were, and are, very heavy.

The vital difference with mountainbikes is that they are made with the lightweight alloys and components generated by BMX technology and the boom in adult sports bikes. The result is a machine that is both lightweight and incredibly tough. It's everything a bike should be. Other than for road racing, if you are to have only one bike then a mountainbike has to be the No. 1 contender. Nothing else on two wheels is so useful, so versatile, and so much fun.

Fun is how it all started. Mountainbikes are an American invention, born in Marin County, California, in the mid-1970s. It's a great story, and the man to tell it is Charles Kelly. He was there, he asked Joe Breeze to build the first ever mountainbikes, and it's all in his fine book: *MOUNTAINBIKE!*. Here's Kelly on the beginnings:

1976
It has been an unseasonably dry winter in Northern California, and the three young men are sweating profusely as they push strangely modified bikes up the steep dirt road in the cool air. The subject of their breathless conversation is a detailed analysis of the condition of the road surface, which resembles an excavation site more than it does a road. On occasion one or another will stop and look searchingly back down the hill, perhaps kicking dirt into a small depression or rolling a rock to the side of the road.

These young men belong to the same adrenalin-driven breed that will always be found exploring the limits of human performance; in other circumstances they might be skiing off cliffs, jumping out of airplanes, or discovering America. In this instance they have developed their own unique athletic challenge, a race whose participation is limited to a few dozen local residents who know about it and have the unusual cycling equipment necessary to take part. The road they are on is the racecourse.

After more than half an hour of hard work, scrambling and pushing but hardly ever riding their bikes, the trio reaches the crest of the hill, where the road they are on intersects another equally rough dirt road. A small crowd of about fifteen other cyclists, similarly equipped and including a couple of high-energy women, is gathered at the intersection. These people have come up by a slightly easier route that follows a paved road up part of the hill, but they have also had to ride a couple of miles of steep and rough road to arrive here. The three recent arrivals casually drop their bikes on the road, which has become a jumble of modified machinery.

Most of the crowd is in their twenties, but there are a few teenagers and one grizzled individual who claims to be fifty. All are wearing heavy shirts and jeans, and most are also wearing leather gloves and heavy boots. None is wearing a helmet.

Although the scene seems to be chaos, order begins to appear. One of the group takes out of his backpack a well-thumbed notebook and a pair of electronic stopwatches. Moving slowly through the crowd, he begins compiling a list of names. The notebook is the combined scoring system, archives, and publicity for the race, since it contains in addition to today's scoring all the previous race results and the telephone numbers of all the participants. Apparently races are not scheduled, they are spontaneously called together when the sun and moon have assumed appropriate aspects.

As names are taken the notetaker assigns a starting order based on the rider's previous performance and experience. Those racing for the first time are first on the list, followed by those with the slowest previous times. The current course record-holder is accorded the honor of starting last. Now starting times are assigned to the names on the list and a copy of the list is made. The watches are started simultaneously and the notetaker hands one copy of the list and one of the watches to an "official timer" whose appearance is undistinguished from the rest of the crowd. The timer takes a moment to tape a bottle-cap over the reset switch on his watch, then he jumps on his bike and disappears down the hill.

For the next ten minutes the adrenalin content of the air builds while riders attend to their pre-race rituals. Some sit quietly eating oranges, some joke nervously or talk excitedly. Others make minute adjustments to their bikes, adjusting brakes, perhaps letting a little air out of the tires, or repeatedly shifting the gears, still undecided about which ratio to use for the start.

After an interval that is too short for some and too long for others the first name on the list is called. Up to the line steps a nervous young man who has by now tried every one of his gears without making a decision. He tries a few more last-second shifts as he rolls his bike to the line, which is a rough scratch inscribed in the road surface by the heel of the starter's boot. This is his first race, and he spends his last few seconds at the top of the hill asking questions about the course faster than anyone can answer, although answers are immaterial because he isn't listening anyway.

The starter props the young man up by holding his rear wheel, and as the rider stands on his pedals his legs are quivering. The starter intones, "Ten seconds...five..." Anticipating the start, the rider tries to explode off the line a second before the starter says, "Go!" But the starter is used to this and he has a firm grip on the wheel, which he releases as he gives the signal. Thrown completely off-balance and draped over the handlebars by his premature jump, the novice wobbles off the line for a few yards before finding the throttle and accelerating to the top of a small rise a hundred yards off and then disappearing from sight.

The sport going on here is so unusual and possibly even dangerous that it is unlikely to catch on with the public as a Sunday recreation, but the participants couldn't care less. They are here to thrill themselves, not a distant crowd, and in that respect this is a pure form of athletic endeavor untainted by any commercial connection.

The bicycles in use are as unique as the sport. They are all old balloon-tire frames dating from the 1930s to the '50s; most of them were built by the Schwinn Company but a few other rugged and otherwise extinct species are represented. The standard set of modifications includes the addition of derailleur gearing systems (either five-speed or ten-speed), front and rear drum brakes, motorcycle brake levers, wide motocross handlebars, handlebar-mounted shift levers, and the biggest knobby bicycle tires available mounted on heavy Schwinn S-2 steel rims. A few reactionaries cling to their one- or two-speed coaster brake models, but the majority have drum brakes and gears, and this looks to be the wave of the future.

The riders affectionately refer to their machines as "Clunkers," "Bombers," or "Cruisers," depending on the owner's local affiliation, and there are not more than two hundred of the advanced models in Northern California.

Certainly people have been riding old bikes on dirt roads in all parts of the world as long as there have been old bikes. These Northern California riders have successfully crossed old newsboy-type bikes with the modern "ten-speed," and the result is a hybrid that is perfectly adapted to the fire roads and trails of the Northern California hills. In the process of field testing their modifications the researchers have shattered every part to be found on a bicycle. Rims, hubs, handlebars, cranksets, seatposts, saddles, gears, chains, derailleurs, stems, pedals and frames have all been ground to fragments along with some exterior portions of a number of clunking enthusiasts, who apparently will make any sacrifice in the name of science.

During the early experimental stage some riders recognized the steep dirt road now known as Repack as an ultimate field test for both bike and rider. This rarely used fire road loses 1300 feet of elevation in less than two miles. In addition to its steepness, it features off-camber blind corners, deep erosion ruts, and a liberal sprinkling of fist-sized rocks. The name "Repack" stems from the coaster-brake era; after a fast trip down the hill the rider would heat the brakes to the point where all the grease in the hub turned to smoke, and it was time to repack the hub.

Returning to the starting line we find that riders have been sent off at two minute intervals. The spacing is to keep riders from catching and having to pass one another. The race evolved out of the downhill dueling that inevitably took place when groups of riders descended. A mass-start format was out of the question, because the narrow roads and blind corners inhibit passing, and any group larger than three was certain to invite mayhem. The time-trial format gives each rider the same chance, undistracted by other riders. By grouping the riders by ability the organizers prevent a slow rider from being followed by an extremely fast one.

The fastest riders are started last so the other finishers can observe their styles, and this starting order leads to an interesting psychological effect. As the number of riders at the line dwindles, those who remain are increasingly the most expert and dedicated riders. They all know each other, and while this is a friendly contest, it is still a contest and these riders are all trying to win it. After the first-time riders leave the line, the chatter dies down, and the air nearly turns blue with the fierce concentration now evident. The only sounds are soft noises of bike adjustments being made, broken now and then by the voice of the starter as he calls the next rider and counts down the start.

What is it like to ride this course? As the rider before you leaves, you have two minutes to prepare yourself, and for a surprising number this means a fast trip to the bushes for an emergency urination. Wheeling up to the line you find that your breathing is already a little strained, fast, and loud in your ears. "Thirty seconds." Squeeze brake levers for the hundredth time to make sure they are adjusted for maximum grab. "Fifteen." You check for the eighth time to make sure you are in the right gear. "Ten." Stand on the pedals as the starter holds your rear wheel. "Five." The world shrinks and becomes twelve feet wide, stretched out in front of you. It takes a conscious effort to hold back from an early start. "GO!" The wheel is released and the bike shoots forward as if propelled by a tightly wound spring.

The first 150 yards are level with a soft surface and a light rise. It is imperative to ride this section as quickly as possible because the fast riders gain two or three seconds on the slower ones here.

Over the rise and into the downhill, and you are already gasping with the effort of the start. No time to let up though, because this section is straight and even though it is steep you are standing on your pedals and stomping your highest gear.

Blind left turn onto the steepest part of the course, covered with ruts and loose rocks. Watch the bump on the corner because at this speed it will launch you into the air and put you out of position for the next corner.

Now the road becomes a series of blind corners which all seem to look alike as you approach. This section favors the experienced Repack rider who can remember which corners to brake for and which can be taken wide open. Since Repack is in more or less a straight line at the top, most of these corners can be taken at full speed, a thrilling prospect in light of the fact that it will take you some distance to stop, unless you hit a tree. At no time should you stop pedaling unless you are jamming on the brakes. As you aproach some of the more wicked curves you are conscious of a few fifty-foot, side to side skid marks laid down by rookie riders. A definite "groove" is visible on most corners, worn into the road surface by the passage of many knobby tires.

A roller-coaster section gives you a new thrill as the bike becomes weightless just when you want the tires on the ground. Into a dip and the bike slides, then corrects itself with no apparent help from the rider, and points in exactly the right direction. Cutting corners as closely as possible, you receive a whack or two from overhanging branches.

Your adrenalin pump goes into overdrive, and your reflexes and vision improve immeasurably. You are aware of every pebble on the road even though they are whipping past. You are completely alone; the only spectators are near the bottom. You dare not lose concentration for an instant, but there is little danger of that.

Sliding into an off-camber, eroded turn you make a slight miscalculation. Out of control, you must make a rapid decision, off the edge or lay the bike down. You lay it down...damn...torn shirt, bloody elbow. No time to check for further damage, since the arm still works; the shirt was old and the elbow was older. How's the bike? It's okay, and a little less paint won't affect the handling...jump back on and feed the chain back on as you coast the first few yards. Back in gear, and now you need to make up time.

Near the bottom of the course you reach the switchbacks, and now you are vaguely aware that you are being photographed as you try to maintain maximum speed through the hairpins. Out of the switchbacks in a cloud of dust and into the final straightaway. Jam on brakes to keep a bump from launching you off the edge. Now several dozen people line the edge of the roadway, earlier riders, girlfriends, and a few locals out to watch the action. Last corner...and speeding past the boulder that marks the finish, you skid to the flashiest possible stop, then throw down the bike and run over to the timer, who immediately gives you your elapsed time. It is the best recorded so far on the day, but your elation is reduced by the arrival of the next rider somewhat less than two minutes later. As the last half dozen riders finish the times continue to go down, and the last finisher records the fastest time of the day, some twenty seconds better than yours. Any time under five minutes is respectable, but the record stands at 4:22.

Now the event is over and the winners are announced, but no prizes are handed out. There are no entry fees, very few rules, and usually no prizes other than a round of beers, but no one seems to care. The finish line is a hubbub as adrenalized riders bounce around, reliving and describing at length their rides and various crashes. "I would have done better, but I crashed..." "I crashed twice and still did better than you did..." "You should have seen it..." But no one did.

The Repack Downhill is gone, the victim of its own success. Originally an underground event, with the increasing numbers of mountain bikers it surfaced on a nationally syndicated television program in 1979. Instead of a couple of dozen friends the field grew to upwards of 100 riders, and the growth attracted the attention of the governmental agencies who owned the property the road runs across. Attempts to work within the system by acquiring all necessary permits failed in the harsh light of the liability and insurance situation. The last Repack race was run in 1984.

In its history from 1976 to 1984, Repack saw no more than two hundred individuals take part. In spite of this, the name has assumed legendary status among mountain bikers. This status may or may not be deserved, but it is certain that this unlikely event was the meeting place and testing site for the people who brought mountain biking to the world. Among the participants were course record-holder Gary Fisher, who helped put gears on Marin's "clunkers," and who is also responsible for some of the standard refinements by adding "thumb-shifters" and the quick-release seatclamp. Joe Breeze holds the second-fastest time, and his designs and frame building were the breakthrough that created the modern mountain bike. Tom Ritchey raced at Repack on a borrowed Schwinn Excelsior before he ever built a mountain bike; Tom's influence can still be seen in the designs of most mass-produced mountain bikes. Another early builder, Erik Koski, raced his designs there. For my part, I was the race organizer, scorer and Keeper of the Records; in 1976 I had a frame built specifically for the purpose of racing there, the first custom mountain bike I know of. (This frame did not live up to my expectations, so I persuaded Joe Breeze to build me another one. Two "his and mine" turned into ten, the prototypes of the modern machine.)

By 1979 several Northern California builders were making major strides in off-road design, inspired by the feedback from each other's efforts. In addition to Joe Breeze, these included Erik Koski, Jeffrey Richman, Jeff Lindsay, and of course Tom Ritchey.

In 1979 Ritchey's frames became the first offered on the market commercially. Even at the staggering price of about $1300 a copy, he could not keep up with the orders. About the same time Marin County brothers Don and Erik Koski designed the "Trailmaster," and shortly afterward Jeff Lindsay introduced his "Mountain Goat." In 1980 Specialized Bicycle Imports of San Jose, California, bought four of Ritchey's bikes and used them as the starting point for the design of the first mass-produced mountain bike, the Japanese-made Stumpjumper, which appeared in 1981. With the appearance of this and other mass-market bikes shortly afterward, the movement took off.

What the early Californian inventors only dimly forsaw was that their creations are the perfect transport for a much nearer wilderness: the urban jungle. Bikes that can zoom along rock-strewn trails and ford streams have no trouble with bumpy, pot-holed streets. With modern tires some of these machines are as at home on the road as on the dirt. In fact, these practical and extremely hardy vehicles have become the No. 1 choice for urban cycling. Today, one in three bikes sold is a mountainbike.

Kinds of Mountainbikes

Mountainbikes are not fettered by UCI regulations or silly ideas about how things should be. Mountainbikes incubate innovation and development, and you can expect to see new things for a long time to come. At this writing, I see four general kinds of mountainbikes:

1. Touring/Downhill. The early Californian riders were famous for 75-foot sideways slides into corners, and speeds of 35-40 mph on rocky trails. The bikes developed to suit this kind of riding are generous on wheelbase and fork rake, and tend to go for strength with, for example, wide 32 mm (1.25 inch) rims and full size 2.125 inch wide tires. The most recent models introduced by builders like Ritchey, Fisher, et al., are moving towards shorter chain stays and a tighter back end, for more kick and better hill climbing ability. The result is a powerful combination of lively, racing-winning performance and "get you home" stability.

2. Sport/Freestyle. Narrow, twisting trails with as much climbing as descending, and freestyle stunts like hopping on and off logs, rocks, and what-else, have led to lighter, tighter designs. On sport mountainbikes, wheelbase, chain stay length, and fork rake are all slightly more compact than on touring models. Rims are usually 28 mm (1.12 inch) and tires range from 1.5 to 2 inches wide. The result is a bike that is responsive and nimble, and that can move fairly quickly on-road as well as off-road. Fitted with a carrier rack and fenders, it is an excellent city bike.

3. Trials. People determined to ride their bikes over or through anything they encounter have evolved designs where the geometry is tight, and the bottom bracket very high. The whole idea with trials is to ride "clean", without the feet touching the ground, and so the bottom bracket is well up to provide clearance over obstacles. People use these bikes to ride over cars, clamber over 5 foot diameter logs, and other incredible stunts.

4. Competition. The emerging style for competition mountainbikes is akin to cyclo-cross machines: very light and tight, often with dropped handlebars. Rims are often a slim 22 mm (0.875 inch), mounting 1.4 inch wide tires, and some riders have gone over to conventional 700C rims and 1.125 tires. The idea is to pare weight to the absolute minimum, sacrificing if necessary some of the strength necessary for gonzo descents. The gains on climbs and over the ground more than make up for the loss of speed downhill.

Selecting a Mountainbike

The classifications I've given are legitimate, but note that races have been won by every kind of bike you can imagine. Different kinds of bikes suit different kinds of riders. You'll get some people who swear a certain bike is the best thing ever, and others who swear it is the worst in all creation. The only good way to find out about mountainbikes is to try them for yourself and see what you like. A big part of the fun is new horizons and new skills. You're exploring, and one cannot say for sure what you are going to find. This said, here are a few general guidelines.

1. Decide what you want the bike for. Are you going to ride all the time in town? Do you like belting down fire roads and gravel tracks? How about coming down the really super-steep, butt well back off the saddle? Do you want to load up with camping gear and explore country roads and trails? Or do you like to go ripping through rolling terrain, zooming up and down like a roller coaster? Would you like to be able to skate over a 12 inch high log? Do you just want a strong, dependable bike?

2. Buy the quality you need. In Toronto, for example, most of the ground is flat. You don't need much of a hot-shot machine if you just want a mountainbike as transportation. Vancouver, on the other hand, has plenty of hills, and even a plain transportation mountainbike wants to be of fairly good quality, to keep down weight.

3. Buy a good name. There are a lot of Johnny-Come-Lately firms cashing in on the mountainbike act, and some of them are big guns with lots of advertizing muscle. Making a good mountainbike is not just a matter of copying what someone else did, or blithely shoving out a bike with a relaxed frame geometry and fat tires. Beware the "hot answer", it may be a lot of hot air. The people who know about mountainbikes are the people who ride them. This is just as true for a New York City messenger as for a Colorado trail blazer. For straight info and fun reading take out a subscription to the magazine Fat Tire Flyer, P.O. Box 757, Fairfax, CA 94930.

4. You will hear a lot of opinions about frame size. I believe that the natural tendency is to go too big. When you take a mountainbike Out There and really push to the limit of what you can do (the bike usually still has a lot in reserve), you'll find that you want to be able to move the machine around underneath you quickly and easily. My advice is to ride the smallest frame that you can comfortably use. You'll grow into it.

5. Your comfort will depend very much on the reach of the handlebars. Most mountainbike handlebars are very wide, and this lengthens the reach. If you are stretched out on a bike, often a good solution is to move your hands inboard. If this does the trick, the controls can be relocated and the bars trimmed with a hacksaw.

The Case for Gonzo

If you are a beginner and want to really hare off into the back of beyond, you are well advised to take a conservative approach and pick a bike that will help take care of you. Something rugged, and kind, that holds a line when you are too tired to see small obstacles. Something with nice low, low gears that can just settle down and chew along if need be. For any beginner who has not had a lot of Out There experience, and who intends serious off-road excursions, the classic California Gonzo, touring/downhill basher bike is an excellent choice.

It's also of course the machine to have if you want to blast along trails and tracks at very high speeds. It's really fun to let it all hang out and go to the limit. Again, when your teeth are rattling at 30 mph and the bike is skittering around a corner, just barely in control, it is comforting to know that the machine was made for the job and will pull through if you do.

The Case for Sport

Most people have to use their bikes for transport as well as off-road fun, and performance on pavement is important. Sport mountainbikes are reasonably lively on-road, and a lot of fun off-road. Like any performance machine, they demand a certain amount of attentiveness and concentration. What this means, for example, is that if you nose into a ditch on a sport model, the timing of your weight transfer to lighten the front has to be a little more precise than with a touring model.

A sport mountainbike is a lot of fun if you like monkeyshines: zipping in and out of hollows, catching air, and sliding the bike a lot in corners, so that it is sort of like freestyle on skis. The "get you home" bikes don't always appreciate fooling around, and many just naturally try to keep matters regular, which is what they were built to do. Sport mountainbikes are a little more finely balanced and responsive - and easier to lose too!

The Case for Trials

Don't look at me. I've got lots of friends who just love playing with their trials style bikes, and I'm always amazed at the things they can do. I keep meaning to get my hands on a trials bike and learn the vital trick of riding over a car, but am always playing with other toys.

The Case for Competition

Personally, I think competition mountainbikes are where it's at. They are really quick, extremely light, and no slouch whatsoever as road and touring bikes. A model from a top custom builder like Charlie Cunningham can pare down to as little as 21-22 lbs. Most good competition models will slip under 25 lbs. This is starting to go into the same class as road racing bikes. Minimum weight makes for easier climbing and snappier acceleration. It also makes the bike easier to handle, whatever you are doing, from fording a stream to boarding an airplane.

A competition mountainbike is dynamite in urban traffic. It's a racing machine that you can use all the time. Flat-out road racing bikes are faster, but racing mountainbikes are a lot tougher. They

can survive time after time, when a road racing bike would be knocked to flinders. A fast mountainbike is stronger and safer. And at 25 lbs or less, with hard, fast tires, they only give away a few minutes on most urban journeys. Often they arrive first, because they don't have to stay on the road.

The countryside touring story is about the same. A full-up, high quality touring bike will make a little more speed on roads. When it comes to climbing, a competition mountainbike is just as good and often better. And once you start exploring trails and open country, the mountainbike has it all.

The handling of a hot mountainbike can be quick, but not if you are used to a responsive road bike. Its vitality is a safety feature of sorts, because it commands more of your attention. It's not a cruiser. It's a bike for going flat out, wherever and whenever you want.

Wheels and Tires

The original gnarlies (knobby tires) for off-road use were heavy, and noisy and stiff when used on pavement. Modern gnarlies are much lighter, and have tread patterns that grip in sand and mud, but roll fairly easily on hard surfaces. For maximum road performance, however, it is better to use tires made for the street. One welcome spillover for mountainbikes from road racing bikes are completely bald tires. These go like stink and are said to have excellent grip. I don't much care for combination tires with a raised center bead for pavement, and knobs on the side for traction in dirt. They are too prone to slide out in a corner.

One good trick is to run two sets of wheels. On my bike, Midnight Express, I use 22 mm wide rims and quick-release hubs. The road wheels have 1.4 inch Specialized Nimbus tires, and the dirt wheels have 2 inch Ibex Panaracers. Funny thing is, the Nimbus tires are pretty good off-road, I only use the gnarlies when there's lots of mud, snow, or very rough terrain.

Fenders

It is a very good idea to keep a mountainbike as simple as possible. If you ride a lot through mud, however, fenders can be really helpful. Mount them for as much clearance as possible, or else the mud may pack up and drag on the tire.

Gearing

Most mountainbikes have triple chainrings and 6-speed freewheels. This gives an even spread of gears over a wide range, and is an excellent way to go. If you get to the point of setting up your own gearing, however, give consideration to the less complex arrangement of double chainrings and a 5-speed freewheel. There is less weight all around, shifting is easier and more certain, a wider, stronger chain can be used, and the rear changer can be more compact and swift.

Toe Clips

I highly recommend the use of toe clips. Stabbing your foot out to maintain balance is usually the beginning of the end. What you want to do is stay with the bike, not

form an ever-widening triangle with the bike as one side, and your leg as the other. If you stay balanced over your bike, then you and the bike move together. The way to develop this kind of skill is to shove your feet into toe clips, and keep them there.

It's also very much a safety feature. When you get to tearing around it is important to stay connected with the bike. If you lose a pedal, you lose a lot of control. One specific hazard is a whop on the shin from a jagged pedal, and that one can really hurt. I promise: the risk of injury is much greater with open pedals than with toe clips.

The Great Outdoors

There is a lot of controversy over the use of mountainbikes in the countryside. In some places they are banned. My views on the subject are pretty simple. Anyone going off the beaten track should have an idea of what is going on, and how to behave. They should be self-sufficient, and not surprised that it becomes colder at night. This applies whether by foot, bike, canoe, skimobile, or flying machine.

As far as mountainbikes themselves are concerned, they do less damage than a horse. Of course, if you come down through a mountain meadow with the back wheel locked up and plowing a deep furrow in the earth, then a lot of harm can be done. The furrow becomes a watercourse, erosion takes place, and bang, no more meadow filled with pretty flowers.

Wilderness and the countryside have to be treated with care and respect, but they should be used. I see mountainbikes as a great help for conservation and the environment. The more people who get outdoors and learn to love natural things, the better. Sure there are gonzo riders who headbang down trails, scaring the wits out of hikers and horseback riders. But the majority of mountainbikers enjoy and love the countryside just as much, if not more, as anyone else.

Restrictions are a horrible fact of life. Prohibited. Not allowed. No swimming. No skiing. No, no, no. It's really very difficult. I've seen a lot of wonderfully beautiful places ruined and turned into rubbish heaps by thoughtless, wantonly destructive people. It's criminal. The concern with preserving the countryside has a good foundation, even if it does seem to attract an awful lot of busybody types who enjoy making up rules for other people.

I think a lot depends on how you go about things. If you slip along quietly and don't make a lot of fuss, then most times things will be all right. If you are rowdy and toss beer cans all over the place, you're more likely to attract trouble. Talk to people: farmers, rangers, hunters, fishers, hikers. Try to hear what they are saying, whatever it is. Once they feel they are being heard, the process is much more likely to work in reverse, and once they know you have feelings and ideas too, matters usually get a lot better.

Riding a trike like the Windcheetah SL can be very athletic. Andy Pegg is showing off by keeping his weight well to the inside, so that the machine is sliding hard - the stress to the outside tire is for real. The fastest way through a corner, however, is a smooth line, with the inside wheel feathered just short of lifting off the ground.

CHAPTER 15

Zzzwwaaammo!

Air is thick stuff. A cyclist moving at 20 mph displaces some 1,000 pounds of air a minute, a task that consumes about 85 percent of the rider's total energy output. The idea of improving performance by reducing aerodynamic drag dates from at least 1895, when a man named Challand built a recumbent bicycle in Belgium. In the period 1912-1933, conventional upright bicycles fitted with egg-shaped fairings set numerous speed records. But the proofs of performance that influenced history came between 1933 and 1938, when a relatively unknown Frenchman, Francois Faure, riding a fully faired recumbent bicycle built by Charles Mochet called a Velocar, shattered speed records

Velocar

for the mile and kilometer. The change these feats provoked, however, was negative: in 1938 the world governing body of cycle racing, the Union Cycliste Internationale (UCI), banned recumbent bicycles and aerodynamic devices from racing.

The lack of competitive incentive for new cycle designs, together with the rise of the motor vehicle into a dominant role in transport, canonized the safety bicycle. The evolution of cycles remained limited to detail improvements in safety bikes until the height of the American Bike Boom in 1974, when two academics in California, Chester Kyle and Jack Lambie, recognized the general need for a 'better bike': a personal vehicle faster, safer, and more convenient than the 1885 safety. They founded the International Human Powered Vehicle Association (IHPVA) in 1975 to stimulate the development of vehicles for land, water and air. In stark contrast to the stringent technical limitations imposed by the UCI, the IHPVA has but one rule: machines must use human power only, with no energy storage devices - otherwise, anything goes.

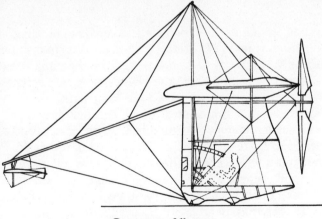

Gossamer Albatross

Machines built under IHPVA auspices have re-written the record books. The ages old dream of human powered flight is a reality many times over, with perhaps the most spectacular accomplishment the crossing of the English Channel in 1979 by Bryan Allen, pedaling Gossamer Albatross to scoop the $100,000 Kremer Prize. An IHPVA machine, Flying Fish, is the first successful human powered hydrofoil and holds the world record for speed on water. But land vehicles are the most popular and widespread portion of IHPVA activites. For over a decade, speed records have fallen one after the other. Pedaling all on their lonesome over level ground, people have exceeded 65 mph in a sprint, and covered more than 41 miles within an hour. The IHPVA's free rein for innovation has resulted in some very wild and wonderful creations, but recumbent designs are the mainstream. Collectively, they're known as human powered vehicles, or HPVs for short.

Broadly, an HPV is defined as any human powered vehicle not allowed to compete in UCI events. Because HPVs are pedal powered there is an automatic tendency to compare them with bikes. But bikes are - bikes. A wonderful, singular design refined and sharpened for over a century. HPVs are a new class of vehicles with different characteristics, in designs that are varied and very much in evolution.

Quest for Speed

The four central elements in the speed of an object through air are frontal area, smoothness, shape, and power. A recumbent cycle has about 20 percent less aerodynamic drag than a conventional upright bicycle. This is mostly due to reduced frontal area and a more streamlined shape. Things begin to cook properly when the flow of air is smoothed with a fairing (body shell). In comparison with an upright bike, a fully faired

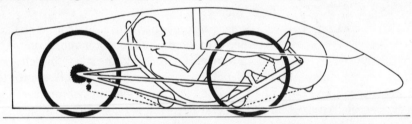

Vector

recumbent has up to 80 percent less aerodynamic drag, or 70 percent less energy consumption. It takes 375 Watts (0.5 horsepower) to maintain 30 mph on an upright bike, and only 150 Watts (0.2 horsepower) for the same speed in a fully faired recumbent.

From this point onward the physics of speed become a good bit more complicated. With the current crop of record breaking machines, shape is a major consideration that can overshadow frontal area, which is sometimes large. And then there's powerplant positioning; different configurations suit different purposes. But the bottom line is pretty clear: HPVs are the most efficient vehicles in the world. Per distance per weight carried they consume less energy than anything else going. Yes they are very fast. No solo UCI bike will ever see 65 mph on level ground, or more than 40 miles in an hour. But the key asset of HPVs, particularly as transportation, is their efficiency. A cyclist fit enough to be classed as an athlete will usually average around 18-19 mph on a racing safety bike. Riding 25 miles within an hour on such a bike is an accomplishment that rates genuine pride. In a good HPV an ordinary person in reasonable health can average 20 mph. If they train and become fit enough to output 0.25 horsepower, which most people can do, average speeds will start climbing toward 30 mph. In other words, in an HPV most people can achieve 25 miles within an hour, and on a regular bike most people cannot.

The fundamental requirement for greater efficiency and speed is a fairing that smoothes and eases the movement of air. In my book, an HPV is more specific than just non-UCI. It is a vehicle with a fairing that reduces aerodynamic drag. Most HPVs are based on recumbent cycle designs, but not necessarily so. Alex Moulton's AM upright bicycle, for example, has exceeded 50 mph fitted with a full fairing.

Hardware

What is a good HPV? The evolutionary history has two strands: competition and street. The first consistently successful HPV in both speed trials and road races was the Vec-

tor, a low-slung recumbent tricycle mounting a smooth, tear-drop shaped body shell. It looked futuristic and fast - and was. In 1980 it set a world speed record at Ontario Speedway of 58.89 mph that stood unbroken for many years. The Vector was also an able contender on road racing circuits. Demonstration runs

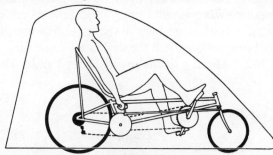

Bluebell I

on public roads produced point to point average speeds that had many people speculating on when they too could buzz the highway patrol on their way to work. By media furor the future had arrived. But although the Vector was offered for sale to the general public it was not a practical street machine. It cost $10,000, rider comfort was poor, both vision and visibility were severely limited, and there was no provision for basics such as lights and signals. It was a racing machine, built to break records and explore new ground in knowledge.

Enter street. Recumbent bicycles were an early line of development for street usable machines that could be produced inexpensively. The configuration is more or less a tandem rearranged to seat one person, and building does not involve untoward

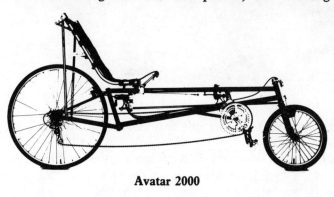

Avatar 2000

problems for anyone familiar with bikes. Building a good recumbent trike, however, is a demanding business that only a few people have accomplished successfully. Essentially, the recumbent bicycle is in-line and does not have to endure any more stress than an ordinary bike. A trike, however, is subject to high lateral forces. The design must be strong, and right: the nuances that give good handling, for example, are more slight and critical than with a recumbent bicycle.

There were a number of people producing recumbent bikes, and yours truly was an early customer for a model designed by David Gordon Wilson, the Avatar 2000. Riding 0012, as she is called after her serial number, I became convinced that the machine could outcorner a Vector on a tight course. Derek Henden designed and built a fairing, the drivetrain was modified with cross-over gearing, and with Tim Gartside as engine we were away. At the 1982 IHPVA Championships in California, Tim and the machine christened Bluebell trounced the Vector, setting a world record bicycle speed of 51.9 mph in the process.

Key to Bluebell's success was Derek Henden's fairing, a three dimensional flow shell shaped like a shark's fin. With a large side area it was a handful in a cross-wind. It was an airfoil: stalled when upright, but given to flight when heeled over in a corner. But the shape was fast and slippery, and the semi-upright riding position good for power.

Bluebell was the first bicycle recumbent to pip the Vector, but other builders had already been working with the design for some time. It wasn't long before Tim Brummer's X-2 Lightning floated by at 57 mph plus. Then the $18,000 DuPont prize for

Bluebell II

the first HPV to crack 65 mph fell to Gardiner Martin's Easy Racer Gold Rush, ridden by Fast Freddy Markham.

The really fast HPVs tend to have ultra-smooth body shells made from exotic materials like Kevlar and carbon fiber. But a significant advantage of the bicycle recumbent is the shape takes easily to a fabric fairing. These are inexpensive and of course very

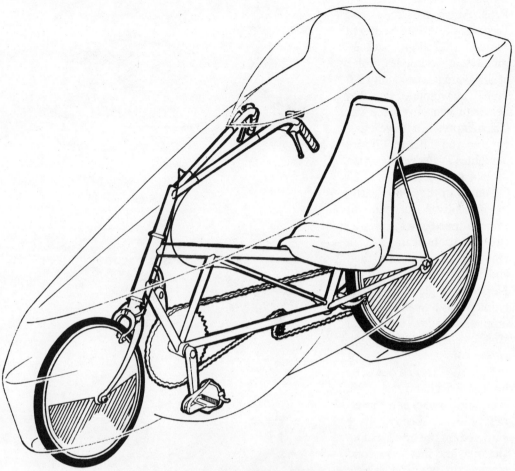

Gold Rush - first HPV to break 65 mph

lightweight. Such machines are still very quick, and deadly on roads and for circuit racing. Relatively at least, bicycle recumbents are readily available, at prices comparable to ordinary bikes. It's a natural process to start with a bare bike, and then gradually streamline it more and more.

Breaking land speed records has become a specialized activity. The push past 65 mph, for example, took place in the mountains at an altitude of around 8,000 feet, where the air is thinner. Mounting such projects is a lot of hard work, and expensive. The IHPVA has increasingly focused on the development of street machines through practical vehicle competitions, circuit racing, and point to point races on open roads held in compliance with traffic laws.

The pattern that has emerged from events in Europe and America is that fully faired bicycle recumbents have the edge for speed, but only if conditions are good. If the weather becomes dirty, or there are bad cross-winds, the faired tricycles have a much higher survival rate. And there often isn't a lot in the difference. Pete Penseyres rode the Lightning X-2 from Seattle to Portand in 7 hours and 30 minutes, covering 192 miles at an average speed of 25.6 mph. The winner of the 1986 Seattle to Vancouver race was Chico Expresso, a tricycle that covered 166 miles in 7 hours 5 minutes at an average speed of 23.4 mph.

Fourth in the 1986 Seattle to Vancouver race at an average speed of 21 mph was the Windcheetah SL, a recumbent tricycle designed and built by Mike Burrows of Norwich, England. Popularly known as a Speedy, it was originally made as a practical street vehicle for training riders of record attempt machines. It turned out to be both practical and fast, with exceptional agility and cornering ability. Speedys have garnered many road racing victories, and first and second placings in practical vehicle competitions.

In the immediate future, bicycle recumbents will be the main line of development. They are inexpensive, easy to build, and fast. I think it will

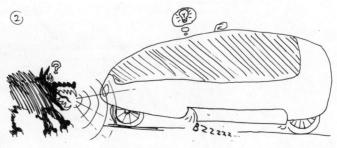

From an HPV enthusiast in Poland

be possible to have faired versions that are practical for street use. In the longer term, tricycle HPVs will prove to be the more versatile all round design for practical vehicles. If you like, the bicycle HPVs will be equivalent to racing safeties, and the tricycle HPVs equivalent to touring safeties.

But Beware! HPV evolution is very much in progress. I know of at least two ultra-low slung trikes in development that have every chance of busting speed and distance records right, left, and center. Anyone who says that a trike or a bike is the final answer is just asking to have to eat their words.

What's It Like?

It depends on what you are riding. Broadly, in comparison with safety bikes, recumbent cycles have superior comfort, braking, handling, and speed. Fully faired HPVs are more like cars.

Comfort

The recumbent position is very relaxed and kind to the body. There's no problem with saddle sores or chafing. In long wheelbase models the ride is like a tandem bicycle - comfortable. In short wheelbase models, bumps are felt with sharp awareness, but there is no harsh shock rammed up the spine. The chest cavity is open and free to breathe fully. There's no pain in the neck, back, arms, or hands. Riding a supine recumbent is literally relaxing in a comfortable chair.

Weather

On a bare recumbent you've got the same exposure to weather as on a regular bike. In an HPV like the Speedy, the weather is immaterial. I normally wear shorts and a shirt. If the temperature falls to freezing, I add another light shirt. If it gets really cold, say below 20° F, I wear a light jacket and full length pants. In the opposite direction, on warm days I open up the convertible top. It can be set in stages: fully closed, half open, or completely open. If it rains I zip up and put a little hood over my head. On a hot day this can get you warm, but not as much as you might imagine. Overall, temperatures inside the Speedy seem to be fairly consistent. Like a car, you jump in and go. If you need more air and coolness, you open a vent scoop, and if you want to be warmer, you zip up.

Stability and accidents

This depends on the vehicle. Long wheelbase recumbent bicycles tend to be light at the front wheel and wag back and forth in cross-winds. There's no real problem, just more movement. Shorter wheelbase bikes like the Lightning P-38 are better balanced and don't have this difficulty. In any case, if something goes amiss it is easy to put down both feet. The prototypical example is a stick through the spokes of the front wheel. A safety bike will cartwheel and send the rider to the ground face first. A recumbent bike will just lock up and come to a stop, landing the rider feet first. If a recumbent bike skids in a corner, there is not far to fall. Most recumbent bikes have wide seats, which tend to bear most of the impact.

Trikes such as the Speedy are completely stable, and this is very handy in heavy traffic. It's also great when you want to go: close to the ground on three wheels that c.n be drifted through a corner, I'm not worried about hitting a pot-hole and destroy-my face, or skidding on an oil patch and collecting strawberry burns or broken bones. A Speedy can be rolled, but only if you really foul up. If you overcook a corner, then by keeping your body weight properly distributed the Speedy can be made to understeer and scrub off speed. I'm one of those people who prays for snow. Sliding through a corner in a plume of crystals isn't just fun, it's ecstacy.

In a proper crash a bare recumbent is a better bet by far than a safety bike, and an HPV is simply another dimension. I've seen lots of crashes in competition and at record attempts, and only rarely has the rider suffered more than a dusting and minor grazing. I'll never forget watching a Speedy crash in a round the houses (criterium) race on London streets. It was an early, development model that was inclined, in a corner, to suddenly tilt up onto two wheels and arrow off in a straight line. In this incident, the luckless rider careened across the road, caromed off a parked car, mounted a 6 inch high curb, hit a parked mountainbike, tossing it well into the air, and finished by smashing into a fence of iron railings. Damage to rider: one cut on the shin needing one stitch. Damage to machine: none. Both were off to see the sights of the town within the hour.

An HPV with a body shell is remarkably safe. At San Diego, Tim Gartside in Bluebell hit a steel pole head-on at well over 40 mph. The machine did a mid-air flip and disintegrated; the fairing was made out of a material essentially similar to McDonald's hamburger boxes. Bluebell came to rest with the forks and head tube torn out by the roots and the fairing shredded to bits. Tim walked away with a few grazes. It's a safe bet that on a safety bike, he would have been critically injured or dead. Nor was the incident a fluke. Richard Crane did exactly the same thing in a later edition of Bluebell, when he hit a stout wooden post head-on at 45 mph while going for the hour record. Like Tim, Dick walked away with a few grazes.

Visibility

The most common objection to recumbents and HPVs is that they are unsafe in traffic because they are too low to be seen. This simply isn't so. Recumbents and HPVs attract a lot of attention. The Speedy, for example, is far more noticeable than any car, however fancy or expensive. For pulling crowds it can cut a $100,000 Ferrari dead. It's got real spirit. More to the point, in traffic other road users notice and make room for the Speedy far more readily than for a safety bike. It's not just that the Speedy is unusual. To other road users, it is a proper vehicle that looks and behaves like a car, and they give it a lot more respect than a bike. I use the Speedy nearly every day in traffic, in no small part because it is the best and safest machine for the job.

There are a few rules. On a bare recumbent you've got more or less the same restrictions as on a regular bike. You don't go snaking through stopped traffic, asking to be caught by an opening door. You're careful when trailing behind a vehicle. On a long wheelbase machine, you nose out carefully at intersections, as you cannot stand up and have a good look at what's coming. If it is a full HPV that takes time to exit, you watch carefully for any idiot in front who might reverse suddenly. This is the one genuine disadvantage of an HPV in traffic, and going through an E. A. Poe routine just once is enough to make you permanently wary of the problem.

Motorists

Most motorists are charmed by recumbents and HPVs. They think the idea is great and cheer you on. A few cluck mournfully and suggest that you are incredibly foolish. A very few are aggressive. The main factor seems to be status. The cars that feel compelled to blow off the Speedy at a traffic light are usually cheap models with go faster paint stripes, Porches, and BMWs. They sometimes get a rude surprise on the next corner.

HPVs are new, and most of the people riding them have had experience at racing and mixing it up at close quarters. When a car bullies and tries to shunt them to one side, they usually push right back. It is not perhaps the sensible thing to do, but a machine like the Speedy is a lot better for an argument with a car than a safety bike. We've had incidents where HPVs have been deliberately hit from behind and then pushed down the road at high speeds. The amazing thing, so far at least, is that the machines have survived unscathed.

Agility

I can't decide which is more fun down a twisting country lane: a recumbent bike or a recumbent trike. Like a regular bike, a recumbent bike banks over. The difference is, you can keep on pedaling, and this gives a completely different dimension of control. On a regular bike, you set up a line for the corner and then ride it out, for better or worse. On a recumbent bike, if you need more bank, you back off the power. If you've room to spare, you screw on the juice.

A trike is stable, and extremely agile. It seems clear that recumbent bikes are awfully fast in corners. I've never seen anything as razor sharp as Fast Freddy Markham whizzing around a road racing circuit on a fabric faired Easy Racer. But then again, I've never seen anyone as good as Andy Pegg in a Speedy. A lot depends on the rider. This said, more than once I've watched bikes and Speedys go into a corner, and seen a bike go down while the Speedys survived.

Summarily, you have to work hard to overcook a recumbent bike in a corner, but they can go down. A trike with a good center of gravity is incredibly agile and a great survivor - but beware off-camber corners!

Braking

A recumbent will outstop a safety bike by a wide margin. You can just put out the anchors for all they are worth. And if they are real stoppers, like the twin drum brakes on the Speedy, then you can stop on a dime. It doesn't do to rely on your brakes to get you out of trouble. Nevertheless, the immense, car-class stopping power of recumbents is a great boost to confidence and morale.

Speed

"How fast can you go?" is a question I get at every other traffic light. The answer is: "Depends on the rider."

Recumbents are faster than regular bikes. They've been whipping them since the 1930s, and that's why recumbents are banned from UCI sanctioned races. Overall, a recumbent is about 10 percent faster than a safety bike. But the point of real advantage is not the speed reached at maximum effort, but rather the speed attained for a given effort. Crudely, 25 mph on a recumbent takes 20 percent less power than 25 mph on a safety bike. In practical terms, for a given effort, the average speed of a recumbent is 1 to 2 mph faster than a safety bike.

HPVs are like recumbents, only much more so. A lot depends on the machine in question. At 30 mph, a machine like Bluebell is just loafing. I doubt if it needs more than 30 percent of the power to drive a safety bike at the same speed; 125 Watts, or about 0.16 hp should do it. For a machine like the Speedy, I'd guess around 175 Watts of 0.23 hp. But it is probably more relevant to answer the question in real life terms.

If I am just going somewhere in the Speedy, it will be at 18 to 19 mph. Any good club rider on a safety bike - and there are many who are curious - can pull up alongside. If I make a slightly more solid effort, the speed notches up to around 21 mph, a rate that I can keep up comfortably for a fair time. The good club rider is now working, oh, noticeably hard. What happens next depends on the distance, and the people involved. Basically, a very good club rider can give me an argument - for a while. If there are hills, they have an advantage. But I'll eventually wear them down. In the normal way, I let them get a little bit tired and then press a bit harder and drift away. They've had enough and since strictly speaking, there has been no race, honor is intact. It's best not to go for sprints, because you're talking speeds of 30 mph or more - on level ground. I've been pulled over by the police a number of times. Downgrades run 35 to 40 mph, and I've been clocked at 55 mph on a steep mountain descent.

The thing to appreciate is that as HPV riders go, I'm not very fast. The interesting point of comparison is that riding a good, lightweight safety bike, I can average 15 to 16 mph, sometimes 17 mph, on a regular urban commuting journey. In the Speedy I can do the same trip at an average speed of 20 mph. And watch what happens when I get my hands on a street version of Bluebell!

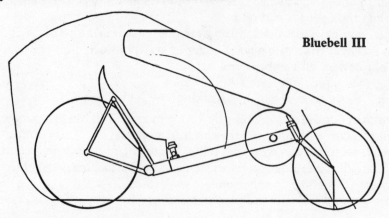

Bluebell III

Power

The foregoing is a frame for the next point. In a recumbent the back is braced, and it is possible to generate much greater thrust and power than with a safety bike. If you want to screw it on for a moment, you can scoot like you wouldn't believe. But the high thrust is strictly momentary. In a recumbent you have none of the advantage of your body weight helping to press down the pedals. It's all down to your legs, and the cadence range for effective power is narrower than with a safety bike. You have to be able to spin, and use gears precisely.

An HPV is a great old man's machine. What you do is ram in the thrust and whiz the thing up to speed, and then jump the gears to a big ratio that you slowly trundle, taking a rest from the burst that got you going. Hardly any effort is needed to conserve momentum.

Hills are supposed to be the weak point for recumbents and HPVs. Depends on the hill, the conditions, and the technique. There isn't that much difference between a safety and a recumbent of equal weights. With the recumbent you must spin. Beware of recumbents that weigh more than 35 lbs, they are just as much hard work as a safety bike of that weight.

With an HPV, there is usually a weight penalty. The works racing Speedy dresses out at 35 lbs, complete with fairing. My street Speedy when equipped with lights, batteries, tools, etc., must go for 55 lbs. If it is a long, long hill I simply settle down and winch my way up. But in the normal course of events the hills are fairly short, or the grade is moderate, and the aerodynamic advantage is still considerable. A short hill can simply be hit with a surge, but a long grade needs consistent delivery of a measured amount of force. What it comes down to is, if I had to climb all through the Alps I'd beg, borrow, or steal the works Speedy. Otherwise, for flat, undulating, or mildly hilly terrain, the aerodynamic efficiency of even a fairly heavy HPV more than offsets the penalty of extra weight.

An HPV for You?

I'm sold many times over on HPVs. Note I didn't say recumbent. You start with a recumbent and learn how it goes before setting it up as an HPV. Machines like the Lightning P-38, Easy Racer, and Windcheetah SL are incredible fun as bare recumbents. But if you're going get into this business, you might as well go all the way. It's only when you have a full fairing that the performance, weather, and safety advantages really come on stream.

I think perhaps the most basic point to appreciate is that an HPV is not comparable to an ordinary bike. It is a personal vehicle, with utility, performance, and safety standards that no upright bicycle can emulate. If you make any comparison, it should be with cars. You shouldn't run an HPV on public roads, for example, unless you can drive a car or motorcycle with reasonable skill.

If you travel 100 miles to and from work every day, or need to climb 5,000 feet at a clip, an HPV isn't much of a bet as transportation. If you are one of the vast majority who take little journeys here and there at distances of 10 miles or less, usually by yourself, then an HPV is an answer that takes a lot of beating. It's simple, quick, safe, easy to park, weatherproof, and gives you healthy, life-giving exercise. Cheap: it runs on milk and cornflakes or any other bio-digestable substances!

I believe that HPVs transform the whole concept of a personal vehicle. They are good for you, and they don't hurt anybody, or damage the environment. I feel good when I ride the Speedy, and proud that I'm the engine. The Speedy is my Icarus suit. I put it on, and I fly. The bottom line is a kind of fun that is really like sprouting wings. I don't want to overdramatize the thing, or make it seem easier than it is. You get out what you put in. But HPVs are the most efficient form of transportation on earth. Within the next 3 years a human being will ride America from coast to coast, entirely on pedal power, within 5 days. And when we see the 21st century, I think HPVs will be all over the place: little and big, solo and tandem, fast and sleek, slow and roomy, each suiting particular people and particular needs - Icarus suits!

Here is a shortlist of some machines I know about at this writing. No prices as they are likely to change. For more information, contact the International Human Powered Vehicle Association, P.O. Box 51255, Indianapolis, Indiana 46251. In Europe, The British Human Power Club, Sec. John Kingsbury, 22 Oakfield Road, Bourne End, Bucks SL8 5QR, England.

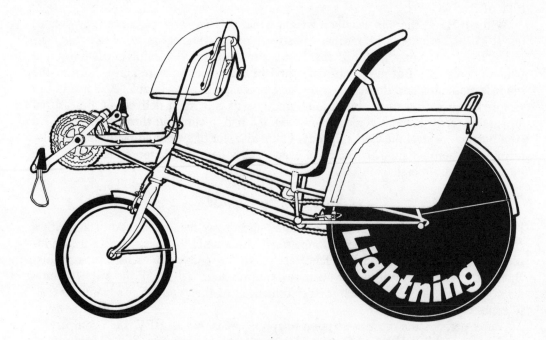

Lightning P-38

Recumbent bicycle, medium wheelbase (chainset above and slightly forward of front wheel axle). Available with a Zzipper windscreen fairing and streamlined panniers. Very able road machine. The full faired HPV Lightning X-2 has done Seattle to Portland at 26 mph average, and claims the low altitude speed record of 64.2 mph. Address: Brummer Engineering, 1500 E. Chestnut Ct., Lompoc, CA 93436.

Moulton AM-14

Upright safety bicycle, but 17 inch wheels allow fitting of full length Zzipper fairing. Very versatile, quick, and comfortable. Deadly in traffic. See Special Bikes and Trikes for more information.

Tour Easy and Easy Racer

Recumbent bicycle, long wheelbase. Upright handlebars. Optional Zzipper fairings in standard and full lengths. Self-build kits, complete bikes, custom framesets, and complete plans. Longest in the business. The full-bore Easy Racer Gold Rush and Fast Freddy Markham hold the world speed record of 65.48 mph. A must see. Address: Easy Racers Inc., P.O. Box 255, Freedom, CA 95019.

Trice

Recumbent tricycle. Weight approximately 45 lbs. Stable, enjoyable, and (relatively) inexpensive. Fully assembled. Address: Crystal Engineering, 13 Pound Crescent, Marlow, Bucks SL7 2BG, England.

Vanguard

Recumbent bicycle, long wheelbase. New machine, very similar to Avatar 2000, with underneath seat handlebars. Address: Ryan Recumbents, 58 Lyle Street, Malden, MA 02148.

Windcheetah SL

The Speedy! Recumbent tricycle. Weight approximately 35 lbs. Very agile and quick, winner of many practical vehicle contests and road races. Best all round street HPV in the world. Available only as a basic kit. Skilled metal machining and standard cycle components required to complete. Not a casual project, but within bounds if you are serious. Full body shell in fiber glass, fabric top available. Address: Burrows Engineering, Green Lane West, Rackheath, Norwich NR13 6LW, England.

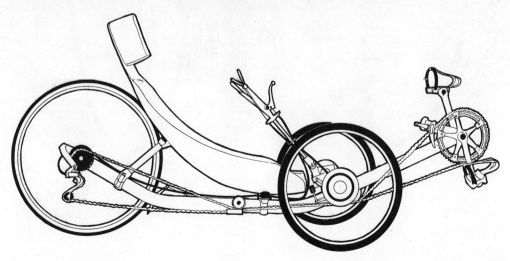

MOORE DEL.

CHAPTER 16

Racing

Bicycle racing is quite specialized and involved. Space and my own limited knowledge of the subject permit only the briefest comments and descriptions.

John Forester's *Effective Cycling* (MIT Press) contains much information of value to the racer. *The Complete Cycle Sport Guide* by Peter Konopka (EP Publishing) is detailed and highly regarded. *Bicycle Road Racing* by Edward Borysewicz with Ed Pavelka (Velo-News) is highly readable and filled with info from the man who led the US team to nine medals in the 1984 Olympics.

To participate in organized road racing you must join a club. Ask at your local bike shop for the one nearest you or write to the United States Cycling Federation, 1750 East Boulder Street, Colorado Springs, CO 80909, and they will advise you. Club level racing does not require a license, but sanctioned races require a United States Cycling Federation (USCF) license, and a hard shell helmet. You compete according to age, sex, and ability, so if you are a beginner do not worry about being trounced first time out - most of the riders will be fairly evenly matched. Some of the greatest bike riders in the world are little shrimps. The less weight to lug around, the better. Big people are not excluded either - on downhills they generally have the edge. What counts in the end is fitness - and heart. Bike racing is an extremely rigorous sport. In skiing, running, football, and most other sports, when you are finished you drop. On a bike a lot of weight is supported by the machine and only a small amount of energy is required to maintain balance. It is quite possible to run your body to the finish and beyond, so that when you stop you are unable to stand on your feet. Any serious racer has to keep fit with a year-round physical conditioning program.

The thing about riding as a racer (in Europe, a club rider) is that the business is riding, pure and simple. It's all down to you and a bike. You are welcome to start as a raw beginner. The clubs and training programs want as broad a base as possible, and only a very few people will evolve into top level competitors. But you are expected to work hard and develop whatever potential you've got. And as you move up the ladder, one of the many rewards is attaining a level of riding ability that is simply in another class.

The three basic types of USCF races are road, track, and cyclo-cross.

Road

Time trial - Individual or team rides against the clock over 10, 25, 50, and 100 mile courses, or rides for the greatest distance covered in 12 or 24 hours. Pure riding ability and stamina count the most. An increasingly popular variation are point-to-point races over fixed routes where you ride for the best time. Some of these are epic, such as the annual Race Across America (RAAM).

THE FINISH OF A RACE

Massed start - Everybody starts together, first human over the finish line wins. The course can be 10 miles, or 2,600, as in the Tour de France. Most single day events are between 50 and 100 miles for amateurs, and 80 to 180 for professionals. Races lasting 2 days or more are called stage races.

In road racing riders are pitted against each other, and the resulting shenanigans are sometimes incredible. Intelligence, strategy, trickiness, and psychology play an equal role with riding ability and strength. Teams work together to launch a strong teammate ahead of the pack to victory, and block opposition riders. In big races like the Tour de France bicycles collide and pedals jam into spokes. In Europe these races go on despite wars, revolutions, or anything else, and are the subject of intense popular interest.

A type of road race popular in America is the criterium. It is usually held on a closed circuit measuring less than 2 miles around, with sharp and narrow corners, over distances ranging from 25 to 62 miles. Very precise riding is needed to cope with the corners and the dense pack of riders created by the narrowness of the streets or road. Criterium bikes tend to have very stiff frames for quick handling, and a high bottom bracket so that pedaling can continue through the corners.

Cyclo-cross

Cross country races from point to point or around a course up to 16 miles in length, run either as a time trial or as a massed start. Courses feature steep climbs and descents, mud, thick woods, streams, and hurdles. Some sections are negotiated on foot. It is a rough sport, physically very demanding, with plenty of spills.

Track

The machine common to a wide variety of track events is the greyhound of bikes: an ultra-light frame with a short wheelbase; a fierce position with the saddle high and handlebars low; a single fixed wheel gear, with no brakes; and tires bonded to the rims with shellac to withstand the stresses of violent track maneuvers. There are no quick release hubs, gears, pumps, cables, etc., making these among the most lovely and functional of bikes.

There are many different kinds of track events. Here are a few:

Sprint - Usually a 1000 meter course with only the last 200 meters timed. Involves all kinds of tricky tactics and scheming. There are times when racers hold their bikes stock still while jockeying for position. *Behind* the leader and in his slipstream until the final dash is the favored winning position.

Pursuit - Two riders or teams start on opposite sides of the track and try to catch each other.

Time Trials - Against the clock, as in road racing.

Devil Take the Hindmost - Last man over the line every 2 or 3 laps is out.

Paced racing - Motorcycles are used as pacesetters for the riders, who stay as close as possible to the pacer's rear wheel so as to minimize wind resistance. Speeds up to 60 mph.

Madison - Two-person teams run in relays. Events run from 50 kilometers or 1 hour to 6 day races. Each team member runs one or two laps and then hands over to a teammate, literally throwing him by the seat of his pants or by a hand-sling. A very spectacular form of racing.

Off-road

Cyclo-cross is formal, and rather like ballet. Mountainbike racing is varied, and while very demanding at the top level, is open to riders of all ability grades. Many 'races' are a wonderful way to see incredible scenery, and even if you come in 545th place it can be an exciting and satisfying accomplishment. For information, contact the National Off-Road Bicycle Association (NORBA), 2175 Holly Lane, Solvang, CA 93463.

THE ROAD RACE

CHAPTER 17

Old Bikes

If you have a little spare space, antique cycles are interesting items to collect and restore. The early models were largely blacksmiths' creations and bringing them up to snuff is a feasible home workshop project. The last part of the 19th century was the heyday of innovation and experimentation in cycles, and many wonderful machines were produced. Some are illustrated in this book. A fascinating read is *King of the Road* by Andrew Ritchie (Ten Speed Press), which traces cycling history in social terms - for example, how the bicycle changed the role of women. Definitive information on hardware and restoration techniques is the forte of *Collecting and Restoring Antique Bicycles* by G. D. Adams (Tab Books). The Wheelmen, 1708 School House Lane, Ambler, PA 19002, is an organization devoted to old bikes, and if you are keen on the subject, The Southern Veteran Cycle Club, membership secretary Sue Duxbury, 42 Parkside Avenue, Winterbourne, Bristol BS17 1LX, England, publishes an engaging magazine *The Boneshaker*.

The best source for old bikes is grandfather's attic. Most machines already on the market are expensive. You need to find an old wreck mouldering in a field or root around in the junk shed of great Uncle Fred the bicycle dealer who unexpectedly kicked the bucket decades ago. What you find is usually a disheartening pile of rust, but it is surprising what elbow grease and rust remover can do.

By 1910 or so, cycle designs had fairly well settled down, and machines from this date onwards can be had for reasonable sums. Many are elegant and mechanically of very high quality.

American bikes made ca. 1930-1950 are now becoming classics. They're an awful lot of fun. Many were kind of mock motorbikes, with gas tanks, decorations, and ornate embellishments. Clear, deep chrome of bell-like quality. The great thing is that there are still a lot of them out there, just waiting to be discovered in barns, attics, and the like. Paying a lot of money in an antique shop for a rare veteran is nowhere near as exciting as making a 'find'. For info, subscribe to *Antique/Classic Bicycle News*, P.O. Box 1049, Ann Arbor, MI 48106, and John Lannis's newsletter, P.O. Box 5600, Pittsburgh, PA 15207.

TRIUMPH 10/C GENT'S 1941 SPORTS MODEL.

RENDEZVOUS

WHEN HITLER'S LITTLE GAME IS FINISHED !

CHAPTER 18

Accessories

Once upon a time, cycle accessories were cheap bits of decorative garb avoided by dedicated cyclists like the plague. There is still nothing quite so beautiful as a clean, no frills racing bike, but for many general functions such as commuting, touring, and utility use, the right accessories can make a crucial difference in efficiency and comfort. Make sure, however, that the item is well made and will stand up to the job, and expect to pay for it. Equipping a rider and a touring or commuting bike can easily equal the cost of the machine.

Anti-puncture products

Punctures are the bane of the cyclist, and not a year passes without the introduction of a new product claimed to eliminate the problem. Here's a brief rundown on the merits and demerits of each type.

1. Liquid sealants. These can be used with clinchers, and tubulars fitted with a two-piece Presta valve. Sealant adds about 2 oz to a tire. The tire is then theoretically proofed against direct punctures, as from a nail or thorn, but not against large slashes or cuts, as from glass. If the tire suffers a major blow-out the sealant can create a thorough mess. It can also put paid to a tire valve. After 6 months to a year the solvent evaporates, reducing the effectiveness of the sealant. In most cases, liquid sealants are more trouble than they are worth. But they do work. On trans-Sahara expeditions and other specific occasions, liquid sealants have drastically reduced the number of punctures. If you do high mileages on littered urban streets and are plagued by punctures, and are prepared to replace the inner tube/sealant combination every 6 months or so, then the product may be worth a try.

2. Tapes. These are thin ribbons of polymer plastic inserted inside the tire between the casing and the inner tube. Extraordinarily tough and pliable, they are effective at warding off punctures from ordinary broken glass, nails, and thorns, but cannot withstand a long, needle-sharp carpet tack. In conventional 1¼ and 1⅜ inch wide 55 to 75 psi tires, tape has little adverse effect on performance - e.g. ride comfort, rolling resistance, and weight. One difficulty, however, is that in some cases tapes can cause rather than prevent punctures.

This appears to happen when the tape changes position away from the central bead of the tire. When using tape it is important to deflate the inner tube once a month or so, and ensure that the tape is correctly positioned. It is also important to use the correct size of tape for a given tire. Problems seem to arise when tape intended for 1¼ inch tires is used in narrow section 1 and 1⅛ inch wide 100 psi tires. In any case, tape in a narrow section tire noticeably diminishes performance - so one might as well use a heavier, more durable 1¼ inch wide tire in the first place.

One advantage of tapes is that they can be re-used from tire to tire. When using tape, reduce air pressure by 5 psi as there will be less room inside the tire.

3. Belted tires. Tires with a belt of Kevlar or wire mesh embedded in the casing are effective at reducing the number of punctures, and do not have the problems of loose tapes. They seem to be the best way to go. They are expensive, and increase weight and rolling resistance, but they do work.

4. Solid inner tubes. No. Fitting a solid inner tube on to a rim is an event that you will remember, with pain, for the rest of your days. More fundamentally, solid tubes are very heavy and magnify the gyroscopic qualities of the wheel - it can be fatally difficult to change direction when riding. Definitely a case of once tried, never again.

5. Solid tires. One hundred percent puncture proof and also the stuff of a Homeric epic to mount on a rim. Once in place, they have such a rough ride that they will destroy the bike, if the rider is not broken first.

Various other anti-puncture nostrums claim to solve the problems of ride, mess or whatever. I don't believe in any of them. The pneumatic tire gives a nice ride and is lightweight. The simple route for more muscle against road litter, thorns, etc., is a heftier, stouter tire. I keep my tires fresh and inflated very hard, try to stay out of trouble, and carry a puncture kit and spare tube. I'd rather rely on myself than on a product that might or might not work. Most punctures can be mended in minutes. If it is pouring cats and dogs I use the spare tube and mend later, when warm and cozy.

Bells and horns

Little bells and horns are forever failing or being stolen. Freon horns contribute to noise pollution. Yelling is quick, reliable, and the most expressive.

Car racks

There are two types of car rack: rear mounted and top mounted. Rear mounted versions are inexpensive, usually quick to attach, and will hold two bikes. The machines tend to scratch each other, and to collect road grit. They are also vulnerable to other cars. Top mounted versions cost more, attach easily enough, and will hold up to six bikes safely out of harm's way. The LP range of car carriers are sturdily constructed, substantial products that perform efficiently, and include a Universal model for attaching to already existing car racks. An original type of bike carrier for cars is the Zulu. This consists of pads which rest on the roof and support the bicycle, and a system of straps to hold it in place. Capacity for two bikes. The whole thing can be set up with bikes inside of 4 minutes, and stores into a compact bag when not in use.

Carriers

The best sort of carrier depends on your needs. Straight handlebar bikes can use the traditional wicker basket, or a wire basket, and these are surprisingly versatile and useful. Avoid the type which uses a support rack where part of the rack rests on the head tube. When the handlebars are turned the support rack scratches the head tube.

A cloth slingbag or musette can go with you on and off the bike and will manage books, papers, and the odd container of milk. For bulkier loads use a knapsack or backpack. Most panniers are quick release and in this respect convenient, but have a zillion straps and drawstrings that are a major production when shopping.

If you like off-road riding, using a backpack keeps the bike limber and versatile. But on-road, and for long distances, it is better to have the bike do the carrying. The possibilities in panniers are numerous: large bags, small bags, itsy bitsy bags, bags that shrink or grow as required, and even bags that convert to backpacks. There are very neat panniers that double as briefcases when off the bike. And big folding basket panniers that will hold an amazing number of things when open. You really have to go along to a bike shop to see what will meet your requirements.

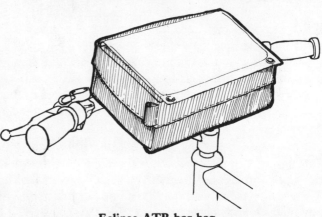

Eclipse ATB bar bag

A bike can be very handy for humping things, for example groceries home, or supplies to a base camp. Fine if you want to take giant watermelons to the beach. But when you want the machine as a bike, resist the temptation to take along the kitchen sink. Boil down everything to the absolute bare minimum, and then discard half of what is left. I like tidy items such as the Eclipse Mini-Wedge, which fits underneath the saddle and holds basics: tools, spare tube, windproof jacket, etc. Their ATB bar bag is another winner. Eclipse is very good on design, quality, and attention to detail. So are many other makers. The shops are filled with goodies. Avoid cheapo imports. Save up your pennies if you have to. Better one good, loyal bag than four that fall apart and become none.

Carrier racks can be very useful. For around town use, a lightweight alloy spring clip carrier rack such as the Pletscher will manage brief-

H. MATTHEWS'S
LUGGAGE CARRIER

Although only introduced this season, thousands are in use. Fits any Rover Safety or Cripper Tricycle.

---÷---

3/6 each, complete
Or Post Free, 4/-.

cases, parcels, and other moderate loads. Steel racks are a bit heavy but are strong, durable, and easily mended. Most people prefer a good quality alloy rack for both lightness and strength. Look for four-point fixing (drop-outs and seat stays), which is better than three-point (drop-outs and brake bridge). Some models are characterized as 'fast', meaning they are weaker. There's no point. The carrier is for loads anyhow, and might as well suffer a few extra ounces to do the job properly. I like the alloy Jim Blackburn racks that started the whole business because they pass a test that the maker would never sanction: carrying a person.

If you're going in for a lot of baggage, for example self-contained cycle camping, then use front and rear racks to even out the load. At the front, use a design such as the Blackburn Low Rider, that locates the panniers alongside the axle. The improvement this gives for handling is enormous.

New ways and means of carrying things on bikes come along rapidly. It's worth checking out the latest models in a bike shop. I'll repeat: quality counts. If you are short of ready green, bash together a rack from salvaged rubbish (discarded lawn chairs, etc.) and stick on an orange crate. Some people have gone around the world with no more.

Catalogs

Catalogs are fun for browsing and seeing what's around. Many are also full of useful tips and information. Whether you should buy mail order or from a shop is your affair. There are cases for both routes. But no fair to examine and inspect in a shop, and then buy mail order as cheaply as possible. Here are a few of many:

Bikecology, P.O. Box 3900, Santa Monica, CA 90403

Cycle Goods, 2735 Hennepin Avenue South, Minneapolis, MN 55408

Bike Nashbar, 4111 Simon Road, Youngstown, OH 44512

Performance Bicycle Shop, P.O. Box 2741, Chapel Hill, NC 27514

Mountain Bike Specialists, 1611 S. College Ave., Fort Collins, CO 80525

Child seats

Rear mounted moulded plastic seats will manage a child weighing up to 40 pounds, and should include a wrap-around spoke guard to prevent feet from tangling in the spokes. These seats will also neatly hold a boxful of groceries. Rear mounted seats are best used with a diamond frame bike; without the support of a crossbar (top tube) the extra weight of the child is likely to cause frame whip and unstable handling. Carrying a child is a good excuse for a mountainbike with robust tires and strong brakes. The mounting hardware for a child seat should be self-contained, and not depend on an existing carrier rack. Models are available that attach and detach in seconds.

One way around the handling problem caused by a heavy load at the rear is a seat which attaches directly to the crossbar and places the child between the adult's arms, thus creating a minimal adverse effect on bike handling. I've a really neat wicker model from China that just slips over the crossbar when needed.

Another route is a trailer. I've used the Cannondale Bugger to cart about two hefty children, and it is a wonder. Some people recoil at the idea of placing their nearest and dearest in a 'vulnerable' trailer. I feel that overall, the detrimental effect on bike handling of a rear mounted carrier creates a greater danger. Further advantages of a trailer are capacity up to one-half the adult rider weight (say 70 to 80 lbs, or two kids), and a quick release hitching which leaves the bike a proper bike when the trailer is not in use.

Once the child is about 4, he or she can ride the back of a tandem and join the fun via a junior pedaling attachment. Tandems, particularly good ones, can be quite expensive. However, although a child aged 8 or so can ride a bike on roads in company with adults, no great distances can be contemplated and the adults will have a full time job in the role of shepherd. Children need to be age 13 or so before they possess a sufficient attention span to be safe when cycling on roads, and the necessary strength to start dusting off the adults. Looked at as a means of family transport for 8 years or so, a tandem is economically a good investment, and a lot of fun. Plus, if you look after it, you will be able to re-sell for a tidy sum.

Clothing

Cycle clothing makes riding a bike a lot more fun. Take a simple thing like touring shorts. A good pair will have a lined crotch for comfort, and pockets with flaps and buttons so things don't get lost. Or pants. They'll be lined also, and fit snugly so that nothing flaps in the wind. Chill weather? There are models faced with nylon at the front to break the wind, but with regular fabric at the back for ventilation and ease of movement.

Cycle clothing is very functional, and also very pretty. A lot of people really get off on the designs and bright colors. But judge for yourself. All I want to say is that the stuff is really worth a look.

Computers

Cycle computers are interesting, and can be very useful for training. Some models have just a few functions, others more than you can count. Speed, distance, and elapsed time are the basics. Maximum speed reached is a nice function to have, because at the time you are usually too busy to be looking at the computer. Average speed as a computer function that can be called up en route is a handy way of checking pace. Perhaps the most useful function is cadence, the rate at which the cranks are spinning. You can experiment with different cadence rates and gears over known distances and terrain, and learn a lot about maximizing performance.

Cycle bags and cases

Large soft cloth bags and hard fiberglass cases designed to hold a bike with the wheels off are a great way to fox the anti-bike contingent when traveling by air, rail, or bus. Most will *not* accept a bike with fenders or a rack. Cloth bags are inexpensive, light, and versatile. You can cram them full of clothes and other gear. At journey's end once the bike is out, the bag can be folded up and carried on the back of the bike, or for a time, over your shoulder. Cloth bags are convenient, but stripping down and swaddling up a bike so that it has a fighting chance against baggage handlers can take a spell. Fiberglass cases are heavier and fairly expensive, but give much better protection for the bike. Very little preparation is necessary. There's usually a set of trundle wheels to help make the case more manageable in airports etc. At journey's end you need a place where the case can be kept.

Fenders

A requirement for tourists and people living in rain forests or at the end of muddy tracks. They do add a lot of air resistance, though, and if you want to go like the clappers and don't mind a strip of dirt up your spine once in a while, then leave them off. The short models are completely useless. Full length plastic mudguards are light, and easy to get on and off the bike (weekend racers, note), but eventually warp and fail. Much better are the ESGE and Bluemels chromoplastic models, which will stand years of abuse. Stainless steel and aluminum mudguards are durable, and offer a mounting point for lights and other gear, but tend to be noisy. This can be cured with undersealing paint (motor accessory shops).

Fairings

At 12 mph on a bike the retarding effect of mechanical drag and air resistance is about the same. Past 20 mph overcoming increased air resistance consumes 85 to 90 percent of pedaling effort. Put another way, in terms of air resistance 20 mph on a bike takes four times the effort required for 10 mph.

The Zzipper fairing is a clear, bubble-like windscreen that mounts to the brake lever hoods in a trice, and claims a 20 percent improvement in aerodynamic efficiency. The beneficial effect is more pronounced at higher speeds, and overall works out to allow the use of a gear 10 inches higher than would otherwise be the case. On long downhills the extra turn of speed is very evident and exciting and, because of the air pressure on the screen, bike handling is actually somewhat steadier. The main drawback is vulnerability to cross-winds, and a large lorry overtaking at speed will put a Zzipper equipped bike out of track by about 12 inches instead of the more usual 6 inches. On a very gusty day you will want to leave it off the bike.

The Zzipper fairing is useful for fending off rain and snow, and helping to keep the rider warm in cold weather. It is the most effective out on the open road; aerodynamic efficiency is not of great moment in stop-and-go town riding. If you often carry your bike up and down stairs, having a Zzipper aboard can make matters awkward. However, it really does mount and dismount within seconds, and on long journeys allows greater distances for noticeably less effort.

Glasses

For urban riding a pair of glasses will spare grit in the eyes, and at speed in the country eliminate burning of the eyes by the wind. This latter seems to be personal: wind causes eye discomfort in some people, and in others, not. But if your commuting route includes heavily trafficked roads, or blustery, dirt raising weather, then glasses are a definite aid to avoiding discomfort. Plain, untinted glasses are available for those who do not want to jaundice their view of the world. Look for glasses that ride clear of the face, to help minimize condensation problems, or that embody an anti-fog element.

Gloves

Over the years I've come to regard gloves as essential. Cycling gloves are fingerless, with ventilated mesh backs and padded leather palms. The padding helps to prevent numb hands from pinched nerves, and affords some protection in the event of a spill.

For winter riding there are full finger gloves made with Gore-Tex or other materials that are wind- and waterproof, but that allow your hands to breathe.

Handlebar tapes

There's quite a dazzling range of handlebar tapes available these days, and if you are at all cosmetically inclined, you should drop by a good bike shop and check out the possibilities. From the functional standpoint of comfort, if your hands numb easily, different tapes offer various degrees of padding to help insulate against road shock. Plastic and cloth tapes are generally cheap and nasty, although they are all that is required on a no-frills racing bike. The exception is Benotto tape, which comes in an outrageous range of colors, and is favored by many top professional riders. A better grip and a range of colors is to be found with suede and cork type finish tapes. For more padding, Bike Ribbon micro-cell strips in a range of plain and metalized colors, and for the ultimate in comfort, foam sleeve Grab-Ons. These are a popular item, and go for the real McCoy. There are a lot of imitation Grab-Ons around, and most of them are distinctly inferior in performance and durability. The style minded may favor leather sleeves, which richly deserve the three full pages of instructions on getting them aboard a bike.

Helmet

In most fatal bicycle accidents the injury is to the head. Even a drop of 2 feet onto a hard surface is enough to fracture the skull. Wear a helmet whenever you cycle. It's inconvenient. So is not being able to think or talk because your head has been pounded into jelly.

A helmet must protect against impact, and simultaneously avoid frying up brain matter through lack of ventilation. Cycling is warm work, and climbing hills while wearing a helmet on even a temperate day can leave you awash in perspiration. (On a long, slow climb, you can take it off.)

The classic cycling 'helmet' consists of a network of padded leather strips, and is great for fresh air but of little use when piling head first into a brick wall or parked car. The best protection is provided by hard shell helmets with a shock-absorbing liner or suspension system. But don't be led down the garden path by sales pitches stressing impact resistance and performance in laboratory tests. Of course the thing must work. But an accident is a one-time proposition that may or may not go according to script. At any level of protection you are

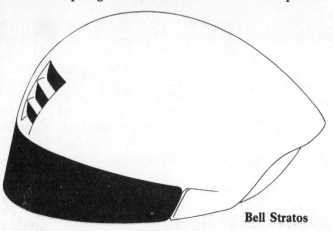

Bell Stratos

still taking your chances. The more basic requirement is that a helmet is on your head in the first place. For this, it must fit snugly and be comfortable.

A snug fit is essential for effectiveness. A loose helmet can do some nasty work in an accident. Most good models have sizing pads or similar means of customizing fit. As for comfort, this is a factor that varies from person to person. For example, I cycle very warm and even in mid-winter my helmet is an open design Skid-Lid. Other people need earmuffs and an extra wool cap. If you perspire easily and tend not to need a lot of clothes when active, pay careful attention to ventilation. One of the most popular open design models is the Bell V-1 Pro (the Skid-Lid is no longer available).

Many people object to using a helmet while cycling. They think it looks foolish, or want to maintain freedom, simplicity, and contact with fresh air. In most cycling accidents it is only the cyclist who is injured or killed. So the wearing of a helmet is largely a matter of personal choice, in which the pleasure of 'freedom' and other intangibles must be weighed against the prospect of death or disablement.

Calculating that prospect is not simple. Children cycle the fewest miles but have the greatest number of accidents, and cyclists on minor rural roads are in less danger than their urban counterparts. There is a statistical case, if one wants to make it, for saying that children and urban and racing cyclists are well advised to wear helmets, while adult touring cyclists are at relatively little risk.

Statistics have none of the enduring imperishability of a tree or stone curb with which your head has come into contact. They do not bleed, talk funny, or spend 6 months in hospital. Some of the people that this has happened to were among the most experienced cyclists around. All too often the accident was in no way their fault.

Initially, wearing a helmet is inconvenient, and can make you feel foolishly over-cautious. I've used helmets for years now, and the only time I feel odd is when I ride without one. There was a great billboard poster around for a while. It showed a man in a wheelchair and the caption read: 'I didn't wear a seatbelt because it was inconvenient.'

Kickstand

A kickstand adds a lot of weight for very little useful function. There is almost always something against which a bike can be leaned. A lightweight cure for the bike falling over because of front wheel movement is a parking brake, which can be made from a clothes pin or other handy bit, and jammed into the brake lever when required. A device specifically for this purpose is the Blackburn Brakestopper.

Lights

Adequate cycle lighting presents a whole series of problems for which there is no single perfect answer. The two basic types of lighting systems are battery and generator.

Generators take power off the wheel, thus increasing pedaling resistance. There is more hardware, wires can snag and break, and the system is permanently attached to the bike. Underway the lights are bright and strong, but unless a storage battery is fitted, they go out when you stop. They also tend to blow out bulbs on fast downhills, although this can be cured by fitting a zener diode to bleed off excess current. Some systems have this feature as standard. Generator lights are initially expensive, but cheap to run.

Bottle generator

There are two types of generators: bottle, which runs on the tire sidewall, and bottom bracket, which runs on the center tread. The bottom bracket models are effective, and have less drag than the bottle type, but get dirty easily and slip in wet weather. No problem if you are a sunshine area cyclist and enjoy consistent attention to keeping the generator clean and lubricated. If you cycle a lot in wet or dirty conditions then while there are various remedies and incantations that will keep a bottom bracket generator going, you are better off with a bottle generator. These are noisier and have more resistance than bottom bracket models, but are more reliable. The idea is to have the thing work when required, and these days people are going for bottle generators and lamps with bright halogen bulbs.

Bottom bracket generator

Standard battery lights are generally not as powerful as generator lights, but are convenient. They stay on when you stop and have no wires or other bits to snag. They can be got on and off the bike easily. This is handy for map reading and roadside repairs, and for other people who happen to have need of a light - it's rare to go through a winter season on just one set of battery lights.

If you ride mostly in town and do not want to lumber your bike with additional weight when not needed, then battery lights will probably be best. The French WonderLites are not so great for seeing, but are readily visible to other road users, and the mounting brackets are versatile. This allows you to easily get the lights up high, where they are properly visible. Set the front beam so that it goes out level, for maximum visibility to motorists. Mounting a lamp on the fork blade casts a pool of light that is good for seeing the road surface ahead, but not so hot for visibility to other road users. At the

The "Microphote" Lamp.

"Silver" King of the Road.

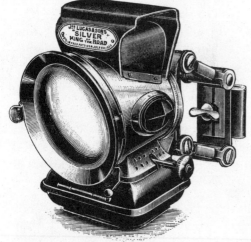

With Silvered Mirror Reflector

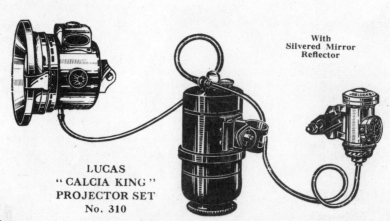

LUCAS
"CALCIA KING"
PROJECTOR SET
No. 310

We make Light of our Labour

KING OF THE ROAD

KING OF THE ROAD

back, the reflector should be low, and the lamp high. A further danger of mounting on forks or stays is that the brackets can loosen and twist the light into the spokes. This has caused some nasty accidents.

I've found that the best combination of economy and power is with specialized rechargeable 6 or 12 volt battery systems. These tend to have a bit of weight, but a lot of moxie. Optional generators are available as a power source when touring. Three good names are Ed Kearney, Bicycle Lighting Systems, P.O. Box 1457, Falls Church, VA 22041, Velo-Lux, 1412 Alice St., Davis, CA 95616, and Brite Lite, P.O. Box 1386, Soquel, CA 95073. You have to keep track of what you are doing with this kind of equipment, but the results are worth it.

A trick favored by mountainbikers is a helmet mounted light that can be directed exactly where needed: down by the wheel when negotiating tricky sections, up and forward for general information, to the side for sign reading, and so on. A halogen beam model called the Cycle Ops is offered by Ibis Cycles, P.O. Box 275, Sebastopol, CA 95472.

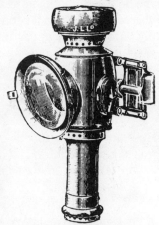

Any lighting system is capable of failing without notice. A second back-up light of some sort is essential. The French Matex light combines a white front and red rear, weighs only 5 ounces, and straps to an arm or leg. Because it is moved around a lot, it is very visible. It's also a handy general light for map reading, camping, etc. It's a sensible complement to a generator system that does not have a storage battery to power the lights when the bike is halted. Much more effective as an eye-catcher, however, is the Belt Beacon, a high intensity light which flashes 60 times a minute, and which can be attached to belt or bike. Research has shown that blinking high intensity lights are the best means of making cyclists visible to motorists.

Lucas candle lamp

Some people object to high intensity lights. One argument is that the need for paying attention rests with the motorist. Another is that high intensity lights can startle a motorist and make them slow down! In some states it is illegal to fasten a flasher light to the bike, but not to the person.

As any study of cycling accident statistics will reveal, the problem at night is to survive. Bicycle lights are diminutive. In cities and towns they are easily lost in the welter of traffic lights, street lights, and neon signs. Out in the country the problem is speed:

a car coming up from behind may be doing 70 mph to your 10 mph. That's an 88 feet per second speed differential, and if the visible range of your rear lights is 300 feet or less, it is under the distance required for a car to stop (315 feet). In short, if the motorist blinks and rubs an eye, or turns for a casual quick glance at a passenger, just for a second or two at the wrong moment, you can be wiped out. A high intensity flasher light is visible from a good distance and may indeed make a motorist slow down, this is exactly what you want. The risk of a fatal accident is nearly four times greater under conditions of darkness. The reason is that motorists do not see cyclists.

Many cyclists think they can be seen when in fact they cannot. They are there, panting away, moving around the place, well in sight, and cannot understand how anyone could fail to see them. But that is exactly what happens.

Fred DeLong took the trouble to replicate a series of car/bike accidents. He used the actual vehicles, equipment, and clothing involved in the original accident, or duplicates in identical condition, at the same location and times of day. In nearly every instance, and despite the use of regulation cycle lights in some cases, the problem was that the motorist could not see the cyclist, *even knowing that the cyclist was there.* Other experiments of cyclists and motorists approaching each other confirm that cyclists think they are visible long before motorists actually see them.

Carbide lamp

Cycling at night is dangerous. The many, many people who do it with no lights at all, in dark clothes, might act otherwise if they understood how closely they are tempting serious injury or death. A little bit of visibility is not good enough. The only sensible way to cycle at night is looking like a Christmas tree gone berserk. See also the reflectors entry in this chapter for more information.

Nail pullers or flint-catchers

These are small half-loops of wire that ride just above the tire and brush off shards of broken glass, pebbles, and other nasty things. Most effective with tubular and narrow section HP tires, and a significant challenge to fit if you use fenders.

Odometer

In the economy version these are little mechanical gizmos ticked over by the spokes. Distance is a function also usually included in electronic speedometer/computers (see separate entry).

Pumps

I long ago tired of fending off little urchins who filch equipment, of seeing expensive aluminum barrel pumps dented and therefore made useless, and of pumps constantly falling about the place while carrying a bike up and down stairs. I keep a large workshop pump at home, which inflates tires with magnificent efficiency, and carry a short pocket model that will serve for emergencies. For touring, however, you will need a decent pump. One of the very best is the Zefal Preset, with a self contained pressure regulator.

A workshop pump will include a pressure gauge, but its readout is likely to have only a passing affinity with reality. For accurate work with modern high pressure tires - essential for peak performance - use a separate tire pressure gauge.

You may also want to possess a tiny Presta/Schrader adaptor, which allows a Presta tire valve to be inflated with a garage air line. If you use this, be very careful; cycle tire pressures are high, but the volume of air is small, and only a moment's inattention is required for the whole thing to blow to smithereens. Personally, I frequently have the opposite problem, i.e. a Schrader valve and only a Presta type pump.

The
HYDROMAC
(R. g.)
**UNIVERSAL
SMOCK
for LADIES**
(as Illustrated).

' *Klossie used it as her only waterproof on our cycling trip to Venice and back, just concluded; and it kept her by far drier and more cosy than any waterproof she has ever had before.*"

Raingear

The kind of raingear you use will depend on conditions in your area. Some places are given to frequent mist and light drizzles. In others, when it rains it is for 3 days non-stop. If you only need light protection, more to ward off chill than to stay strictly dry, then a light nylon windbreaker will fit tidily under the saddle and always be available if needed. One trick if you are caught out is to use a large garbage bag, tearing holes for your head and arms. An ordinary shopping bag will do as a bonnet for your head.

The classic cycling cape drapes over the shoulders, back and handlebars, allowing air to circulate up from underneath. Also circulated is road spray from your tires, and those of other vehicles. This kind of garment is as outmoded as the Dodo bird, although for reasons of simple economy capes still have many adherents.

The problem when cycling in the rain is to keep away wet from both without and within. Conventional waterproofs that seal out the rain also seal in body perspiration, and of the two types of drenching, the former is preferable. The answer is a breathable fabric such as Gore-Tex that prevents large water molecules from coming in, but lets out the smaller molecules of perspiration vapor.

Be sure to buy garments made for cycling. Those made for hiking are too baggy and long and short in the wrong places. A cycling jacket should have long sleeves with adjustable wrist closures, and a long back. Detachable hoods are always missing when you need them, I much prefer the kind that live in a little zip pouch, ready at the moment. Make sure the hood is compact enough so that your vision is not impaired when you turn your head, but large enough to cover a helmet if you use one. (Helmet and hood is very effective. The helmet keeps the hood from touching your skin and becoming all clammy. If the helmet has a visor, you can tilt your head so the visor keeps the rain out of your eyes. Relatively, at least, you'll be quite comfy.)

Ride All Day Long in Slashing Rain!

NECK COMFORT
STRAP & BUCKLE
NON-STICKY PATENT FINISH
THUMB LOOPS
ALL LEG COVER. 126" min.

8/9

Popular Yellow
Quality.. .. 5/11
Leggings .. 4/11
Sou'wester .. 1/9

Pants need to be cut with room for knee movement, and be large enough to fit over other clothes. I prefer the kind that have a full front held up with shoulder straps.

A full size cycling rainsuit is a fairly substantial item. It's fine when touring but something of a pain when riding around in town or off on a tear. Around town I usually leave it at a plain Gore-Tex fabric jacket. Off on a tear it may be a specialized shirt and pants with waterproof panels at the front to keep off the worst of any rain and wind. There are many interim points between a full suit and a converted garbage bag; to case them out call by a good bike shop.

Rearview mirror

Little mirrors that mount to the back of the wrist or attach to eyeglasses have a small field of vision, and are not good enough for certain knowledge of what is going on behind. Infinitely superior for drop handlebar bikes is the Mirrycle mirror, which mounts on the brake lever hood, leaves the handlebars clear and unobstructed, and provides excellent visibility to the rear. The information provided not only serves as a warning of impending danger, but is also a great aid to faster, safer riding in traffic. The Mirrycle mirror is easily one of the best aids to cycling comfort to come along in years.

Reflectors

Good lights are your main defense system at night, but do not always identify you as a cyclist to the motorist. It is difficult to judge distance to a single rear light, and the dazzle of the light itself may obscure clear sight of the cyclist. Plus, lights can fail. Reflectors provide a good back-up that always works, and with proper use will help identify you as a cyclist.

Rear, front, wheel spoke, and pedal reflectors are a legal requirement. A big, red rear reflector is very useful. Mount it as low as possible, so that car headlights catch it easily. A white front reflector is useless. So are spoke reflectors, which are visible only when the cyclist is already broadside on to the motorist. The exception is when wheel reflectors are mounted to return illumination fore and aft; they then have a stroboscopic intensity which is very effective. Wheel reflectors unbalance the wheel. When setting up a bike I throw them away.

Pedal reflectors are very good. Their low position is readily picked up by headlights, and their attention getting distinctive pattern of movement readily identifies the presence of a cyclist. Active, moving reflectors and lights are four times more eye-catching than static reflectors and lights.

Most reflectors are limited in mechanical effectiveness. Far better are retro-reflective materials, which will reflect light back to a source regardless of the angle of incidence. Millions of microscopic prisms per square inch do the trick. They must be sealed under plastic or other clear covering for effectiveness when wet. An excellent product when made of retro-reflective material is the Sam Brown belt, a lightweight combined belt and shoulder slash that can be used with whatever you are wearing. Another good item are retro-reflective trouser/arm bands, which, like pedal reflectors, are very eye-catching. Panniers, jackets, gloves, and so on can all be highlighted with retro-reflective tape, dots, and stickers. These all help to tell the motorist who and what you are - the more, the better.

The compleat night-time cyclist wants both active and static lights and reflectors. Front and rear lights, and a moving or blinking light that can serve as a back-up if one of the static lights fails. A big rear reflector, and pedal reflectors or other type that move around.

Shoes, toe clips, and cleats

Ordinary street shoes do not provide sufficient support for the foot unless used with rubber or metal platform pedals. Cycling shoes have reinforced soles to distribute the impact of the thin edges of the commonly used cage type pedals. Shoes for racing have no heels, and are not intended for walking. Shoes for touring have heels, and will stand casual walking about. Dual purpose shoes with partially stiffened soles are designed for both cycling and walking, and for many people, excel at both functions. You can now have a cycling shoe which can stand a 2000 mile tour and yet looks perfectly in order with formal clothes.

Toe clips and straps elevate cycling into a new dimension, and ensure that your feet will remain on the pedals in the event of a mis-shifted gear or unexpected bump. Many ordinary shoes and most cycling/walking shoes have soles with sufficient texture to grip

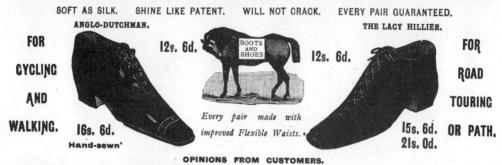

CIVIL & MILITARY CYCLE SUPPLY

WATKINS' PATENTS.

56, QUEEN VICTORIA ST., LONDON, E.C.

The only machines that can be easily converted from military to private uses.

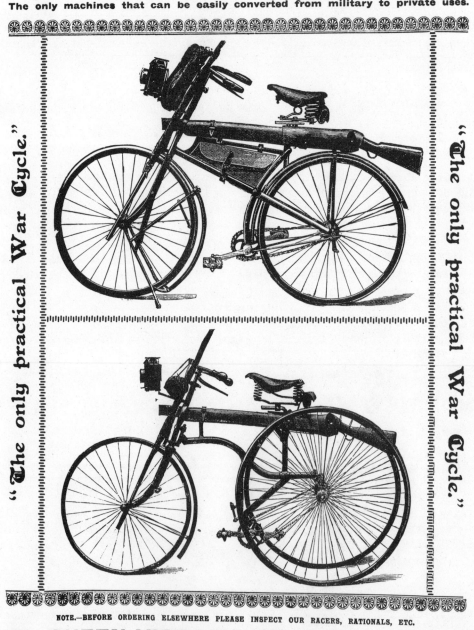

"The only practical War Cycle."

"The only practical War Cycle."

NOTE.—BEFORE ORDERING ELSEWHERE PLEASE INSPECT OUR RACERS, RATIONALS, ETC.

56, QUEEN VICTORIA ST., LONDON, E.C.

the pedals when snugged down with straps, but can be slipped out with ease when required. Some dual purpose shoes have ridges molded into the soles to help grip the pedal. Fine if the alignment is in accord with that of your foot, but if not, a slight twist of your foot can damage your leg.

Cleats attach to the sole of the shoe and then in turn lock to the pedal. They give tremendous get up and go and are a must for racing and fast riding, but can be inconvenient on a tour when you want to stop and stroll around (you'll have to change shoes or go barefoot), and can be dangerous in traffic. Traditional cleats are nailed to the shoe. Many modern cycling shoes have adjustable cleats mounted to the shoe with screws. These allow you to set up the cleat exactly as you like, and to change the setting if you switch to another machine with different pedals.

Even with cleats on, a healthy yank will usually get the foot off the pedal. For safety and effectiveness the toe straps have to be quite snug. This can lead to chafing and foot pains. A very good answer for this problem are system pedals and cleats, such as made by Look, Adidas and AeroLite. These are special design pedals and cleats that mate and lock together, like step-in ski bindings. They're wonderful. So long as the pedaling forces are in the plane of crank rotation, it is difficult or impossible to lose the pedal. But when you do need to detach, a lateral roll of the foot does the trick at once. It's a lighter, safer, and more effective method than regular cleats and toe straps. An important bonus is greater comfort. There is more stress on

AEoleus Butterfly

the shoe, which must be a good fit. I particularly like shoes that fasten with Velcro straps, because they are easy to adjust. System pedals are the current rage and you should see what new offerings are in the shops. At this writing the neatest and lightest is the AeroLite, a little gem about the size of your thumb, that runs on nice long roller bearings. The cleat mounts with four bolts, or via a conversion plate for shoes tapped for Look cleats.

There are practical difficulties in specific recommendations for shoes. The first is that shoes, like saddles, are personal. Bliss for one person may be agony for another. The second is that there are too many for anyone to have tried them all. These points noted, a popular general purpose cycling shoe for use without cleats is the Sidi Comfort. The sole is thick and hard and comfortable for long hours in the saddle. I've also used it often for mountainbiking, but only with toe clips and straps. The hard sole is slippery and unsafe on open pedals. In cleated shoes the Sidi Performance with Velcro straps is a popular model often seen at race meetings. For a general purpose shoe good for walking and safe on open pedals, I'm quite happy with the Adidas Tourmalet.

For winter riding lined cycling boots are available, and for wet weather there are slip on booties that will go over regular shoes. One can also fit toe warmers over the toe clips.

Speedometer

Tire drive models are generally inaccurate and increase drag. Electronic models offer many other functions, such as elapsed time, journey distance, average speed, maximum speed reached, cadence rate,and so on, according to make. Setting one of these up to be accurate can be a chore. However, they can be a very useful training aid when practicing for competition or riding for fitness.

Spoke guard

This is a thin plate mounted on the rear wheel that prevents the rear derailleur from catching in the spokes. With a properly adjusted derailleur this should never happen, but should the derailleur malfunction or break (as has happened to me), then down you go, and with the back of the bike twisted into spaghetti.

Trailers

Trailers are absolutely super for hauling around groceries, laundry, children, and all manner of heavy gear. Most models attach and detach from the bike in seconds and can free you of the need for racks and panniers - very nice if you are running a high performance machine.

All-up trailer and load weight should not exceed one half bike rider body weight. Best machine for the job is a mountainbike. Be cautious when descending hills and over rough ground. It is difficult to overturn a properly designed and loaded trailer, but it can be done.

Turn signals

The kind that mount on a bike are silly. There isn't enough distance between the lights to clearly indicate direction. Hand signals are more definite and effective. What can be very useful at night is a strip of retro-reflective material around the wrist or on the back of a glove. Often when cyclists signal a turn at night, their arm is lifted above the spread of dimmed car headlights and absorbed by the general ink of night. The signal is literally invisible.

Water bottle

Don't ignore this common item. Vigorous cycling dehydrates the body, and a drink may not be readily to hand unless carried on the bike. Drink before you get thirsty. There are any number of patent concoctions available that variously contain glucose and/or salts. Personally, I find that a little honey in plain water is just the ticket for a lift when nearing the end of a long ride. Caffeine will also give a momentary blast. Thermal bottles are also available for a warm drink of soup.

Wheel discs

In HPV racing wheel discs are SOP. Everyone knows that spokes churn air like an egg-beater, increasing turbulence and drag. If you want to go fast, you use discs.

In UCI sanctioned races for conventional safety bikes, wheel discs are allowed only if the disc is an integral part of the wheel structure. This means heavy weight and ruinous cost. In UCI races, you don't go fast unless you have big money.

In the everyday world there are cheaper options. Many a time I've used light cardboard or plastic and tape to create temporary discs for an event. Leave a hole for the valve and cover it with tape. There are also pre-formed plastic discs available, but all the ones I've seen so far are heavy and crude.

The best discs I know of are the Quick Disc made by MSR, Box 3978, Terminal Station, Seattle, WA 98124. They use adjustable aluminum rings and a stretch fabric. This makes them very light and easy to work with. The fabric can be put on or removed in a twinkling. Perhaps more importantly, the fabric is semi-porous. In practical terms, air flows over stretched fabric nearly as efficiently as over a smooth, polished surface. But cross-wind forces are reduced because they are able to partially pass through the fabric. You'll appreciate just how important this is the first time you ride a safety bike with wheel discs. It's not so bad at the rear wheel, but at the front wheel a sudden gust of wind from the side can have a major effect on steering and course. The problem is worse if the bike is a criterium racer with a steep head tube angle. Some people feel that a front disc is too dangerous for general use. I think it is more a question of getting used to very different handling, and developing the appropriate reflexes. With time and experience you learn where and when gusts are likely to come. In any case, if conditions become too difficult it is literally a snap to remove the fabric and eliminate the problem.

Summary

The right selection of accessories can make a vital difference to your cycling efficiency, comfort, and safety. Do not be afraid to spend a healthy wad of money, as the return on investment will probably be excellent. But be aware also that there are many people who have climbed aboard some beat-up old bike outfitted catch-as-catch-can, and traversed entire continents. You can always improvise; the virtue of purpose designed equipment is usually that it is very much better.

"CROW'S NEST"
The tide refuge on the
way to HOLY ISLAND.

Book Two

Maintenance and Repair

Contents

Maintenance and Repair

Working on bikes is often regarded as an unwelcome chore. This is a basic mistake. The extent to which you get involved in working on your bike should be a direct function of how you ride. One follows the other like night and day. The awareness that riding a bike precipitates usually includes an awareness and interest in the bike itself. How the bike responds is very much a function of maintenance. Ideally, you are going to work on your own bike because you want a together, tight machine under you, i.e. you will do it because *you want to.*

As with all things, you get back in proportion to what you put in. It is essentially a question of fineness. It is the nature of bikes that they are at their best when well-lubricated and carefully adjusted. A sensitivity to this sort of refinement does not happen the instant you mount up. Give it time. As you ride you will become increasingly aware of your bike's characteristics. A well set-up bike fits you like a suit of clothes, and you will soon develop an 'ear' for the sound of bearings and a 'feel' for other parts, such as the brakes. The development of this sensitivity - the result of personal and direct participation - is part of the reason for owning a bike in the first place. Eventually, you will find that increased riding pleasure and heightened mechanical sensitivity are synonymous.

As I say, this is all something that you should grow into. The idea of having a bike is to have fun. A fair amount of latitude is possible in servicing bikes and you have hopefully chosen a machine suited to your level of interest. So you can minimize or maximize maintenance as per your own inclinations. But bear in mind that most machines, and certainly bicycles, need a certain amount of lubrication and adjustment if they are to function at all. Without it, they rust away, and because the parts are unlubricated and out of kilter, they slowly chew themselves to bits when ridden. I have seen 'old dependables' that have been left out in the rain for years and have never seen an oil can or a mechanic. They make it for years - and then snap a chain in the middle of a tour or a brake cable at the start of a long hill. Or eventually the rust destroys them. There is no need for this. A properly maintained bike will easily last a lifetime (one of mine was made in 1920 and has seen plenty of hard service to boot). For reasons of simple economy and safety, if you can't be bothered to do routine maintenance then take your machine to a bike shop for servicing at least twice a year.

You should of course have an on-going relationship with a bike shop, as a source of components and bits and pieces, advice, and servicing. If you are really determined you can do every job on the bike yourself. But many jobs are far better done with specialized, expensive tools, while others (such as wheel truing) come more easily to people who do them often. A good bike shop is a professional outfit.

It can be great fun to hand a bike over for servicing and get it back in apple pie order, but you'll find that this is more successful if you look after your bike by keeping it clean, lubricated and properly adjusted. Shops dread ill-looked after, rusty bikes, because they are difficult and time consuming to work on. This sends the labor charge zooming upwards, when often the bike is not worth much. A machine that has been regularly looked after is much easier and quicker to work on, and this helps keep cost down. Cleaning a bike is not a mechanic's job!

The conventional starting point for a job with a bike shop is a written estimate specifying the work, parts, and cost. This is for the shop's protection as much as yours. When the relationship is more established you can leave matters on a more open basis, so that if the shop sees something that needs doing, they know they can go ahead and do it.

But minor adjustments and fine points are best carried out by you. Only you know exactly where you like the brake lever to engage, for example. Also, it is kind of silly to leave your bike at the shop for 3 days for a job that takes 10 minutes to do.

But the most important reason for doing your own work is that it makes preventive maintenance almost automatic. Preventive maintenance is replacing parts before they wear out and break, usually at an inopportune time and miles from any bike store. If you pay attention to the various parts of your bike and keep it in tune, breakdowns will be fairly well eliminated. This is the easiest and most efficient approach. It's more fun to work on a bike at the moment and place of your choosing, and more fun to ride a bike in which you have complete confidence.

Here is my approach: each major component system of the bicycle such as brakes, wheels, gears, etc., is broken down into four areas:

How It Works
Routine Adjustments
Replacing Parts
Troubleshooting

The idea is to give you a basic understanding of what is happening - and make you a mechanic! How It Works for each section is required reading. It does no good for you to diddle with this or adjust that if you have no idea of how it works. And if something is broken it is impossible for you to fix it unless you know how it works in the first place.

CYCLES TO MEND! TYRES TO ME—END!

It will help a lot if as you read, you look at and feel the corresponding parts of your bike.

I don't cover everything. One wheel is pretty much the same as another. I have tried to include representative types of equipment currently in use but there are bound to be exceptions. If this happens to you try to find the item in this book which most closely resembles the part you are servicing or fixing. Pay particular attention to *function* and then analyze your own part the same way. It is more important to understand the concept than to have step-by-step directions. This should get you through most anything.

Most components are accompanied by instructions from the manufacturer. You often do not get these when buying a complete bike, but a request to the shop (and a handy copying machine) should turn up what you need.

There are also some tasks which are just not worth doing. Getting into the innards of a coaster brake multi-speed hub is one of these. It takes a long, long time and isn't fun at all. Even most bike shops refuse to overhaul these units and simply replace them - it's actually cheaper this way. If you insist on doing this sort of work (some people say it has therapeutic value) detailed instructions are available from the bicycle manufacturer or from the hub manufacturer.

Tools

You can get by with amazingly little in the way of tools. However, for some kinds of work there are a few you will just have to get. Also, what you need depends on what kind of bike you have.

Before going into particulars a word on tool quality: do yourself a favor and buy good tools. The cheap tools sold by dime stores, supermarkets, and even hardware stores are a false economy for they are made of inferior metals that will break or bend under stress, or they are made badly enough so that they don't even work. In the long run good tools are well worth the investment.

Many bike shops sell pre-assembled tool kits. Be sure your tools are the correct size. Foreign made bikes, and American bikes with foreign components, use metric system nuts and bolts.

It is a good idea to check tool requirements when you buy a bike. Many components can only be serviced with special tools supplied by the manufacturer. The following list is necessarily rather general:

Tire levers (plastic are light and smooth).
Tube patches and glue.
8" or 6" adjustable end wrench.
Pliers.
¼" tip, 4-5" shank screwdriver.
⅛" tip, 2-3" shank screwdriver.
Set of wrenches (inch or metric, as required).
Set of metric Allen keys (if required, will really be needed).
Cable cutters/wire clippers.
6" mill bastard file.
Thin hub wrenches, 13mm x 14mm and 15mm x 16mm.
Spoke key.
Chain rivet remover.

Freewheel remover. Each make of freewheel has its own pattern of remover; make sure you have the right one for your freewheel. If you have a cassette freewheel, then you don't need a remover.

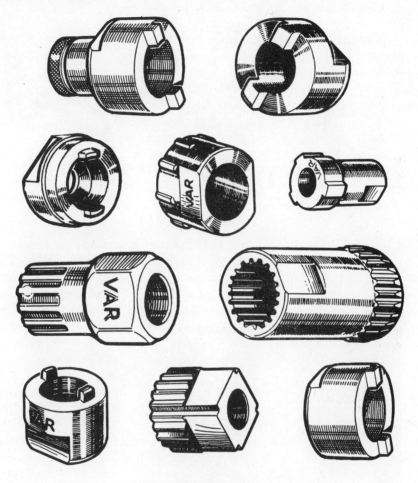

Freewheel removers

For cotterless cranks, crank removing tool as per brand of crank.

Headset wrenches, as per make and type of headset.

There are many other tools and gadgets that can be handy to have. Channel lock pliers or vise-grips are perennial favorites. So is a big (12'' or so) adjustable wrench for really having a go at things. A small portable vise is very useful. A hammer will be needed sometimes. But as you can see, many of the tools are for specialized jobs so you do not have to acquire them all at once. But at the minimum, have a small 'essentials' toolkit, with tire levers and either a patch kit or a spare tube.

If you have difficulty obtaining tools from local shops, or would just like to read over a good tool catalog, write to The Third Hand, 3101 N. Old Stage Road, Mt. Shasta, CA 96067.

You will need some means of holding the bike steady. One method is to simply turn the bike upside down. With downswept handlebars use a narrow cardboard or wood box with slots cut in the side to support the handlebars and keep the brake cables from being bent against the ground. It's better if the bike is upright. A nail driven into a doorjam with a rope to hang the bike by will suffice, but best by far is a proper work stand. These cost a bit but perhaps you could share one with friends. Make sure the one you buy can handle bikes with large tubing (mountainbikes, aluminium bikes, BMX bikes). For inflating tires I highly recommend a track pump that stands on the floor and has a handle for both hands. Frame pumps carried on bikes have a job to reach the high pressures required by many modern tires, and a track pump makes life a whole lot easier.

Lubrication

This is a general discussion of lubrication. For details look under the part in question, e.g. brakes, hubs, gears, etc. There are a number of different types and forms of

lubricants. Each has advantages and drawbacks depending on the kind of machinery and riding involved.

Oil is the old standby. Be sure to use a good grade such as motorist's SAE 30, or Sturmey-Archer cycle oil. Do not use ordinary household oils. Many will leave behind a sticky residue that gums up the works.

Grease is used for bearings. Ordinary grease from a motorist's shop will work well enough. Lithium greases such as Filtrate and Cycle Pro are less likely to be washed away by water. Also good in this respect is Bardahl Multi-purpose grease. Best of all is Phil Wood Waterproof Bicycle Grease.

Generally, a white lithium grease such as Filtrate or Sta-Lube will run more freely

222

than a water-resistant grease such as Phil Wood or LPS-100. You'll find that many racing people favor the lighter greases, and often brew up exotic mixtures of their own design. Powdered graphite is a popular additive. Remember, however, that these people usually think little of stripping down and re-lubing a bike for nearly every race. The tourist, commuter, and recreational rider will usually prefer the longer interval between services provided by the stiffer waterproof greases.

Your bicycle has upwards of 200 ball bearings held in place by cups and cones:

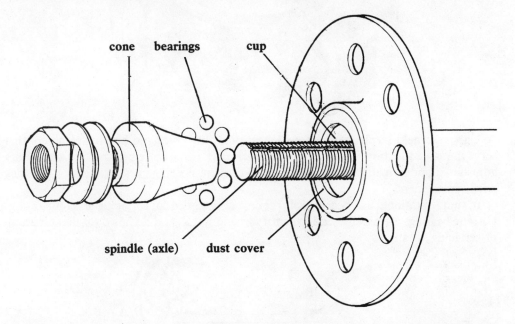

The cone remains stationary while the cup, and whatever part is attached to it - in this example it would be a wheel - rides on the ball bearings and spins around. The distance between the cone and the cup is adjustable and must not be too tight or too loose. Sometimes the ball bearings are held in a clip called a *race*:

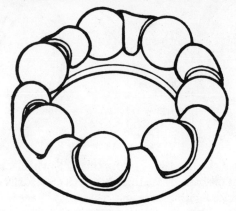

Typically, this is positioned so that the balls are against the cup.

Another type of bearing is a sealed unit known as a cassette or cartridge:

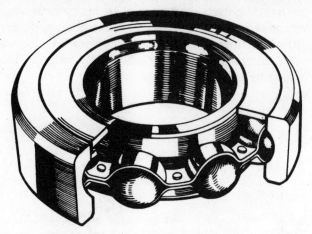

These are held in place in various ways: press fit, glue, and bearing retainers that serve the same function as a cone. Mechanisms that use cassette bearings are sometimes adjustable, and sometimes not. In general, cassette bearings are left alone until they need replacement.

In sum, traditional ball bearings and cones are designed for servicing and lubricating. Cassette bearings are usually sealed against dirt and water, and designed for the minimum of servicing, if any.

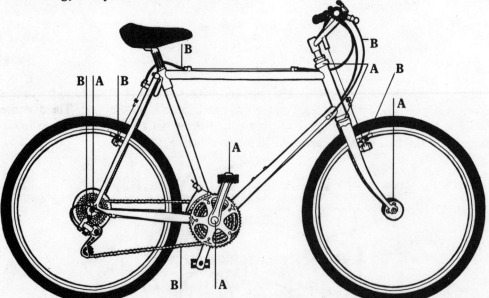

You will find bearings at the headset, bottom bracket, wheels, and pedals (A). When lubricated with lightweight oil-base grease these bearings are usually disassembled, cleaned thoroughly in solvent, packed with grease and reassembled every 6 months. (See under relevant section for disassembly technique.) With good waterporoof grease the job can be left for 3 years if the bike is in moderate service (2000 miles a year or less). High mileage bikes (5000 + miles a year), and bikes with heavy, hard riders will need servicing annually. A bearing which runs rough or tight requires immediate servicing.

Some bearings are both greased and oiled, and in particular, 2- and 3-speed hubs and hubs on ultra-fancy racing bikes. You can tell these by the fact that the hub has a small oil cap or clip:

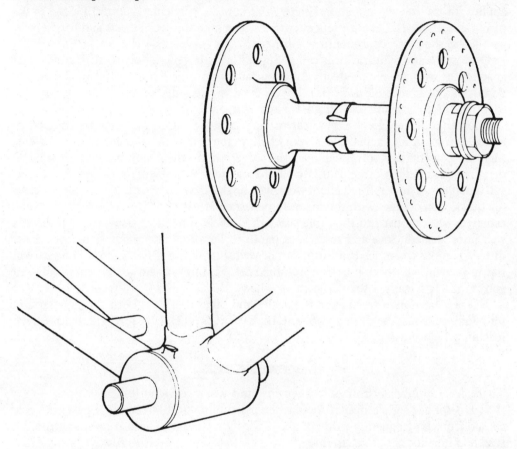

These need lubricating once a month: multi-speed internal gear hubs a teaspoonful, regular hubs about half a teaspoonful, and coaster brake hubs 2 tablespoonfuls. Some bottom brackets are set up to use fluid as well as grease. A teaspoonful once a month. Use fluid wherever you find oil caps or clips. Too little is better than too much. If fluid leaks out of the sides of the bearings and dribbles all over your crankset or wheels, you are using too much.

I prefer the use of a dry lubricant for the chain, freewheel, derailleurs, brake pivots, cables, and any other parts which do not use grease (B). Dry lubricants usually come in spray form and contain an exotic and sometimes secret blend of ingredients. Often included is molybdenum disulfide. The important thing is that the lubricants are dry. The trouble with oil is that it attracts dirt, which then mixes with the oil and forms

225

a gooey abrasive mess, greatly increasing mechanical wear. Everything gets dirty, including you. In the case of the chain, for example, this means that once a month you have to remove it, soak it clean in a solvent, dry it, oil it, and then reinstall it. It's time consuming and messy. If you use a dry lubricant you need do this job only once every 2 or 3 months. You must lubricate more often - bi-weekly in normal service, weekly in hard service - but with a spray this job takes only a few seconds. The same rationale applies for the freewheel and derailleur. The spray is particularly useful for the brake pivots and all cables. Oil has a tendency to leak out onto the brake levers and handlebars, and brake shoes. Once a month is sufficient.

One excellent dry lubricant is called Super Lube. It's incredible stuff. I've also had good results with Tri-Flo products. An important point to note is that some dry lubricants do not mix well with oil or grease. If you want to use a dry lubricant on a chain, for example, first clean off the old grease and gunge.

Another extremely good, very cheap dry lubricant is paraffin wax, available in grocery stores. It is great for chains. Clean your chain in the conventional manner with solvent. Melt the paraffin in a coffee can over the stove. Dump the chain in and then hang so that drippings fall back into can. Use oil or spray for the brake pivot points, freewheel, and derailleur. The paraffin will not work well on these parts because it cools and hardens too quickly on contact with the metal to penetrate effectively. It is excellent for brake cables, however. Just run the cable through a block of paraffin a few times until it is well impregnated. Save and re-use old paraffin. Paraffin, like spray, does not attract dirt. When the chain needs a fresh shot of wax, just dump it in the pot. The dirt will rise to the surface where it can be skimmed off. Hang the chain to drip and cool, and you're off. It's really a very efficient method.

NOTE: New bikes fresh from the dealer and bikes that have been standing around for a long time may be dry as a bone. OIL EVAPORATES! Be sure to lubricate such machines before using.

General Words

There are a number of things to keep in mind when servicing bikes.

1. Do not use a great deal of force when assembling or disassembling parts. Bicycle components are frequently made of alloys for light weight. These are not as strong as steel and it is not hard to strip threads or otherwise damage parts. Always be sure that things fit. Be careful and delicate. Snug down bolts, nuts, and screws firmly, not with all your might.

2. Most parts turn clockwise to tighten and counter-clockwise to loosen. This is called a right-hand thread. A left-hand thread tightens counter-clockwise and loosens clockwise. Left-hand threads are not used often. The left side pedal and the right side bottom bracket cup and lock ring are usually left-hand threads.

3. When fitting together threaded parts hold them as perfectly aligned as you can, and turn one backwards (loosen) until you hear and feel a slight click. Then reverse and tighten. If this is new to you, practice on a nut and bolt until you have the feel of it perfectly.

4. If you get stuck with a rust-frozen bolt or nut, soak it in penetrating oil, give it a few taps to help the oil work in, and then try to undo it again with a tool that fits

exactly. If this fails, try a cold chisel and hammer. Go at this carefully since if you slip you may gouge a chunk out of your bicycle. If this fails, hacksaw or file the nut or bolt off. How did it get this rusty in the first place?

5. When assembling or disassembling try to be neat and organized. Lay parts out in the order which they came apart or go together. Put tiny parts in boxes or jars. There's always a temptation to whiz ahead. Be methodical, it's usually quicker.

6. Allow time for working. One thing often leads to another, especially if the bike hasn't been tended to for a while. A simple brake shoe replacement, for example, may also see you overhauling the brake mechanism and installing a new cable.

7. There are a number of little nuts and bolts on your bike for racks, brake lever mounts, gear shift lever mounts, and the like. These tend to get loose and need tightening about once a month.

8. The left side of the bike is as if you and the bike both point forward.

9. Solvents. Although gasoline is to be found sloshing around at a zillion gas stations, no one will ever tell you to use it as a solvent. The reason is that every once in a while someone gets blown to kingdom come. The gasoline itself is not so bad, but the vapor it gives off is very volatile.

Kerosene can be used as a solvent, but contains water. On a part that you can clean and wipe dry with a rag, no problem. Something with lots of fiddly bits like a chain however, can be damaged unless you carefully dry it out, like in an oven. You can also use degreasers like Spray Away and Gunk, though these once again involve water.

10. Finish: a good quality automobile paste wax will preserve your paint job and make it easier to keep the bike clean. Do not wax wheel rims where brake shoes contact.

It is a good idea to wipe the bike clean once a week. A high pressure hose can be used to clean a very dirty machine, such as a mud-encrusted mountainbike, but be sure to re-lubricate the bike at once. Before putting away a bike that has gotten very wet, run it around a bit to help drive water out of the bearings and other bits.

11. If you need to trim a new cable to size, use wire snips and not pliers. After cutting, solder the cable end or dip it in glue to prevent fraying. File away excess solder or glue. In a pinch, wrap the cable end with tape.

Ordinary cables and housings work very well but when replacement time comes consider using braided cables. These are extra strong cables running through housings lined with Teflon and do not require lubrication.

12. Last but by no means least, do not be afraid! The whole idea of mechanical things is that they go together and come apart. A feeling that something is delicate and might break if you mess with it is a symptom of uncertainty. Get with it, get greasy, and stay with it until you *know* you've got it together.

Brakes

Contents

General

Bicycle brakes come in three basic types: hub, disc, and caliper. The hub coaster brake is inferior on several counts. Under conditions requiring a quick stop it tends to lock up the rear wheel, causing the bike to skid rather than slow down. It has poor heat dissipating qualities and can burn out on a long downhill. It is difficult to service. It is for the rear wheel only, cutting braking efficiency below 50 percent, as it is the front wheel that gives the greatest braking power. In fact, on dry pavement it is difficult if not impossible to lock up a front wheel. This is because braking throws the weight forward, increasing traction. If you have a bike which has only a coaster brake equip it with a caliper brake for the front wheel. Only children whose hands are not strong enough to operate caliper brakes should have a coaster brake, and they should not ride in any situation requiring quick stops or sustained braking.

If something goes wrong with your coaster brake, simply remove the entire rear wheel and take it to a bicycle shop for overhaul or replacement. It is complicated to fix, and infinitely more trouble than it is worth.

Hand operated hub drum brakes are sensitive and powerful, but not in the models so far offered by mainstream cycle manufacturers. Disc brakes give good stopping power in both wet and dry conditions, but are heavy, and easily go out of whack.

Caliper brakes offer a good balance between weight and stopping power. Modern brake shoes give reasonable performance under wet conditions and very good performance under dry conditions. Caliper brakes are relatively simple to service.

How Caliper Brakes Work

Caliper brake systems all work on the same basic principle. There is a hollow, flexible tube called a cable housing between the brake lever mount and the cable hanger. The cable housing is flexible so that the handlebars can turn back and forth. Through the cable housing passes a cable, attached to the brake lever at one end, and to the brake mechanism at the other. The brake mechanism is fastened to the bicycle frame and functions like a pair of ice tongs. When the brake lever is operated, it pulls the cable through the housing, thereby pulling together the arms (or *yokes*) of the brake mechanism, causing the two brake shoes attached to the yokes to press against the wheel rim and stop the wheel.

When the lever is released, a spring in the brake mechanism forces the yoke arms away from the wheel rim, and returns the brake lever to the off position. The illustrations opposite are for a center pull brake with two yoke arms, each rotating on a separate pivot point.

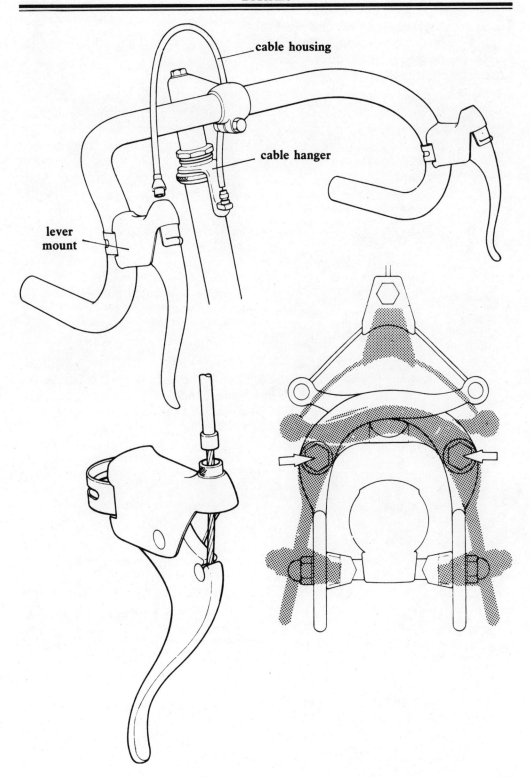

cable housing

cable hanger

lever
mount

The side pull brake uses only one pivot point, with the cable housing attached directly to one yoke, and the cable to the other. The effect is the same.

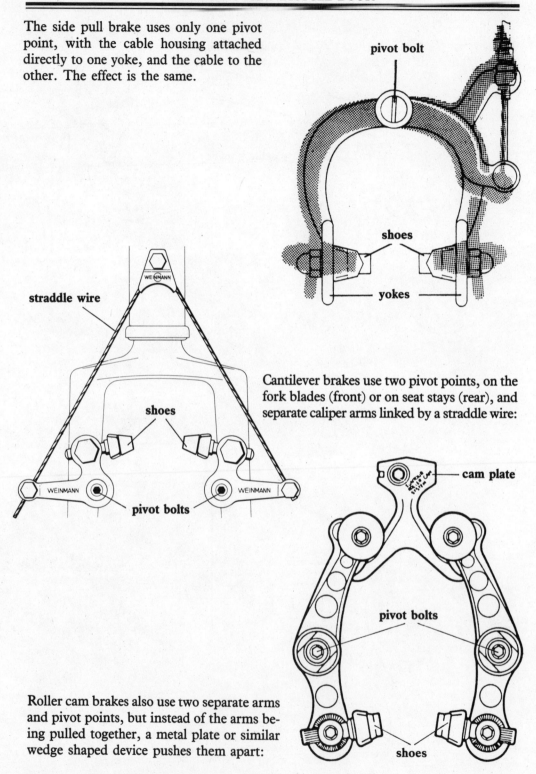

pivot bolt

shoes

yokes

straddle wire

shoes

pivot bolts

Cantilever brakes use two pivot points, on the fork blades (front) or on seat stays (rear), and separate caliper arms linked by a straddle wire:

cam plate

pivot bolts

Roller cam brakes also use two separate arms and pivot points, but instead of the arms being pulled together, a metal plate or similar wedge shaped device pushes them apart:

shoes

All caliper brake systems have a cable adjusting bolt for changing the relationship of the cable housing and the brake cable. On a side pull brake it is usually on the yoke to which the cable housing is attached (A), while on center pull and cantilever brakes it is usually at the brake lever (B) or the cable hanger (C):

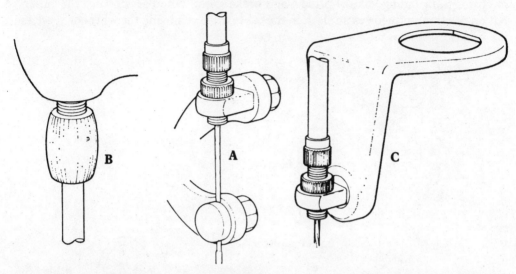

In most cases properly adjusted brake shoes are close enough to the rim so that the tire will not slide between them when removing the wheel. Accordingly, many brake systems have a means for creating a little extra slack in the brake cable. This can be a small button which allows the brake lever to open more; or a cam plate device on the cable hanger or the brake mechanism:

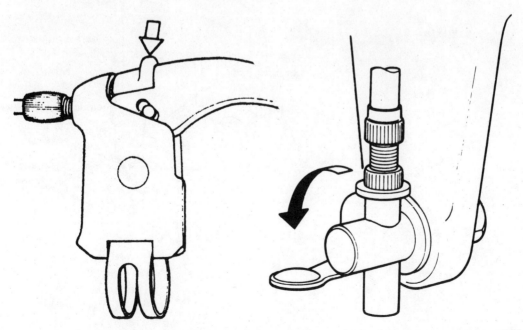

Cantilever and roller cam brakes are easily opened apart by disconnecting the yoke cable or cam plate.

The basics of caliper brake systems are: a brake lever, a brake cable and housing with adjustor barrel, a cable hanger for center pull and cantilever systems, and the brake mechanism, including yokes, springs, and brake shoes. Some designs include either a button or cam to provide extra slack in the cable when removing the wheel or servicing the brakes.

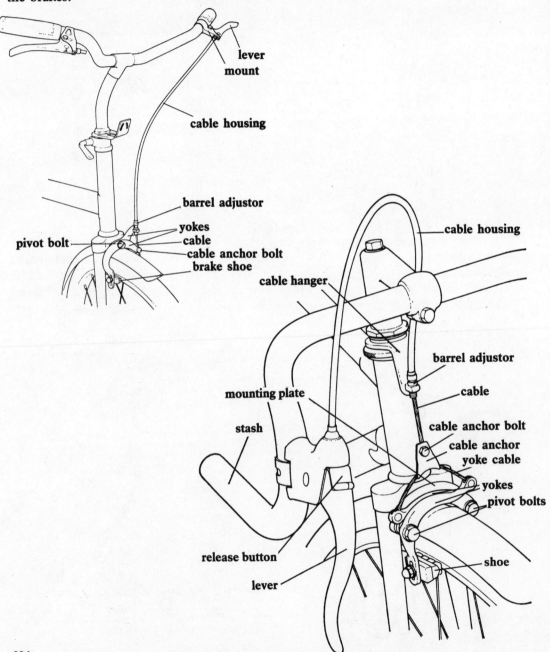

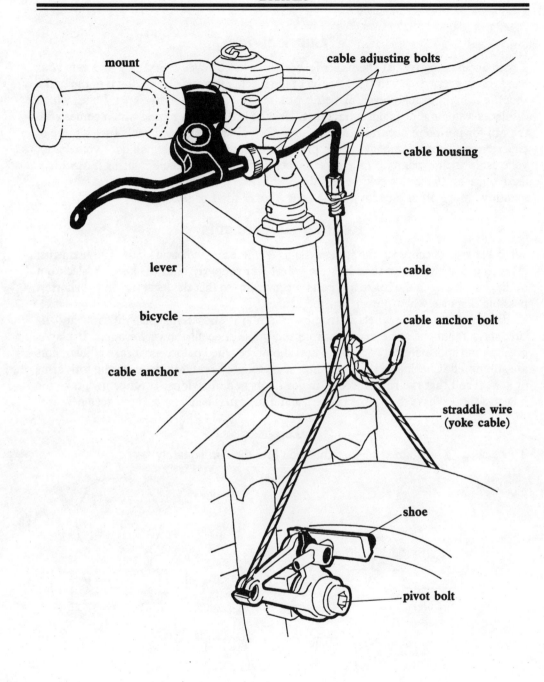

mount

cable adjusting bolts

cable housing

lever

cable

bicycle

cable anchor bolt

cable anchor

straddle wire
(yoke cable)

shoe

pivot bolt

Lubrication

Try to avoid using oil. At the brake levers it works out over everything and gets your hands dirty every time you ride. At the brake mechanism it dribbles down to the brake shoes, cutting braking power. A better product is a spray such as Super Lube, which displaces water and does not attract dirt. Use the little plastic nozzle which comes with the can for pin-point accuracy, and spray pivot bolts, all exposed cable (use a piece of paper or cardboard as a backstop to prevent the spray from going all over your bike), yoke cable anchor points, brake lever pivots, and inside the cable housings. Machines used once or twice a week need lubrication every 2 months, those in daily use, monthly. More often on tours, or if your bike is fond of swims.

Routine Adjustments

Whatever kind of caliper brake system you have, there are two basic kinds of adjustments: (1) seeing that the brake shoe hits the wheel rim properly, and (2) keeping slack out of the cable between the brake lever and mechanism, so that the lever travels the shortest possible distance when putting on the brakes.

First check that the wheel is true by spinning it and seeing that the rim, not the tire, stays about the same distance from the brake shoe all the way around. If play is greater than approximately ⅛" the wheel should be trued before any brake adjustments are attempted. Check also that the wheel is reasonably centered between the fork arms or stays, and that the rim is free of major dents and abrasions. If off center, take the bike to a shop to have the frame checked, and if the rim is badly banged up, get a new one.

Brake shoes

These need to be aligned so that the shoe hits the rim squarely:

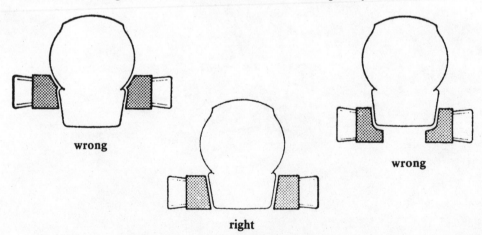

wrong

right

wrong

An important point to note with cantilever brakes is that they arc downwards and not upwards like other caliper brakes. Keep the shoes positioned so that they hit high on the rim, close to the edge with the tire. If the contact point is low on the rim, toward the inside of the wheel, then under heavy braking the shoe can compress slightly and

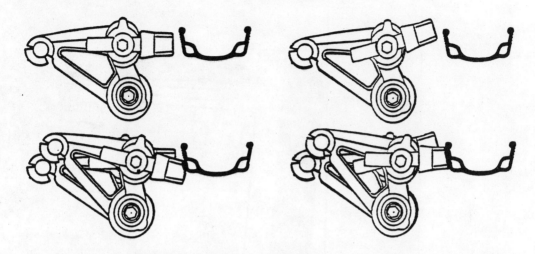

slip off the rim — surprise, no brakes. (But thankfully so far, no shoe in the spokes.) Brake shoes wear out steadily, and are also sometimes put out of adjustment by a chance knock; make a habit of checking them often.

Brake shoes are held on by a conventional bolt or an eyebolt:

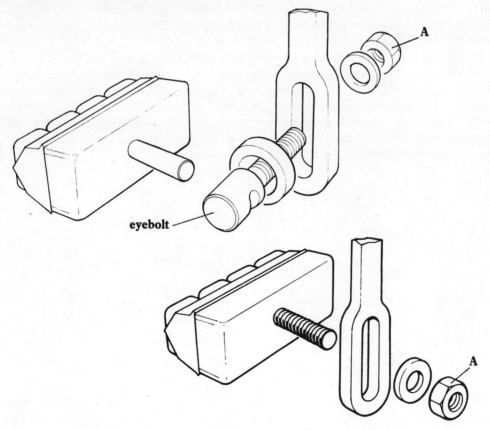

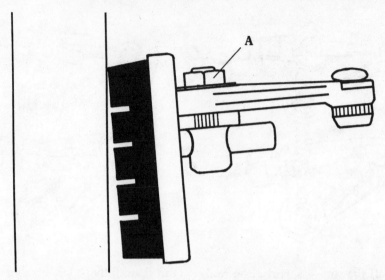

Loosen nut A, adjust brake shoes to meet rim, and tighten. One method is to loosen nut A just a little bit and gently tap the shoe into the proper position with the wrench handle. With conventional bolts you'll find that the brake shoe twists to the right when you tighten the nut back down. A good trick is to set it slightly counter-clockwise so that the final tightening brings it perfectly into position. Do not use too much force. Brake bolt screws strip easily.

Eyebolt type shoes are easy to adjust so that the face of the shoe is flush with the rim. Achieving this effect with a conventional bolt brake shoe sometimes requires bending the yoke. CAUTION: alloy fatigues easily. Slight, gentle bending is usually all right, but hard bending can make the alloy brittle and prone to break. It is better to position and face a brake block by shaving it with a razor or sandpaper, or by using a tapered washer to tilt it in the right direction. Note also that new brake shoes frequently wear into correct alignment after a few days:

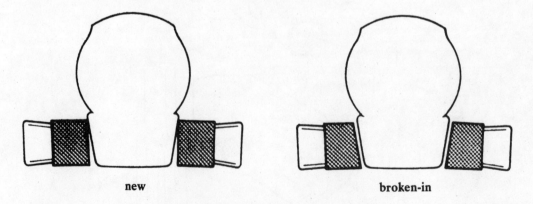

new   broken-in

If bending is the only way, remove the brake shoe altogether and fit an adjustable end wrench snugly over the end of the yoke:

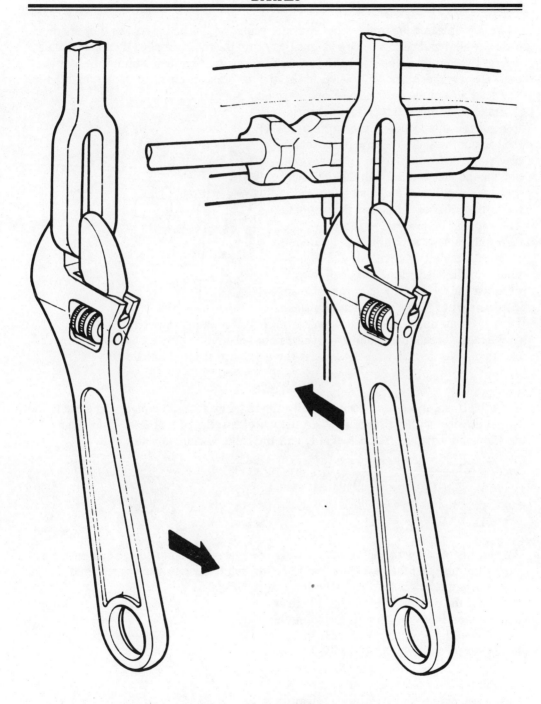

If the yoke needs to be bent outward, simply pull on the handle of the wrench. If the yoke needs to be bent inward, provide a pivot point by wedging another wrench, screwdriver handle, or other object between the yoke and tire, and push in the wrench handle.

If you are replacing the brake shoes consider using the synthetic type, as they are much better for all round performance and sensitivity than the shoes supplied by brake manufacturers. Do so only if you have good quality brakes in crisp, firm condition. Synthetic shoes are very quick, and will snatch and grab if the brake mechanism is loose and sloppy. The leading brands are Atzec, Kool Stop, and Mathauser.

Brake shoes must be toed-in, so that the front of the shoe contacts the rim before the back of the shoe. Because of twist and play in the brake mechanism, under actual braking the shoe is flush with the rim. Synthetic shoes and extra long shoes need more toe-in than rubber shoes and short shoes. The gap can be as large as 0.5 mm. Try 0.25 mm to start and adjust as needed.

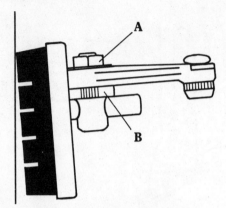

Most if not all synthetic shoes are supplied with beveled washers that allow you to adjust the toe-in. The feature is also an integral part of many brake mechanisms. Loosen fixing nut A and rotate control washer B to adjust toe-in.

When the brake shoe mounts with a straight bolt and no beveled washer is provided, use an adjustable end wrench to twist the yoke arm itself. Be delicate.

Cables

Once the brake shoes have been properly aligned they should be placed as close to the rim as possible without rubbing when the wheel is spun, ⅛" or less. This is done via the cable adjusting bolt and locknut, and the cable anchor nut and bolt:

 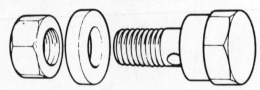

The idea is to screw in the cable adjusting bolt, take up as much slack as possible at the anchor nut, and then use the cable adjusting bolt to take up slack as required. When the cable adjusting bolt reaches the limit of its travel, the process is repeated. There are a number of different methods for doing this job, depending on the type of tools that you have. A very handy gadget is called a third hand and is a spring-like affair for compressing brake shoes together. Bike stores have them. The reason for this tool, or substitute, is that if you loosen the anchor cable nut the spring tension of the brake yoke arms will pull the cable through and you will have a hard time getting it back in.

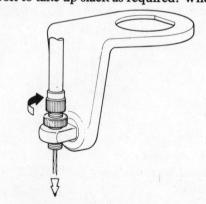

Undo locknut and screw cable adjusting bolt all the way home. If there is a brake release button or cam, check that it is set for normal operation. If you have a third hand, mount it. Or use a C-clamp. Or even string. If you have none of these things, squeeze the brake yoke arms together with your hand. With the other hand, pull the cable at the brake mechanism out so the brake lever is fully home, as it would be if the brakes were not on. Make sure the cable housing has not caught on the outside lip of the cable adjusting bolt. Now look at the amount of slack in the cable. For center pull and cantilever brakes this is the distance between the yoke cable and the cable anchor A:

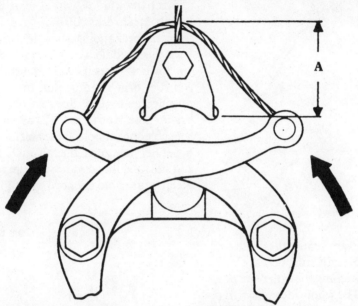

and for side pull systems, it is the amount of new cable protruding beneath the yoke A: Estimate the amount of slack to be taken up with a ruler, tool handle, or finger. Disengage the yoke cable from the cable anchor (center pulls/cantilevers). Eliminate this step if you have a third hand or similar device. Use two wrenches to slacken the cable anchor nut. Avoid twisting the cable. Pass the cable the required distance through the hole in the cable anchor bolt.

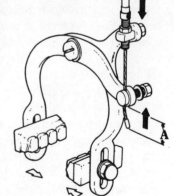

If it is sticky use a pair of pliers to pull it. Tighten cable anchor nut. If no third hand, hold brake yoke arms together again and slip yoke cable back over cable anchor, or cable back into yoke. If you have the feature, now is the time to use the brake button or cam to give you that little bit of extra slack you need. Release the second or third hand, as the case may be. Only one or two turns of the cable adjusting bolt should bring the brake shoes as close as possible to the wheel rim without actually touching when the wheel is spun. If you have gotten it right (it usually takes a couple of tries), use wirecutters to snip off the excess cable for a neat job. Cover the cable end with a cap (bike shops), dip it in glue or solder, or tape it. Frayed cable ends have a habit of snagging fingers and clothing.

Straddle wires and cam plates (but easy on the mustard)

With a center pull brake the yoke cable is usually fixed in length, which means adjusting shoe and rim clearance as per above. With a cantilever brake the yoke cable (also called a straddle wire) is adjustable for length. Together with the eyebolt mounting for the brake shoe, and the cable anchor bolt for the brake cable, there are three means of adjusting shoe and rim clearance. Each has a fair bit of latitude, but try to keep the whole thing in balance.

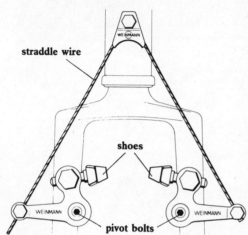

straddle wire

shoes

pivot bolts

Keep the straddle wire at a fairly generous length. If it breaks you may have enough left to get the brake going again. More important-ly, if the straddle wire is short and the cable anchor bolt loses its grip, the straddle wire can be drawn into the tire — instant unwelcome brakes. See that the end of the brake cable protrudes for 2 to 3 inches out of the cable anchor bolt. If the bolt loosens it will hopefully slide down the cable a short distance and still keep the straddle wire clear of the tire. Keep your cable anchor bolts tight!

With a roller cam brake, the cable anchor bolt and the cable adjusting bolt are both for the purpose of keeping the cam plate proper-ly positioned. The whole idea of a cam plate is that there is a moment of maximum mechanical advantage as the rollers move up the cam, which is when the brake shoes should be set to strike the rim. It sounds fiddly, and it is. The problem with giving specific instruc-tions is that there are different makes, and then within those makes, different successive models. They all differ, and how the brake is set up also depends on rim size. What you want are the manufacturer's specific instruc-tions for the model you have, with details of arm width, shoe clearance, and so on. If

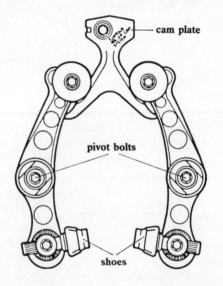

cam plate

pivot bolts

shoes

you need to work by eyeball, use the cable anchor bolt and the cable adjusting bolt to position the cam plate so that the two rollers on each brake arm nest into the indentations in the cam plate.

Then use the eyebolt adjustment to position the brake shoes about 4 mm from the rim. Test the brake and if it works, then leave it alone until you can find a set of instructions for your particular model. It's really worth doing this, because a properly tuned up roller cam brake delivers a lot of performance.

Pivot bolt adjustment

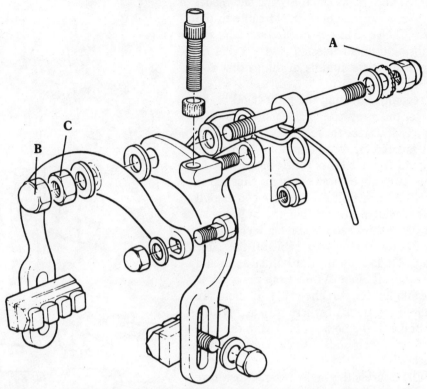

Make sure nut A is tight. Turn in locknut C one half turn while holding acorn adjusting nut B still with another wrench. Turn both B and C in flush against brake yoke arm. Back B off one half turn, hold in place and lock locknut C against it.
Center pull brakes: see under Troubleshooting

Replacing and Disassembling Parts

Cables

The frequency with which you will need to replace brake (and other) cables depends on how you use your bike. Machines consistently left out in the rain, or used hard every day, are going to need them sooner than well cared for or average use machines. There is no hard and fast rule. Any obvious defect, such as a frayed cable, is immediate grounds

for replacement, as is stickiness in the motion of the cable through the cable housing (see Troubleshooting). It is a good idea to replace both brake cables at the same time. They are cheap, and if one has run its course, it is likely that the other has too. The inconvenience of a broken cable is not worth the gain of a month's extra use. If you have purchased a used bike I would replace cables all around unless you know they are relatively new and obviously in good condition. Good condition means they are clean, have no kinks or frayed spots, and pass easily through the cable housings.

Unless you can specify the brand and model of brake, take your bike or old cable to the store. Cables come in different shapes, lengths, and thicknesses. It is very irritating to discover in the middle of things that you have the wrong part.

I recommend using the right-hand brake lever for the rear brake. This follows standard practice, and since the rear brake is generally more favored for routine braking, leaves the left hand free for cross traffic signals.

For any caliper brake system, first screw home the barrel adjustor. With a center pull or cantilever, push together the brake yoke arms (use a third hand or similar device if you have it) and slip the yoke cable off the cable anchor. Undo cable anchor bolt and nut and slide same off cable. With a front brake, slide the cable housing off the cable. If there are ferrules keep track of where they go. With a rear brake, if the housing is held to the bike with clips, then slide the cable out of the housing.

Fully depress the brake lever. Most have a provision for disconnecting the cable by sliding it through a slot:

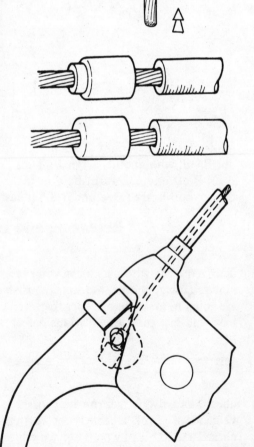

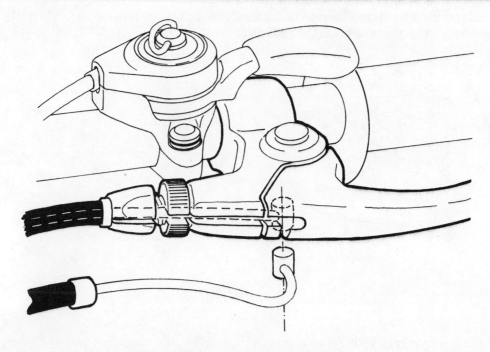

If not, simply thread the cable back out of the brake lever.

Before installing new cable, check the cable housings to see if they need replacement. Are they kinked or broken?

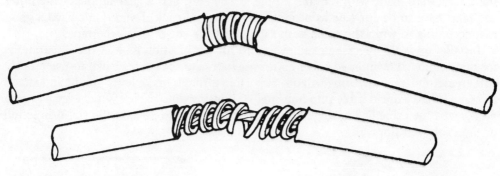

Are the ends free from burrs?
You can eliminate a burr by
1. snipping off the cable housing end with a strong pair of wire cutters (pliers are not good enough);
2. clamping the cable housing end in a vise and filing it down; or
3. using a tool called a taper ream, which you insert in the cable housing end and twist until the burr has gone.

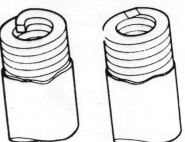

If you use wire cutters be sure to get the cutting edges in between the coils of the housing or else you will mash the ends flat:

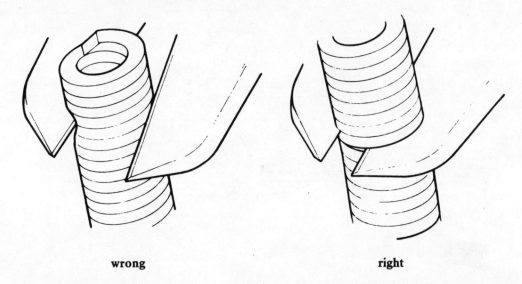

wrong   right

Cable housings lined with Teflon eliminate the need for lubrication but eventually wear out. They will survive one or two cable changes before needing replacement.

When installing new cable, save any cutting for last. Cutting invariably frays the cable end and makes it hard to slide through the housing and cable anchor bolt. However, some cables are made with a brake nipple at one end, and a gear nipple at the other end, and have to be cut - be as neat as possible. One trick if you don't have a good cutting tool is to wrap the cable with tape and then cut through the tape.

Installation is the reverse of removal, and for clarification look at the illustrations for that section. For unlined cable housings, lubricate the cable. I like to use a fairly stiff grease, tho most anything will do. Slip cable through brake lever mount and attach to brake lever. Thread cable into housing, or housing onto cable. Whichever way you do it, twist the cable or housing as you go, and be sure to do it in the right direction or the cable will unravel.

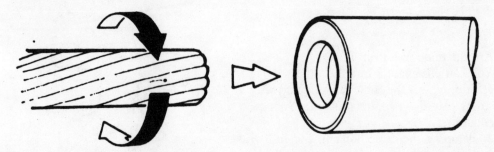

Push free cable end through cable hanger (center pulls and cantilevers), or through cable adjusting bolt at yoke (side pulls), and then through cable anchor bolt hole. To adjust see Adjustment, this section.

Levers

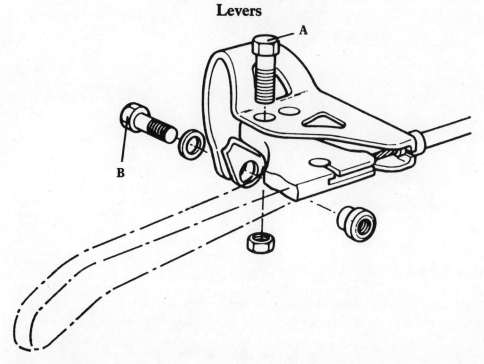

To adjust, slacken A and move. To remove, take off bolt B. May have to be slid off handlebar in which case grip must be removed. If the grip is stuck, a little soap and water will do the trick.

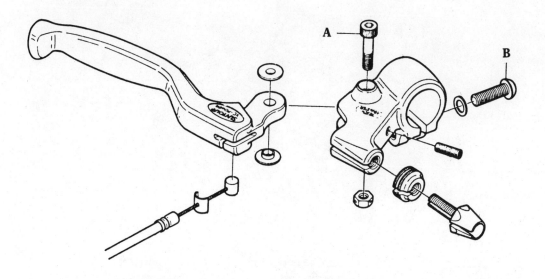

A is the bolt for the lever, and B is the mounting bolt.

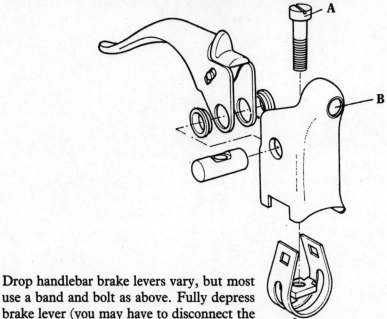

Drop handlebar brake levers vary, but most use a band and bolt as above. Fully depress brake lever (you may have to disconnect the cable for enough room) and use a screwdriver or socket wrench on bolt A.

Brake Mechanism
Side pull

First disconnect brake cable. To remove entire brake from bike, undo nut A. Disassembly should be done only to replace a specific part if it won't work. Start with brake mechanism on bike, or end of pivot bolt clamped in a vise. Undo the brake spring by prising it off with a screwdriver. Careful of fingers. Separate nut B from nut C, and take them both off the pivot bolt. Then the rest of the stuff. Keep the parts lined up in the order in which you remove them. If you are replacing the pivot bolt, undo nut A and take off bolt. Reverse procedure for reassembly.

Center pull

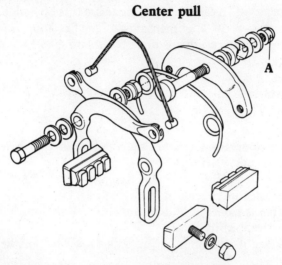

First disconnect brake cable. To remove unit from bike, undo nut A, remove washers and seating pads, and then brake mechanism. Full disassembly varies considerably from model to model and is covered for three types in Troubleshooting, below.

Cantilever and roller cam

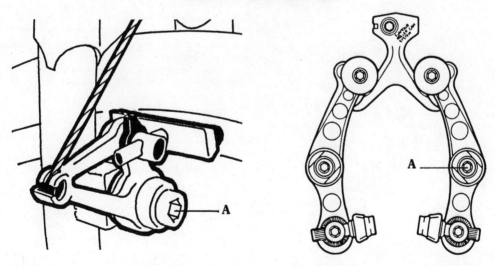

Undo pivot bolt A, and be meticulous about keeping track of the bits and pieces as they come off. Each marque has a different assortment, but there is a reason for every part. Know which way is right side up, and don't mix the parts from one side with the other. The right and left springs, for example, are different.

Troubleshooting

Before using this section please read How It Works and Adjustments. You have to know how it works in the first place in order to figure out what's wrong. Brake problems come in three broad categories. In each category there are three possible areas in which the trouble may be: brake lever, cable, or mechanism. The first thing is to find in which of these the problem originates, and this is done by isolating and actuating each unit separately.

Category 1 — No or very weak brakes.

• Is rim oily?
• Are shoes hitting rim?
• Will brake mechanism compress when you squeeze it with your hand? If no, go to Category 3, sticky brakes, below. If yes,
• Does lever move freely? Yes? Broken cable. Replace.
• Lever will not move. Disconnect cable at brake mechanism end. Will cable housing slide off cable? No? Cable is frozen inside housing. Get if off somehow and replace. If cable and housing separate easily then,
• Lever is frozen. First see if your unit has an adjustable bolt for the lever (B):

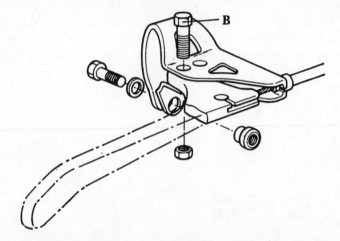

and if so give it a try. No? A major bash may have pinched together the sides of the brake lever mount housing.

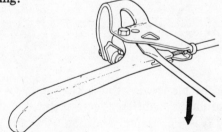

Examine it carefully and bend out dented parts with a big screwdriver.

Or the lever itself may be bent. If the damage is slight, bend it back. If the damage is severe, replace the lever or unit. Metal which has been bent a lot may look perfectly OK but be fatigued and weak, and snap under pressure of a hard stop.

Category 2 — Brakes work, but unevenly or make noises.

● Juddering. Can be caused by a loose brake mechanism, uneven rims, or sometimes by a loose headset. If it is the brake mechanism, tighten up the pivot bolt(s) A:

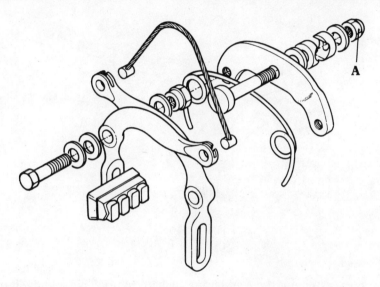

With a side pull, undo locknut C from acorn adjusting nut B and screw both in flush against brake yoke arm. Back off B one half turn and lock into place with locknut C:

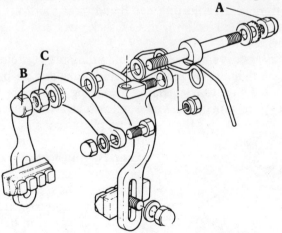

● Squealing. Brake shoes may be old and hard. Sometimes rubber from shoes has streaked rim. Clean with a strong solvent like benzene or cleaning fluid in a WELL VEN-TILATED AREA. Squealing brakes can sometimes be fixed by toeing in the brake shoes (see Adjustments) and sometimes this problem just can't be eliminated.

Category 3 — Sticky or dragging brakes.

This is the most common problem. First determine if it is the lever, cable, or mechanism which is at fault.

- If it is the lever, see Frozen lever(above).
- If it is the cable, replace it (Replacement, further above).
- Brake mechanism.

Side pull

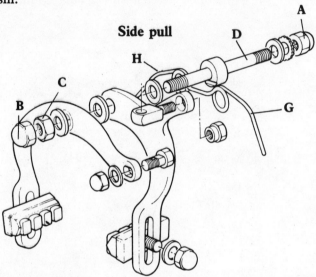

First make sure everything is there and properly hooked up. This sounds simple minded, but there is a reason for each of the parts and the mechanism won't work without them. Is the spring complete and attached to both yoke arms? Make sure nut A is tight. Undo locknut C from acorn adjusting nut B and screw both flush against yoke arm. Back B off one half turn and lock it with C. Check pivot bolt D is straight and replace if necessary. Lubricate.

If one shoe drags against rim: loosen the mounting nut A, hold brake yokes in correct position, and re-tighten. No soap? Examine brake seating pad F. If it has a slot for the spring you will have to try bending the spring. There are two ways to do this. One is to prise the spring arm off the brake yoke which is dragging and bend it outward

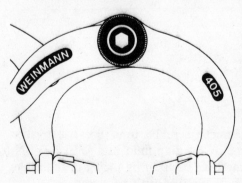

using pliers or a similar tool. The second is to take a big screwdriver and poise it against G or H, whichever is OPPOSITE the dragging shoe, and give it a sharp bash with a hammer. This second method is quicker, but of course a little riskier.

Many Weinmann brakes have a little recessed hex bolt for making this adjustment. Clever, but the tool to fix the hex bolt is usually tinny and more likely to break than not. Better to just slacken pivot mounting nut A.

Still no soap? Check to see that the brake yokes are not rubbing against each other. If so, bend them apart with a screwdriver, or slide in a piece of fine emery cloth (like sandpaper) and file it down.

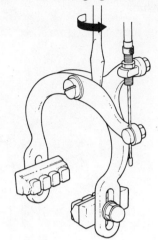

If this is not the problem and you have tried everything else a complete disassembly (see above) is necessary. Study each part to see if it obviously needs replacing (like a washer bent out of shape). It may be that the yoke cannot rotate on the pivot bolt. File down and polish the bolt, or enlarge the holes in the yokes (with a taper ream, or emery cloth wrapped around a nail). If none of these things work get a new brake mechanism.

Center pull

● Is cable adjusted correctly?
● Are all parts there? Is spring intact and properly mounted?
● Is mounting nut A tight?

If one shoe is dragging against rim, slack off A, center brake mechanism, and re-tighten A.

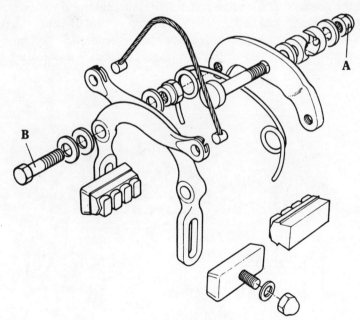

If both shoes stick try lubricating the pivot bolts B while wiggling the yokes back and forth. No? You will have to get into the pivot bolts.

First disconnect the spring. Study the bolts to see if they are type 1, where the pivot bolt screws into the brake arm bridge H; type 2, where the pivot bolt screws into a post which comes off the brake arm bridge and on which the yoke rotates; or type 3, where the pivot bolt simply goes through the brake arm bridge and the yoke rotates on a bushing.

Type 1

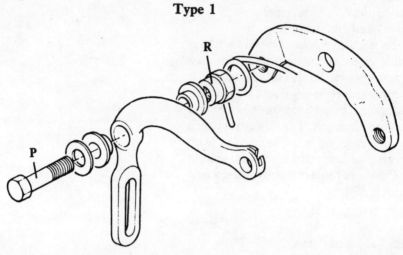

First try slacking off the locknut R and undoing the pivot bolt P one quarter to one half turn. On some models the locknut R is on the other side of the brake arm bridge H. If yoke will now pivot, retighten locknut R. If not, remove pivot bolt P altogether. Keep track of all the washers. Is the pivot bolt P straight? Look for dirt or scarred surfaces on the pivot bolt P and inside the yoke. Clean and polish. If yoke will not turn freely on pivot bolt, enlarge yoke hole with a taper file or ream, drill, or emery cloth wrapped around a nail. Or sand down the pivot bolt. Lubricate and reassemble.

Type 2

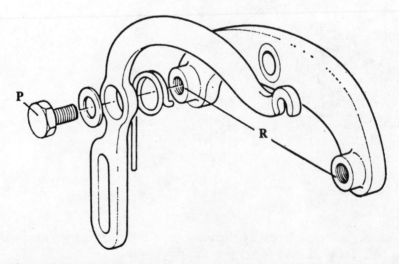

Undo spring and remove pivot bolt P. Remove yoke and keep track of washers. Check for grit and clean. Is post R scarred? Polish with fine sandpaper or steel wool until yoke will rotate freely on it. Lubricate and reassemble.

Type 3

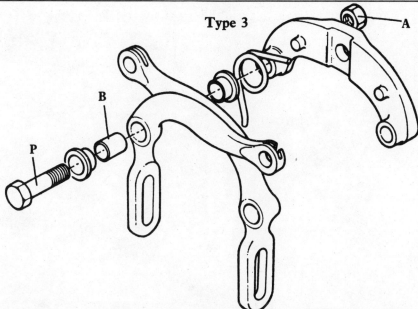

Undo nut A and remove pivot bolt P. Keep track of bushings and washers. Is pivot bolt straight? Is bushing B in good condition? Check for grit and clean. If yoke still sticks, try polishing pivot bolt with steel wool. Lubricate and reassemble.

Cantilever

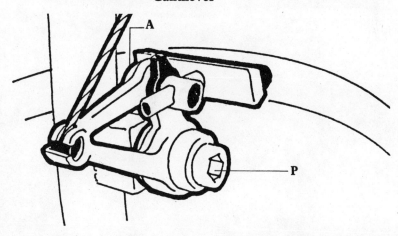

First check that the cables are all OK and properly adjusted. Sometimes dirt, or a kink in the straddle wire, will cause uneven pull on the arms. Disconnect the straddle wire and check the movement of each arm. If rough, then it is probably dirty and needs cleaning. Undo pivot bolt P, take apart in orderly sequence, clean and lubricate, and reassemble. If spring tension is weak, then unwind the arm and bend the spring until it is stronger, or replace the spring. If the springs won't pull the arms away, see if you can move the brake shoes away from the rim (eyebolt nut A) so that the springs engage sooner when the arms are compressed.

SWITCHBACK

Staying Aboard

Contents

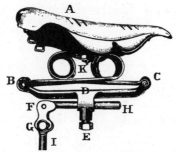

Saddles

General

Saddle design is a balance between supporting weight and reducing friction between the legs. The more actively you ride, the narrrower the saddle. Roadsters and cruisers tend toward wide, pillow like saddles that often have big coil springs. At the other extreme, racing bikes tend toward sparse, lean saddles that are little more than a rail. Between these two points are a galaxy of saddles in varying widths and materials, many with padding or other insulation.

I don't know you, how you ride, and least of all anything about your behind. If you are just starting out, an anatomic design saddle with some padding is probably a safe bet. If you are female, be sure to get a woman's model. Later on you can slim things down. Cindy Whitehead was a mile along in a punishing 50 mile off-road race when the saddle fell off. She finished the remaining 49 miles standing up - and won the race.

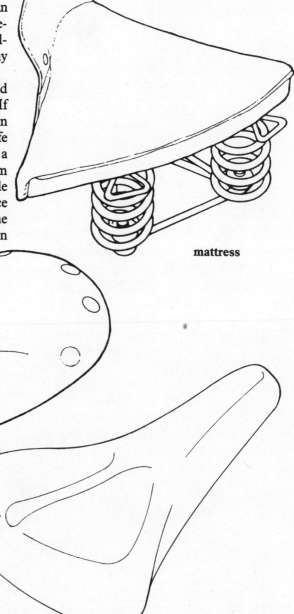

mattress

racing

anatomic

Adjustment

Saddles with a plastic base rarely have any provision for adjusting cover tension. Good leather saddles do, at nut A:

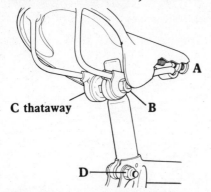

To raise or lower the saddle, loosen the binder bolt D. Be sure to use a tool that fits the nut precisely. It has to be tight, and the wrong tool can tear up the nut. On a mountainbike there will often be a quick release lever. If it is not tight enough, open the lever, hold the opposite side nut still, and wind the lever on until it is tight enough when closed. The seat post should be lightly greased to prevent corrosion and ensure that you can get it back out.

The seat post above is the most basic kind. To remove the saddle from the seat post, adjust it backward, forward, or to tilt it, loosen nuts B and C. More sophisticated seat posts have micro-adjusting bolts: loosen bolt or screw on end to be raised, tighten bolt or screw on end to be lowered. Loosen both an identical number of turns to slide saddle backward or forward. For proper saddle position refer to Fitting.

Leather saddles need a bit of care. Brooks Proofide is good stuff. If you want to speed up the break-in process, saturate the saddle with neatsfoot oil from UNDERNEATH.

Troubleshooting

If the seat post keeps sinking slowly into the frame as you ride, no matter how tightly you draw up the binder bolt, then the post is almost certainly too small in diameter for the seat tube. Pop around to a bike shop and see what can be done.

Some bikes are ultra-minimalist and just want to be kept going at zero expense. You can stop a seat post from sinking by installing a thin bolt through the frame and seat post at point P:

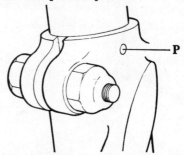

Turn the bike upside down while drilling the hole, or metal shavings will fall down the seat tube and make hash of the bottom bracket bearings. Make more than one hole in the seat post if you want height to be adjustable, and make them in a spiral pattern if you want to be fancy:

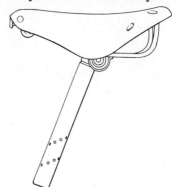

Handlebars

Adjustment

To change handlebar position loosen
binder bolt(s) A on stem and reset bars:

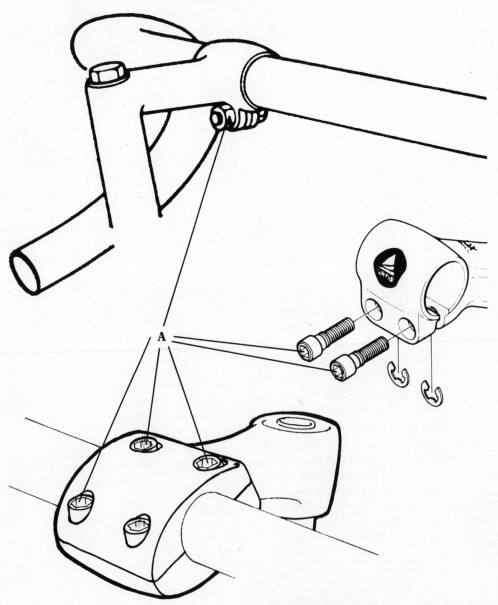

Height adjustments are made with the
stem (next section).

Taping

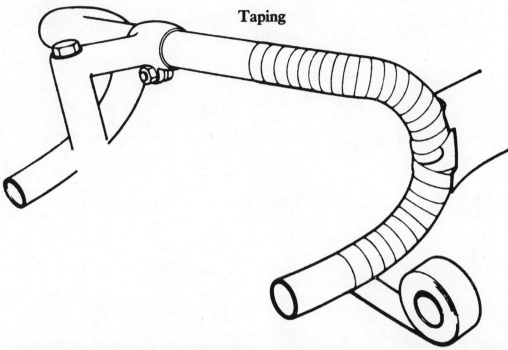

I prefer non-adhesive tapes. Adhesive tapes gum everything up with a sticky residue which ultimately leaks out all over the place. There are many options in tapes, see Accessories for information.

Be sure that the brakes are in the position you want. Start about 2'' from the stem. Use a small piece of scotch tape to hold down the end of the tape where you start. Work directly from the roll to minimize confusion, and maintain a continuous light tension as you apply the tape. First take a couple of turns at the starting point and then start down the bar, overlapping ½ to ⅓ of the tape. At the bends you will have to overlap more on the inside than the outside. For a neat job, loosen the brake lever mount, tape underneath, and retighten. When you reach the end of the bar leave an extra 2-3'' of tape. Fold this over and push it inside the handlebar.

Finish off with a bar plug (bike stores) to hold tape securely. If plug is difficult to insert, rub some soap on it and tap it in with a hammer. Bar plugs can also be made from champagne corks. Use something - if you spill, an open bar end can make a hole in you.

Troubleshooting

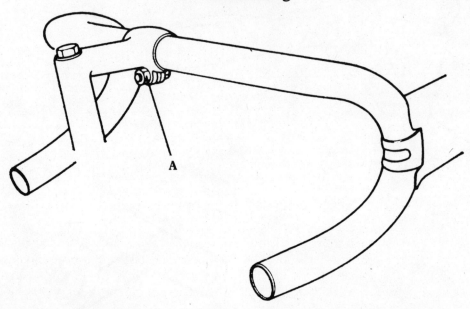

A

● Bar spins around on stem: tighten binder bolt A. If binder bolt still spins uselessly, remove it and see if the little protrusion on it has been worn off, or if the corresponding slot on the stem into which it fits has been damaged. If the problem is the bolt, get a new one. If it is the stem, get a proper bolt with a hex nut that you can grip with a wrench or Allen key. In a pinch, you can use pliers or vise-grips to hold the round part of the old bolt.

If the binder bolt is in working order, check and see that the lips of the stem do not meet:

If they do, it's either a new stem or new bars (expensive) or a shim (cheap). Shimming: find a small piece of flat metal slightly longer than the width of the stem lips. Something that won't rust, like aluminum, is preferable (hardware stores, machine shop litter, junk lying around), but part of a tin can or a finishing nail will do. Remove binder bolt. Using a screwdriver, prise apart the lips of the stem, slip the shim into the gap between the handlebar and the stem, and reinstall binder bolt.

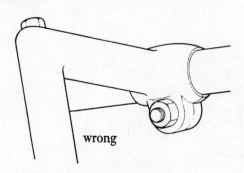

wrong

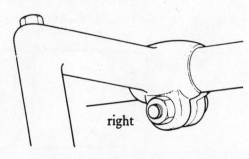

right

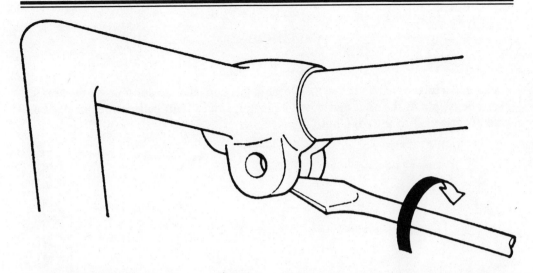

● Bent bars. Steel bars can be bent back into shape. Bent aluminum bars should be used for sculpture. Bending them back into shape risks fatigue and an unexpected failure that could kill you. It's obviously very tempting to bend expensive aluminum bars back into shape. I'm telling you on the basis of experience that you should not.

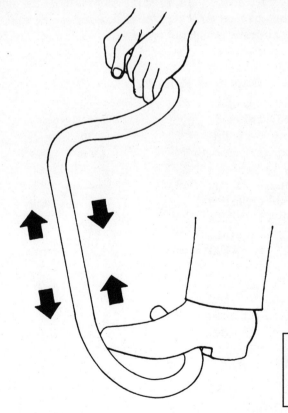

MECHANIC GENERAL'S WARNING: Bending Aluminum Bars Causes Fatigue, And May Complicate Riding.

Stem

How It Works

The stem is a tube which holds the handlebar in position, and fits down inside the headset. The tube is split at the end, and down its length runs a bolt, called an expander bolt, which is attached to a wedge nut (A):

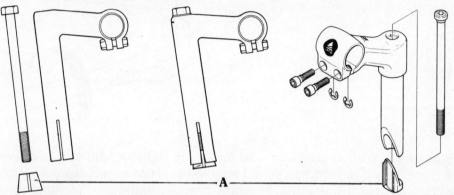

A

When the expander bolt is tightened, it draws the wedge nut into the tube, and this in turn forces apart the split sides of the stem, pressing them against the sides of the headset and holding everything in place. Another type of design does not split the tube, but uses a slanting washer to force the wedge nut against the head tube. The basic idea is the same.

Adjust or Remove

Undo expander bolt two turns. Using a wooden block or piece of cardboard held against the expander bolt to protect the finish, tap it with a hammer or heavy object. Repeat as necessary to get stem loose. Adjust height or remove. If you remove altogether and reassemble, note that some wedge nuts have a dog guide which must fit into a corresponding slot on the stem. KEEP AT LEAST 2½'' OF STEM IN THE HEAD TUBE.

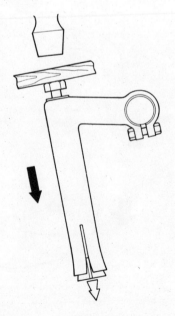

Retighten expander bolt so that when you stand in front of the bike with the wheel clasped between your legs, you can twist the handlebar and stem in the head tube. That way, if you take a spill the bars will give instead of bending or breaking.

Troubleshooting

● Stem is loose and expander bolt comes out freely: wedge nut has come off. Take out stem, turn bike upside down, and shake wedge nut out. Reassemble.

● Stem is frozen in place and expander bolt spins uselessly: threads on wedge nut have stripped (1), or expander bolt has snapped (2).

(1) Separate expander bolt from wedge nut by grasping it with pliers or vise-grips and maintaining a continuous upward pressure while twisting it. If it is obstinate, help it along by wedging a screwdriver between the expander bolt head and the stem:

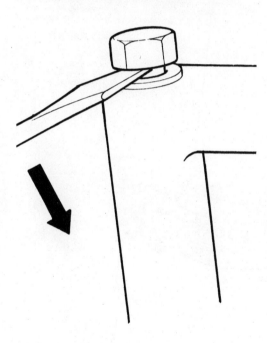

Once the expander bolt is free of wedge nut leave it inside the stem.

(2) Remove top half of snapped expander bolt. Find a rod or bolt which will fit inside stem and touch wedge nut while still protruding an inch or two above the stem. (1) and (2): Use a hammer to lightly tap the expander bolt or rod, working the end in-

side the stem around the edges of the wedge nut:

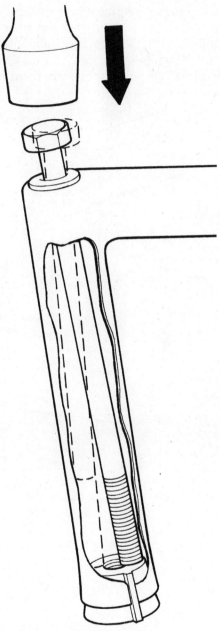

Work firmly but gently; too hard a blow will jam the whole thing. When stem comes loose, turn bike upside down and shake out wedge nut.

● Stem tube cracked. Replace it.

Headset

How It Works

The headset connects the front forks to the head tube of the bicycle frame. The fork is held solidly to the bicycle but allowed to turn freely by using ball bearing sets at the top and bottom of the head tube. Starting at the bottom, the crown of the fork has a fork crown bearing race (A), then come the ball bearings (B), and next is the bottom set race (C), screwed or force-fitted into the head tube:

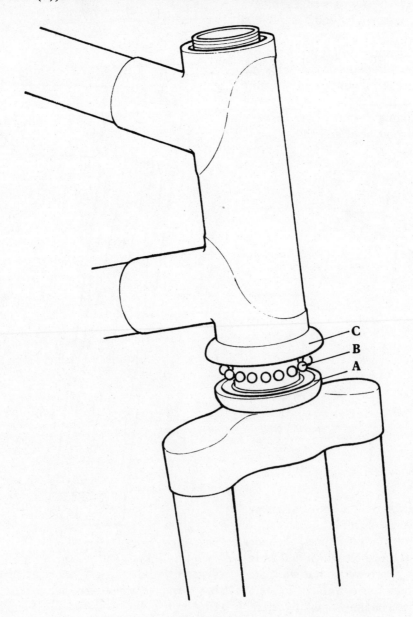

Put together, it looks like this:

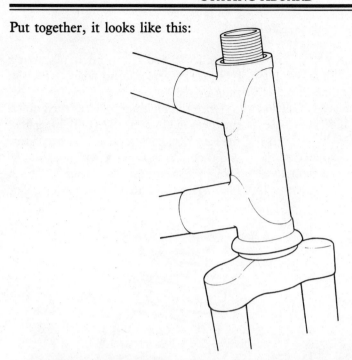

To keep the forks inside the head tube and evenly positioned, a second set of races is used at the top of the head tube. There is a top set race, screwed or force-fitted into the head tube, more ball bearings, and the key to whole business, the top race, which is threaded onto the fork tube:

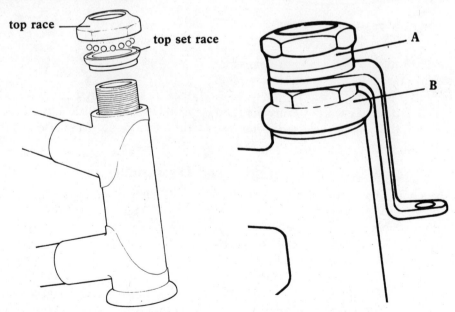

This is capped by a washer, the cable hanger and/or other accessory mounts, if used, and a locknut to keep the top threaded race exactly in place.

Adjustments

Forks should turn freely but without excessive up and down play. A simple test for looseness is to lock the front brake and rock the bike forward and backward. A clicking noise from the headset indicates loose bearings. To adjust, loosen locknut A. Sometimes this locknut is designed with notches. If you haven't got the right tool to fit, it can be loosened with a hammer and center punch or screwdriver.

wrenches borrowed from a plumber's toolbox, be very careful not to bend the nuts or races.

Once the locknut is loose, turn down the threaded top race B handtight against the bearings, back it off one quarter turn, and then lock it in place with locknut A, using a medium amount of force. Check play again. If things are looking good,

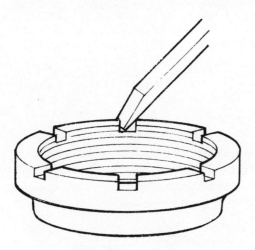
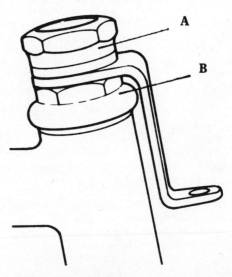

There are also many special designs that manufacturers have cleverly arranged to require a tool made only by themselves. It is unfortunately worth having the right tool for the job. If you go in for big

then lock up the system firmly. The trick is to have just a little extra slack so that the final lock up gives perfect adjustment.

Lubrication and Disassembly

The headset should be dismantled, cleaned, and regreased about once a year. Remove stem (see above). Lay bike down on side with newspaper or white rag under the headset. This is to catch falling ball bearings. There are many different headsets, and no way for me to tell you how many bearings are in yours. So don't lose any.

Undo and remove the locknut, washer,

cable clamp (if you have one), and anything else necessary to get to the threaded top race. Secure the fork to the frame. You can do this with rubber bands, elastic carrier straps, shoelaces, etc., but the simplest way is to hold it with your hand. Be sure to do something, or what you do next will cause the fork to fall out with a rain of ball bearings. Next: undo the threaded top race A:

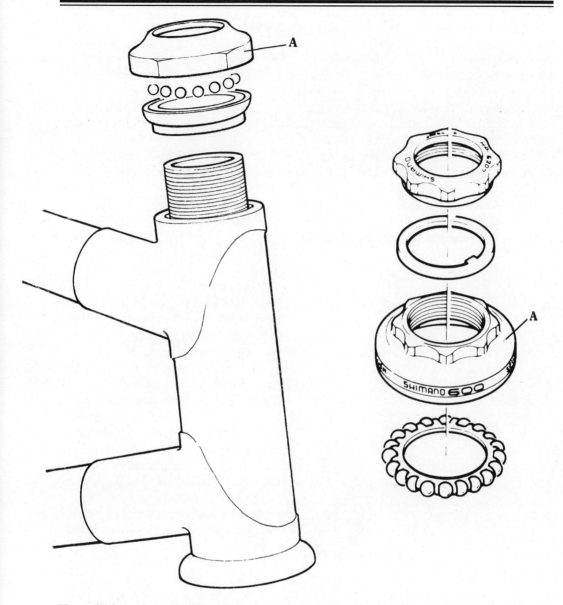

You will have loose ball bearings and are to follow instructions for (1), or bearings in a clip, in which case follow (2).

(1) A few may stick to the threaded race, a few may fall on the newspaper, and most will probably stay in the top set race. Gather them all together, count them, and put bearings and race into box or jar. Next: make sure head tube is positioned over newspaper or rag. Slowly draw out fork tube. Ball bearings will fall out. Gather and count them, including any that are still stuck to the bottom set race, the fork tube, or whatever, and put them in a jar.

(2) Clipped bearings: Lucky you. Remove clip, noting carefully which side goes down against the top set race, and put in a jar or box. Now draw out fork tube and lift out

clip for bottom race. Further disassembly for routine lubrication is not necessary.

(1) & (2) Soak and clean thoroughly all parts in solvent. Use a rag to clean out the top and bottom set races, and the fork crown race. Ball bearings should be smooth and un-pitted. Clipped bearings should be securely in place. Races should be evenly colored all the way around where the balls run. Place them on a glass surface to see if they are bent or warped. Replace any defective parts.

Reassembly: pack fresh grease in the top and bottom set races. Just fill the grooves; excessive grease will attract dirt.

(1) Push ball bearings into grease on bottom set race. Grease will hold them in place.

(2) Put some grease inside the clip. Slip it down over the fork tube to rest on the fork crown race.

(1) & (2) Carefully insert fork tube into head tube. Keeping it snug against the bearings, check that it turns freely. Hang onto fork so that it does not fall back out.

(1) Stick ball bearings into grease of top set race.

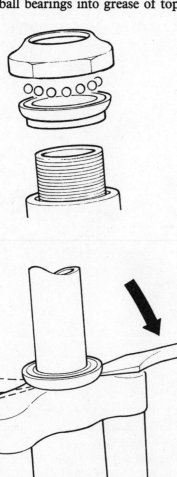

(2) Grease and slip on clipped bearings.

(1) & (2) Screw down top threaded race. These threads are fine, so do it carefully (see General Notes for best technique). Set it hand tight, and then back it off one quarter turn. Pile on washer, cable anchor mount, etc., and locknut. Be careful to keep threaded top race in position when tightening locknut. Check for play.

If the bike has been in a smash-up or if rust has got to the bearings, it may be necessary to do a complete disassembly. This is a job better left to a bike shop, because the head tube itself should be checked and faced with a special (quite expensive) tool to ensure that everything is correctly sized and positioned. If the frame is new, this work is essential before installing a headset.

Take fork and ball bearings out as per for lubrication. Remove crown fork race from fork. If it is stuck, pry it up *gently* with a screwdriver, working around the edges a little at a time. Be careful, it is easy to bend:

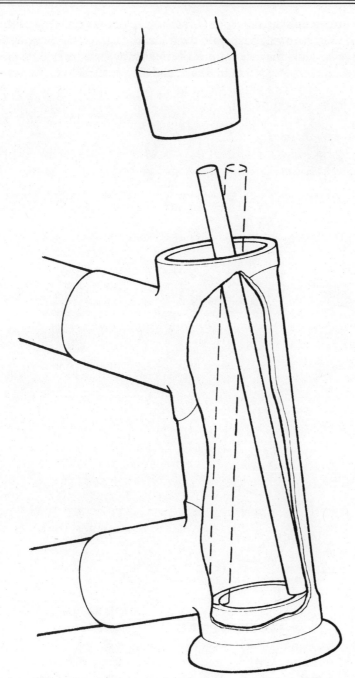

Remove top and bottom set races. You may possibly have threaded set races, in which case simply unscrew them. For force set races, insert a large screwdriver, piece of pipe, or stiff rod into the head tube and tap around the edges of the race.

Clean all parts with solvent. Test races for uniformity by seeing if they lie flat on glass or other smooth surface.

Reassembly: screw in threaded set races. For force set races it is best to use a wooden block to avoid denting or bending the race and hammer:

Make sure that the race is seated fully into the frame. Use a wooden block also on the fork crown race if it is balky but be very delicate, and tap evenly all the way around the race.

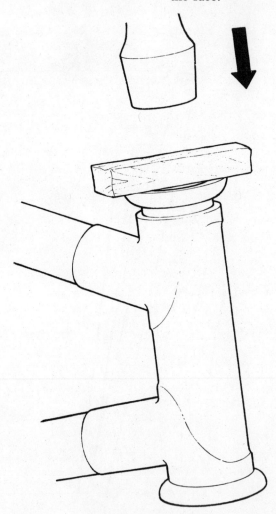

Troubleshooting

● Fork tube is extremely loose in the head tube. May just need adjustment, but if things have come to that pass I suggest dismantling and checking condition of parts.

● Adjustment does not work: top threaded race or fork is stripped. Dismantle and see. It is unlikely that this is the result of

excessive tightening, and likely the top threaded race was screwed down off center. When you have your new parts review General Notes, Threading, before starting.

● Fork binds or catches, or makes grating and rasping noises when you turn handlebars. Adjust as per above. No go? Something is broken or bent, completely worn out, or there are too many or too few bearings. Review the possibilities. Has fork or headset been whacked severely lately? A couple of months ago? Did you or someone else service the headset and lose a bearing or two, or place too many in one race and not enough in the other? Or perhaps the bike is simply ancient, and needs new races? In any case, disassemble, clean, and check all parts. Are bearings evenly distributed (ask your bike shop how many should be in your headset), and free of dents, cracks, and pitting? Do races lie flat on a glass surface? Replace defective parts and reassemble. If you can find nothing wrong take the parts down to your bike shop and see what they say.

Forks

How They Work

The fork holds the front wheel in place and allows the bike to be steered. The fork arms are curved, raking the axle drop-outs away from a line drawn through the fork tube:

The amount of rake varies according to the purpose of the bike. Broadly, touring and mountainbikes have more rake, racing bikes have less. The more rake, the more stable the handling, although this is also a function of head tube angle.

The main problem that can arise with forks is if they are bent in an accident. The best thing is to replace them. Bending fatigues metal and makes it weak. The weakness does not show. What happens is that the fork suddenly gives up while you are tearing along at 30 mph. This does not happen very often, but once is enough.

On the other hand, bike shops do have special tools for straightening bent forks and if the bend in yours is slight, you may want to try it. Go by the advice of the shop. Be aware that you are taking a calculated risk, however small.

Tests for bent forks: the bike will ride funny. If forks are bent to one side, the bike will always want to turn to the left or right. Test by taking your hands off the handlebars. Any decently set-up bike can be ridden hands off for miles. Forks which have been bent in, usually through a head-on collision, make the bike's ride choppy and harsh, and make it feel like it wants to dive in the corners. A sure sign of bent-in forks is wrinkled paint on the upper fork arms, or at the join of the fork tube and

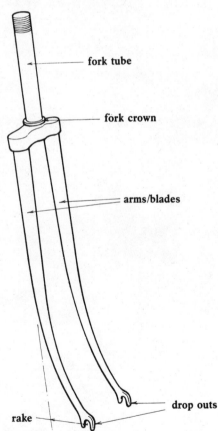

fork crown. Forks which have been bent out (rare) manifest themselves in a sloppy, mushy ride, and curious, long arcing turns. Again, there will probably be paint wrinkles at the bend point.

273

Wheels

Contents

Wheel Removal

Wheels need to be removed often, for a variety of reasons, and sometimes on the road. So you can and will do this with a free-standing bike, but it is much easier if it is hung up. Most bikes can simply be turned upside down on handlebars and seat, as long as cables or shift selectors are not damaged. Bikes with caliper brakes in proper adjustment should require some slacking of the brakes so that the tire will pass between the brake shoes.

Front wheel, any bike

Wheel will be held to fork by hex nuts, wing nuts, or a quick-release lever:

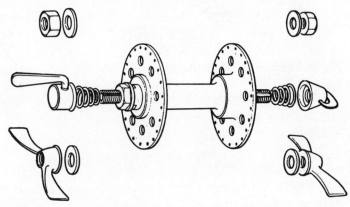

For nuts, undo both simultaneously (counter-clockwise) and unwind a turn or two. Levers, pull open, rotate slightly to loosen if necessary. Remove wheel. Note washers go outside fork drop-outs.

Rear Wheel

Derailleur gear bikes

Run chain to smallest sprocket. Undo nuts or lever as for front wheel, and push wheel down and out. If you have a free hand hold back the derailleur so that the freewheel clears it easily, otherwise just gently wiggle it by.

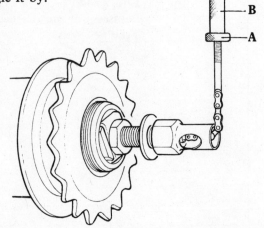

Hub gear bikes

Shift to 3rd gear. Disconnect shift cable at rear hub by undoing locknut A and unscrewing adjustor sleeve B from pole: Undo nuts simultaneously (counter-clockwise). Remove wheel, and note washers are outside drop-outs.

Coaster brake bikes

Disconnect coaster brake bracket from bike frame (metal arm at left end of rear axle), undo nuts (counter-clockwise), and remove wheel.

Replacing Wheels

Front, any bike

Axle with nuts: back off nuts a few turns and slip axle onto drop-outs. Washers go outside drop-outs. Set nuts finger tight and check that rim is centered between fork arms before snugging them down. Re-set caliper brakes if you have them.

Levers: slip axle onto drop-outs with lever on left side of bike. If this is difficult, hold knurled cone with one hand and unwind lever a couple of turns with the other. Slip axle on drop-outs and wind lever down just short of finger tight. Check that wheel rim is centered between fork arms, and close lever so that it points upwards and backwards. It should be firmly shut but not hysterically so. Re-set caliper brakes.

Rear wheel

Derailleur gear bikes

Work axle into drop-outs, slipping chain over smallest sprocket on freewheel. Set nuts or lever for light tension. Pull wheel toward rear of bike until right end of axle hits the back of the drop-out. Use this as a pivot point to center the rim between the chain-stays, and tighten nuts or lever. Re-set caliper brake.

Hub gear bikes

Work axle into drop-outs, slipping chain over sprocket. Lightly tighten nuts (washers are outside drop-outs), and pull back wheel so chain has ½'' play up and down:

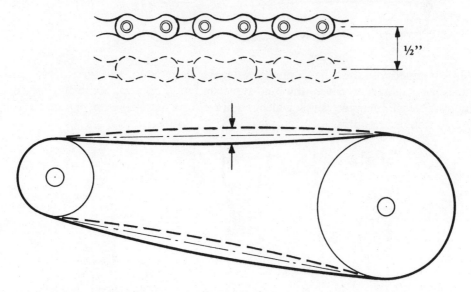

Center rim between chain-stays and tighten down nuts. Check chain tension. If coaster brake, reconnect brake bracket to frame. If hub gears, move gear selector to 3rd (H), reconnect barrel sleeve to hub gear chain, and set locknut with cable slightly slack. Test gears and adjust if necessary. Re-set caliper brake.

Tires

How They Work

Any pneumatic tire works by supporting a casing, the part touching the road, with an inside tube which is filled with air like a balloon. With tubular tires the tube is fully encased by the casing; with clincher tires the tube is held in place by a combination of two wire beads which run around the outside edges of the tire, and the rim sides:

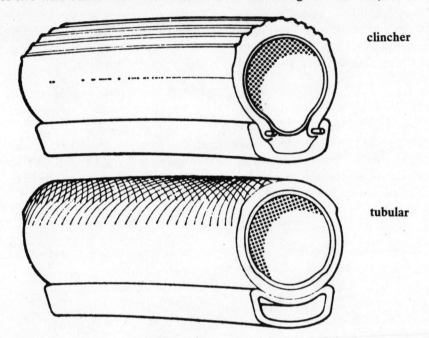

clincher

tubular

Air is pumped into the tube through a valve which comes in two types. Most clincher tubes have Schraeder valves, the kind typically found on cars. Some clinchers and all tubulars have Presta type valves, which require either a bicycle pump, or a special adaptor for gas station air pumps.

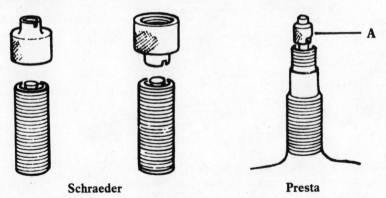

Schraeder   Presta

On a Presta, undo the locknut A in order to add or remove air.

Routine Adjustments

Tire pressure

It is best to use your own tire pressure gauge (bike shops). The right pressure within 5 psi makes a big difference in performance. Gas station gauges are unreliable. When filling your tires at a gas station do it yourself. The proper pressure for your tire may be as high as 100 pounds per square inch, but the total volume of air is small, and it takes only seconds to blow a tire out. Some air pumps take a few moments to fill the tire; others will do it instantaneously. Jab the air hose down on the valve for just a second, then release and test. Tires should be hard enough so you can barely dent them with a finger, and bulge only very slightly when ridden.

Bicycle pump and Schraeder valve: draw hose fitting out of pump handle and fit to pump and valve. Check connections periodically as you pump. Alternatively, the pump may just fit over the valve and lock in place with a lever. Presta valve: undo valve locknut, push pump on valve, hold firmly to tire with one hand, and pump with the other. Keep pump perpendicular to valve. Disengage with a sharp downward knock of the hand; wiggling will lose air and possibly bend valve. Close valve locknut.

Know the recommended pressure for your tires. This can vary from 30 to 110 psi depending on tire size and model. A difference of as little as 5 psi from recommended pressure can adversely affect performance

Increase pressure for heavy riders and/or heavy touring loads, bad conditions, and riotous living. The best protection for a tire is plenty of air. A 200 lb weight rider will need 15 to 20 psi more than a 125 lb weight rider with low to medium range 40 to 70 psi tires, and 5 to 10 psi more with high range 90 to 100 psi tires. Keep an eye on matters. Sometimes a rim and tire combination is loose, and the tire can blow off the rim if grossly over-inflated. Other times you can safely double the manufacturer's recommended pressure. It all depends - look and see.

Hot weather in the 80's and up may require that you bleed some air from the tire to avoid over-inflation and a possible blowout. In very slippery conditions some people reduce pressure in an effort to obtain better traction. This trick works, especially with wide mountainbike tires, but increases the risk of pinching the tube and puncturing it in a distinctive 'snakebite' pattern. I like to keep air in the tires.

Riding

Some people are more puncture-prone than others. Most tire problems are the result of picked-up debris working into the casing as you ride. Going over rocks, through pot-holes and on and off curbs will cause ruptures. Cultivate an eye for these hazards, and if you are forced to go through a patch of broken glass, for example, check and see that the tire has not picked any up. Be aware of your tires and - the fates willing - you will have less trouble. A useful gadget for tubular tires is a nail-catcher (bike shops) which rides lightly over the tire and brushes off particles before they can cause damage:

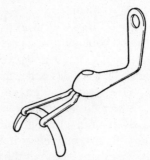

Keep oil away from tires. It rots rubber. Grease, do not oil bicycle pumps. Oiled bicycle pumps can vaporize and blow oil inside the tube. Check cement on tubulars about once a week.

Care and Storage

Keep clincher spares in a dry place. Tubular spares should be carried folded so the tread is on the outside and not folded back on itself. Under the seat is a dandy place. Secure with straps or rubber bands:

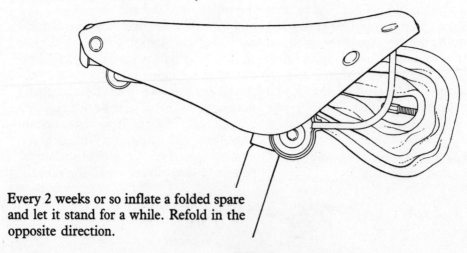

Every 2 weeks or so inflate a folded spare and let it stand for a while. Refold in the opposite direction.

Flats

Flats take the form of violent blow-outs (rare), or punctures (common) which leak air with varying degrees of speed. Blow outs are usually terminal, doing so much damage that the tube and sometimes the tire must be replaced. Punctures which are not gaping wounds can be repaired. There is debate as to proper policy for this. Some people patch until the tube looks like calico. Others, myself included, assign a tube to spare status once it has had a couple of punctures.

Clincher tires

You will need a tube patch kit containing patches, glue, an abrasive surface, tire levers (the kind which hook onto spokes are handiest), and chalk.

First check valve by inflating tire slightly and placing a drop of spit on the end of the valve stem. A leaky valve will bubble or spit back. Tighten valve if necessary with valve cap or suitable part of pressure gauge:

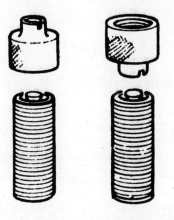

Hooray if the problem was a loose or defective valve. If not, spin the wheel and look for an obvious cause like a nail or piece of glass. Yes? Dig it out and mark the spot.

What you do next depends on circumstances. It is easier to work on a puncture with the wheel off the bike. However, you may not have the tools to remove the wheel, or be in a hurry. If you know where the puncture is, the wheel does not have to be removed. At any rate, the basic procedure is the same.

Deflate tire and remove valve stem locknut if you have one. Work the tire back and forth with your hands to get the bead free of the rim. If the tire is a loose fit on the rim you may be able to get it off with your hands. This is best, because tire levers may pinch the tube and cause additional punctures. The secret of the trick is work the casing with your fingers, moving it away from the rim sides and down into the deeper groove where the spokes are held. When everything is loosened up, take a healthy grip on the tire with both hands and pull it up so that one bead comes over the rim:

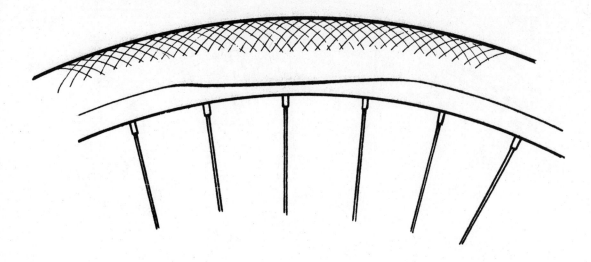

Then go around the rim working the bead completely off.

You will probably need to use tire levers. Use tire levers, not screwdrivers, as these are likely to cut the tube. An alternative are small ring wrenches, so long as they are smooth and free from burrs. Free bead from rim, as per above. Insert tire lever under bead, being careful not to pinch the tube, and lever it over the side.

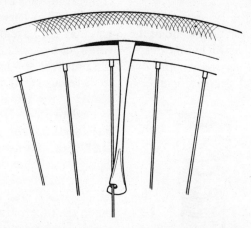

Insert second lever 2" or 3" away from first lever, and past where bead is over side of rim. Lever lever. For most tires this will do the job. No? A third lever. If this doesn't work, use the now free 2nd lever for a fourth attempt, repeating process as often as necessary:

If you don't have tire levers which will hook onto the spokes, then you will need to use elbows, knees, etc., to hold down the levers as you work away. Be careful not to inadvertently crush a spoke, and keep your face away in case something slips and tire levers start jumping about.

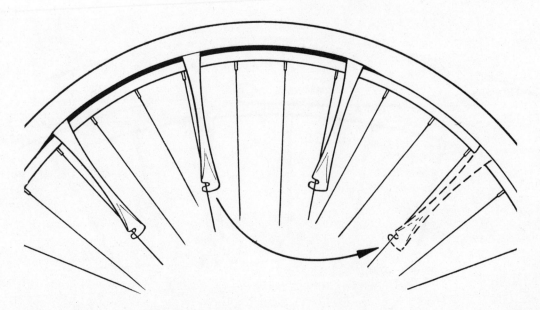

If you have only two tire levers and need a third, scrounge something up. In the country a flat rock or a stick. In the city a pencil, a beer can opener, or something from the garbage. Look around. At any hour there will be something. Prise up bead with a tire lever. Insert foraged tool between bead and rim and wiggle lever out:

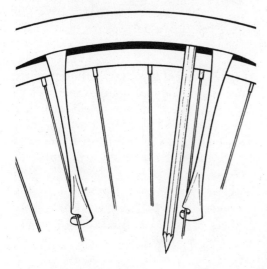

Use tire levers to make two prises on either side of foraged tool.

When one bead is off the rim, push valve stem up into tire, and remove tube. Use chalk or eidetic memory to make note of which way tube was in the tire. Inflate tube and rotate it past your ear. If you can locate the puncture through the hiss of escaping air, mark it with chalk. No? Immerse tube in water and look for escaping air bubbles. Dry tube with a rag while holding finger over puncture, then mark with chalk.

Take sandpaper or metal abrader supplied with patch kit and rough up the area around the puncture. Spread a layer of cement over this area and let dry tacky. Peel the paper backing off a patch without touching the surface thus exposed, and press it firmly on the puncture. Set tube aside to dry.

If puncture was on inside of tube, probably a protruding spoke caused it:

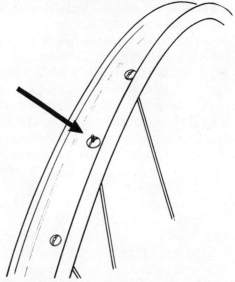

File the spoke flush with the rim. Check other spokes.

If puncture was on inside of tube, probably a protruding spoke caused it: fingers around inside the casing. Check the rest of the casing for embedded particles, and for ruptures or breaks:

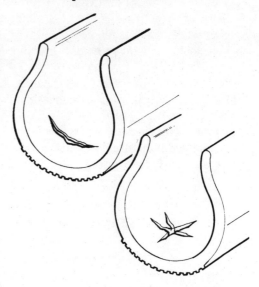

Replace the tire at the first opportunity if it has these.

To install the tube, first inflate it slightly to prevent it from folding and pinching itself. Push the part of the tube with the valve stem into the tire, and the valve stem through its hole on the rim. Fit valve stem locknut loosely. Stuff rest of tube into tire being careful not to pinch or tear it. Check that valve stem is still straight.

Push valve stem partway out, and slip bead of tire at that point back over the rim. It is important that you hold the base of the valve stem clear of the rim as you do this, or the bead may catch on it, creating a bulge in the tire.

Work around the rim replacing the bead and always taking care not to pinch the tube. Ideally you can do the entire job with your hands. Check that the valve stem is still straight. The last bit will be hard. Just

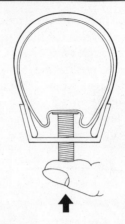

keep working at it with your thumbs, first from one side, then from the other. When about 2'' of bead remains give it the grand mal effort. Don't wonder if it will go over; decide it will. If you have to use a tire lever, be very careful not to pinch the tube.

Tubular tires

You will need:

Patches	Needle
Thread	Rubber cement
Sandpaper	Talcum powder
Chalk	Screwdriver

Sharp knife or razor blade.

Remove wheel. Deflate tire completely by opening locknut A on valve and holding down.

Remove tire from rim with your hands. Inflate and immerse in water a little at a time. Do not be misled by air bubbles coming out by the valve. Since the tire is sewn, the valve hold and puncture hold are the only places air can escape. Hold finger over

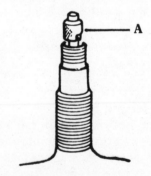

puncture when located, dry tire, and mark puncture with chalk.

With a screwdriver or similar implement pry away about 5'' to 6'' of the tape on the inner side of the tire at the puncture area:

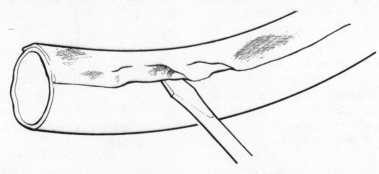

Next cut stitching about 2'' to either side of puncture. Make only two cuts to avoid numerous bits of thread, and cut upwards to miss tire:

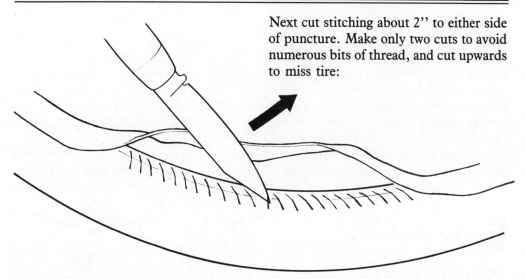

Gently remove tube and locate leak. A mixture of soap and water will pinpoint elusive ones. Dry tube if wet. Abrade area around puncture with sandpaper. Apply cement and let dry. Peel protective paper from patch without touching surface thus exposed and apply to puncture. Dust with talc to prevent tube from sticking to casing. Get whatever caused puncture out of casing. Insert tube, inflate, and check for leaks. Do this carefully. You are going to be mad if you get it all back together only to discover it still leaks.

Thread the needle and knot the two loose ends of thread. In a pinch 12 lb linen thread or silk fishing line will do. Using the old holes, start with an overlap of about half an inch past where thread was cut. Pinch the sides of the casing between thumb and forefinger to keep the tube out of the way:

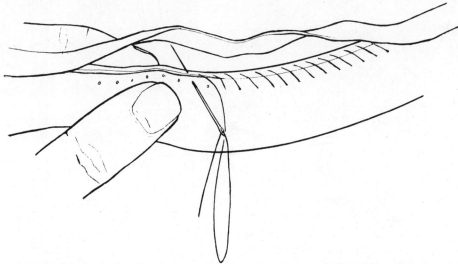

Pull stitches firm, but not so tight as to cut casing. Finish with a half inch overlap into original stitching. Layer cement on casing and inside of peeled-away tape and keep apart until dry. Position carefully and press together firmly.

Mounting a tubular

Oh fun. Stretch a new tire by inflating it off the rim, and then on the rim. If the rim cement is old and gungy, clean it off with shellac thinner or solvent (bike shops). There are two methods for mounting a tubular: double-sided rim tape, and cement. Cement is doubtless stronger, but I've had no problems with double-sided tape, which has the advantage in convenience. Whichever product is used, there are two basic ways of doing the job.

(1) Slow but sure. If using tape, apply one side to rim and leave protective paper on other side. Deflate tire. Insert valve. Stand rim on soft surface with valve stem up, and working from above, work tire down over rim.

Be careful to distribute tire evenly round rim. Finish by grabbing with both hands and getting the last bit over by main force:

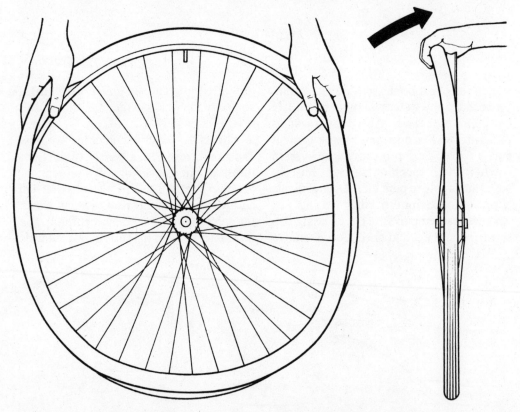

Inflate tire and check that it is evenly distributed and centered on rim. Deflate. If tape, pull away protective paper wrapping, feeding tire into place as you go. If cement, roll back a portion of the tire and brush glue on rim and lining. Repeat all the way around and from both sides. Check again for evenness. Inflate hard. Allow half a day to dry before using or tire may creep (bunch up in spots) or simply come off the rim in a corner.

(2) Fast method. Apply glue to rim and tire and allow to dry tacky. Or the tape. Wear old clothes and assemble as above.

Road repairs: use the old cement on the rim and don't lean hard into corners going home. Or, double-sided tape.

SPORT and PLAY

Rims and Spokes
How They Work

The rim which supports the tire is laced in position by the spokes, which are held fast at the hub and screw into the rim, so that they are adjustable:

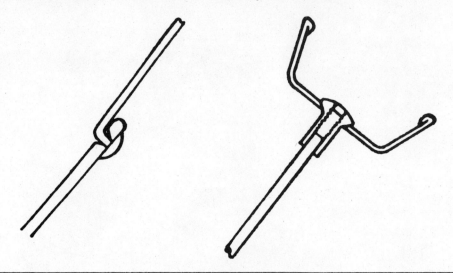

Adjustments

The tension on the spokes relative to each other determines both the strength and position of the rim. Positioning the rim correctly, both up and down, and side to side, is a long job requiring lots of patience and skill. Some people develop more skill than others. A good wheelbuilder is a craftperson well worth using. But one should still be able to do up a wheel if need be, and make minor adjustments without much fuss.

Have a spoke key. Emergency repairs can be made with a small adjustable wrench, but a spoke key is far superior. Hang up the bike or place the wheel in a jig. Spin the wheel holding a pencil or some-such at a fixed point like the fork arm or a seat stay with the point near the rim to see how bad the wobble is. If it is over one half inch pack up the entire project and take the wheel to a bike shop. If they think they can save the wheel, fine, otherwise get a new wheel.

With less than one half inch wobble: deflate tire. If job looks to be major, it will be easier if you just remove the tire altogether. Pluck the spokes with your fingers - they should all 'ping' - and tighten any that are slack so that they all have an even tension. Spokes are tightened by turning counter-clockwise. If in the course of doing this you find spokes with frozen nipples (the part that holds the spoke to the rim) they must be replaced (see below). If it more than three or four spokes I once again suggest resorting to your friendly bike shop.

Hold a chalk or pencil at the outer edge of the rim while you spin the wheel so that the high spots are marked. (Up and down, not sideways.) Working one half to one turn at a time, tighten the spokes at the chalk mark (counter-clockwise) and loosen them opposite the chalk mark. Continue until the wheel is round.

Hold pencil or chalk at side of rim so that side to side wobbles are marked. Working one half to one turn at a time, and in groups of four to six spokes, tighten up the spokes opposite the chalk mark and loosen the ones next to it:

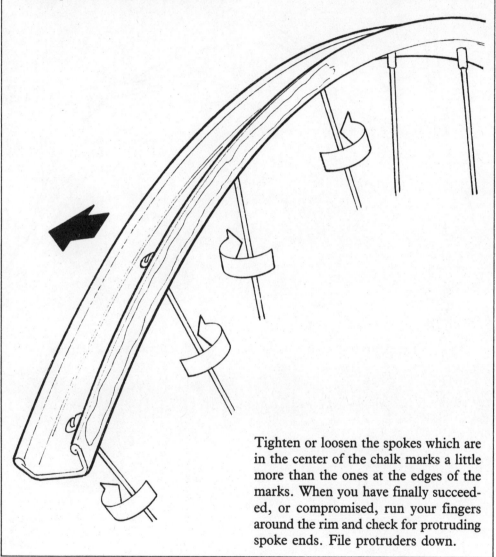

Tighten or loosen the spokes which are in the center of the chalk marks a little more than the ones at the edges of the marks. When you have finally succeeded, or compromised, run your fingers around the rim and check for protruding spoke ends. File protruders down.

Replacing Spokes

Remove tire. If you are dealing with spokes on the freewheel side of a rear wheel, the freewheel will have to be removed. Take broken spokes out of hub and rim. Get replacements which are exactly the same; many different kinds are available.

New spokes should go into hub so that head is on the opposite side of hub from adjoining spokes and spoke is pointed in opposite direction:

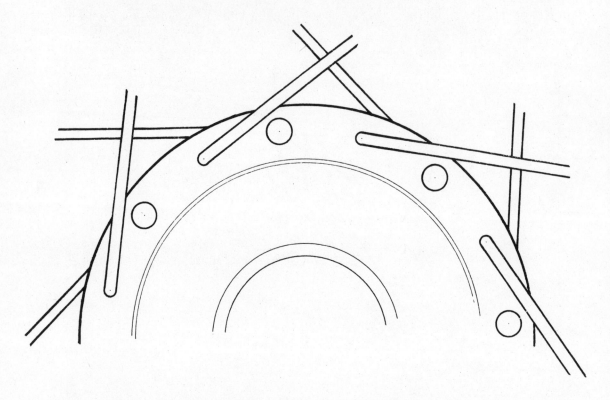

Be sure that it is correctly positioned in the hub with respect to the bevels:

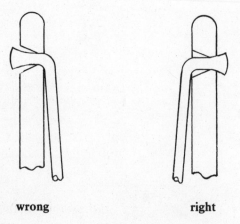

wrong   right

On almost all bikes the spokes touch where they cross. Weave new spokes through old as per other spokes on wheel. Place nipples on spokes and tighten. True wheel (see above), file down any protruding spokes which might puncture the tube, and remount tire.

Troubleshooting

- For side-to-side wobbles and elliptical wheels, see above.
- For straightening bulges in the rim caused by piling into curbs, stones, etc., you will need vise-grips, channel-lock pliers, a C-clamp, a small vise, or similar. If bulge is equal on both sides of rim, place implement over bulge and squeeze gently until the rim is even again:

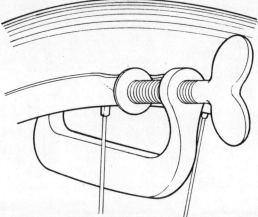

If the bulge is on the side of the rim, distribute the pinching force of your implement on the non-bulge side with a block of wood or some-such:

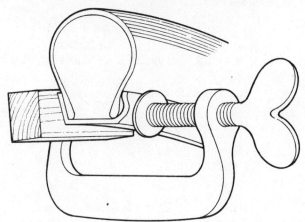

Fixing bulges almost invariably leaves a slight dimple because the metal itself was stretched, but the wheel will probably be usable.

Wheel Building

You may want to go the whole route and build your own wheels. This is at once straightforward, and an art. A good book on the subject is *Building Bicycle Wheels* by Robert Wright (World Publications). *The Bicycle Wheel* by Jobst Brandt (Avocet, Inc.) is an engaging general scientific appraisal of the wheel, and has excellent building and repair instructions.

Hubs

How They Work

A hub consists of an axle, two sets of bearings, and a casing or shell. The axle is attached to the frame drop-outs, and the casing, to which the spokes are attached, spins around it riding on the ball bearings. The method of dealing with the ball bearings gives two broad types of hubs: loose bearing and cassette (cartridge) bearing. Loose or caged bearings ride around in a cup that is part of the hub shell, and are held in place by an adjustable cone:

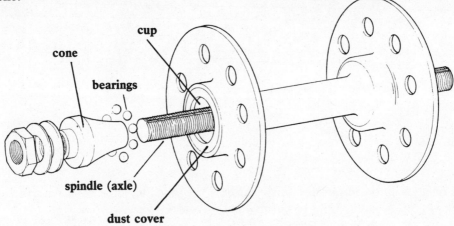

Cassette bearings are self-contained in a mechanism that includes the cup and cone functions. The cassette is pressed into the hub shell, and the axle rides on the inner part of the cassette. In most cases the design includes seals to keep out water and dirt.

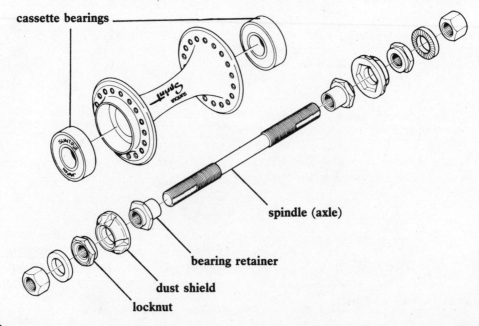

Adjustment

You need thin hub wrenches (bike shops). Hubs with loose ball bearings and adjustable cones are simple and easy to service. Some cassette bearing hubs are adjustable, and others are not. Many that are adjustable, such as SunTour hubs, need a special tool or a bit of ingenuity for the job. If you've got a sealed, cassette bearing hub - a likely possibility - check with a bike shop for instructions and any special tools.

Wheel bearings are out of adjustment if, with the axle held firmly in place, the wheel can be wiggled from side to side (usually with a clicking noise), or if the wheel will not turn easily.

Loose bearings

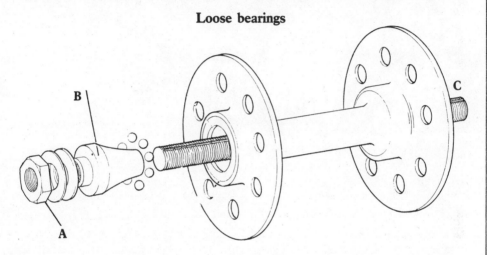

Remove wheel. Undo locknut A from cone B. Holding axle still with wrench at locknut C, screw one quarter turn. Lock in place with locknut A. Test for side-to-side play. Wheel should spin freely, and on good hubs the weight of the tire valve will pull the wheel around so that the valve rests in the 6 o'clock position. NOTE: tightening the skewer on a quick release hub compresses the axle and can make the bearing adjustment too tight. Always give a hub bearing adjustment a final check with the wheel mounted in place.

On a 3-speed hub adjustment is made on the side opposite the hub gear chain and sprocket. Loosen locknut A turn cone B fully home, back off one quarter turn, re-set locknut A:

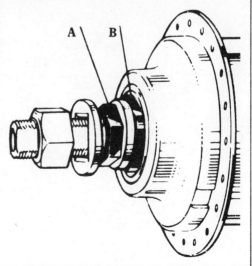

On a Sturmey-Archer SC coaster hub loosen locknut B, then turn C clockwise to tighten, counter-clockwise to loosen. Re-set locknut B:

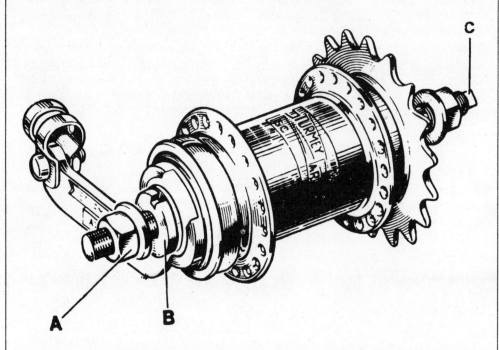

Odd information department: front wheel 'dynohubs' are adjusted at the left side, away from the dynamo, while rear 'dynohubs' are adjusted at the left side, next to the dynamo:

In both cases loosen locknut A, turn slotted washer B fully home, back off one quarter turn, and re-set locknut A.

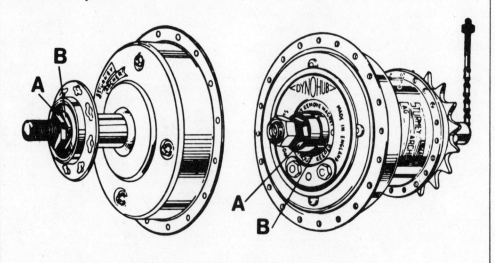

Cassette bearings

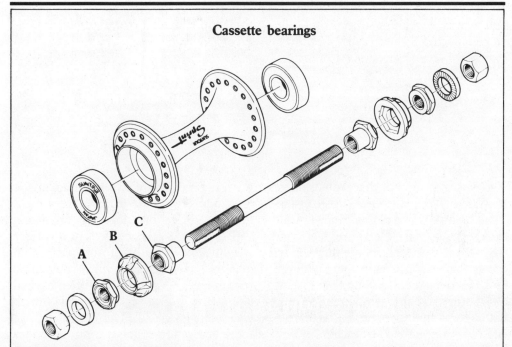

Remove wheel. Undo and remove quick release skewer or axle nuts. Remove locknut A while holding dust shield B still with special SunTour tool, or a pin tool. Undo dust shield B; the bearing retainer C will come with it. The bearings should stay in place. Screw in C and B finger tight against bearing. Hold B still and tighten locknut A against it.

Lubrication

How you lubricate a hub depends on how it is set up in the first place, and on what you want. Many hubs are fully sealed and do not need any lubrication at all. They run until they drop and are then discarded or rebuilt. At the other extreme are hubs set up for regular lubrication with oil or grease. These have oil clips or grease nipples:

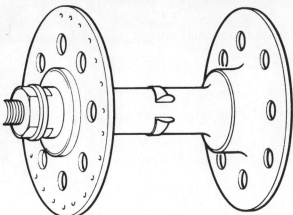

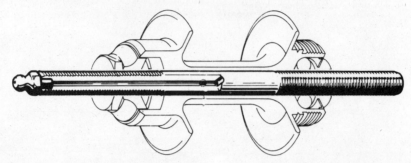

The most common of this type of hub is Ye Olde Faithful Hub Gear, which can use about a teaspoonful a month of good quality cycle or motor oil. (Don't use household oils.) Coaster brake hubs are thirstier and can go for a tablespoon or more a month. Hubs for derailleur gear bikes are sparing: a few drops to half a teaspoonful. You're not likely to find these except on classics, and hubs customized for racing.

The majority of hubs just use grease. There are a few oddball hubs with grease nipples (ram the stuff in until it bleeds out the sides, hopefully carrying away any dirt in the bearings), but most must be taken apart. As you might imagine, the racing crowd like thinner greases and don't mind whipping a hub apart and back together fairly frequently. Off-road and utility riders generally prefer a thick, waterproof grease that endures for a long time. The frequency of lubrication depends on many variables: mileage, conditions of use, rider weight, etc. Broadly, if you use a thin grease you should know when you plan to take the hub apart again, not often beyond 6 months. With good quality, thick waterproof grease (like Phil Wood), you can more or less forget about it until the idea returns from atavistic memory. I don't want you to be too casual about this, but many hubs run for 2, 3 and more years without a hitch. Especially with fixed cassette bearings, many mechanics regard bearing wear and lubrication as synonymous: when the bearing starts to run loose and rough, it's time for a new cassette and fresh packing of grease.

Disassembly and Replacement

Loose or caged bearings

Remove wheel from bike. Derailleur gear rear wheels, remove freewheel. Lay wheel down on rags or newspaper to catch ball bearings. Undo locknut A from cone B and remove both while holding on to axle at C.

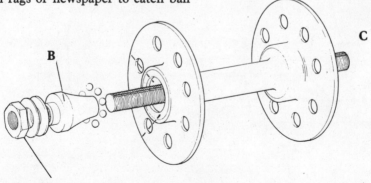

Remove dust cover D. To do this it may be necessary to let the axle drop in just a little way so you can pry the dust cover off with a screwdriver.

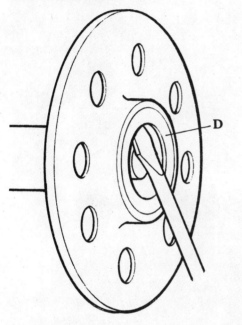

Prise out the loose or clipped ball bearings

(or turn the wheel over and dump them out), count, and place in jar. Now slide axle all the way out and dump out remaining bearings. Garner and count. Undo remaining locknut and cone and remove from axle. Clean all parts in solvent. Examine bearings to see that they are not cracked or pitted. Clipped bearings should be secure in clip. Cups and cones should be even in color all around where bearings run and free of pitting. Test axle for straightness by rolling on glass surface. Replace any defective parts.

Reassembly: pack cups with grease. If ordinary grease, then not too much as excess will attract grit. If a waterproof grease then really pack it in so that grease seals out water (which it will do until it gets dirty). Lock a cone and locknut on axle. Slip dust cover on axle. Pack bearings into cup on one side of wheel. The grease will hold them in place. Gracefully insert axle and turn wheel over. Pack bearings into cup, replace dust cover, screw on cone and locknut, and adjust as per above.

Cassette bearings

If you undo and remove the locknut, dust shield, and bearing retainer (see SunTour above) then the axle can be drawn out of the hub shell. The bearing cassettes can then be flushed out with solvent and repacked with grease, but it is a tedious job and there is always the worry of missing nooks and crannies with the grease. Best is to take out the bearings, but in most cases the manufacturer says not to do this, citing need for special tools, precise alignment, and experience. It is indeed easier and usually more practical to leave this kind of job to someone who does it regularly and has all the particular tools for the job. But it can certainly be done. The basic technique is to expose the cassette, get something behind it, and tap it out. Specialized make a cassette bearing removal tool that works very well. If you go this far, it will probably be worth simply putting in new bearings.

Troubleshooting

If something goes wrong it is usually because a cone and locknut have come adrift, something has cracked, broken or bent, or there has been an invasion of grit. In all instances if routine adjustment will not solve the problem, completely disassemble hub and replace broken or defective parts per above.

PAST AND PRESENT.

Power Train

Contents

Pedals

A pedal consists of a platform for the foot, an axle (called a spindle), which screws into the crank, and two sets of bearings on which the platform rides as it spins around the spindle. The bearings may be loose and held in place with an adjustable cone, or they may be cassette type, pressed into place and sometimes held with glue, and not adjustable.

Adjustments

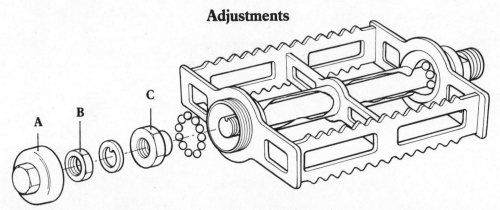

If the pedal can be wiggled back and forth on the spindle and clicks it needs tightening. Remove dustcap A (pry with a screwdriver if it is the wedge type). Undo locknut B from cone C. Screw cone C fully home and back off a quarter turn. Secure with locknut B. Check for play and that pedal spins easily. Replace dustcap A.

Pedals need cleaning and re-greasing every 6 months, more often if you ride a lot or favor wet weather. Remove pedals from crank. NOTE: right-hand pedal unscrews by turning counter-clockwise, but left-hand pedal unscrews by turning CLOCKWISE. Work with pedal over newspaper or rag to catch ball bearings. Remove dustcap A (see illustration above). Undo and remove locknut B and cone C while holding platform and spindle together with hand. Get all bearings out of dust cover end and place in jar. Remove spindle and place all bearings from crank end in jar. Clean all parts in solvent. Check ball bearings for pitting, cracks, disorderly conduct; cups and cones for uneven wear, pitting, spindle for straightness.

Reassembly: pack grease into cups on platform. Pack ball bearings into cup on crank side of platform (grease will hold them in place), and slide on spindle. Pack bearings into dust cap side cup. Screw down cone C fully home and back off one-quarter turn. Secure with locknut B. Check for play and that pedal spins easily. Replace dustcap. NOTE: Pedal stamped 'L' on end of spindle shaft goes to left side and screws on counter-clockwise. Pedal stamped 'R' screws on clockwise.

Troubleshooting

● Pedal is tight to crank but askew. Bent spindle. Replace immediately.

● Grinding noises, hard to turn pedal. Try routine adjustment as above. No? Something is probably broken. Disassemble as above and replace defective parts.

● Loose pedal Check that it is tight to crank. Left pedal tightens counter-clockwise, right pedal tightens clockwise. No? Loose bearings. Adjust as above.

Cranks

Cranks support the pedals and transmit pedaling power to the chainrings. They are attached to a bottom bracket axle which rides on two sets of ball bearings inside the bottom bracket shell. There are three types of cranks: one-piece; cottered three-piece; and cotterless three-piece:

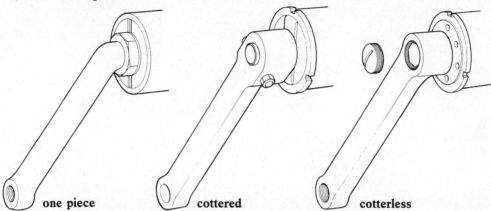

one piece   cottered   cotterless

Since one-piece cranks include the bottom bracket axle, they are covered under Bottom Brackets. To test a cottered or cotterless crank for tightness, position the pedals equidistant from the ground. Press firmly on both pedals with hands and release. Rotate crankset one-half turn and press pedals again. If something gives, one of the cranks is loose.

Adjustment
Cottered Cranks

Support the crank with a block of wood which has a hole or V-notch into which the cotter pin A fits. Be sure that the support block touches only the crank and is firmly in place. Otherwise what you do next will damage your bearings by driving the balls into the sides of the cup and scoring it (called brinelling). Next: if you are tightening, give the head of the cotter pin two or three moderate blows with a wooden mallet or hammer and wooden block combination. Then snug down nut firmly, but not with all your might or you will strip it. If you are removing, undo cotter pin nut two or three turns and then tap threaded end of cotter pin. Repeat if necessary. Be careful not to damage the threads as you will want to use the pin again. If you use a new pin and it does not fit, file down the flat side until it does.

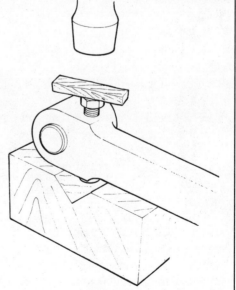

Cotterless Cranks

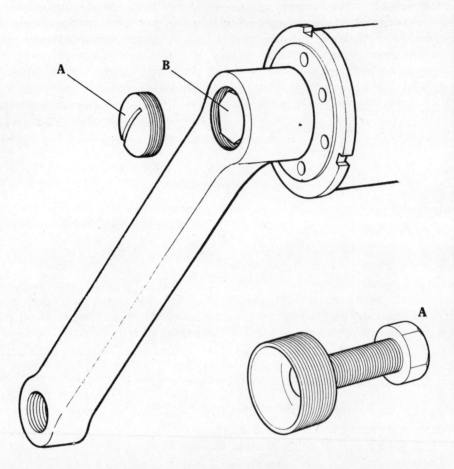

You will need a crank installer and extractor which fits your particular brand of crank. Cotterless cranks are made of alloy and must not be tightened with the same force as steel parts. To tighten or loosen, first remove the dust cover A.

To tighten, apply socket wrench of installer to nut B and turn down, wiggling crank arm to make sure it is seated all the way. For new cranks retighten every 25 miles for the first 200 miles of use. To remove, first get chain out of way. Remove nut B. Back inner bolt A of extractor all the way out. Screw extractor into crank, and then tighten down inner bolt A. Do not do this with all of your might or you may strip the threads. If the crank does not come loose with a firm tightening on the extractor bolt, give it two or three taps with a hammer, and tighten it one-eighth of a turn. Repeat until crank comes free. When replacing crank, lightly lubricate axle. Wiggle crank back and forth and make sure it is fully home before you give it the final tightening.

Troubleshooting

● There is a 'click' as you bring the pedal around on the upstroke and then a momentary dead spot and another 'click' as you push it down. It may be a loose pedal, bottom bracket, or crank. If it looks to be the crank, test and tighten if necessary as per above.

● Stripped holding bolt on a cotterless crank. Get a new bottom bracket axle. If this is impossible, a machine shop may be able to re-thread the axle to accept a larger bolt. Be sure that the head of the larger bolt is small enough so that you can still use an extractor.

● Stripped thread for the extractor on a cotterless crank. A bike shop should be able to solve the problem. You may be able to find a substitute tool which will do the job. I have one which looks like this:

It probably has to do with flywheels or plumbing. Anyway, the arms A will hook onto the crank or sprocket while the bolt passes against the bottom bracket axle.

If you can't find a substitute tool a machine shop may be able to make an extractor. Explain that you want a steel plate or bar threaded in the center for an extractor bolt, and with holes drilled so that other bolts can be slid through and in turn be attached to metal plates which will hook behind the chainset:

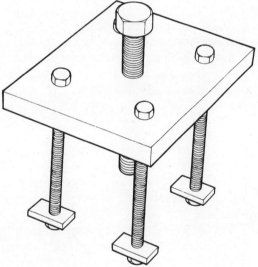

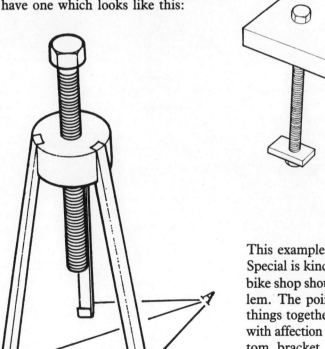

This example of whizzing up a Backyard Special is kind of funny on account of any bike shop should be able to solve the problem. The point is that you can get these things together yourself. I still remember with affection managing an emergency bottom bracket overhaul with a beer can opener, rock, and piece of string.

● Bent crank. Should be fixed by a bike shop with a special tool for the job.

Bottom Bracket

How It Works

The bottom bracket axle (called a spindle) spins on two sets of bearings inside the bottom bracket shell, and holds the cranks. On the Ashtabula type one-piece crankset, the two cranks and spindle are one unit. Three-piece cranksets (cottered and cotterless) consist of two cranks and a separate spindle. The bearings may be loose and run in adjustable cups and cones threaded into the bottom bracket shell itself, or be in cassettes that are fixed in place and are not adjustable. Many bottom bracket units are self-contained units that fit into the bottom bracket shell, and are held in place with lockrings. This is an easy remedy for crossed or stripped bottom bracket threads, and also eliminates any maintenance. After a couple of years the unit is simply replaced, at less cost than overhauling a conventional bottom bracket.

Ashtabula one-piece crankset

Adjustment

If axle is hard to turn, or slips from side-to-side in bottom bracket shell, first remove chain, and then loosen locknut A by turning it clockwise:

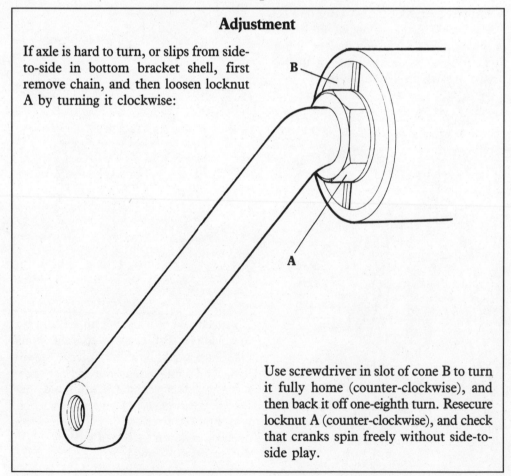

Use screwdriver in slot of cone B to turn it fully home (counter-clockwise), and then back it off one-eighth turn. Resecure locknut A (counter-clockwise), and check that cranks spin freely without side-to-side play.

Lubrication and Disassembly

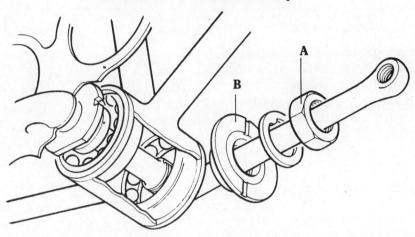

Bottom bracket axles should be cleaned and re-greased once a year. This requires disassembly. Bearings for one-piece cranksets are held in clips so don't worry about losing them. Remove left pedal (clockwise) and chain from chainring. Undo locknut A (clockwise), and unscrew cone B (clockwise). Remove ball bearing clip. Slide all parts off crank and place in a jar. Now move axle to right and tilt to slide whole unit through bottom bracket and out of frame. Take right side bearing clip off axle. Clean everything thoroughly with solvent. See that ball bearings are secure in clips and free from pitting or cracks; cups and cones are even in color where ball bearings run and free from pitting or scoring. If cups are deeply grooved replace them. Remove with hammer and steel rod or screwdriver:

and make sure the new cups are well seated by tapping them in with a hammer and wooden block:

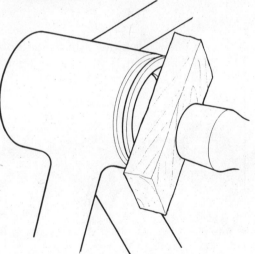

To reassemble: pack grease into bearing clips and cups. Slide one clip on axle with solid side against right cone. Gracefully insert crankset through bottom shell from right side. Slide on ball bearing clips with balls in, solid side out. Screw on cone (counter-clockwise). Check that crankset spins freely without side-to-side play. Replace pedal (counter-clockwise) and chain.

305

Three-piece Cranksets

Adjustment

Bottom bracket axle (spindle) should be free from side-to-side play and spin easily. To adjust, first disconnect chain from front sprocket. Loosen notched lockring C on left side of bracket with a 'C' wrench (bike stores) or

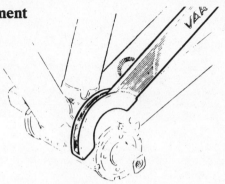

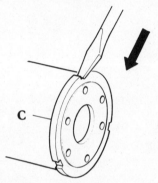

hammer and screwdriver combination (counter-clockwise):

Then tighten (clockwise) adjustable cup D fully home with a pin tool or light

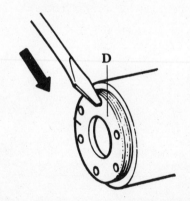

taps of a hammer on a screwdriver or center-punch inserted in hole or slot. Back off one-eighth turn and secure with lockring C. Check that spindle spins freely and has no side-to-side play.

Lubrication and Disassembly
Ball bearings and cones

A conventional bottom bracket should be cleaned and re-greased once a year. Disconnect chain and remove cranks. You can do the job with the bike on a workstand, or lay it right side down on newspaper or rags

to catch loose ball bearings. Undo lockring C with 'C' wrench or hammer and screwdriver combination and remove. Carefully holding axle in place against right side bearings, remove adjustable cup D.

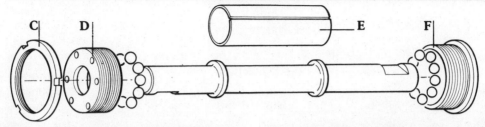

Look out for the ball bearings! Some will fall out, others will stick to various parts. Gather, count, and place in jar. Make sure you have them all. If your bearings are clipped, lucky you. Now pull spindle straight out. Garner all the right side ball bearings and jar 'em.

There may be a plastic tube (E, above) inside the bottom bracket shell. This is to prevent grit in the frame tubes from falling into the bearings. Take it out and clean it off. Clean out inside of bottom bracket shell with solvent. Examine the fixed cup F with a flashlight. If it is unpitted and wear is reasonably even, leave it alone. Otherwise unscrew and replace. It has a left-hand thread and unscrews CLOCKWISE. Clean all other parts in solvent. See that ball bearings have no pits or cracks, and if clipped are secure in retainers; inside of adjustable cup and cones on spindle also have no pits and wear is even; spindle is straight. Replace defective parts.

Reassembly: pack cups with grease. If ball bearings are clipped, pack retainers. Replace plastic sleeve. Pack ball bearings into cups. Grease will hold in place. Clipped bearings go with solid side on cone (balls face out). Carefully insert spindle, long end to chainwheel side of bottom bracket shell. Without jarring loose ball bearings, fit on adjustable cup and screw home. Rotate spindle as you do this to make sure it goes in all the way. Back off one-eighth turn and secure with lockring. Be careful threading this on as it is easy to strip. Check that spindle spins easily with no side play. Replace cranks and chain.

Sealed bottom bracket

Undo left side lockring A (counterclockwise). Ditto right side lock ring B , which has left-hand thread and unscrews CLOCKWISE. Next the left cup C (counter-clockwise) and right cup D (another CLOCKWISE) Remove spindle unit. If the bearings are replaceable, the job should be done at a bike shop with a special tool. Improvising stands an excellent chance of ruining the bearings.

Replacement: mount right side cup D (counter-clockwise). Insert spindle unit. If it is a SunTour, as in illustration, the letter R side of the brand name is the end that goes against the right cup D. Set the chainline by moving cup D in or out as required. Remember, it is a left-hand thread, and tightens by rotating counter-clockwise. Onward: tighten left cup C (clockwise) until it is snug, but not tight. Lock right cup D in place with lockring (counter-clockwise), and left cup C also with lockring (but clockwise). Check that spindle rotates freely.

Chainring(s)

Chainrings are the business with all the teeth attached to the right crank that pull the chain around to deliver power to the rear wheel.

Adjustment

Check periodically for bent or chipped teeth. Remove chain. With a strong light behind the chainwheel, rotate it, looking from the side for chipped teeth, and from above or in front for bent teeth:

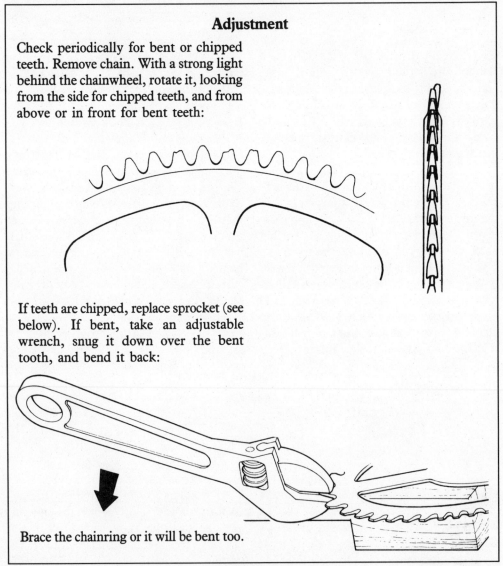

If teeth are chipped, replace sprocket (see below). If bent, take an adjustable wrench, snug it down over the bent tooth, and bend it back:

Brace the chainring or it will be bent too.

Replacement

It's replacement time when the chainring teeth start sharpening up and looking like waves:

This is a good moment to review your gearing options (see Fitting and Gears). One-piece crank and chainring units have to be replaced completely. Good chainsets have detachable chainrings held with bolts. Simply undo the bolts (most will need an Allen key), and keep track of all the washers and spacers. When you mount the new chainrings (replace them all at the same time), snug down the bolts, ride the bike for a few miles, and then check the bolts again. Chainring bolts are one of those items that like to sneak up on you, spring a surprise, and then run away and hide in a deep drain. I like to break in and seat the chainring bolts, and then do them up again with a product like Loctite.

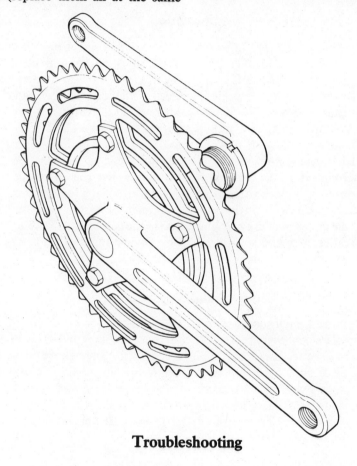

Troubleshooting

● There is a 'clunk' every time you bring the chainwheel around. One possible cause is a bent tooth. Check by hanging bike up and slowly running chainset. If chain suddenly jumps up where it meets the chainring - bent tooth. Fix as above.
● Chainset wobbles from side-to-side, hitting front derailleur cage or rubbing chainstays. If this is not due to incredibly loose bottom bracket bearings, or loose chainring bolts, the sprocket is warped. Fixing is a job requiring both great delicacy and considerable force. Techniques vary so much according to the exact problem that I strongly suggest you leave it to a bike shop.

Chain

The chain is that innocent and simple looking business which transmits power to the rear wheel. There are two kinds: one is used on non-derailleur bikes, is ⅛" wide, and held together with a master link which can be taken apart without special tools; the other for derailleur equipped bikes, is 3/32" wide, and has no master link (it would catch in the rear gear cluster), so that a special chain riveting tool is needed to take it apart or put it together.

Lubrication

Dry film lubricants such as Super Lube are clean, do not attract dirt, and go on in flash. A lot of people just pile on the stuff every time they think of it, or after an especially wet or muddy ride, and don't bother to remove the chain until it needs replacement.

Oil is the traditional lubricant and is cheap (free if scrounged from a gas station wastebin). The problem is that it attracts grit and the solution is to add more oil in the hope that it will float the grit away. Oil every link once a week, and remove and soak clean the chain in solvent once a month.

The most economical lubricant is paraffin wax, available in grocery stores. It is cleaner than oil. Remove and clean chain. Melt wax in coffee can or similar grade container, toss in the chain, and then hang it to dry so that drippings fall back into can. Save the can as is. One beauty of this method is that you only have to clean the chain with solvent the first time. Thereafter you can just toss it in the wax. The dirt will rise to the surface where it can be skimmed off. Once a month.

Removal and Replacement

Chains on bikes that see constant use will probably need replacement every two years, and on bikes in average service, every three years. It depends on how hard the chain is worked, and on how well it is lubricated. Although the chain may look perfectly sound, the tiny bit of wear on each rivet and plate adds up to a considerable alteration in size. A worn chain will chip teeth on gear sprockets and in general be a pain. To test for wear, remove chain (see below) and lay on table with rollers parallel to surface. Hold chain with both hands about 4-5" apart. Push hands together, and then pull apart. If you can feel slack, replace chain.

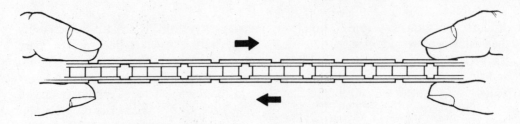

Another simple test for chain wear is to lift the chain away from the front chainring. If the chain will clear the teeth it is more than time for replacement.

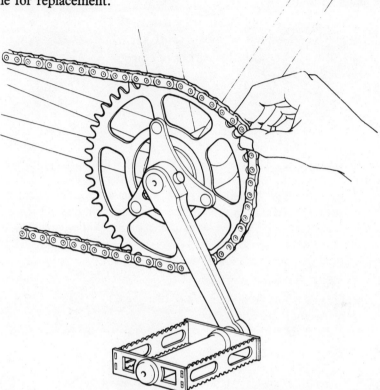

Test also for side-to-side deflection. It should not be more than 1'':

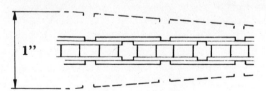

To remove and replace a master link chain find the master link and pry it off with a screwdriver.

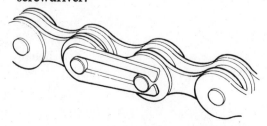

To remove a derailleur chain drive out a rivet with a chain tool:

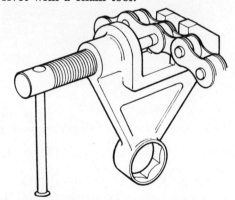

Be sure that the point of the chain tool centers exactly on the rivet. DO NOT DRIVE THE RIVET ALL THE WAY OUT. Go only as far as the outside plate.

Stop frequently to check progress. Once rivet is near chain plate, free the link by slightly twisting the chain. To replace the rivet, reverse chain in tool:

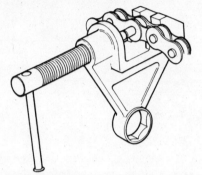

Again, be careful how far you go. The link will be tight. Use the spreader slot on the chain tool.

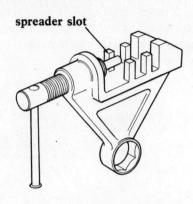

spreader slot

All you need is a little bit of pressure to free up the link. It is an excellent idea to practice breaking and joining chain with some old bit of chain that doesn't matter. It's an easy knack once you've done it a few times.

Fitting

Most new chains need to be shortened in order to fit properly. On a non-derailleur bike it should be set so that there is ½" up-and-down play in the chain with the rear wheel in proper position.

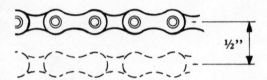

½"

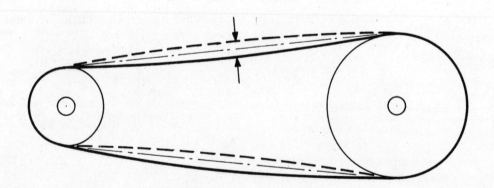

On a derailleur bike, the law says that the chain must be long enough to fit over the large front chainring and large back cog, and short enough to fit on the small front chainring and small rear cog. Sometimes this is asking an awful lot, especially with widely spaced triple chainrings. You should never go big to big or little to little anyhow.

Personally, I set the chain up so that it moves across the chainrings and cogs as a unit: little to big, medium to medium, and big to little.

A more relevant factor than personal preferences is the type of derailleur. Some of the fancier indexed changers are very specific about the amount of chain to be used. Well, if you are putting on a new chain, you'll have the old chain to go by. If you are mounting a new changer, there will be specific instructions with it.

If you just want to check how you are going, thread the chain through everything and over the big chainring and big rear cog. Pull it to a length that, at maximum, has the derailleur arm pointing at the ground. Keeping the chain at the same length, put it over the small chainring and small cog. If the derailleur does not wrap up and bite itself, you've no problem. If it does, shorten the chain, and never shift big to big.

Troubleshooting

● Jammed link. Use chain tool to free tight links by working the rivet back and forth a quarter-turn on the chain tool at a time. If your chain tool has a spreader slot, use it.

● 'Clunk' sounds and/or chain jumping sprockets. Test chain for excessive wear as per above. May also be a bent tooth.

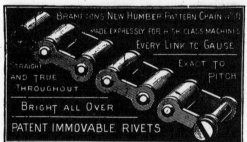

Freewheel
How It Works

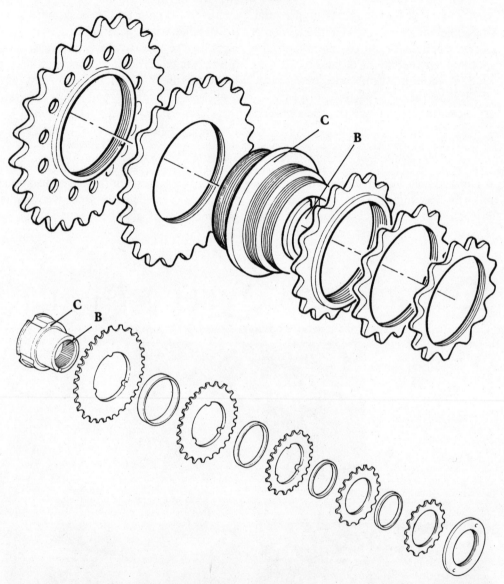

The cogs are threaded and/or slide onto the freewheel body. The exact combination varies from model to model. The freewheel body itself is in two main parts. The inside part B threads or slides onto the hub. The cogs go on the outside part C. The freewheel is ratcheted so that when the outside part C is moved clockwise by the chain, the inside part B (and hence the wheel) also moves. But when the chain is stationary, part C holds still while part B rolls merrily along. The ratcheting is accomplished through the use of a clever maze of ball bearings, pins, springs, and other minute parts inside the freewheel. Looky:

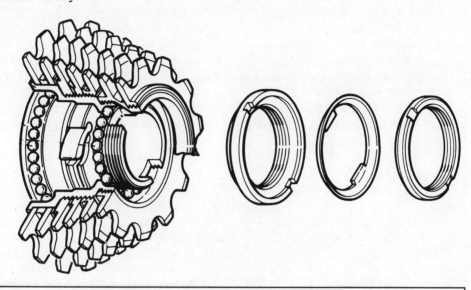

Adjustment

Periodically check the cogs for chipped or bent teeth by looking at them in profile:

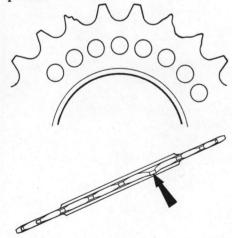

Replace cogs that have chipped or broken teeth, or uneven gaps between teeth. If things have come to this pass it is probably best to replace all the cogs, and the chain as well. A stretched chain will kick up on new sprockets. If it's the odd bent tooth, straighten it by removing the cog

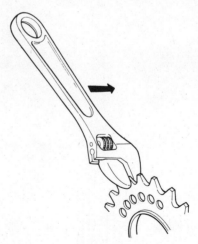

(see below), gripping the bent tooth with an adjustable end wrench, and straightening.

315

Alignment between chainrings and back cogs: standing at the front of the bike and sighting between the two front sprockets (double) or in line with the middle ring (triple), you should see the center cog of the back gear cluster.

One way of adjusting chain alignment is at the front, with longer or shorter bottom bracket axles, or with adjustments of the bottom bracket unit if it is the type that can be moved. Other problems may arise, though, such as crank arms hitting the chainstays, and the front changer will need re-setting.

At the back, the freewheel can be moved out with spacers (in, if there are spacers already there). Ah, but then a spacer will probably be needed on the other side, to keep everything in balance, and then perhaps the wheel won't fit into the drop-outs. I don't want to make you give up entirely, but it usually better to let a bike shop deal with problems of this sort.

There's no adjustment for the freewheel as such. Keep it clean, and lubricated. Some models like the Sun-Tour Winner have an oil hole:

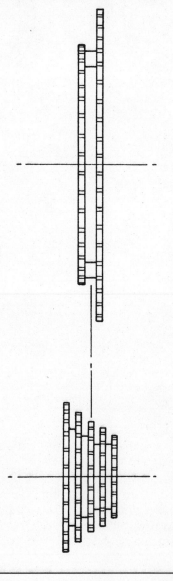

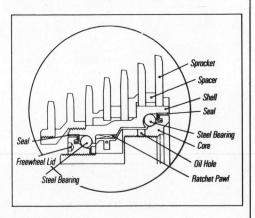

Use oil or a liquid lubricant, and not grease, which may lock up the pawls and cause the freewheel to not freewheel. About once a year remove the freewheel and soak it clean in solvent.

Removal and Disassembly

There are two kinds of freewheels: threaded and splined, or cassette. With the latter type you invariably need a special tool to undo the locknut holding the freewheel body on the spline. Undo the locknut and the rest is easy.

With a conventional threaded freewheel you must have a remover that fits your particular make and model of freewheel. It's no good trying to improvise. Freewheels can be tough to remove and a tool that doesn't quite fit is sure to tear everything to bits.

Remove wheel: Remove nut and washers from freewheel side of axle. Quick release hubs: remove conical nut and spring from shaft of skewer and place spring in a jar. Fit freewheel remover. If it won't go on you may have a spacer nut. Remove with a wrench while holding axle stationary with another wrench on the left side cone or locknut. Fit freewheel remover into slots or splines. Replace nut on axle or skewer and screw down hand-tight. Use a wrench on the freewheel remover to break the freewheel loose. If it won't go, try putting the freewheel remover in a vise and turning the wheel. The moment the freewheel breaks loose, slack the axle or skewer and spin the freewheel off by hand.

To replace a freewheel put a little grease on the threads and screw it on, being very, very careful not to cross thread it or strip the threads. Snug it down with the freewheel remover but don't worry about tightening hard; this happens automatically as you ride.

To change cogs you need a couple of cog removers, and if you are removing all the cogs, a freewheel vise. The technique varies with the design of tool. Follow the instructions given with your particular tools. This is another one of those jobs best left to a bike shop.

If you have a new freewheel with cogs that screw onto the block, then on your first ride, use the chain to systematically tighten the cogs in the order with which they are mounted. If you tighten them out of order, there may be unexpected gaps.

Dismantle freewheel: Nah. If you want to do it for fun sometime, all right. It's logical enough inside, but there are a lot of tiny ball bearings and such-like. Getting them all to stay in place while you reassemble the freewheel can be quite a trick. If you want an education, by all means. But if you need a freewheel and yours doesn't work after being cleaned in solvent, buy another one.

Troubleshooting

● A 'clunk' two or three times per complete revolution of the front sprocket. May be a bent tooth on a freewheel cog. Check as per above.

● Freewheel won't freewheel. Try soaking in solvent to free innards. No? Replace it.

● Freewheel turns but hub doesn't. Spin cranks while holding bike stationary and look carefully at freewheel. If both parts spin around the hub, threads on hub are stripped. Ohh. New hub. If outside part of freewheel spins around inside part, freewheel is clogged up (frozen) or broken. Try soaking in solvent. No? Replace.

Gear Changer Systems

Except for pedal-operated rear hubs, gear changer systems typically include a shift trigger, lever, or twistgrip, a cable, and the gear changing mechanism, of which there are two kinds: internal rear hub, and derailleur.

Hub Gears

These come in 2-, 3-, and 5-speed versions, with planetary or sun gears inside the hub. I consider these units too complicated to be worth disassembling, and so does any bike shop I have asked about doing such work. Here, for example is an exploded view of a 3-speed hub:

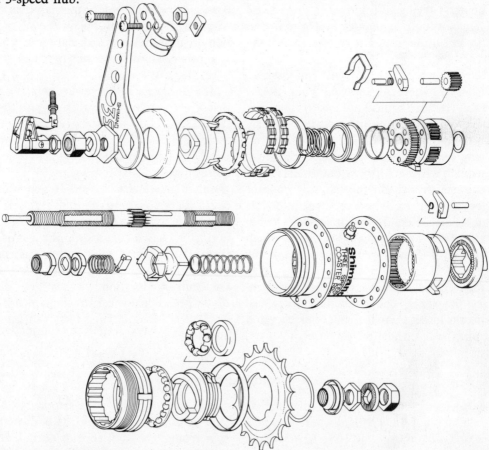

Believe me, if you run into trouble with your hub and can't solve it with routine adjustment or troubleshooting (below), the best thing to do is remove the wheel and take it to a bike shop. The chance of problems arising is quite small. A regularly lubricated hub should last the life of your bike.

There are several brands of hub gears. Most are essentially similar to the original, the Sturmey-Archer discussed here.

How They Work

Shift trigger A connects to cable B, which in turn connects to toggle chain C on hub. Position of trigger determines gear.

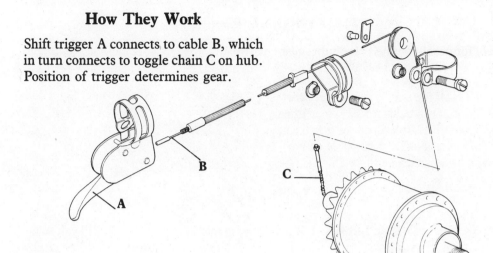

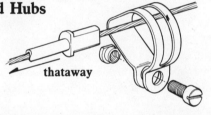

Adjustment
Three-speed Hubs

First move the shift lever to 3rd or H. Then take up slack in cable by loosening locknut A and screwing down barrel sleeve adjustor B:

thataway

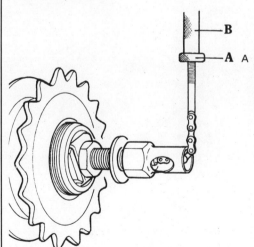

Test gears. No? Check position of indicator rod by looking through the hole in the side of the right hub nut. With the shift lever in 2nd or N position it should be exactly even with the end of the axle:

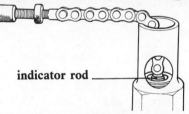

indicator rod

Leave cable very slightly slack. If barrel sleeve cannot do job, move the fulcrum clip which holds the cable housing on the bike frame forward:

Adjust if necessary with barrel sleeve. Test gears. No? Remove barrel sleeve altogether. Check that indicator rod is screwed finger-tight fully into hub. Reassemble and adjust as above. No? Turn to Troubleshooting, this section.

Five-speed Hubs

There are two shift levers. For the right-hand lever, follow procedure for 3-speed hub as above. For left-hand shift lever, set it all the way forward and screw cable connector to bellcrank B two or three turns. Then run shift lever all the way back, take slack out of cable with cable connector, and secure with locknut C.

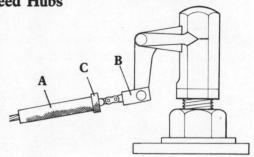

Lubrication

A teaspoon to a tablespoon of oil inside hub once a month. Less for a little used bike, more for a much used bike. If it starts dribbling around the place, less. Use a quality cycle oil, or motorist's SAE 30 oil. Some household and other cheap oils leave behind a sticky residue when the oil evaporates. This is the last thing in the world you want. Once a month use a spray like Super Lube or a few drops of oil on the trigger control, cable, and inside the cable housing.

Disassembly and Replacement

Hub: Remove wheel and take it to a bike shop.
Cable: Needs replacement when it becomes frayed, the housing kinked or broken, or exhibits suspicious political tendencies:

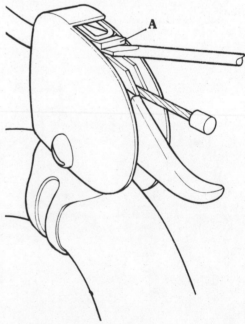

Run shift selector to 3rd or H. Disconnect barrel sleeve from indicator and loosen fulcrum clip (for illustration, see above). The method for freeing the cable depends on the type of shift lever.
Trigger: shift to 1st or L, pry up holding plate A with a small screwdriver, and push cable in until nipple clears ratchet plate: and then pull cable out. Remove entire cable and housing assembly from bike and set aside fulcrum sleeve.

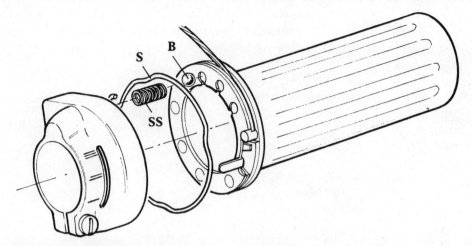

Twist grip: first take off the spring S with a screwdriver. Slide the twist grip off the handlebar and catch the ball bearing B and spring SS if they fall out. Release nipple from slot and remove cable housing assembly from bike.

Top tube lever: undo the cable anchor bolt near the hub. Unscrew the two shift lever halves A and B, and lift casing C away from bike. Push cable in to free nipple from slot and thread out cable.

Take the old cable with you to the shop when getting a replacement. This kind of cable comes in a variety of lengths.

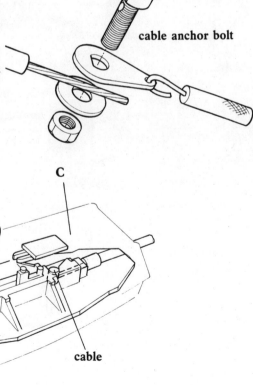

cable anchor bolt

cable

Trigger: place the fulcrum sleeve on cable housing and thread through fulcrum clip. Pry up trigger control plate, insert cable through hole in trigger casing, and slip nipple into slot on ratchet. Run cable over pulley wheel if you have one, and attach to toggle chain. Shift to 3rd or H. Position fulcrum clip so cable is just slightly slack and tighten. Adjust if necessary as per above.

Twist grip: insert nipple into slot. Grease and replace spring and ball bearing. Slide twist-grip on handlebar and secure with spring clip. Use a small screwdriver to work the spring clip in. Run cable over pulley wheel if you have one, and attach to toggle chain. Shift selector to 3rd or H and adjust as per above.

To top tube lever: thread through slot until nipple catches. Replace cable housing or run cable over pulley wheel, depending on the kind of system you have. Connect cable to anchor bolt, shift to 3rd or H, and adjust as per above. Replace casing, and screw together handle halves.

If you have a bashed or recalcitrant shift control the best thing is to replace it. They are not expensive.

Trigger: disconnect cable (see above) and undo bolt B:

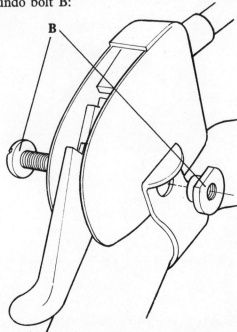

Twist-grip or top tube lever: I recommend replacing with a standard handlebar trigger, which is a much better mechanical design and more reliable. To remove old unit disconnect cable (see above) and undo bolt B:

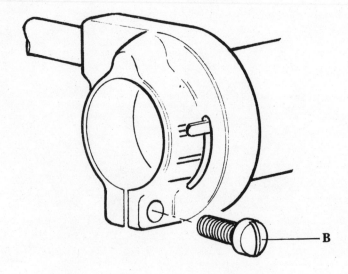

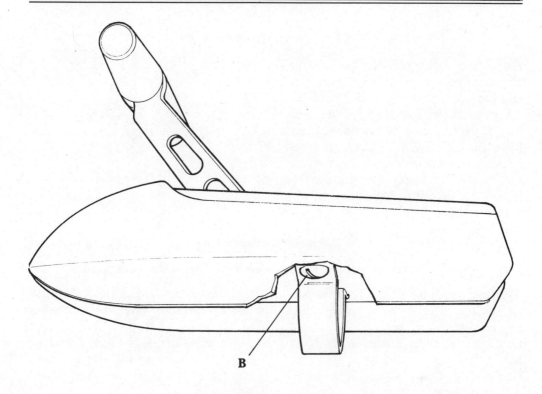

B

Troubleshooting

No gear at all (pedals spin freely) or slips in and out of gear.
- Is gear in proper adjustment?
- Is cable binding? Check by disconnecting barrel sleeve at hub and working cable back and forth through housing. Replace if it binds.
- Is shift mechanism together and functioning? Stick and twist-grip models are especially prone to slippage after the track for the ball bearing becomes worn.
- Insides of hubs may have gotten gunked up through the use of too heavy or household oils so that pawls are stuck. Try putting in kerosene or penetrating oil and

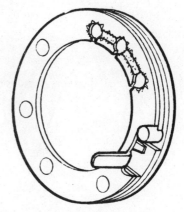

jiggling everything around. No?
- Remove wheel and take to a bike shop.

Derailleur Systems

A derailleur system consists of a shift lever connected via a cable to a front or rear gear changer (derailleur) through which the chain passes. When the shift lever is actuated, the derailleur moves sideways and forces the chain onto a different sprocket.

Although we are dealing here with a system, it will simplify everything to take it piece by piece first, and then deal with it as a whole.

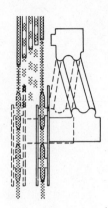

Shift Levers

How It Works - Adjustment - Lubrication - Replacement

The function of the shift lever is to position the derailleur in line with the selected cog or chainring. There are three basic mechanisms: friction, ratchet or clutch, and semi-automatic. Friction types have a tension screw A. Some tension screws have a slot for a screwdriver or coin, some have wings, and others have wire loops. They all work the same way. The shift lever needs to be set so that you can move it without undue strain, but be stiff enough to hold fast against spring pressure from the derailleur. Just loosen or tighten A until it works OK.

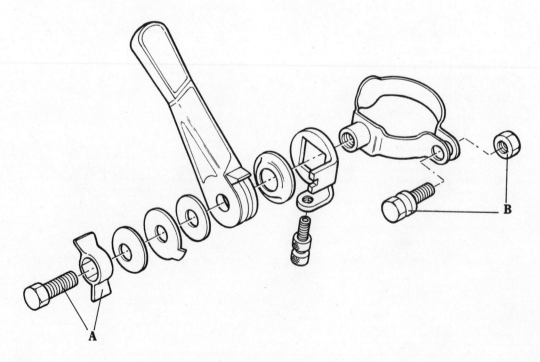

Take apart the unit for cleaning by removing A, being sure to keep everything in order, as there can be a fair number of bits:

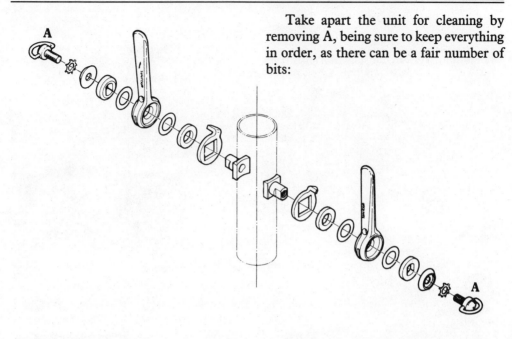

Periodically clean the mechanism, but don't lubricate it.

Ratchet and clutch type levers are more complex, and although frictionless, there is still a bolt (A) for the lever to rotate on, which also serves as a tension screw:

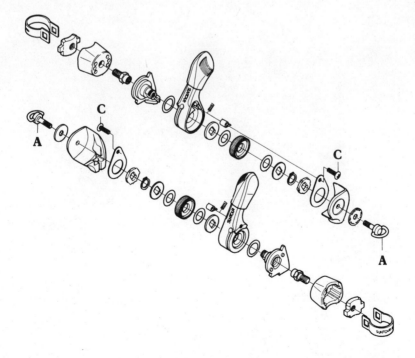

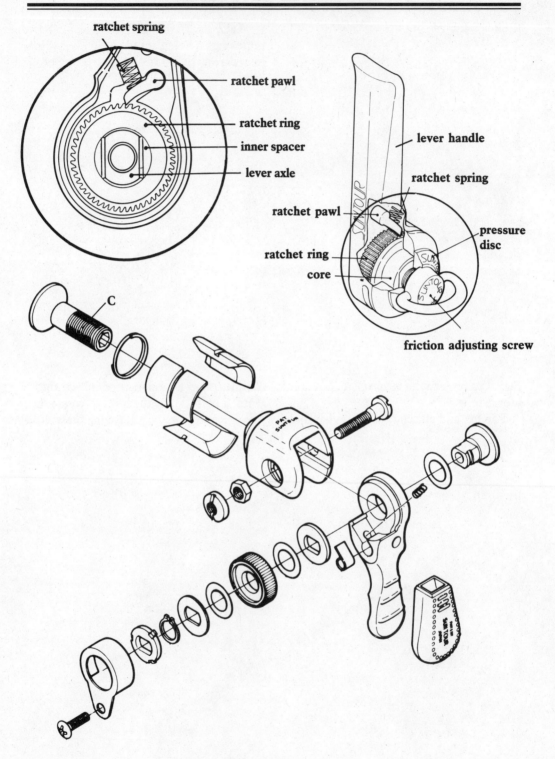

ratchet spring

ratchet pawl

ratchet ring

inner spacer

lever axle

lever handle

ratchet spring

ratchet pawl

ratchet ring

core

pressure disc

friction adjusting screw

C

To get the lever off entirely, remove bolt A and cover screw B. For the Bar-Con, the expander bolt C has to be undone (clockwise) with an Allen key.

Ratchet and clutch levers need cleaning and lubrication with grease or a spray like Super Lube. There are a lot of bits, little springs, and whatnot, and if you prefer, the whole unit can be sloshed in solvent, dried, and relubed. Or you can take it all apart, keeping careful track of the order of parts. There are literally hundreds of different models and no way to show them all. It's not difficult (do watch out for the spring) so long as you're careful.

Semi-automatic shift levers are similar in appearance to ratchet levers:

This is because levers for semi-automatic systems use ratchet and friction mechanisms when not in semi-auto mode. But factory instructions abound with strict injunctions against removing ratchet mechanisms, or disassembling them or the semi-auto mechanism, on pain of voiding warranty.

By and large, servicing semi-automatic shifting systems has to be left to a (well) qualified bike shop. Many stipulations must be met for such systems to work well: frame alignment, drop-out configuration, cable type, cable housing type, hub dimensions, freewheel spacing, and chain, among others. "Variance from these measurements by as little as 1mm (1/25th of an inch) can disrupt adjustment and performance," is but one gem of many. One twenty-fifth of an inch is not very far. In servicing terms, the price of semi-automatic shifting is a royal P.I.A.

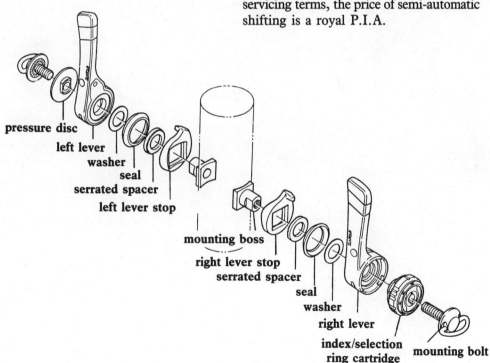

pressure disc
left lever
washer
seal
serrated spacer
left lever stop

mounting boss
right lever stop
serrated spacer
seal
washer
right lever
index/selection ring cartridge
mounting bolt

Cables

Derailleur cables are thin and take a beating. Check them often for fraying:

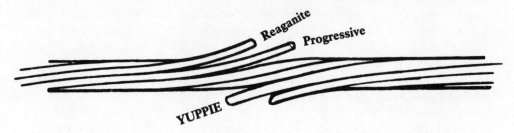

Adjustment

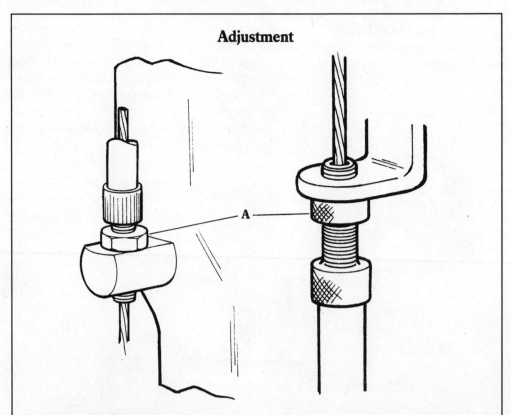

Adjustment is needed when the shift lever has to be pulled all the way back to engage the large sprocket. Place the shift lever forward so that the chain is on the smallest sprocket. Some systems have a cable adjusting bolt, either at the derailleur or at the shift lever. Undo the locknut A and move the cable adjusting bolt up until slack is removed from cable. If this will not do the job, turn it back down fully home, and reset cable anchor bolt. All derailleurs, front and back, use a cable anchor bolt or screw to hold the cable.

Here is the location (CB) on some representative types:

CB

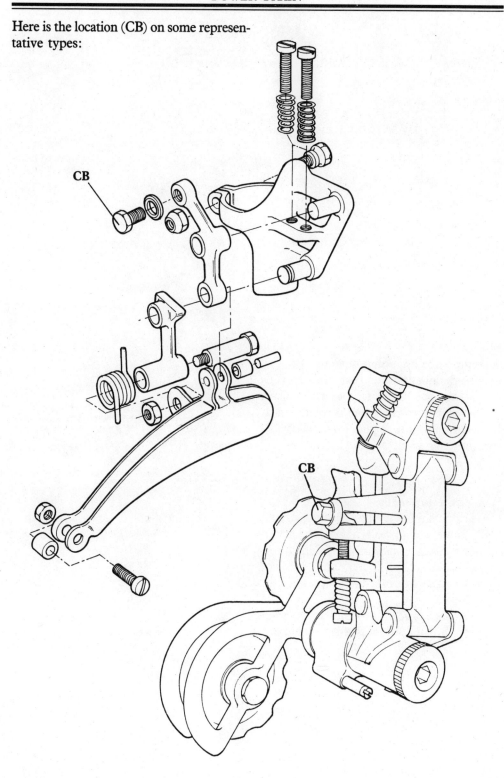

CB

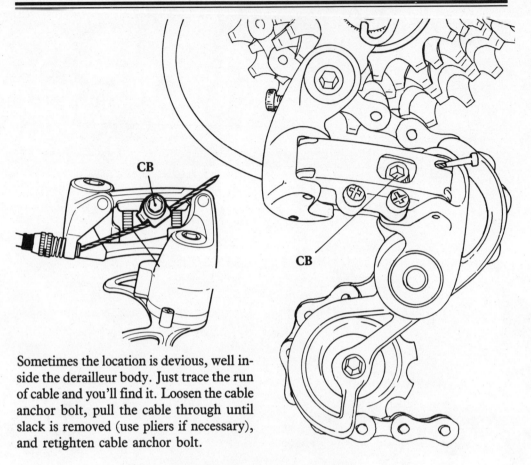

CB

CB

Sometimes the location is devious, well inside the derailleur body. Just trace the run of cable and you'll find it. Loosen the cable anchor bolt, pull the cable through until slack is removed (use pliers if necessary), and retighten cable anchor bolt.

Removal and Replacement

Run chain to smallest sprocket. Screw home cable adjusting bolt, if there is one. Undo cable anchor bolt and thread cable out of derailleur. Check cable housings (not on all models) for kinks and breaks. Remove cable from lever by threading it out.

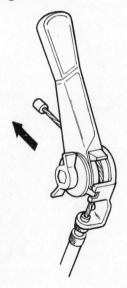

The exact procedure varies from lever to lever, but the basic idea is the same.

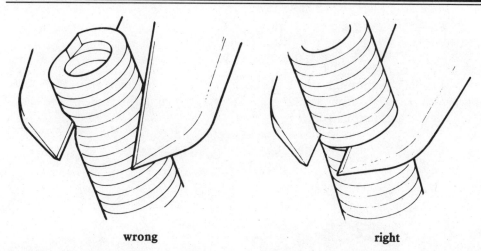

wrong   right

Replacement: do not cut new cable to size until it is installed or it may fray and jam when going into cable housing. If you are cutting new cable housing, be sure to get the jaws of the cutter between the wire coils of the housing.

Start by threading through the shift lever, and then through down tube tunnel, cable stops, cable housings, and whatever else is in your particular system. As you pass the cable through cable housings, be sure to twist it so that the strands do not unravel:

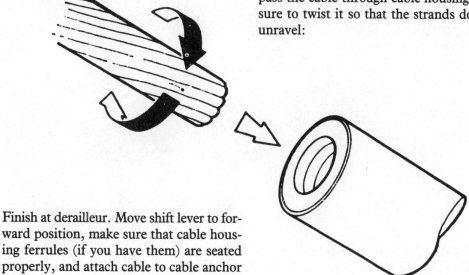

Finish at derailleur. Move shift lever to forward position, make sure that cable housing ferrules (if you have them) are seated properly, and attach cable to cable anchor bolt.

Troubleshooting

Cable problems are evinced by delayed shifts, or no shifts at all. In any case, the procedure is the same: undo the cable anchor bolt and slide the cable around by hand, looking for sticky spots. Check carefully for fraying, and for kinks in the cable housing.

Derailleurs - Front
How They Work

There is a metal cage through which the chain passes as it feeds onto the chainrings. The cage can be moved from side-to-side, and by pressing on the side of the chain, shifts it from chainring to chainring:

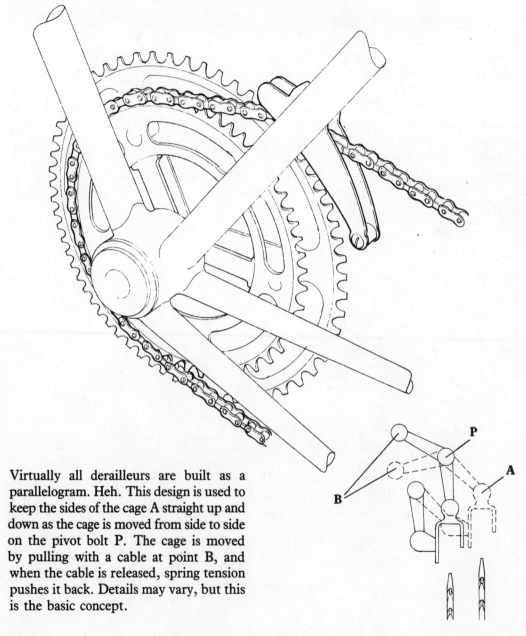

Virtually all derailleurs are built as a parallelogram. Heh. This design is used to keep the sides of the cage A straight up and down as the cage is moved from side to side on the pivot bolt P. The cage is moved by pulling with a cable at point B, and when the cable is released, spring tension pushes it back. Details may vary, but this is the basic concept.

Adjustment

The changer as a whole must be properly positioned with the outer side of the cage about ¼'' above the sprocket.

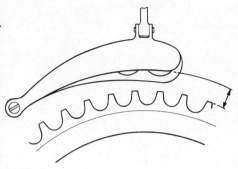

There are many nuances for this setting. For example, some front changers are designed to be used with triple chainsets where the difference between chainrings is at least six teeth or more. If the difference is less, say four teeth, then raising the changer a little higher may do the trick. Move the changer by loosening the mounting bolt B:

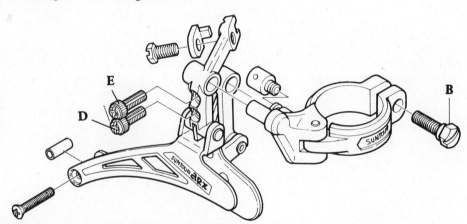

Side-to-side travel of the cage must be set. First check that cable is properly adjusted. Then locate the high and low adjusting screws.

The adjusting screws are sometimes hidden, but they can't go far. Push the changer back and forth and see what things go bump.

Run chain to largest rear cog and smallest front chainring. The left side of the changer cage should just clear the chain. If not, adjust the low adjusting screw D until it does. Then run the chain to the smallest back cog and largest front chainring. The right side of the cage should just clear the chain. Adjust high screw E until it does.

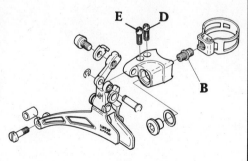

Test operation of gears. If you don't have the bike up on a workstand, get a friend to hold the rear wheel off the ground while you turn the cranks and run through the gears. This is an important safety check. If you take the bike out on the road and something tangles, both you and the bike can be badly hurt.

You're almost certain to find that the changer needs further adjustment and diddling of one kind or another, for example to stay clear of a crank. It is also frequently necessary to overset the travel of the changer to get the chain to move over, and this can have the chain rubbing the cage unless you remember to reverse the shift lever slightly after making a shift. When you get to the sometimes it shifts/sometimes it doesn't stage, move the adjusting screw only a quarter turn at a time.

Lubrication

A little Super Lube or a few drops of oil on the pivot bolts once a month. If the unit becomes dirty, take it off and soak it clean in solvent.

Replacement

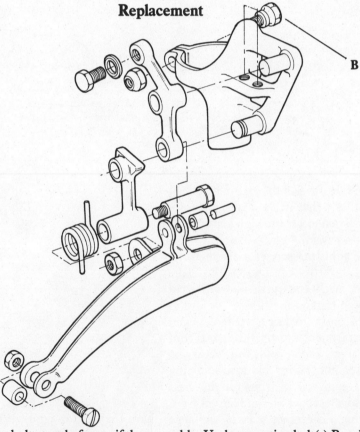

Remove chain or bolt at end of cage, if there is one. Undo cable anchor bolt and slip off cable. Undo mounting bolt(s) B and remove unit.

Troubleshooting

Most of the difficulties experienced with the front changer are actually caused by problems elsewhere in the power train. I am assuming that you have already set your changer as per Adjustment, above.

Chain throws off sprocket.
● Is shift lever tight?
● Cage travel may be set too far out. Adjust it slightly.
● Is chain old? Is a link frozen?
● Are sprocket teeth bent?
● Are front and rear sprockets in alignment?
● If chain continually overrides big front sprocket, take an adjustable wrench and bend the leading tip of the outside cage in very slightly - about 1/16'':

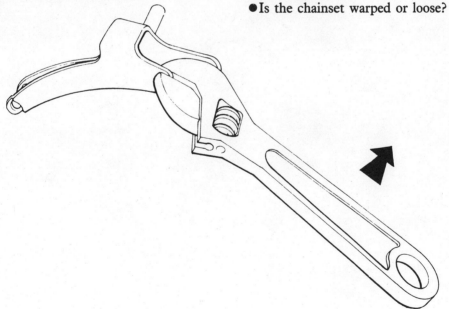

Delayed shifts or no shifts at all.
● Are pivot bolts clean? Try a little spray or oil.
● Is spring intact and in place?
● Is cable sticking or broken?

Chain rubs side of cage.
● Is shift lever tight?
● Can you stop rubbing by diddling with shift lever? For example, the amount of right travel necessary to shift the chain from the small chainring to the large chainring may leave the cage too far to the right when the chain is on the large back cog, and cause the chain to rub the left side of the cage. It is common with front changers to move the cage back just a trifle after a shift has been completed.
● Is the chainset warped or loose?

Derailleurs - Rear
How They Work

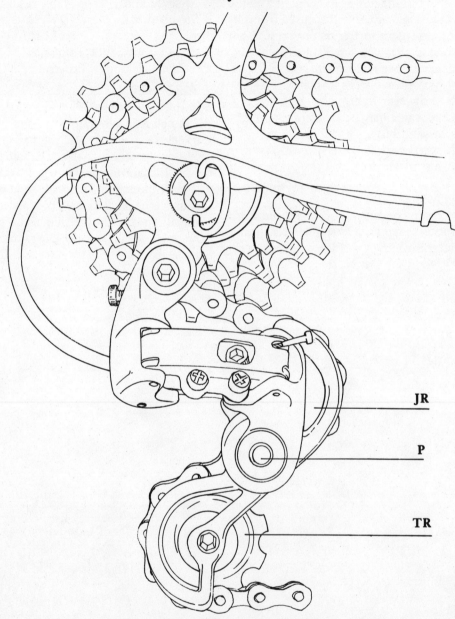

JR

P

TR

As the chain comes back off the bottom of the front chainset it passes through the rear derailleur on two chain rollers. The cage holding the rollers is fastened to the main body of the changer by a pivot bolt P, and is under constant spring tension so as to keep the chain taut.

The lower roller is the tension roller (TR), the upper the jockey roller (JR). The position of the cage, and hence of the chain on the rear gear cluster, is determined by the changer body.

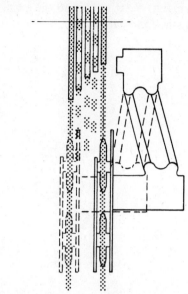

The changer body is under constant spring tension to carry it to the smallest sprocket. It is restrained from doing so by a cable and shift lever.

Derailleurs come in an assortment of designs. Some are simple, others have compound articulation points. The more complex models are usually designed with the intention of keeping the jockey roller at an even distance from each cog. The best way to see and understand what is happening is to put the bike up on a workstand and run it back and forth through the gears, watching how the derailleur moves. Alternatively, disconnect the chain and push the changer around with your hands.

Adjustment

Changer body

Most modern derailleurs are set on the frame so that the main body of the changer is parallel with the chainstay. Often there is an angle adjusting screw A.

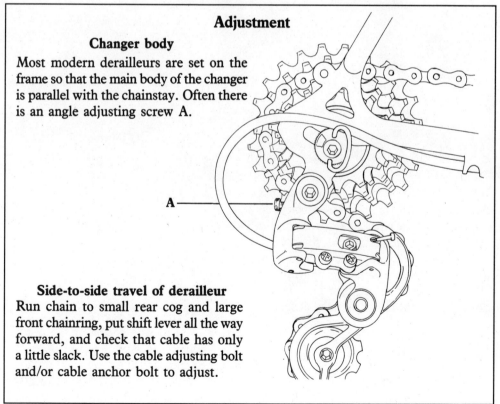

Side-to-side travel of derailleur

Run chain to small rear cog and large front chainring, put shift lever all the way forward, and check that cable has only a little slack. Use the cable adjusting bolt and/or cable anchor bolt to adjust.

The derailleur needs to be set so that side-to-side travel does not throw the chain into the wheel, or off the small cog. This is done with the high (E) and low (D) adjusting screws:

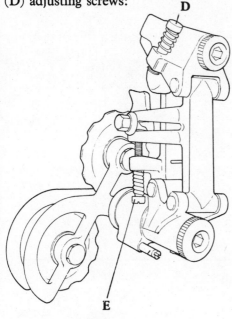

If derailleur goes too far, throwing chain off, set in position with shift lever so that jockey wheel lines up with sprocket on the side you are working on, and turn in appropriate adjusting screw until resistance is felt. Stop. If derailleur does not go far enough, back the appropriate adjusting screw off until it does. If this does not work, check to make absolutely sure adjusting screw is backed off. Yes? Turn to Troubleshooting for what to do next.

Spring for cage

On most modern derailleurs the spring tension of the roller cage cannot be adjusted. Many use a spring of the spiral type, which has a wide range of even pressure and should not need attention. Other changers use coil or lever springs, and these can often be adjusted. Spring tension on the roller cage should be sufficient to keep the chain taut when in high gear. Excess tension will cause unnecessary drag and rapid wear. On the other hand, too loose a chain will skip and/or whip. If your chain is skipping and the tension seems OK, check the chain itself for wear. Worn chains skip.

Adjustment procedure varies according to type of derailleur. Some have the spring set on a hook on the cage:

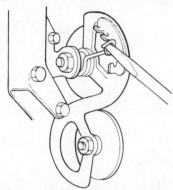

Move it with pliers or a screwdriver, although often it is better to disassemble the unit (see below).

Another method is a choice of holes, as on the old Campagnolo:

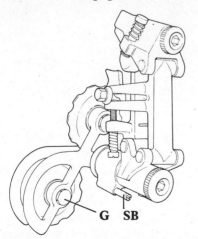

Remove tension roller by undoing bolt G. Use one hand to hang onto the chain

roller cage and prevent it from spinning, and unscrew the cage stop bolt SB. Now let the cage unwind (about one-half to three-quarters of a turn). Remove cage pivot bolt with Allen wrench and lift off cage. Note that protruding spring end engages one of a series of small holes in the cage. Rotate cage forward until spring fits into next hole:

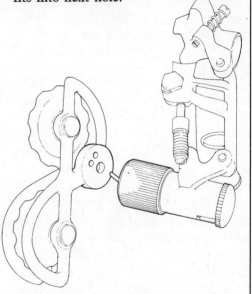

Replace pivot bolt. Wind cage back one-half to three-quarters of a turn and replace cage stop bolt. Replace tension roller and go back to the races. A fair number of changers have a serrated nut for holding the coil spring that gives different tension settings:

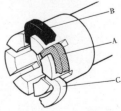

The basic technique is to undo the cage stop bolt SB, let the cage unwind, undo the pivot bolt B, and change the slot in which the spring nests.

Lubrication

Pivot points on the changer body should be kept clean, and lightly lubricated with a spray like Super Lube, or a tiny amount of oil. The main pivot bolts are usually greased, although Super Lube can also be used. Treatment for the roller wheels is something of a personal decision. On most changers the makers claim that the wheels are self-lubricating. You can just leave them. But those poor roller wheels really get a lot of grit and wet, and I like to clean and juice them up often. Super Lube is good. Grease is good. Anything clean and slippery is good. Another alternative is to use replacement pulley wheels with sealed bearings. These work well, but removing,

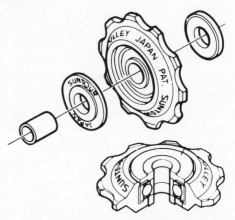

cleaning, and lubricating a standard roller is easily and quickly done, and then you know the thing is in good shape.

Removal and Disassembly

Disconnect cable from anchor bolt. Remove tension roller or slip off chain, if you have a half cage. Undo the frame mounting bolt B:

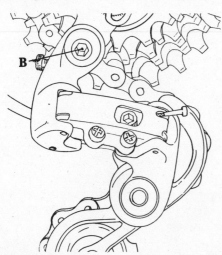

Disassembly: the parts that need this regularly are the chain rollers. Otherwise do it only to replace parts. There are two

kinds of chain rollers, those with washers and a bushing, and those with a hub and ball bearings:

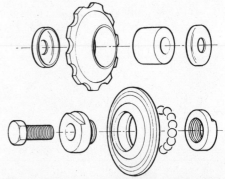

The majority are straightforward and only need the axle bolt removed with a wrench. With a few others you've got to get past a clever maze of springs.

After the chain rollers, the amount of disassembly that can be done varies from model to model. We'll do two: a museum Campagnolo and the archetypal Sun Tour ARX.

The Campagnolo

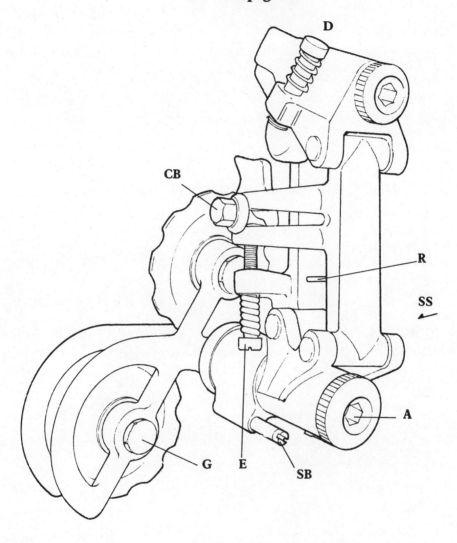

Hang onto chain roller cage to prevent it spinning and remove cage stop bolt SB. Let cage unwind (about one-half to three-quarters of a turn). Remove cage pivot bolt with Allen wrench and lift off cage. Slide out pivot bolt A and spring. Back off high gear adjusting screw E to minimize changer body spring tension, and undo spring bolt SS. Replace parts, clean everything in solvent.

Reassembly: screw in spring bolt SS while holding changer body spring R in position. Replace cage spring and slide in pivot bolt. Put cage on changer with two half-moon sides next to changer. Put nut on pivot bolt. Rotate cage back one-half to three-quarters of a turn and screw in cage stop bolt SB. Replace jockey roller. Mount derailleur on frame. Replace tension roller, cable. Adjust side-to-side travel.

The ARX

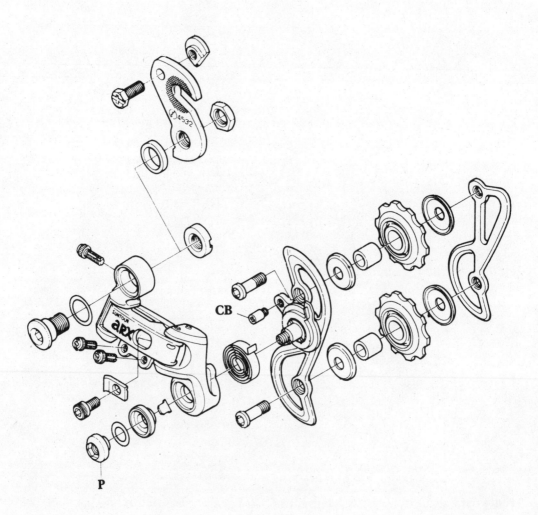

Wind up cage and body, hold tight, remove cage stop screw CB, and allow cage and body to unwind. Undo cage pivot bolt nut P and separate cage and body. Clean everything, replacing spring if necessary. Rejoin body and cage, fitting spring into slot on pivot bolt, replace nut P. Wind cage up clockwise and fit cage stop screw CB.

Troubleshooting

Derailleur is sticky, won't shift, sometimes shifts unexpectedly:
● Is shift lever working smoothly but with enough friction to hold derailleur in place?
● Are cables sticking?
● Are pivot bolts lubricated and clean? On a very few models (Mavic, Campagnolo) these bolts can be adjusted.

Derailleur will not go far enough:
● Is cable slightly slack with shift lever all the way forward?
● Are adjusting screws properly set?
● Does cable slide easily?
● Is pivot or main changer spring broken?
● Are chain rollers lined up with chain?
● Try to wiggle the derailleur unit by hand. Can you push it to the desired position? Yes:
Works are gummed up. Clean in solvent and lubricate with spray or oil. Adjust (not possible with all models) by undoing pivot bolts one-eighth of a turn and re-setting. No:
If it won't reach the big rear cog and the adjusting screw is backed off, go to a bike shop.
If it won't reach the little rear cog and the adjusting screw is backed off, a spacer washer at the mounting bolt may help.

Chain throws off cogs:
● Are adjusting screws set properly?
● Are any teeth worn or bent?
● Is chain good?
● If chain is skipping, is spring tension for roller cage sufficient?
● Is roller cage aligned with chain?

Power Train - Troubleshooting Index

Noises
First make sure that noise is coming from power train by coasting bike. If noise continues it is probably a brake or hub problem. If noise persists, try to determine if it comes from the front (crankset), the chain, or the rear sprocket(s). Do this by disconnecting the chain and spinning the various parts.

Grinding noises:
Front -
● Bottom bracket bearings OK?
● Pedal bearings OK?
● Chain rubbing derailleur?
● Front sprocket rubbing cage or chainstays?

Back -
● Wheel bearings OK?
● Freewheel OK?

Clicks or Clunks:
One for every revolution of crankset -
● Pedal tight?
● Crank(s) tight?
● Bottom bracket bearings OK?
● Are teeth on sprocket(s) bent?

Two or three for every revolution of the crankset -
● Are teeth on rear sprocket(s) bent?
● Is chain worn or frozen?

For all other problems consult the troubleshooting section for the part which is malfunctioning.

CHAPTER 6

Dream
Ramode
Sunfighter
Birthright

Everybody has dreams and here is one of mine: motor vehicles exist only in memory and museums. Cycles are used for local personal transport and light goods carriage, and mass transit systems are used for long journeys and bulk loads.

The efficiency of such an arrangement in terms of money and energy expenditure is tremendous. A cycle factory is a low-technology operation that is far easier to initiate and maintain than an automobile factory. Cycle production and use does not necessitate vast support industries in petroleum, metals, rubbers, plastics, and textiles. Road requirements are minimal. There is no need for traffic regulation, licensing, courts, lawyers, and expensive insurance. There are no 50,000 loved and cherished people dead and gone each year, and no hundreds of thousands of maimed people requiring expensive hospitalization, emergency, and other medical services.

A dream? In China, there are about 25,000 people for each motor vehicle, as against three people per motor vehicle in Britain and the United States. People cycle or use public transportation. A direct comparison would of course be misguided. China is culturally very different, and is a developing country that is austere by Western standards. Much work is done by hand, including crop irrigation, waste disposal, and movement of goods up to several hundred pounds in weight. A bicycle is a serious piece of equipment that can cost up to 2 years' wages, and requires a government permit to purchase. At the moment there is about one bike for every five people in China. But production has been increasing at about 15 percent annually and by now is clipping 40 million bikes a year. In terms of sheer transportation efficiency China has got it right.

A dream? This is the U.S.A., home, rampart, bastion, and citadel of rampant consumerism. The freeways and highways regularly jam to surfeit with massive automobiles conveying just one human each. CB'ers play spot Smoky the Bear to the ripping howl of 400 cubic inch engines. In Russia, 89 percent of journeys are by public transport. In America it is exactly the reverse: 89 percent of journeys are by car. The situation in America is the result of deliberate policy carried out by industry and government. And thanks to advertising and consumerism, the system has lots of fans. But not everyone likes the game.

Little more than a decade ago, bikes were toys. If you started talking about the importance of bikes, most people thought you were touched. Harmless, but not all there.

Today things are very, very different. You can earn a living working in the area of cycling, and with far healthier long-term prospects than in the automotive industry. Cycles are an established feature in transportation engineering, and cycle planning and activism is intense at many levels, from small towns and municipalities through to Washington, D.C. and nationwide Federal programs. Colleges and universities now give degrees in cycle and cycle-related subjects. If you want to charge the world on a bicycle, you can do it.

In cycle activism *Bicycle Transportation* by John Forester (MIT Press) is required reading. Forester is an original, a fighting crusader who has laid down many important guidelines in cycle transportation engineering. Another useful book is *A Handbook for Cycle Activists* by Ernest Del (Stanford Law School). *Energy and Equity* and *Tools for Conviviality* by Ivan Illich (Harper) are wonderful books for relating philosophy to nuts and bolts.

The organizations to contact are:

Bikecentennial, P.O. Box 8308, Missoula, MT 59807-9988

Bicycle USA, Suite 209, 6707 Whitestone Rd., Baltimore, MD 21207.

Promulgating a single attitude toward bikes in America is difficult, because conditions, problems, and solutions vary from place to place. Some towns have really good cycleway systems, and there are country networks that cover considerable distances. There are also a lot of ill-conceived facilities for cyclists that have increased rather than decreased the accident rate. One of the most notorious was the attempt in New York City to create bike lanes using low concrete dividers down one side of major avenues. The result of this folly was chaos and the dividers had to be torn out. One cannot help but wonder if the project was launched as a deliberate failure. In major metropolitan towns like New York you either devise a set of rules for all vehicles, or take your choice of stopping the cars or building elevated cycleways.

All too many cycling facilities have been devised to merely sweep bikes under the carpet. But the activist act is coming together. One project worth keeping track of is the Rails-to-Trails Conservancy (Suite 304, 1701 K Street N.W., Washington, D.C. 20006). The RTC is devoted to converting abandoned railroad rights of way into trails for public use. This is an idea with fabulous potential. The country is honeycombed with disused railroads that can easily be made into ideal cycle and walking paths. Railroad routes are gently graded and often pass through lovely countryside, but of course connect urban locations and other logical journey points. With an already existing roadbed, laying down pavement is a relatively simple and cheap business. In England, the first cycleways of this type are a solid success for both cyclists and pedestrians. They are lovely: paved ribbons meandering through countryside and farmlands, not a gas station or other rancid commercial enterprise in sight. And of course, no cars. They are safe for children.

Transportation systems in which the needs of different kinds of road users are met separately and without conflict are very pleasant. The classic example of building an entire town with provision for cyclists is Stevenage, England. Stevenage has a popula-

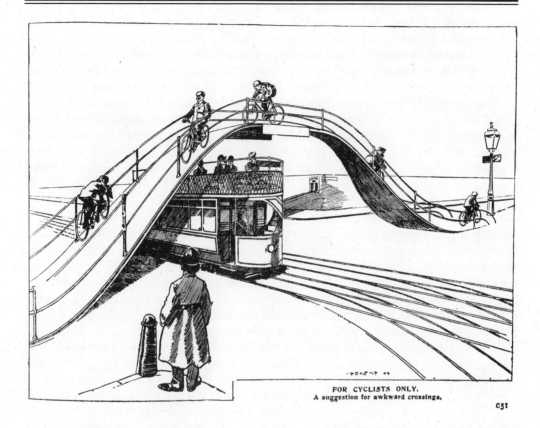

FOR CYCLISTS ONLY.
A suggestion for awkward crossings.

C31

tion density greater than that of Central London, and yet there is not one single traffic, cycle, or pedestrian light in the entire town. Even at rush hour the flow of traffic is so even and smooth that there does not appear to be anybody around. The reason is that there are no conflict points and no impediment to movement whether you are driving a car, riding a bike, or walking. There are independent roads for motor vehicles, cyclists, and pedestrians. Use of one particular type of road is not obligatory; the charm of the system is that it works so well that most road users prefer to use the road designed for them.

You can cycle or walk anywhere you wish in Stevenage and never encounter a motor vehicle. The offical cycleways system is shared by all types of cycles, mopeds up to 50cc capacity, and pedestrians. The cycleways frequently run alongside main roads but are separated by grass verges and trees from both the roads and footpaths. Conflict at cross points is resolved by the generous use of underpasses. These are a study in sensitive design. An overpass for cycles has to rise at least 16 feet, which involves steep gradients and a lot of hardware. An underpass for cycles only needs seven and a half feet of clearance and in Stevenage and other British towns they are made by excavating to a depth of 6 feet, and using the excavation material to raise the road by 3 feet.

There are also cycleways that are completely independent routes. Additionally, cycles make free use of the footpaths so that most cycle journeys are door-to-door. Despite mixing cyclists and pedestrians, accidents are very rare, and minor. So far as I know, the worst in 25 years has been a broken arm. There are no rules and regula-tions for the cycleways and footpaths, and no need for police involvement. There's no silly business about bikes having to use the cycleways. Cyclists are free to use the roads if they prefer, and that's exactly what racers and the odd HPVs do.

The benefits of a system such as Stevenage's are often intangible and not easily reckoned on a balance sheet. What is the worth of never, ever, having an obstruction or aggrava-tion in traveling? That whole series of abrasions, conflicts, and problems for which most of us armor up each day just doesn't exist in Stevenage. What price a mother's peace of mind, knowing that her children can walk or cycle anywhere and never encounter a motor vehicle? Sixty percent of the workers in town go home for lunch. How do you measure the value and effect of this increased family life? These are alterations in the quality of life with some similarity to the pastoral peacefulness of a 'primitive' society, but with full technological benefits!

In the Netherlands the idea that people come first is more advanced. They've of course got cycleways like you wouldn't believe. You can get anywhere just on a bike. They've also got residential districts called *woonerfs* that are designed primarily for people. Cars can gain access, but only very slowly and not in numbers. Landspace in a woonerf belongs to the people, and is safe for children to play in. Such an arrangement gives a far wider dimension to the concept of home. It's definitely the sort of thing we should work towards. Woonerfs demonstrate the key concept in planning for people - territory. Fully half the space in American cities is given over to motor vehicles. People are secondary to routing cars around the place. And four out of every ten cars that you see on the street will someday kill or injure a human being, or have already done so. It's crazy.

Will we see a world in which cars are just a memory? Will we see an end to the bomb? The idea of vaporizing the planet many times over also does not make a lot of sense. The war establishment is vast and it seems inevitable that one day, the world will go bang. But you don't give up. You don't quit living just because living might end. Cars as a transportation necessity are as much of a hoax as bombs are for peace. The ten largest companies in the world all produce oil or cars. They routinely buy and sell govern-ments. The vested interest in cars is colossal. And nowhere is the car more important, more a fundamental cornerstone of transport, than in the U.S.A. You still don't quit. In fact, sometimes you win a few.

There are many different strands in American society that signify change. Look at people like Ralph Nader. He's had a few really good bites out of the auto industry, and transformed the concept of consumer advocacy. Look at organizations like Mothers Against Drunk Drivers (MADD). There's a long way to go yet, but drinking and driv-ing is no longer a tacitly approved sport.

People do want to live. To be themselves. And that's my vision of the future. I keep seeing people in PVs (personal vehicles) that are essentially extensions of their bodies. Icarus suits. Transportation not just as something that happens, but as a conscious ac-tivity that people do, each in their own way and for their own purposes. In my mind's eye it looks like many fish swimming in the sea: little and big, slow and fast, all orbiting and moving - and open. That's the most important feature. Not people wrapped in metal shells, but people part of their environment, moving with it and using it.

That's my faith, and I live it a lot in a world of bikes and HPVs and all the adven-tures large and small that can be devised. It has a richness and a texture that I am mortally convinced is right for people. I've loved bikes for most of my life simply because they are fun, rewarding, and kind. They go with human life, human contact, loving relationships - and even worthwhile work!

And it is also a war. Every day out might be the last. The dead in our cemetaries and the maimed in our hospitals are still embraced with glee by the supporters of motor transport. Few ask if it is necessary, and still fewer put the financial support behind alternative schemes necessary to create a choice. It is very difficult to find a workable perspective for this kind of situation. But in the end it is my life, and yours, that is on the line.

Some gonzo madman comes running down the street, shooting people dead left and right, and unless he runs out of ammunition there isn't much choice - you blow him away. Like a mad dog. Now Hymie Dunderhead comes along driving his 140-mph Turbo-Dynamic Special. Hymie has worked hard to get his idiot crate. From day one he's listened to his parents, to the boob tube, to his school masters - Hymie has cooperated with his society, however insane, and now he wants his reward, some kind of evidence of his cooperation as a sop to a malformed ego - and that just happens to be a 140-mph Turbo-Dynamic Special that in Hymie's hands is far more dangerous and indiscriminate than a gun. What do you do with Hymie - shoot him like a mad dog? According to his lights he's playing by the rules, however crazy. If you do something drastic he'll come back for more, carrying a deep anger inflamed by the fact that basically, he's wrong.

But so what? A lot of people are wrong in the head. We've got a long history of wars, genocides, and other destructive madnesses. Self-preservation has to come into effect at some point. You're on your bike and a motorist endangers your life? Go for his throat. The cars ignore a 15 mph speed limit past the local school? Blow up the road. Too dangerous? You might go to jail? Then that is the price you place on your child's life. And yours.

The right to live is a birthright - but you must fight for it. There's no matter of right or wrong, good guys or bad guys. It is a very simple situation: motor vehicles are filling the air with deadly fumes and noise, recklessly wasting a dwindling supply of natural resources, *and killing and injuring people.* Some people blow up the road. Others speak nicely to the motorists. (But most effective are speed bumps that force the cars to slow down.)

Where you pick up on the situation is up to you. There are many fronts and strategies. Each moment of opportunity is a matter of individual assessment and decision. It might be fun, it might be hard, it might be little, it might be great. We all move according to our best understanding of right and wrong, and act in accordance with our ability to do so. But if a good chance comes your way,
Take it.